HISTORIC PHOTOS OF
LAKE MICHIGAN

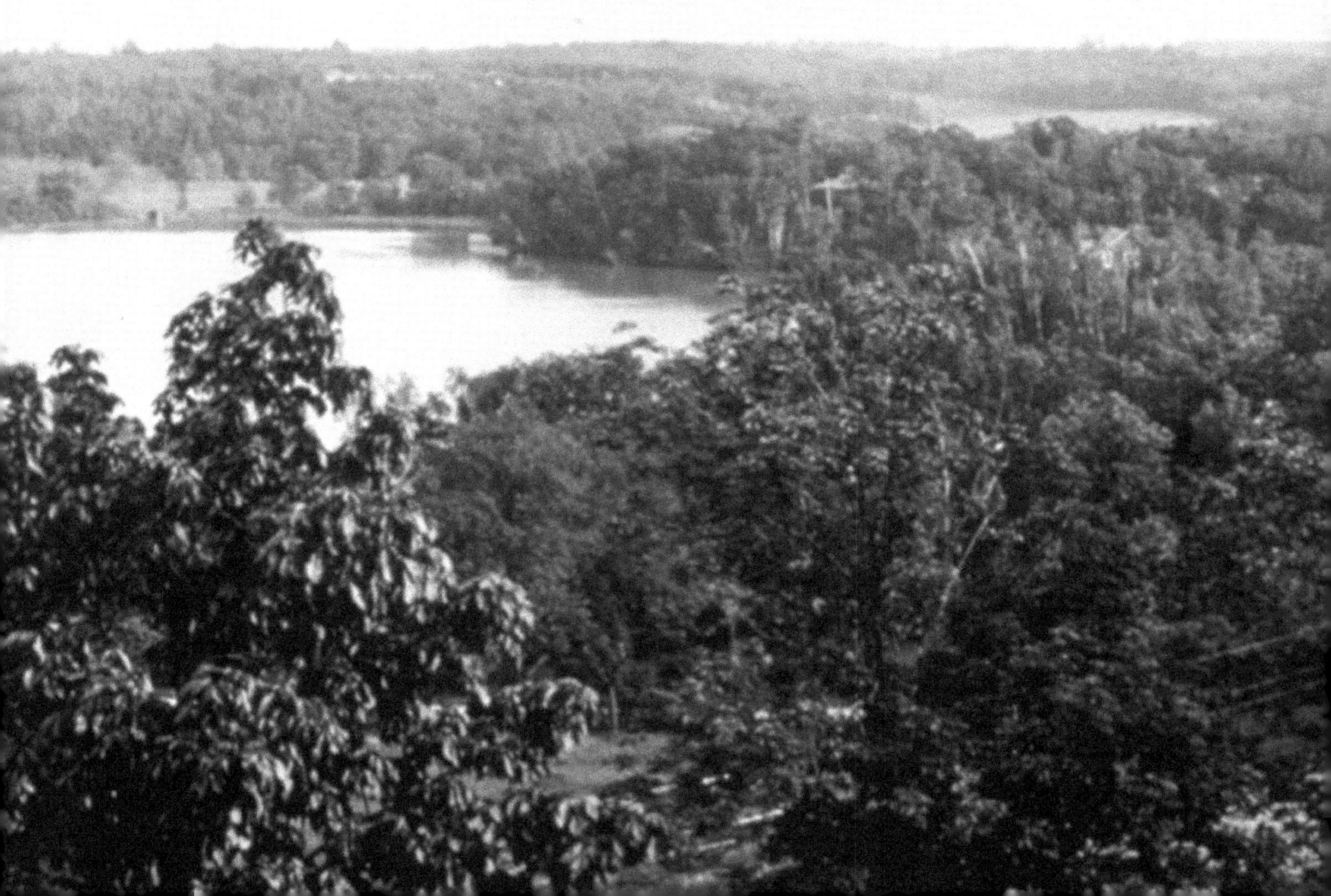

Turner Publishing Company
www.turnerpublishing.com

Historic Photos of Lake Michigan

Library of Congress Control Number: 2009921193

ISBN: 978-1-59652-532-0

Printed in the United States of America

ISBN 978-1-68442-087-2 (hc)

HISTORIC PHOTOS OF
LAKE MICHIGAN

TEXT AND CAPTIONS BY LYNDA TWARDOWSKI

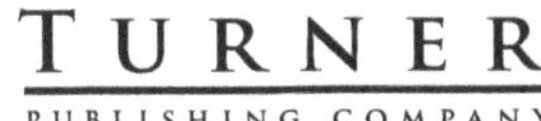

Sheboygan County's Crystal Lake, pictured here in 1912, is one reservoir of the 75-mile Sheboygan River, which empties into Lake Michigan at Milwaukee.

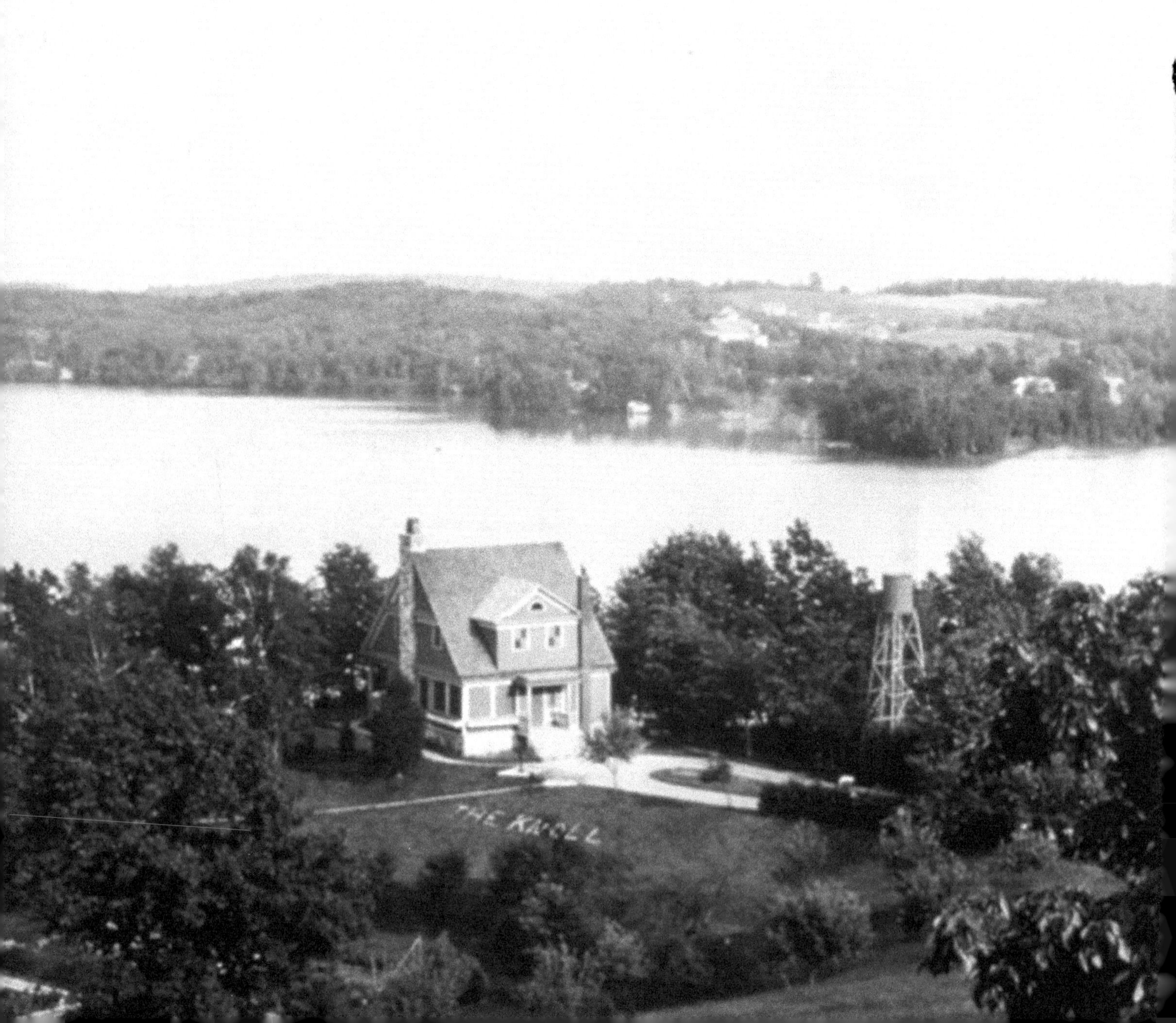

Contents

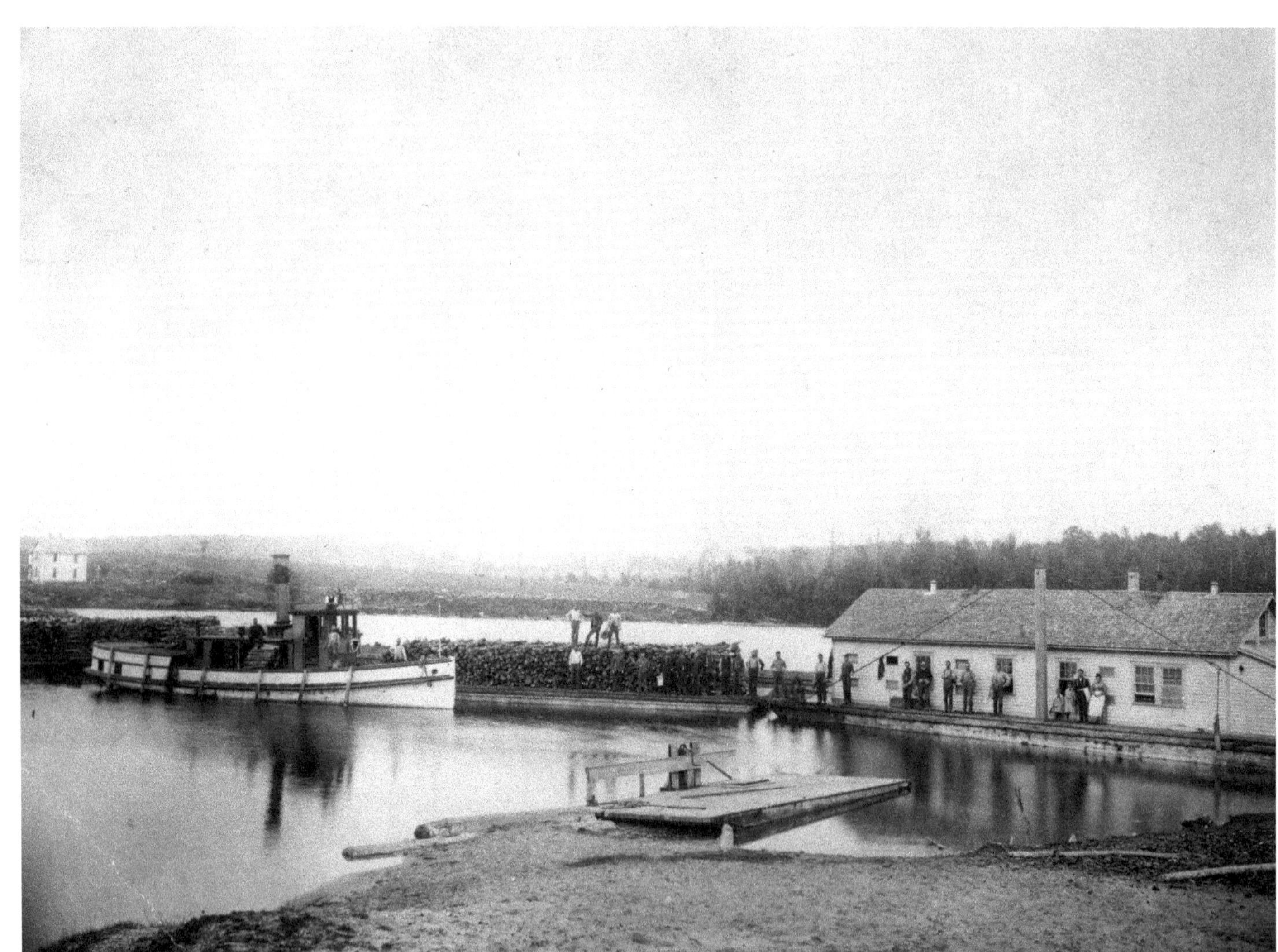

A floating boardinghouse and tug in the harbor of Elk Rapids, Michigan—likely those of the firm Dexter & Noble, who owned an immense timber operation in the village. Floating boardinghouses typically served two purposes: transporting logs tied together in rafts—a safer method than driving separated logs—and housing the men who "rafted" the logs.

Acknowledgments

This volume, *Historic Photos of Lake Michigan,* is the result of the cooperation and efforts of many individuals and organizations. It is with great thanks that we acknowledge the valuable contribution of the following for their generous support:

Bentley Historic Library
Library of Congress
Wisconsin Historical Society

With the exception of touching up imperfections that have accrued with the passage of time and cropping where necessary, no changes have been made. The focus and clarity of many images are limited to the technology and the ability of the photographer at the time they were recorded.

Preface

Imagine, if you can, a time when Lake Michigan didn't exist. Nearly 20,000 years ago, it didn't—not a drop. Where now there is a freshwater vastness of cerulean blue, there was then nothing but a gigantic white sheet of ice, nearly two miles thick. The ice would ultimately vanish without a trace, but an indelible map of the glacier's existence on the earth was etched into the terrain beneath. As the world around it warmed, the glacier retreated, carving deep gouges—the deepest of which would become enormous basins into which the glacial melt would pour, filling them and falling, then rising and falling again as the land and water worked to find balance over the next 10,000 years.

The Lake Michigan we know today, more than 100 miles wide, 300 miles long, and filled with nearly 1,180 cubic miles of water, took more than 6,000 years to ease into its current shape and volume. But glacially slow though its first 200 centuries moved, this third-largest of the Great Lakes, in recent centuries, seems to have evolved as quickly as a sudden Lake Michigan storm can chase away the sun.

Ancient peoples and Woodland Indians settled early on the dried landscape beside the new waters, and European explorers followed in the early seventeenth century. French explorer Jean Nicolet is considered the first European to discover Lake Michigan, but he would not be the last to traverse its waters and coast. Louis Jolliet, Jacques Marquette, and Robert de La Salle and a host of traders and missionaries came to the region, one after another, establishing scores of small ports and settlements along the coast through the late seventeenth and eighteenth centuries.

Some say the first permanent settlement on Lake Michigan was at the site of present-day Chicago by Jean Baptiste Point du Sable in 1779; others assert Green Bay has a rightful claim to that distinction, noting the mission established by Father Allouez in present-day Green Bay, Wisconsin, in 1669. Much like its bitterly contested claims to "firsts," the Lake Michigan region, as part of the resource-rich Northwest Territory, inspired countless battles for control between the French, English, and Native Americans, but by 1796 it was in the hands of the newly formed United States—and the American way of growth, expansion, and innovation would kick-start the nineteenth century's progress along the Lake Michigan shoreline like none before.

With Lake Michigan as the anchor to trade throughout the otherwise remote and largely isolated region, ships plied its waters, giving birth to city after city along its coast. The year 1837 brought the founding of Chicago, Illinois. The city of Manistee, Michigan, was founded four years later. Milwaukee, Wisconsin, settled since 1818, officially became a city in 1846. Green Bay followed in 1854. The growth in commerce spurred the cities on, fueling their expansion and attracting waves of immigrants seeking a livelihood and making their way from the Atlantic Coast to the burgeoning cities, farms, and orchards around Lake Michigan. As time advanced, so too did technology, bringing steam power to Lake Michigan's ships, then to the railroad lines stretching out along its shores. Timber from Michigan's hinterlands was shipped to build (and, in some cases, rebuild) growing cities along the lake's western coast. In return, the west coast cities and ports shipped beef and grain from their outlying farming regions east to Michigan and beyond.

By the early 1900s, lumbering had reached its peak and bottomed out, felling many a boomtown, but many established towns and cities remained, as well as the wealth that timber and the railroad and car-ferry links between them had fostered. Those who had prospered took advantage of their leisure, exploring coastal towns and cities they hadn't seen before and bringing more prosperity—along the lengthening railroad lines they inspired—to farther and farther reaches of the region. Summer resort towns and yacht clubs followed—from Milwaukee to Chicago to Michigan's Benton Harbor and Harbor Springs. The growing population, from the well-heeled to the average citizen, found excitement in the emergence of coliseums, halls, rinks, and stadiums—home to great gatherings for music and sport—in their shoreside cities and towns.

As elsewhere around the nation, the advent of the automobile and its associated industries brought more freedom and prosperity, and a call for greater innovation that would define the twentieth century around the great lake. No more would people rely on the rails and car ferries to ship themselves and so many goods east and west. Dirt roads would give way to highways and tarmac, and automobiles and airplanes would lead the way toward a new economy, forcing rails and ships out of favor and changing once again the way the region relied on the great lake. Today twelve million Americans, residing in the surrounding states of Michigan, Wisconsin, Illinois, and Indiana, call Lake Michigan's lakeshore communities home.

The one thing that hasn't changed? The beauty and majesty of Lake Michigan, and the indelible imprint it has left on our times.

—Lynda Twardowski

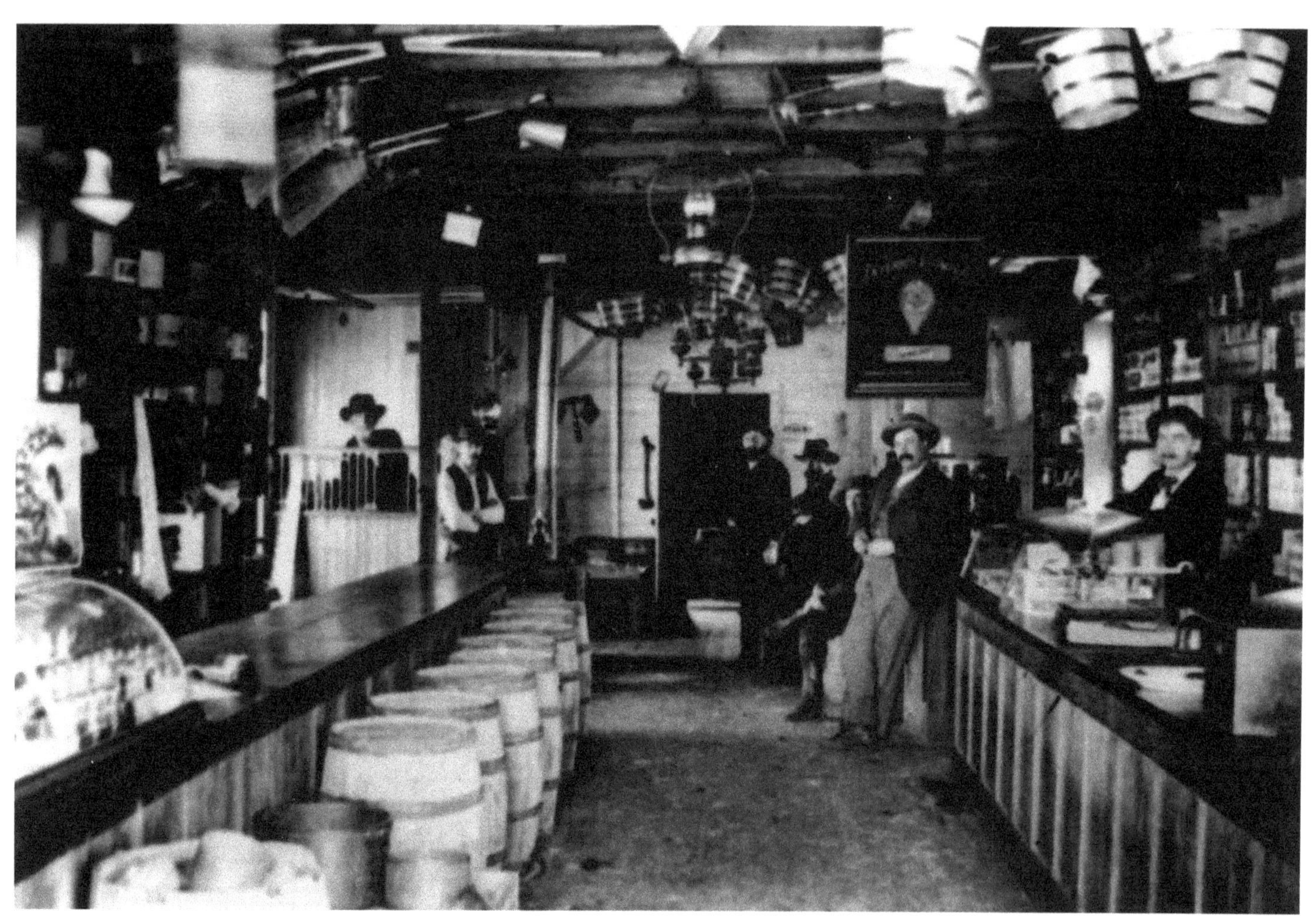

The interior of a small merchant store in Charlevoix, Michigan, around 1885.

Settlement of the Great Water

(1861–1880)

Inside a jagged circumference of craggy rocks, towering dunes, deep forests, sandy shores, and dozens of modern midwestern towns and cities, there glimmers a glacial footprint of eons past: Lake Michigan, one of the largest freshwater lakes in the world and the only one of the United States' five Great Lakes that sits entirely within the nation's borders. Christened Mishigami—meaning Great Water—by the Ojibwe Indians who once roamed its shores, Lake Michigan's storied history is as epic as its native name.

Long before the New World became a nation, the Great Water had brought both sustenance and struggle to centuries of Native Americans, European explorers, fur traders, and missionaries. Early on, the progress of the people and places along Lake Michigan's shores trickled forward, but after the birth of the United States and particularly in the nineteenth century, it became a flood. The Civil War was the impetus for the most significant wave. In the early 1860s, the war between North and South stymied cargo transport in and out of cities farther south, places like Cincinnati, Ohio, and St. Louis, Missouri. To continue moving cargo, northern states quickly turned to Chicago, Illinois, and Wisconsin's Green Bay and Milwaukee—burgeoning cities of the north surrounded by Lake Michigan and the Midwest's farms and prairies.

Over the next decade more and more schooners took to the freshwater sea, ferrying tons of the Midwest's wheat, hay, flour, and meats a hundred miles across the waters to the state of Michigan, and on through the interconnected chain of the Great Lakes to the eastern states of Ohio, Pennsylvania, and New York. Those same schooners returned west with city-building cargo: coal, immigrants, fruit, and—especially after the Great Chicago Fire of 1871—massive loads of lumber.

As lake traffic and commerce boomed, the lake's coastal cities and settlements did too—expanding and improving to accommodate their growing populations and industries, and linking, by way of ever-lengthening railroad lines, each state's farthest reaches. As would be expected, the shoreline itself evolved: harbors were improved, channels dredged, and scads of lighthouses erected. By 1880, Lake Michigan's coastline—more than 1,600 miles rimming Wisconsin, Illinois, Indiana, and Michigan's Upper and Lower Peninsulas—bore the indelible footprint of modern man.

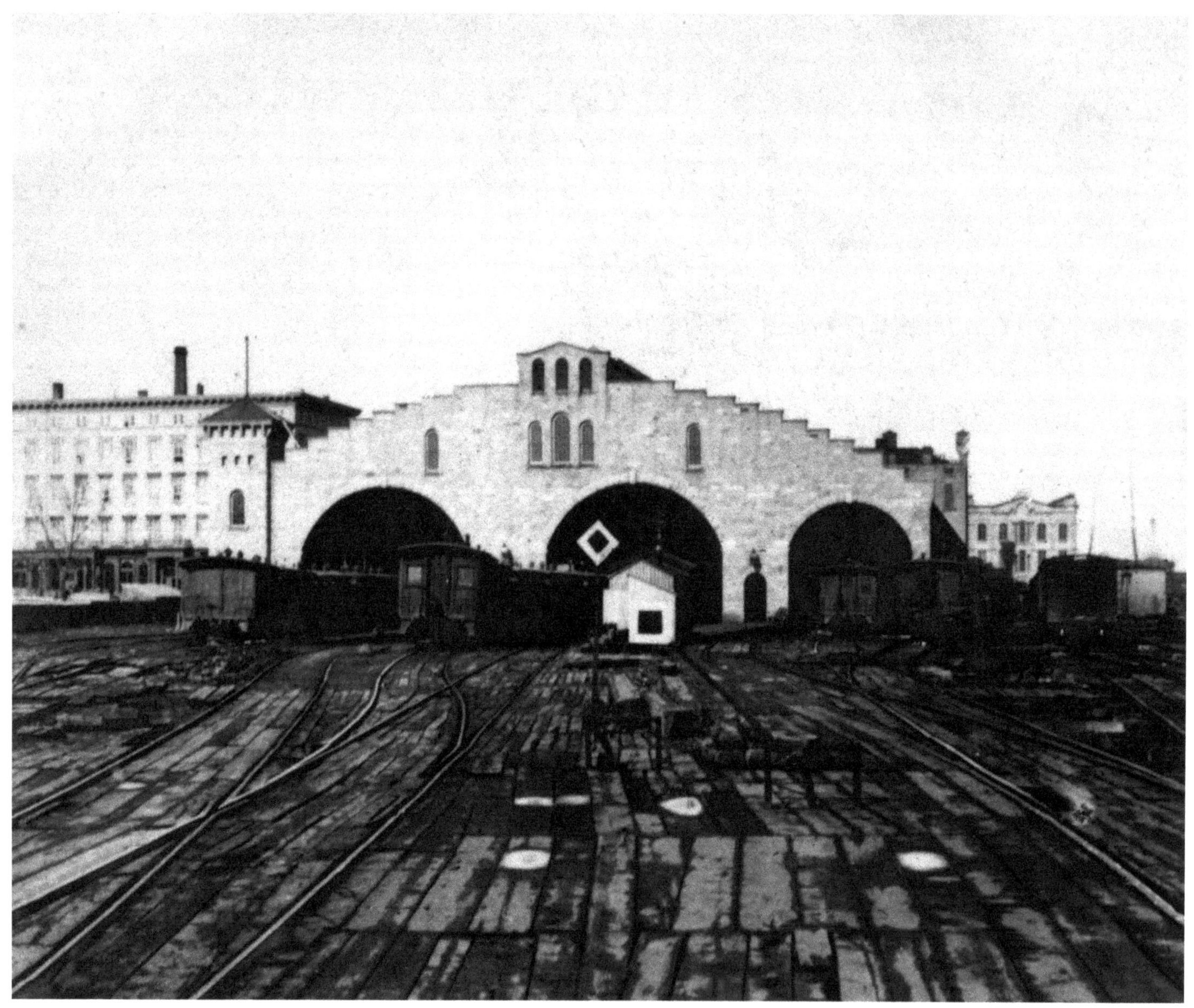

In Chicago, south of the Chicago River and north of what would later become—when filled with earth—Grant Park, stands the Great Central Depot of the Illinois Central Railroad in 1863. The Illinois Central, known as the Maine Line of Mid-America, was the first U.S. railroad aided by a large—more than two-million-acre—federal land grant. Stretching more than 700 miles, it was the longest road in the world when completed in 1856.

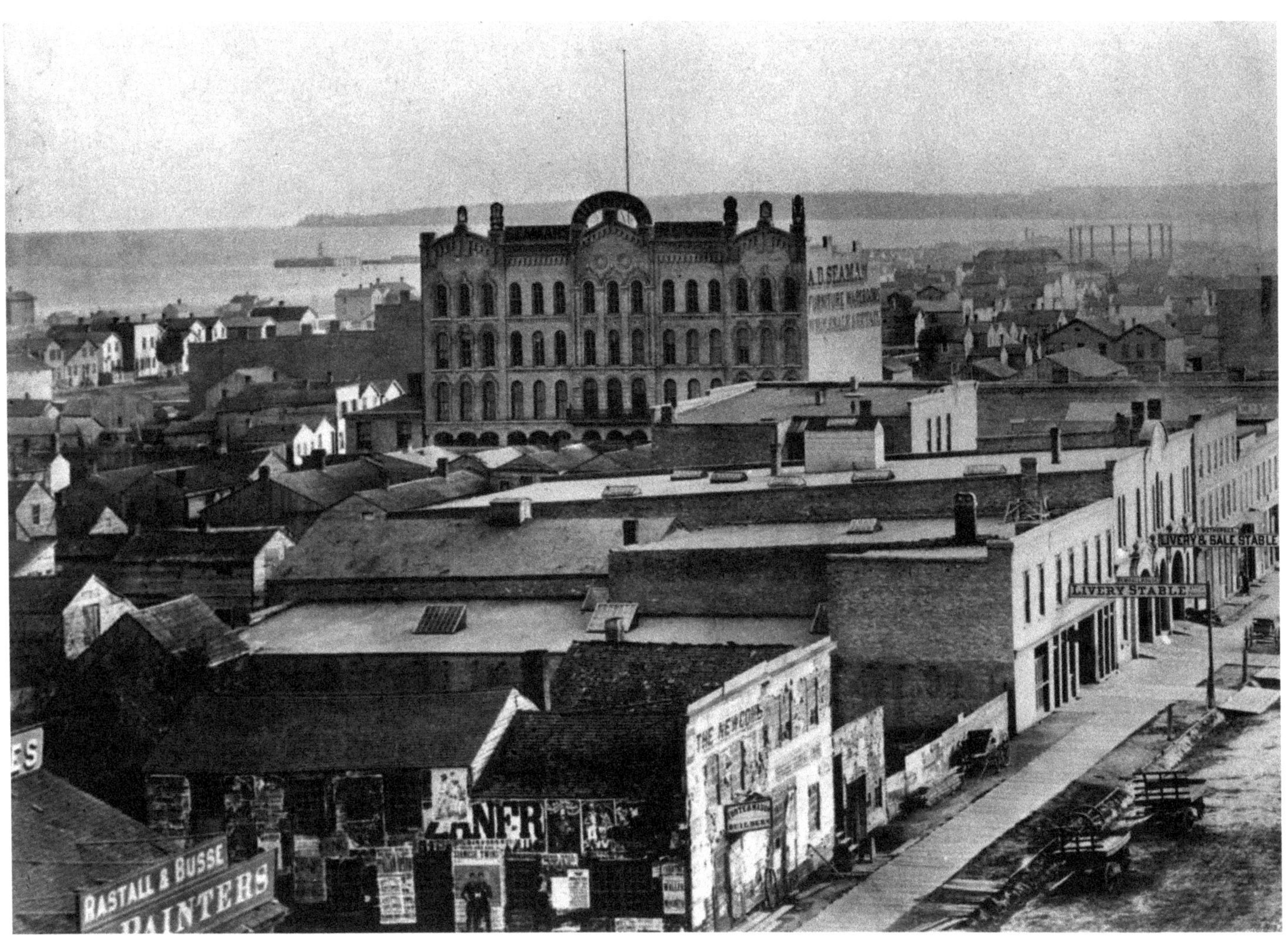

Alonzo D. Seaman's Furniture and Rooms company rises above carriage- and cart-dotted streets of downtown Milwaukee in 1868. As the automobile industry grew around the turn of the century, Alonzo's son William, who had inherited his father's furniture manufacturing empire in 1881, began building wooden automobile frames, among them the first Rambler runabout chassis. Nash Motors—the precursor to American Motors and General Motors—eventually purchased Seaman Body Corporation.

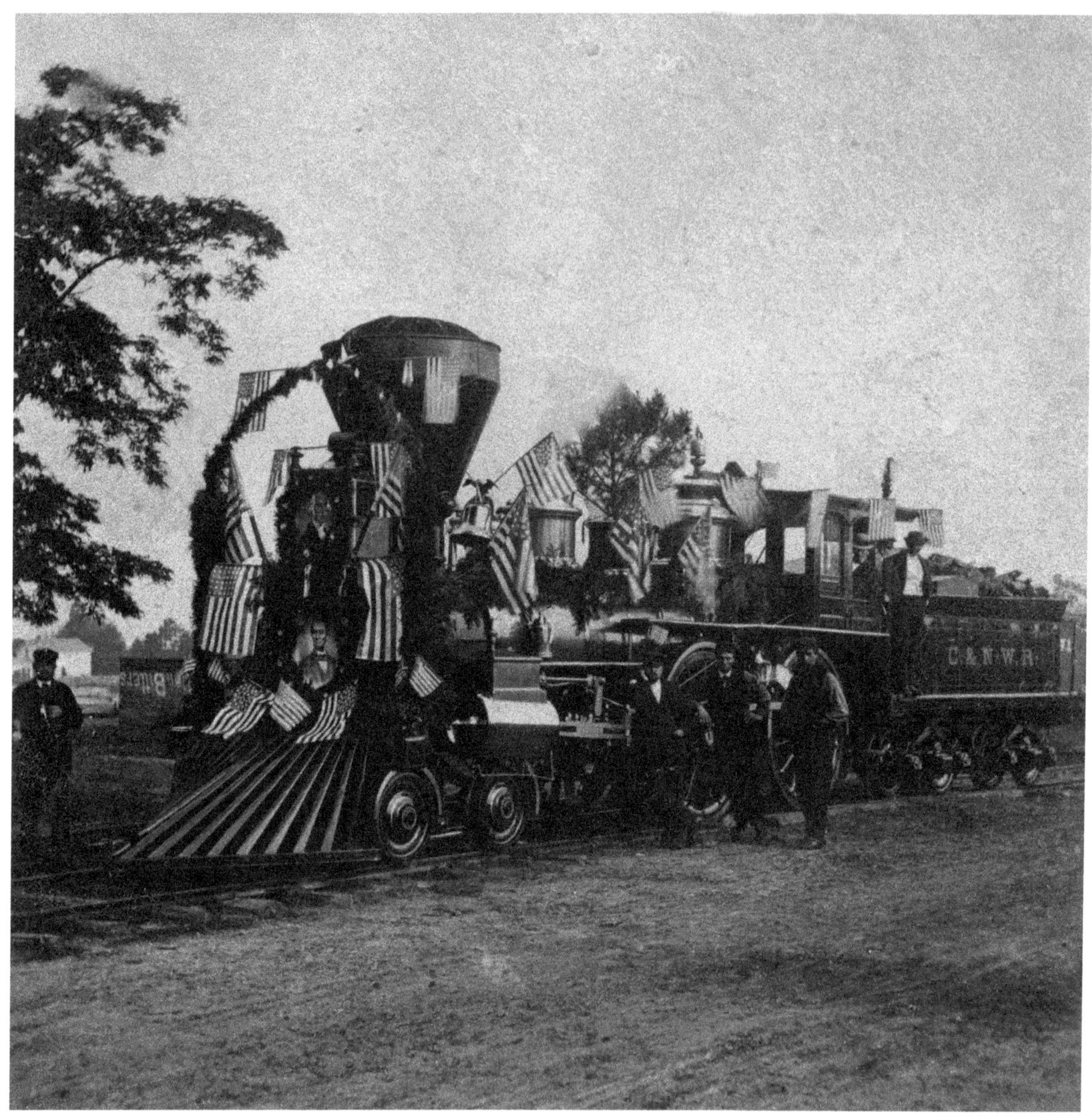

Decorated in 4th of July finery, the *Camilla*, a wood-burning locomotive belonging to the Chicago & Northwestern Railway, trundles down the tracks in Kenosha, Wisconsin, in 1869. By 1870, wood-burning locomotives would begin falling out of favor owing to an abundance of coal and ever-diminishing forests.

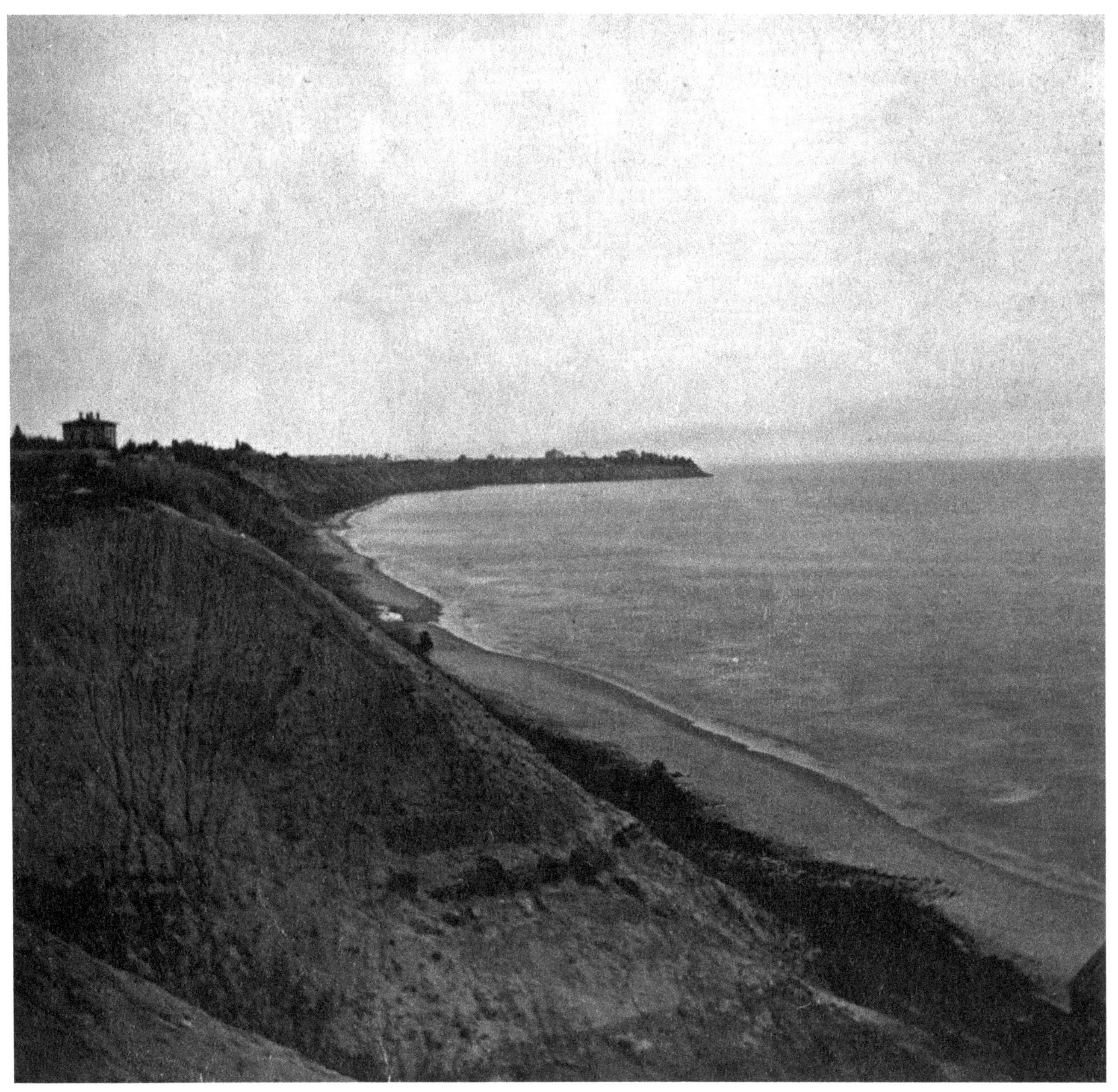

This view of Lake Michigan faces northward along the Milwaukee coast from the end of Oneida Street, now East Wells Street, in 1870.

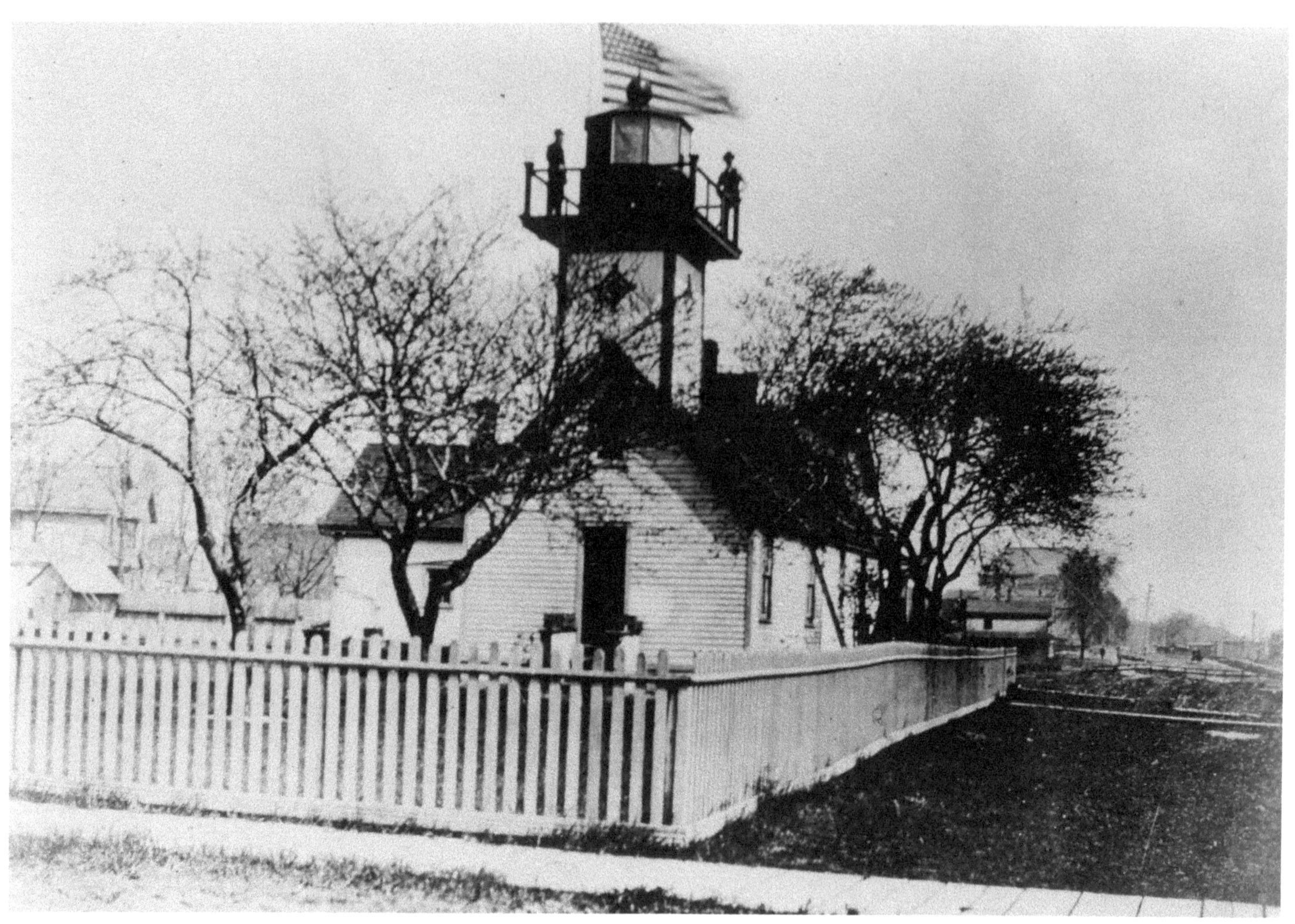

While awaiting completion of a harbor breakwater and iron pierhead beacon at Little Fort, Illinois, in the early 1850s, Congress offered $1,000 to keep the light of the new but crumbling Little Fort Lighthouse shining in the interim. The solution was to demolish the failing brick tower and top the existing keeper's house roof with a wooden tower and temporary cast-iron lantern. That "temporary" solution shone until the breakwater's completion much later in 1898.

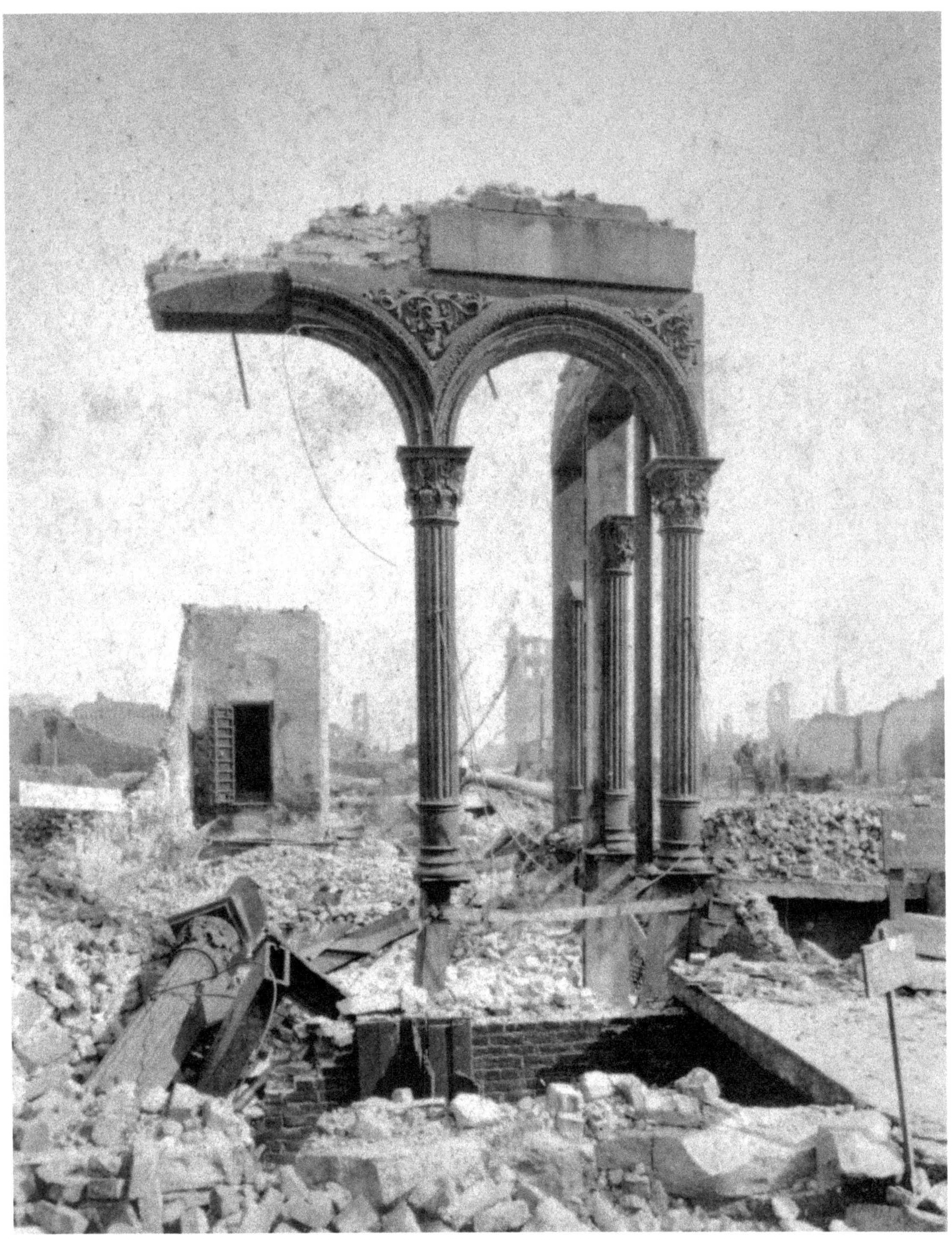

On the northeast corner of Clark and Washington streets, the skeletal remains of the Number 18 Fifth National Bank smolder eerily after the Great Fire of Chicago tore through the city. The fire destroyed more than 17,000 buildings and $200,000 in property, between Sunday, October 8, and Tuesday, October 10, 1871, taking hundreds of lives. While the Chicago fire was in progress, other Lake Michigan communities suffered devastating fires, including Wisconsin's Green Bay town of Peshtigo, which experienced what remains the deadliest fire in American history.

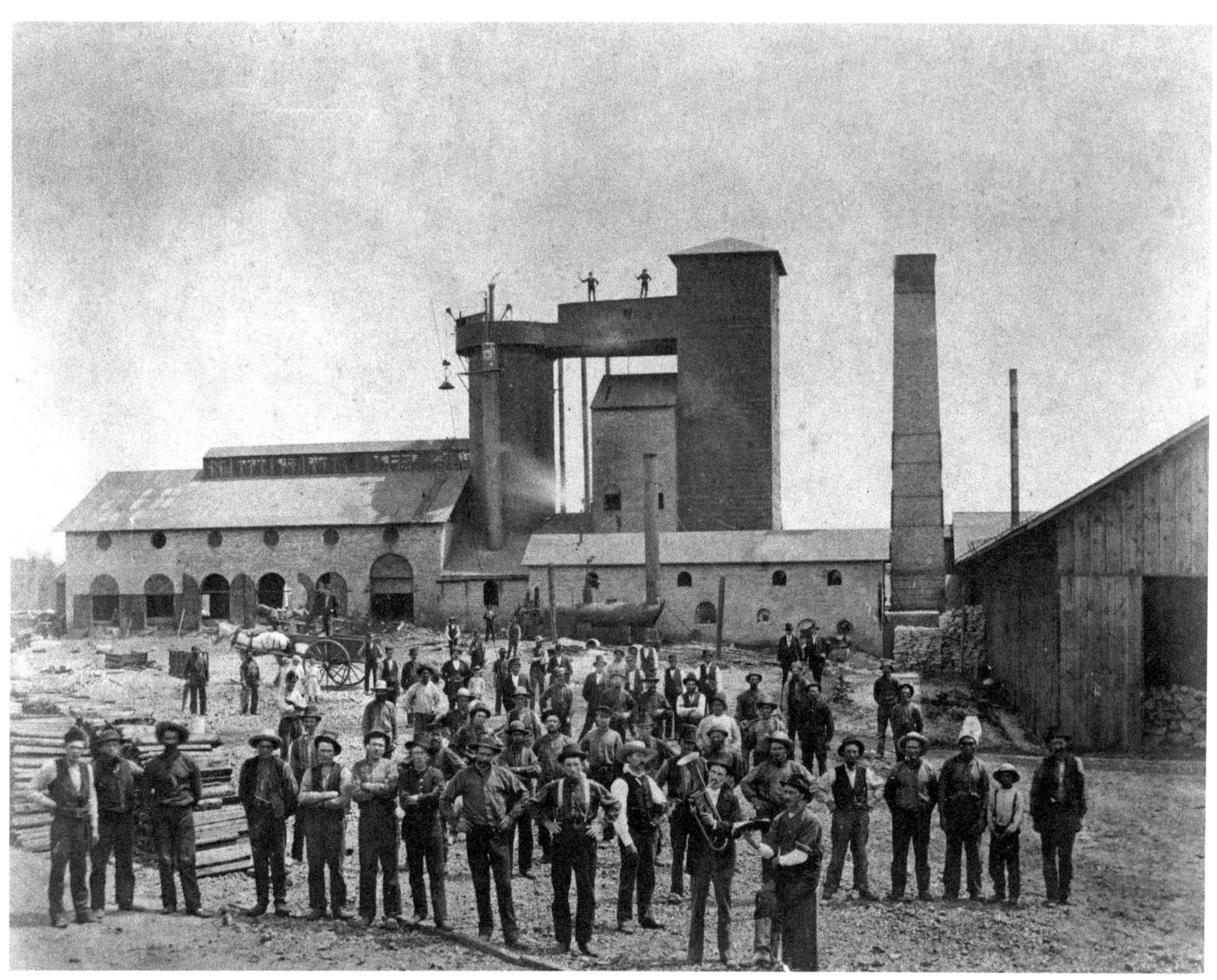

With Northern Michigan's pine supply dwindling, the Elk Rapids Iron Company in Elk Rapids was organized in 1873. Its giant iron-smelting furnaces—at the time the biggest in the country—made use of the area's still-abundant hardwood trees, manufacturing an average 30 tons of pig iron daily.

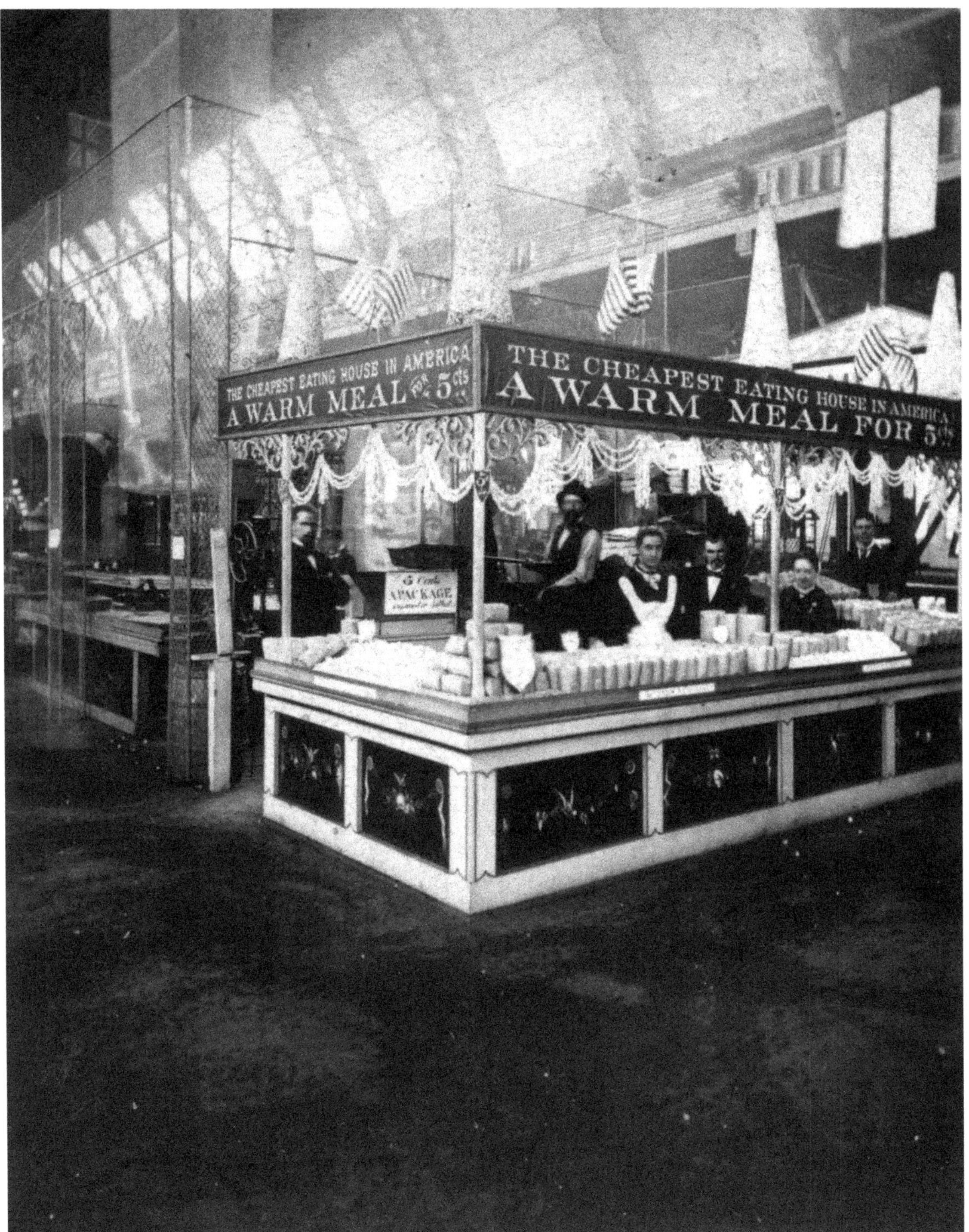

Booth vendors in Chicago during 1873 hawk "a warm meal for 5 cents" at the self-proclaimed "Cheapest Eating House in America." The photograph's date and scene suggests that it records a view of the city's first Interstate Industrial Exposition, kicked off to build city commerce and confidence after the Great Fire.

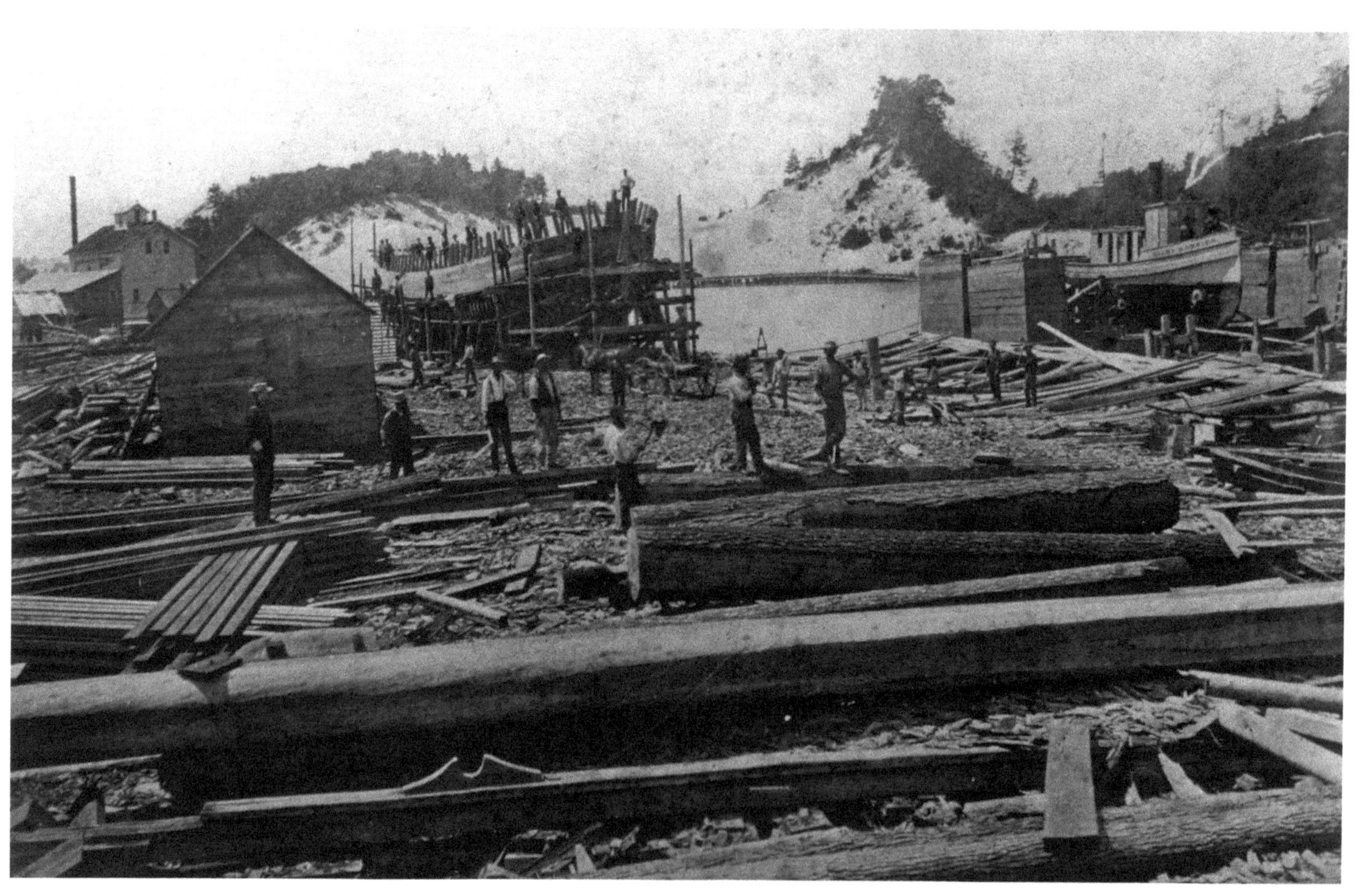

One of the hard-working Grand River shipyards at Grand Haven, Michigan, shown here around 1875. Rising behind the yard are the Grand Haven sand dunes later known as Dewey Hill.

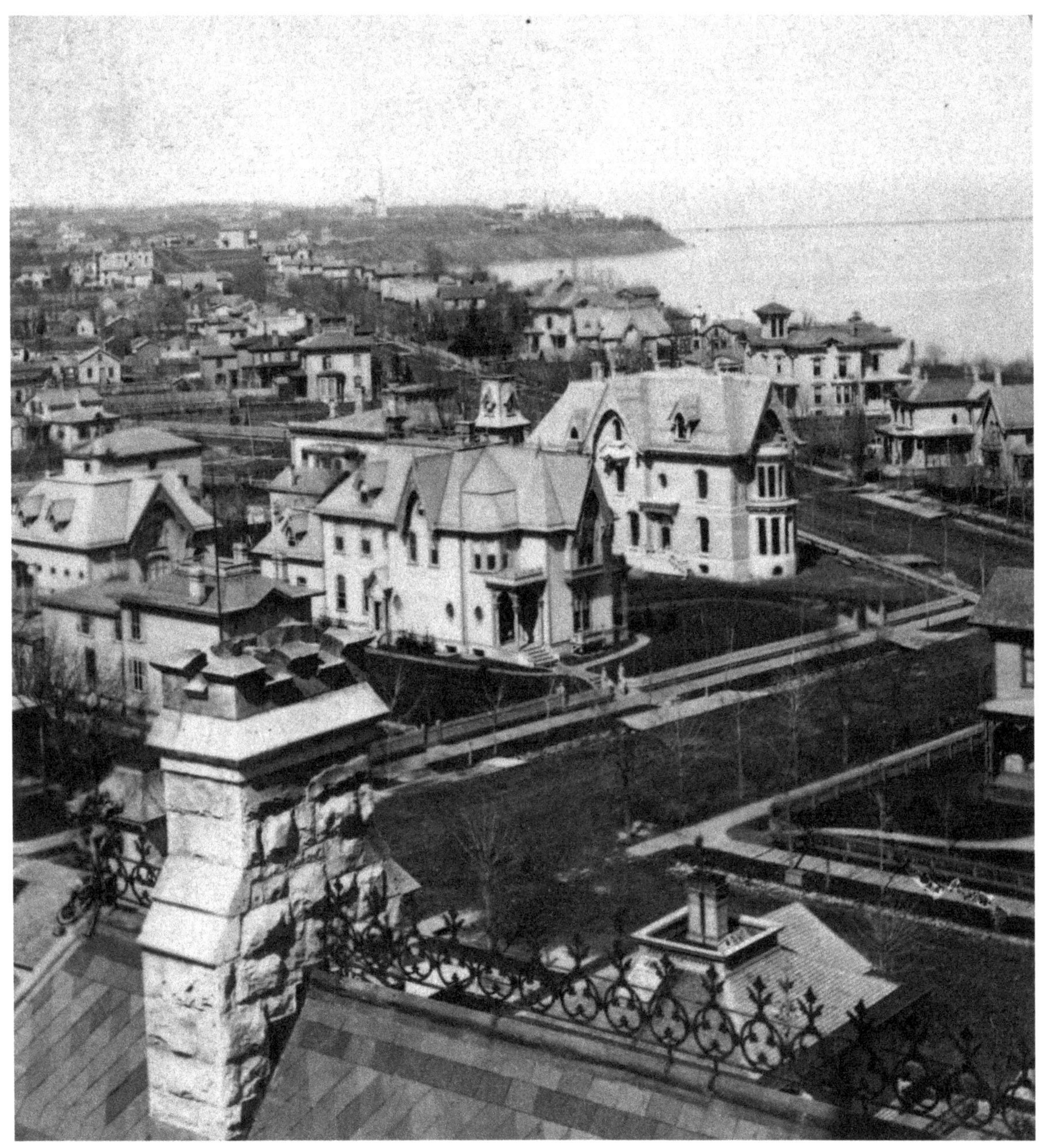

This stereograph image, recorded sometime before 1876, captures a lofty view of a Milwaukee neighborhood and, in the distance, the Lake Michigan shoreline.

Buildings and a railroad are shown nestled against the bluffs along Milwaukee's Lake Michigan shore in 1877.

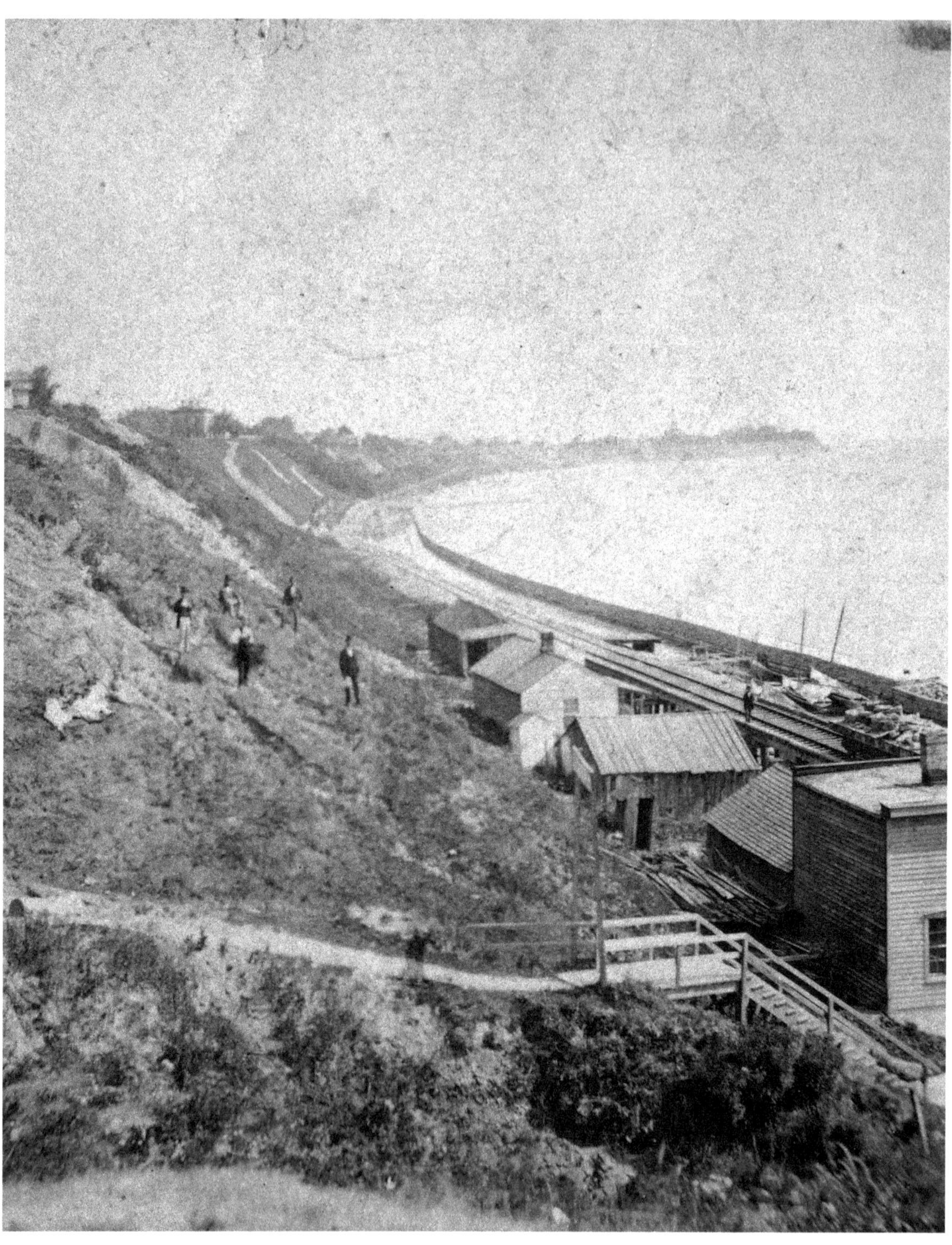

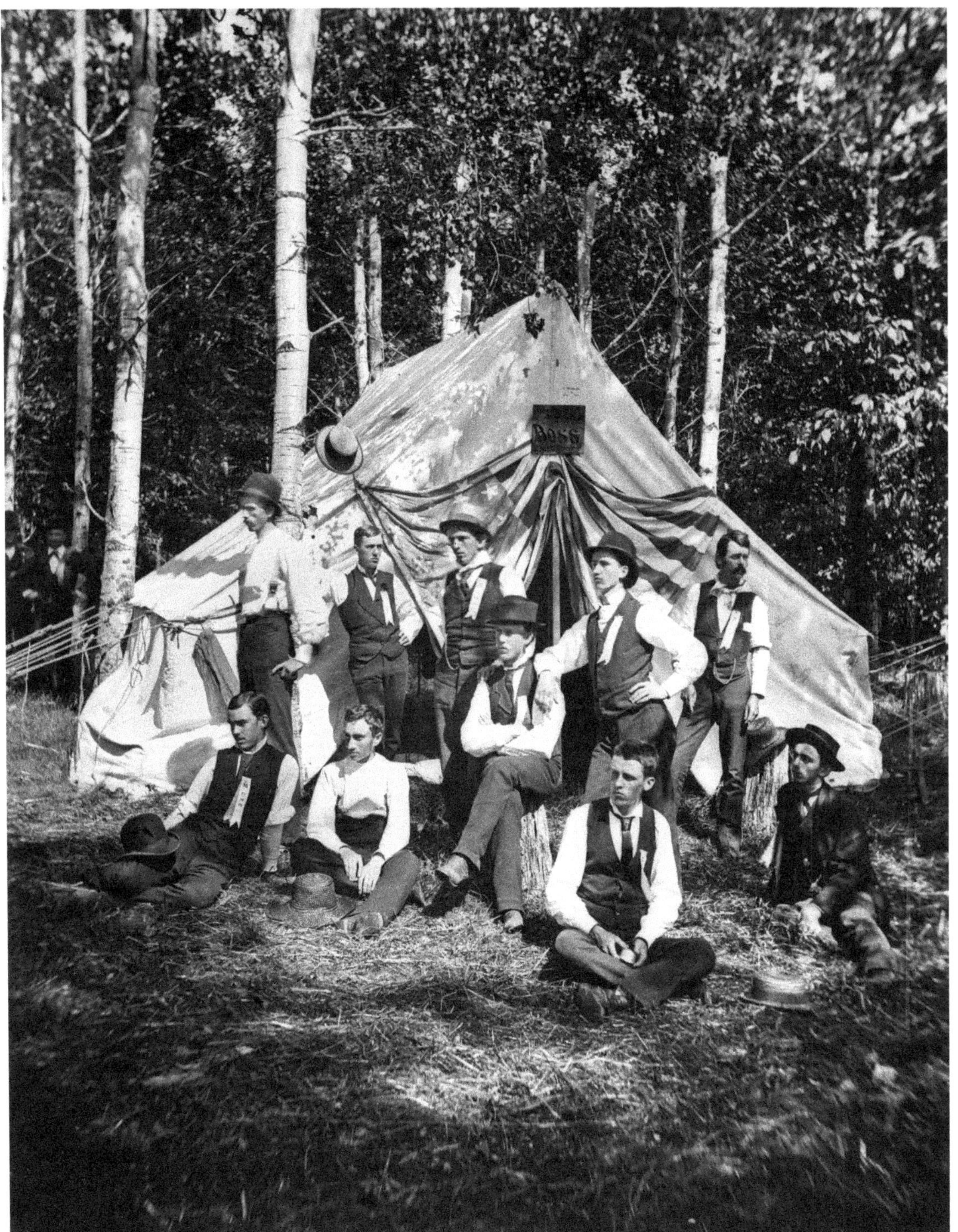

Members of the Chicago Traveling Club pose outside their tent on a trip to Twin Lakes in Kenosha County, Wisconsin, in 1878.

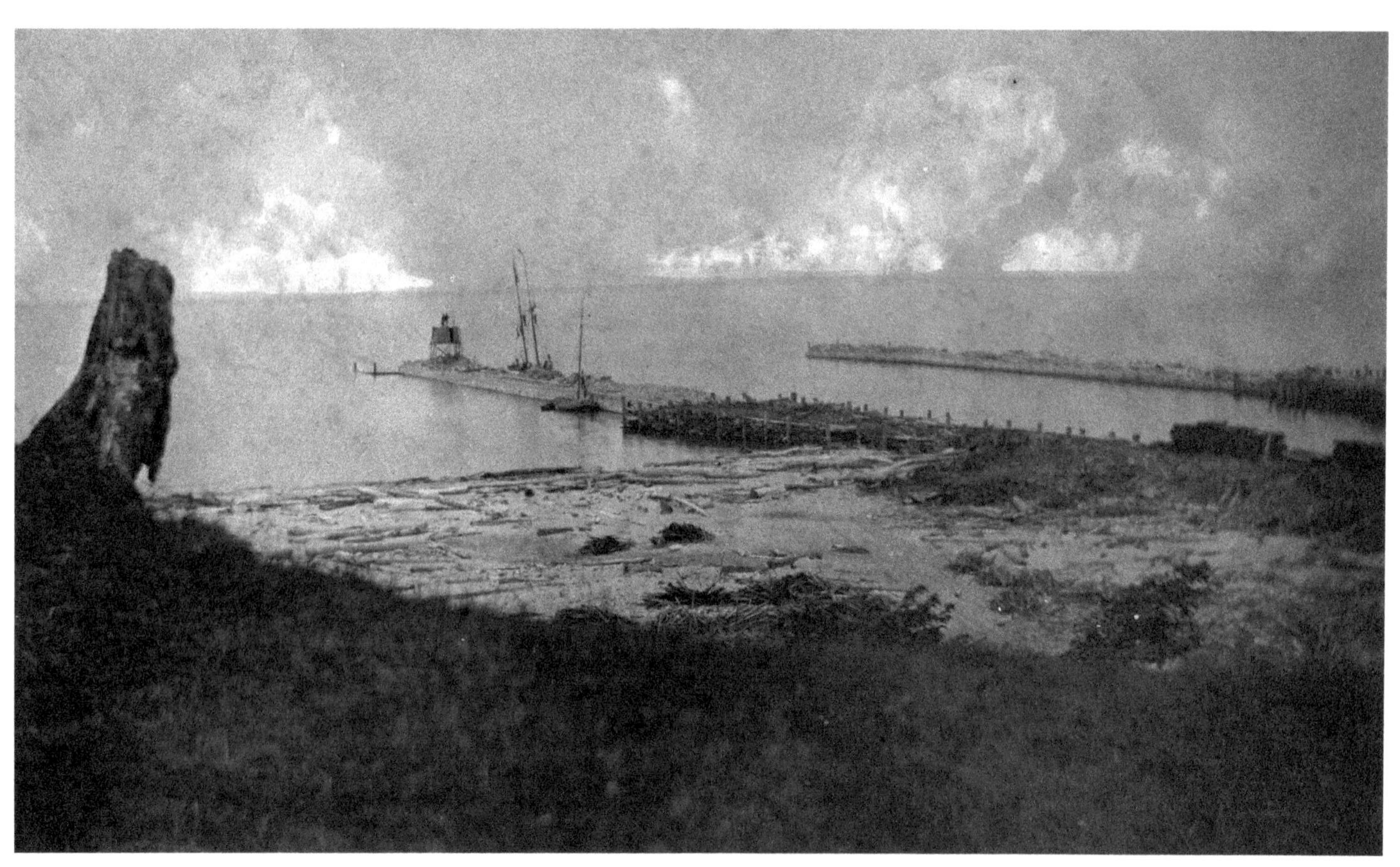

Home to Ottawa, Miami, and Pottawattamie tribes long before modern settlement, Michigan's sublime stretch of Lake Michigan coast at South Haven exemplified—here in the 1880s—the meaning of "Ni-Ko-Nong," the name ascribed to it by the early inhabitants: "beautiful sunsets."

Through Timber Boom and Bust

(1881–1900)

Logging in the Great Lakes states—most notably Michigan and Wisconsin—got its start early in the nineteenth century, driven by a few rugged souls who set out into the woods to fell its giant white pines and erect small sawmills to turn their logs into lumber. But by the 1880s, the ranks of those lone lumbermen had multiplied exponentially, the savviest among them building and buying more and more mills, snapping up hundreds of acres of timberland, organizing their own lumberyards, and creating an explosion of wealth and commerce on and around Lake Michigan.

Credit the boom to several factors: the many miles of free-flowing rivers stretching to the Great Lake—Michigan's Muskegon and Manistee rivers, and Wisconsin's Fox and Wolf rivers among them; the post–Civil War boom of coastal cities and settlements in dire need of lumber for everything from firewood and fence posts to home framing and furniture; and the construction and maintenance of the nation's rapidly expanding railroads—roughly 73 million ties needed annually by 1890.

The voracious appetite for timber far outpaced the forests' ability to generate new growth. For a time lumber companies moved inland into tougher reaches of woods; then, when those lands were stripped bare of the choice white pine, they moved on to other species of trees. But as the turn of the century approached, the swaths of majestic forests surrounding Lake Michigan and its hinterlands grew fewer and farther between. One after another, lumber companies and young boomtowns folded, as bankrupt as the landscape they left behind.

The lumber boom's decline, however, did not extinguish all the progress that had been made. In its wake remained dozens of strong cities and towns, vast stretches of railroad, greater prosperity, and, most meaningful for the times, the promise afforded by a glimpse of what man—given the freedom to improve his circumstances—could make possible.

In 1897, Lake Michigan welcomed its first car ferry—which transported railroad freight cars across the giant inland lake in four to seven hours, a faster and cheaper means than hauling freight all the way around it. The easy connections between railroad and water, coupled with the birth and betterment of coastal cities and towns, enabled average folks to do something no generation had done before: set out across the wide water to explore—for pure pleasure—the opposite shores.

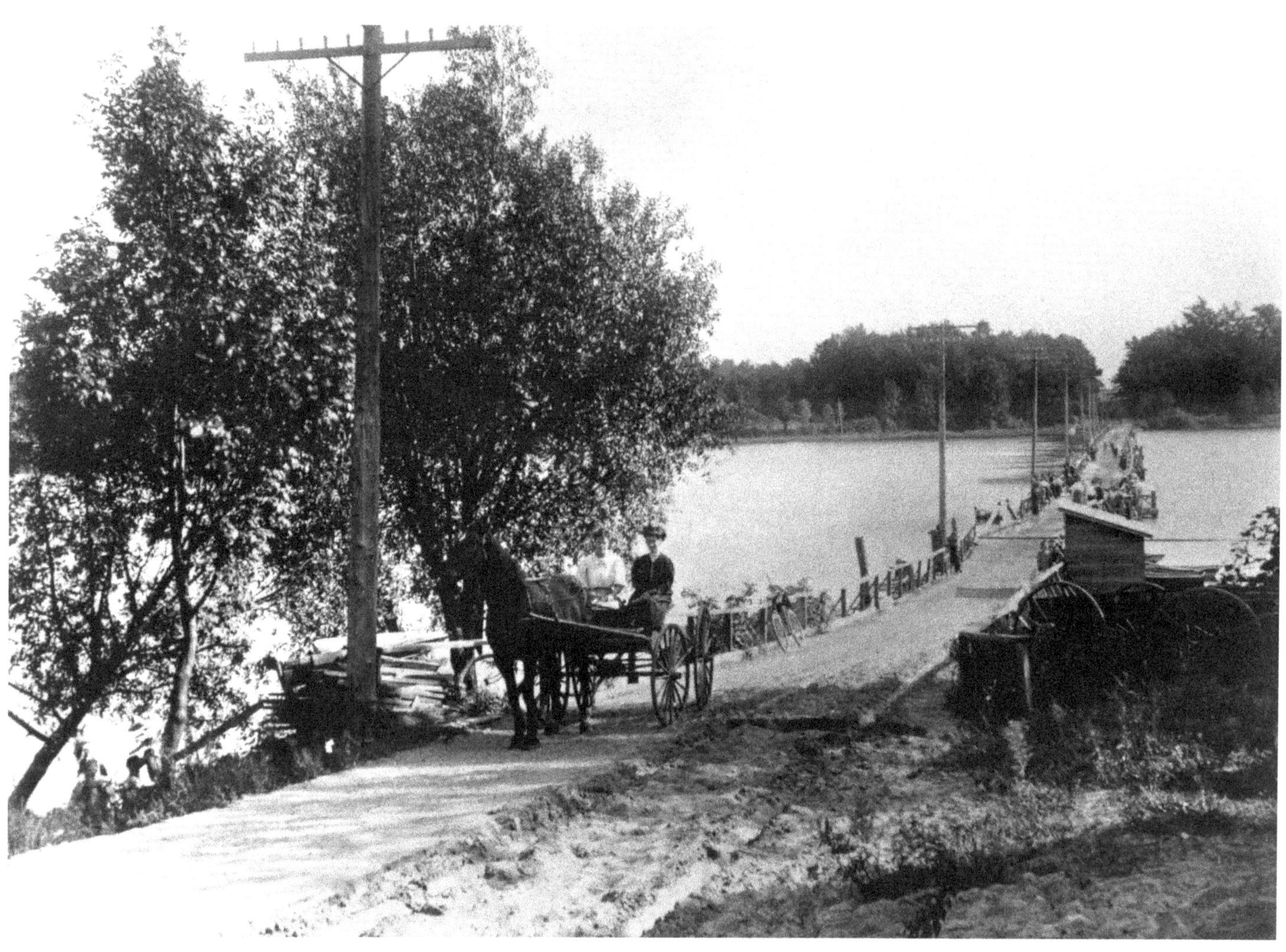

Long, skinny Black Lake (now Mona Lake) in Norton Shores, Michigan, emptied straight into Lake Michigan, making it easy for boats to enter and circle the inland lake, picking up and transporting wares from the town's sawmills, box factory, and fruit orchards to cities on the other side of Lake Michigan. However, in 1881 it was decided that the snaked shape of the lake also required this floating bridge, for those who wished to cross it on wheels.

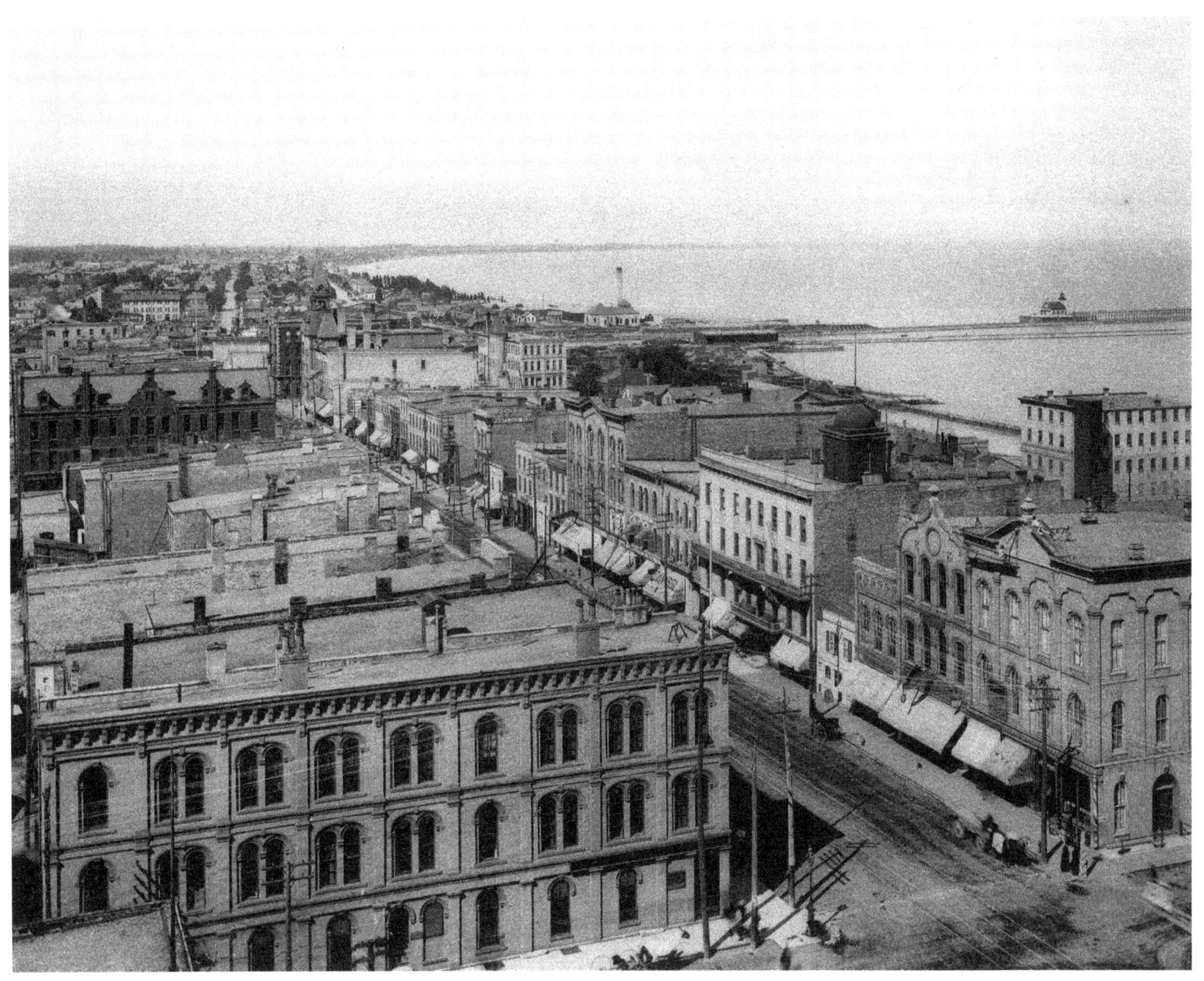

A view from the Racine Court House tower, facing northeast toward Lake Michigan, early in the decade of the 1880s. Construction of the courthouse, Racine's second, began with the laying of its cornerstone on July 4, 1876.

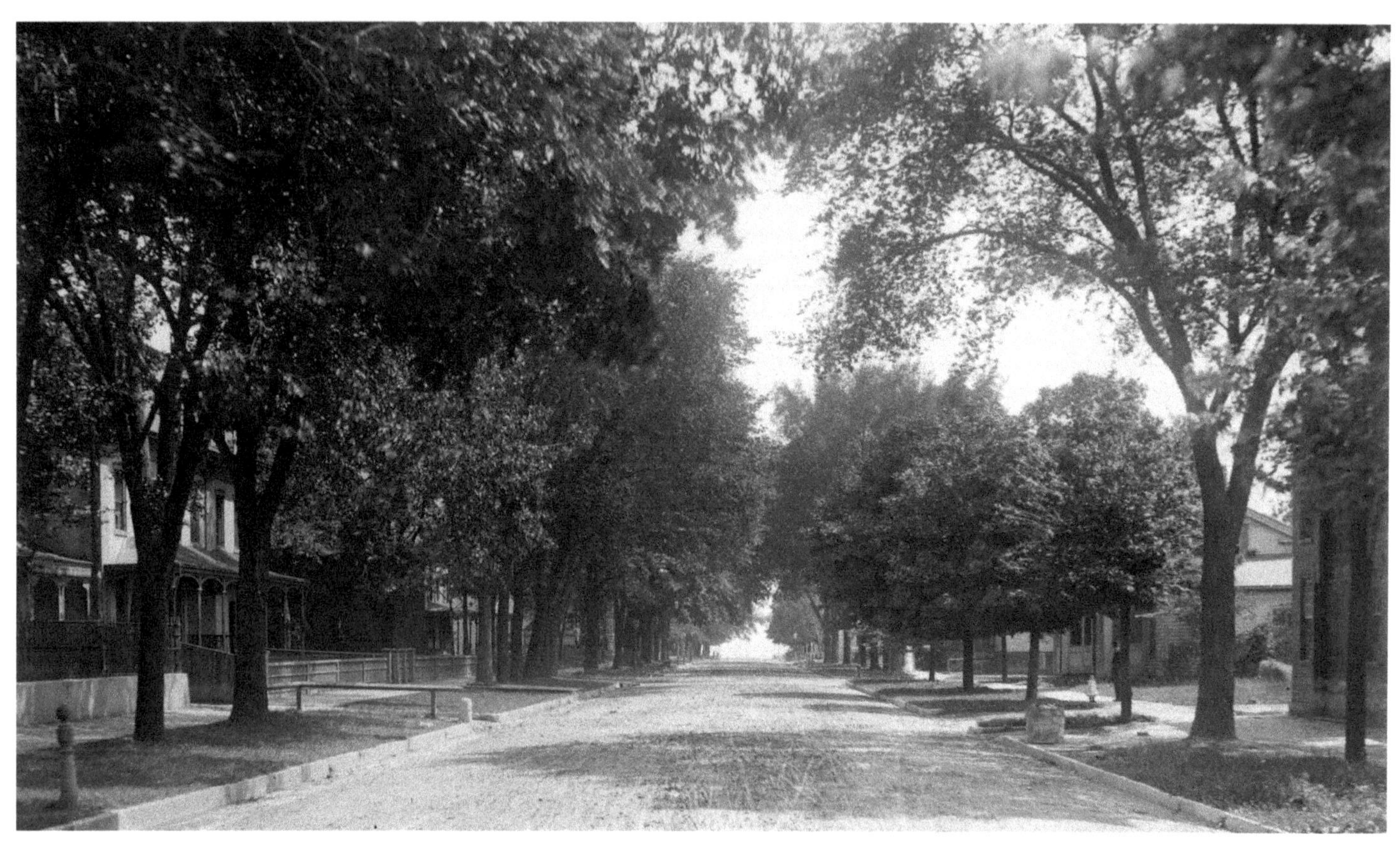

A look down one of the prettiest streets in Milwaukee in 1889, Mason Street, whose wide expanse, lined generously with trees and homes, slopes gently toward Lake Michigan. In 1842, a hill along Mason Street provided the earth needed to fill a large, swampy section of East Water Street.

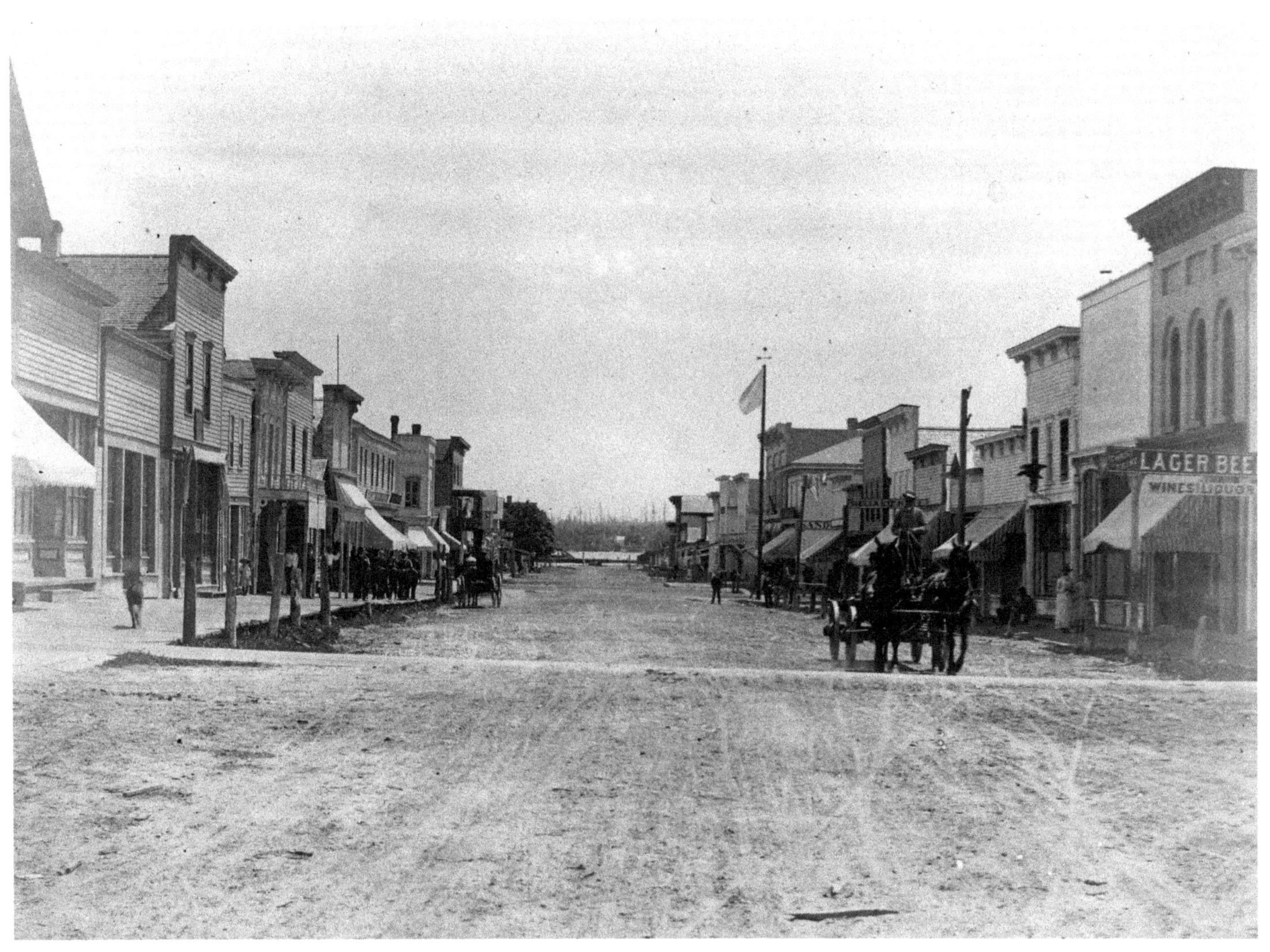

An 1888 image of Main Street (now Hancock Street) in Pentwater, Michigan, between Fifth and Fourth streets. To the right are Weidensee's Saloon, Bunyea's Grocery, Bird's store, Schmidt's Saloon, Haughey's store, and Moody's Pool Room. In the distance is what is now Snug Harbor on Lake Michigan.

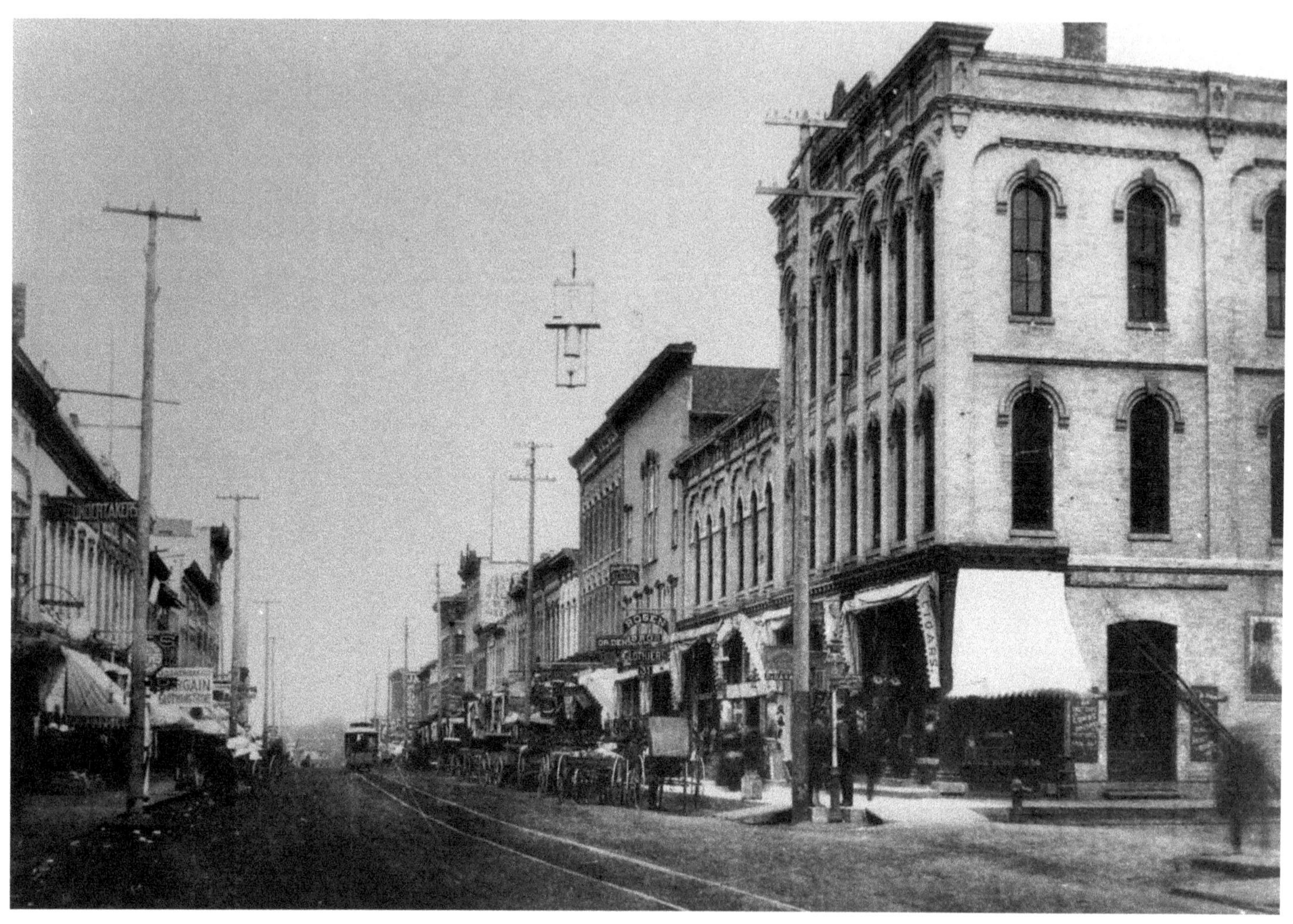

Formerly a marshy spot of natural impounded rivers, harbors, and windswept dunes along Michigan's west coast, Muskegon—derived from the Ottawa Indian term *Masquigon,* which means "marshy river"—would become a hotbed of industry by the time of this photograph in 1889, which showcases the city's then-commercial center, Western Avenue.

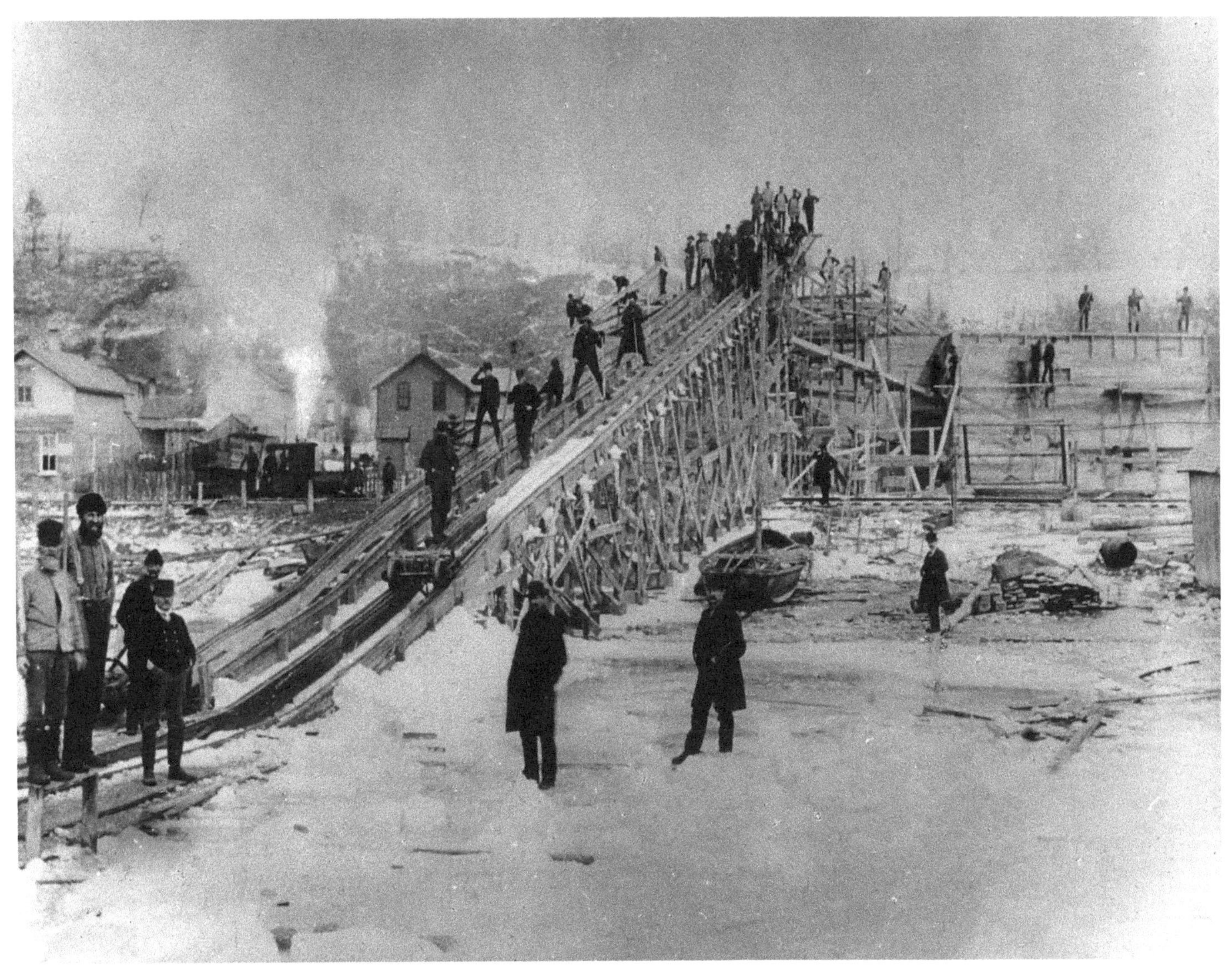

The Harbor Springs branch of New York's Knickerbocker Ice Company kept the iceboxes of the small Michigan town filled with frozen blocks carved from Little Traverse Bay each winter. Here, in 1889, workers stand on the tramway over which ice was hauled. In the background is local inventor Ephraim Shay's first and most famous engine, Baby Number 1.

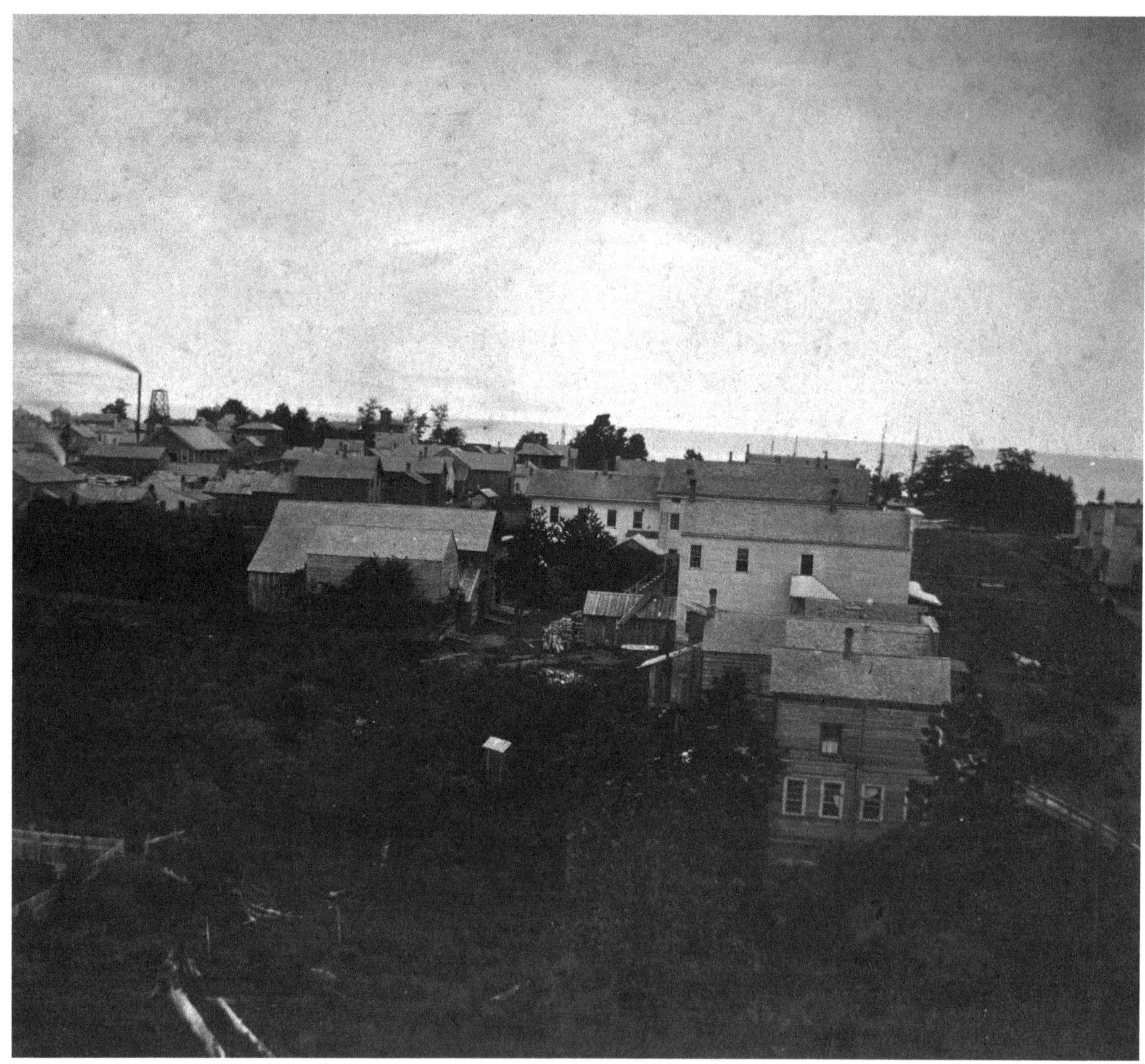

Perched on the eastern shore of Lake Michigan at the mouth of the Black River, Michigan's South Haven sprang to life as a lumber town in the mid-1800s. Fortunes made from shipping its wares to Chicago and Milwaukee gave rise to the harbor town's homes, stores, and school, as well as an opera house, theaters, hotels, and a casino. By the early 1900s, an estimated 2,000 visitors arrived aboard luxury steamships from Chicago each weekend.

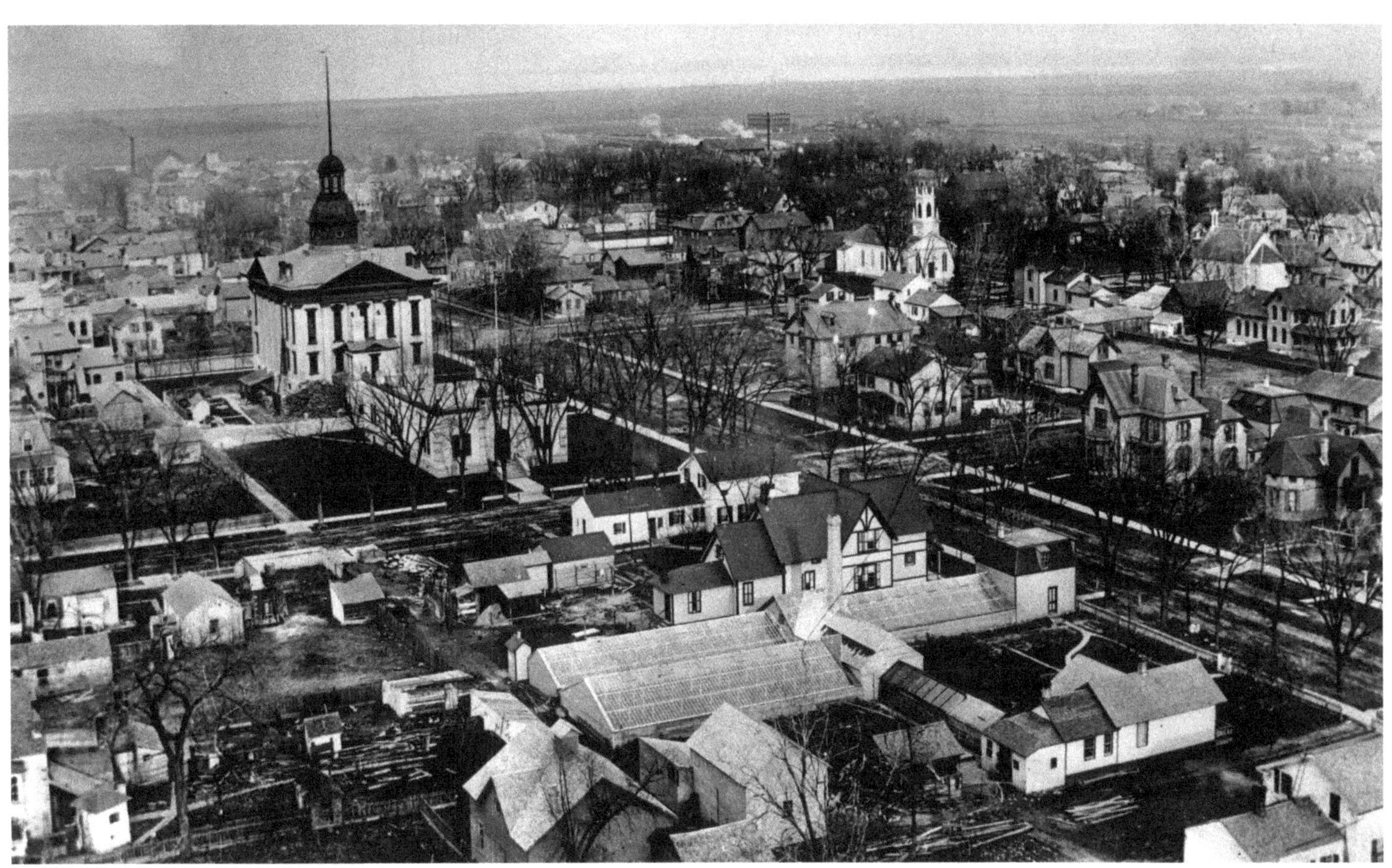

Wresting the Brown County seat from De Pere was a victory for Green Bay; holding court in the cramped town hall was not. Finally, in 1866, after plans to build a new courthouse stalled during the 1857 depression, Green Bay got its courthouse—a stone-and-brick beauty crowned by a grand cupola. Without indoor plumbing or central heat, however, the old courthouse would be abandoned in 1911 for the new and current courthouse.

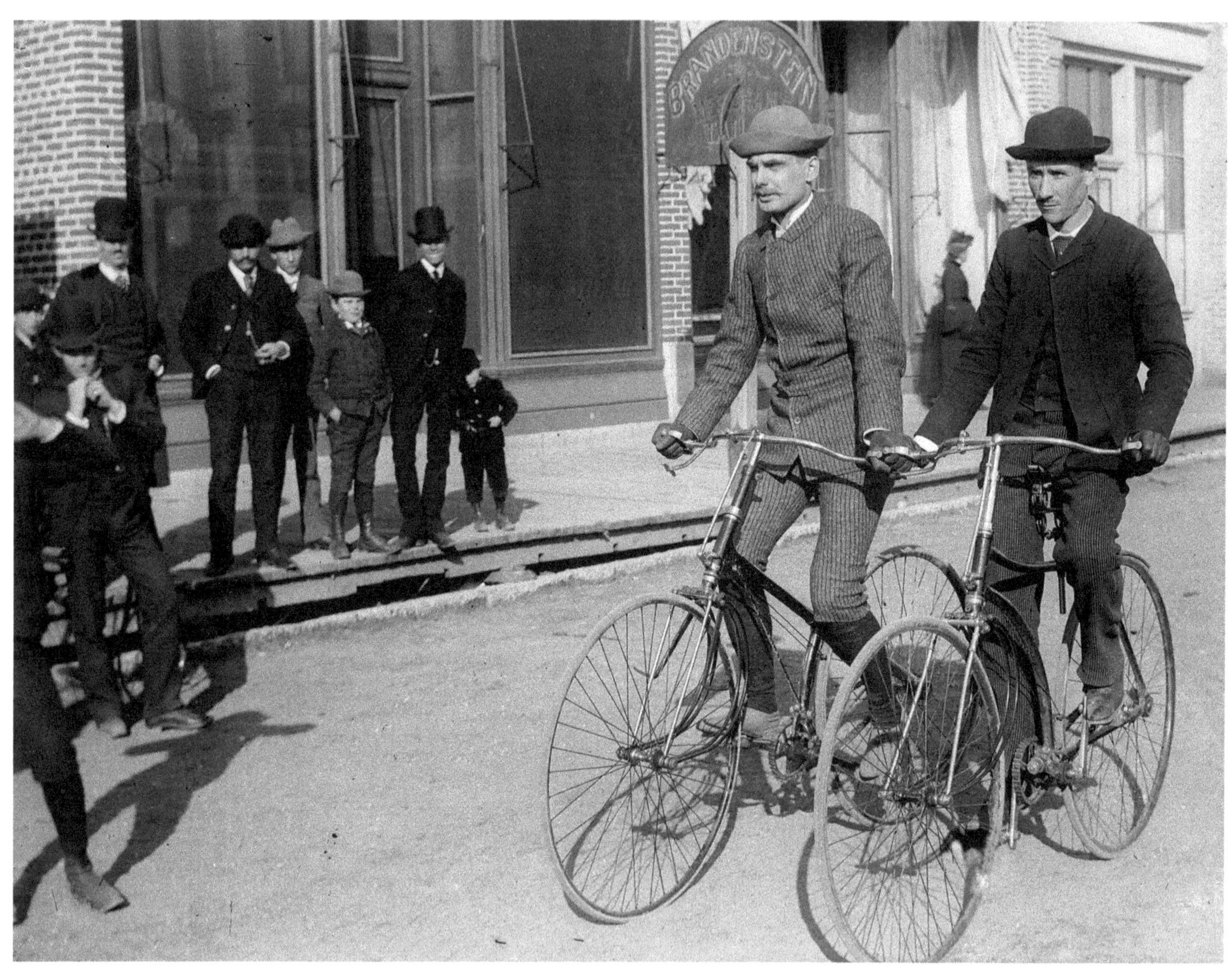

A pair of cyclists pedals past a sidewalk of curious onlookers in Green Bay in this view from 1890.

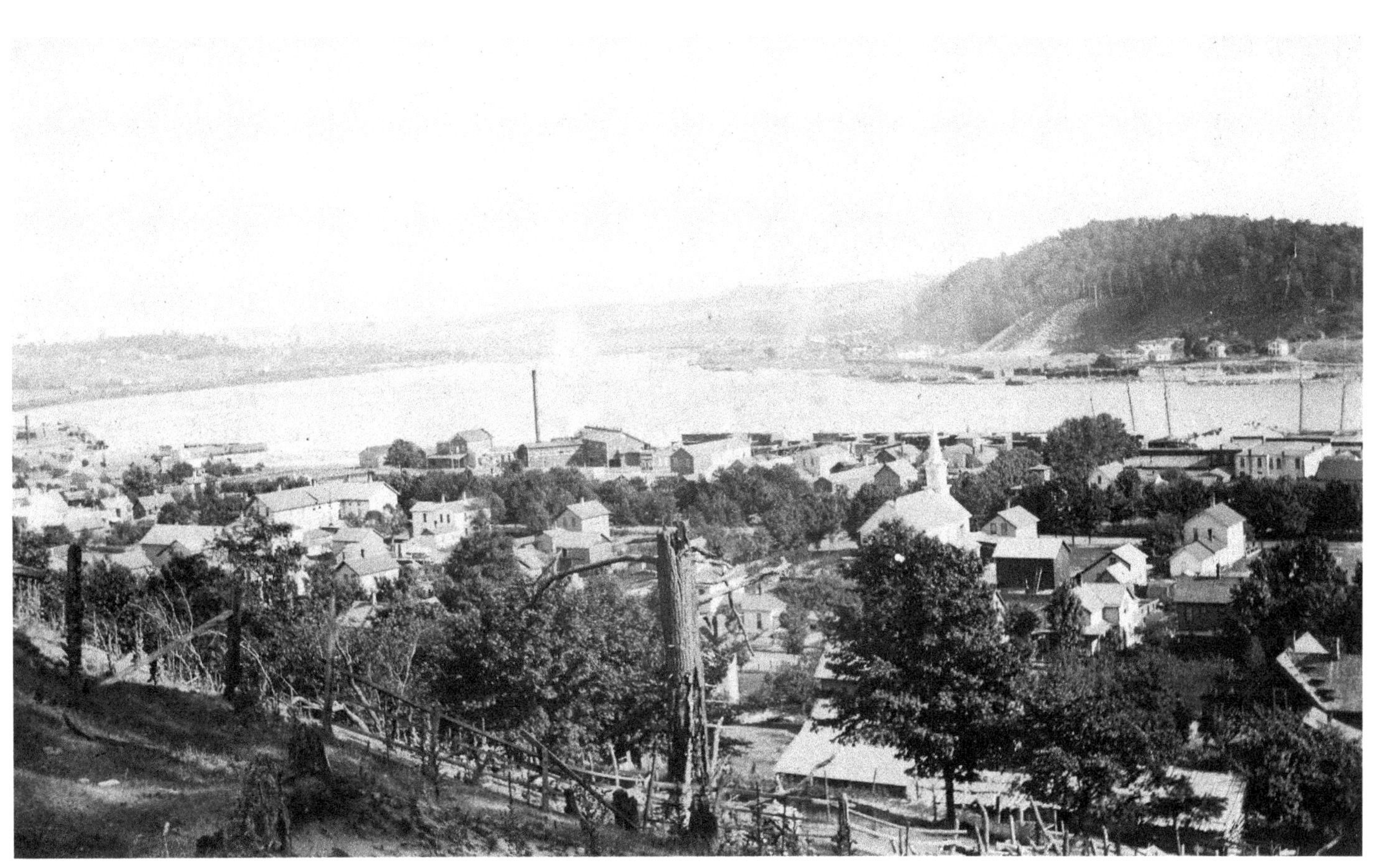

Looking from Frankfort, Michigan, over Betsie Bay toward Elberta—then called South Frankfort—around 1892, the year the Ann Arbor Marine Terminal began ferrying its railcars full of goods through the bay's channel to Lake Michigan, then on to cities along the lake's west coast. Elberta's last car ferry, the SS *City of Milwaukee,* ceased operating in 1982.

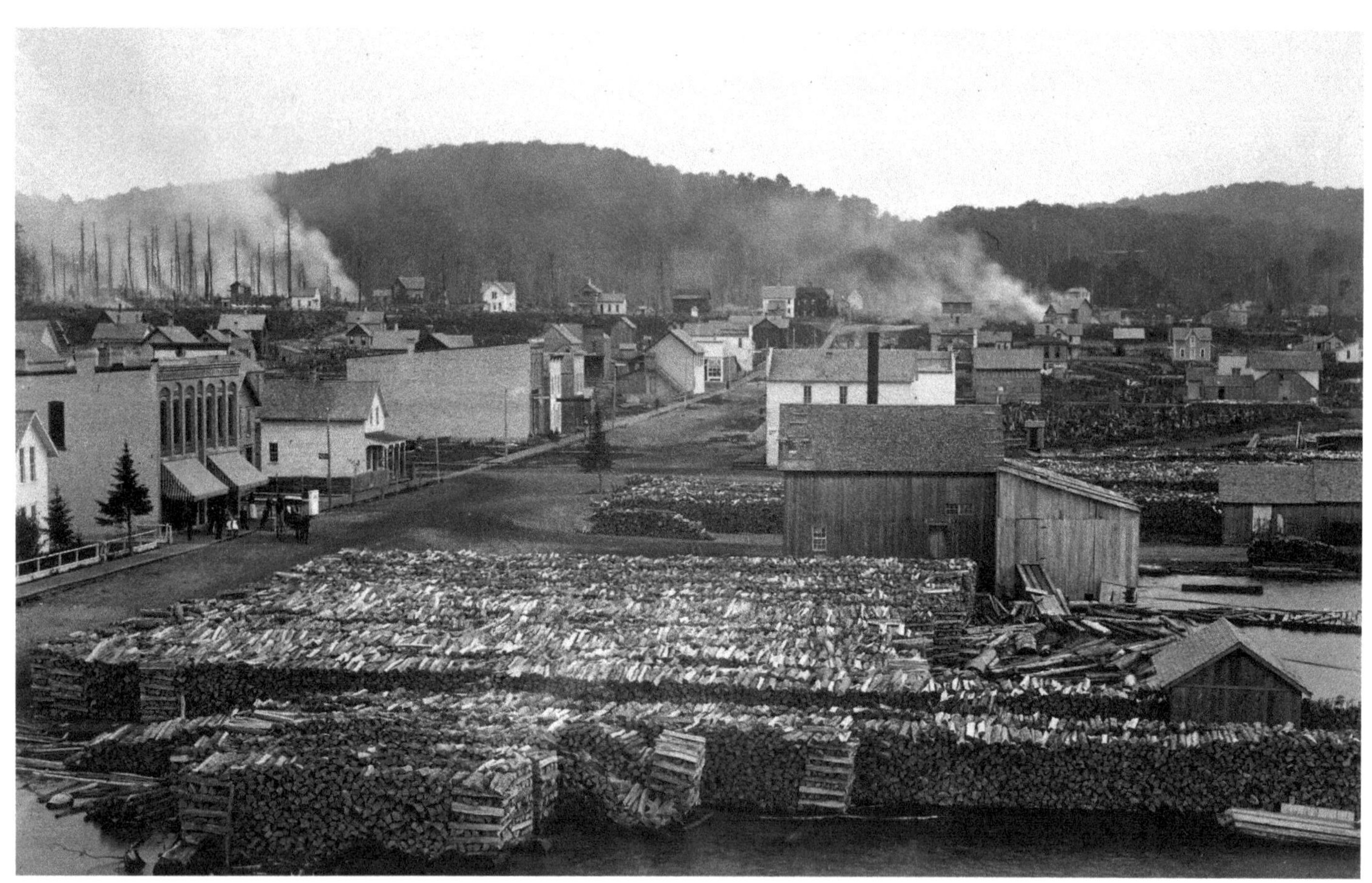

Thanks to Round and Charlevoix lakes' fringe of giant pines, and the hand dredging of the Pine River channel between Round Lake and Lake Michigan in 1873, Charlevoix, Michigan, was a booming lumber town and popular summer destination for wealthy Chicagoans. Notable among this group were the University of Chicago professors who began the tony Chicago Club summer association here in the 1880s, shortly before this photograph was taken.

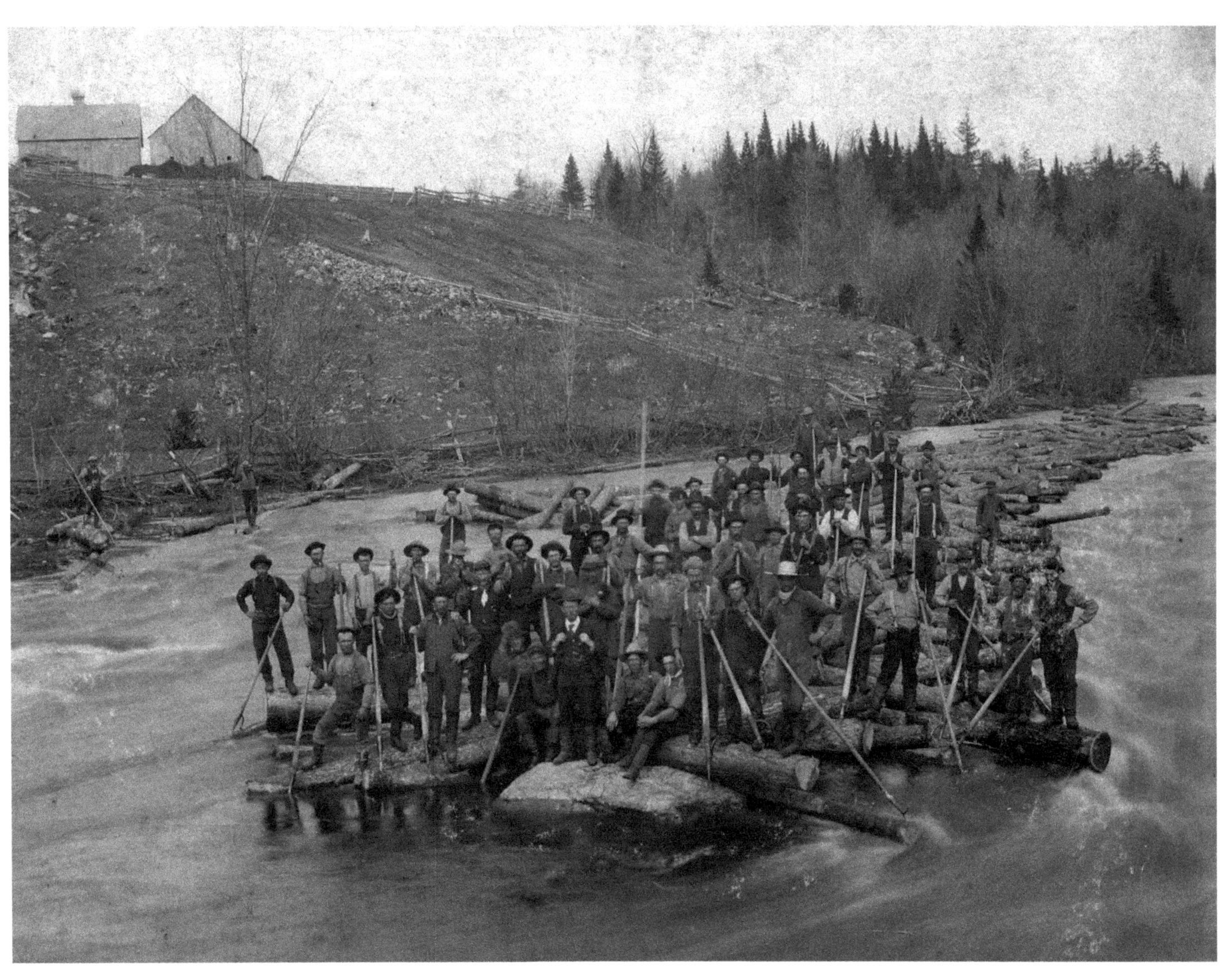

Loggers pose atop a drive along Michigan's 200-mile-long Muskegon River, which moved so much timber between 1880 and 1910, the port town at its mouth, Muskegon, was nicknamed "Lumber Queen of the World."

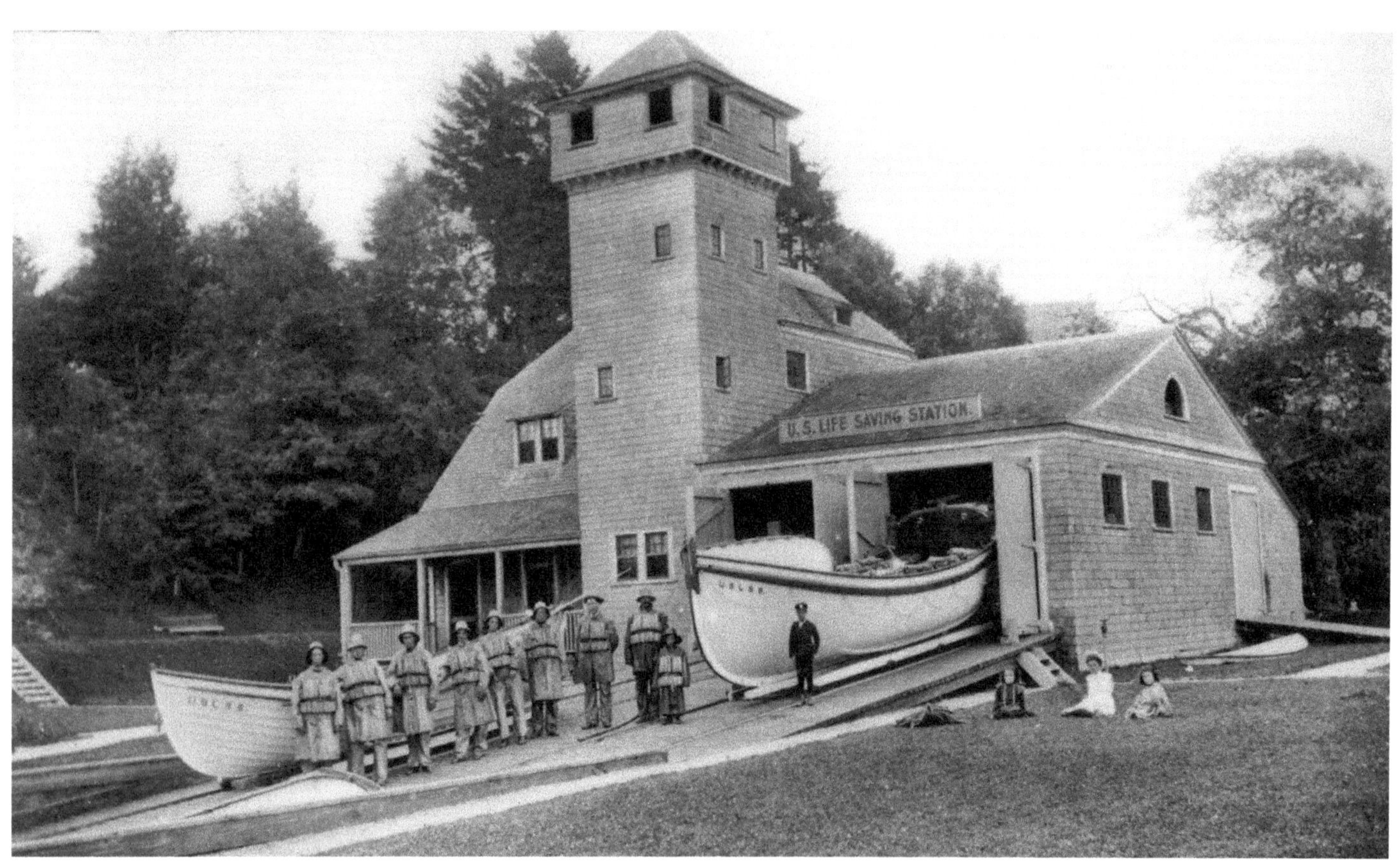

Michigan's U.S. Life Saving Station Charlevoix, built in 1898 on the south break wall of the Pine River Channel to Lake Michigan, was in use until 1965. Seven years earlier, the Coast Guard sent a lifeboat from the station to the sinking SS *Carl D. Bradley,* whose hull had broken in a wild November storm southwest of Gull Island, but extreme wind and waves made rescue impossible. Only 2 of 35 *Bradley* crewmembers survived.

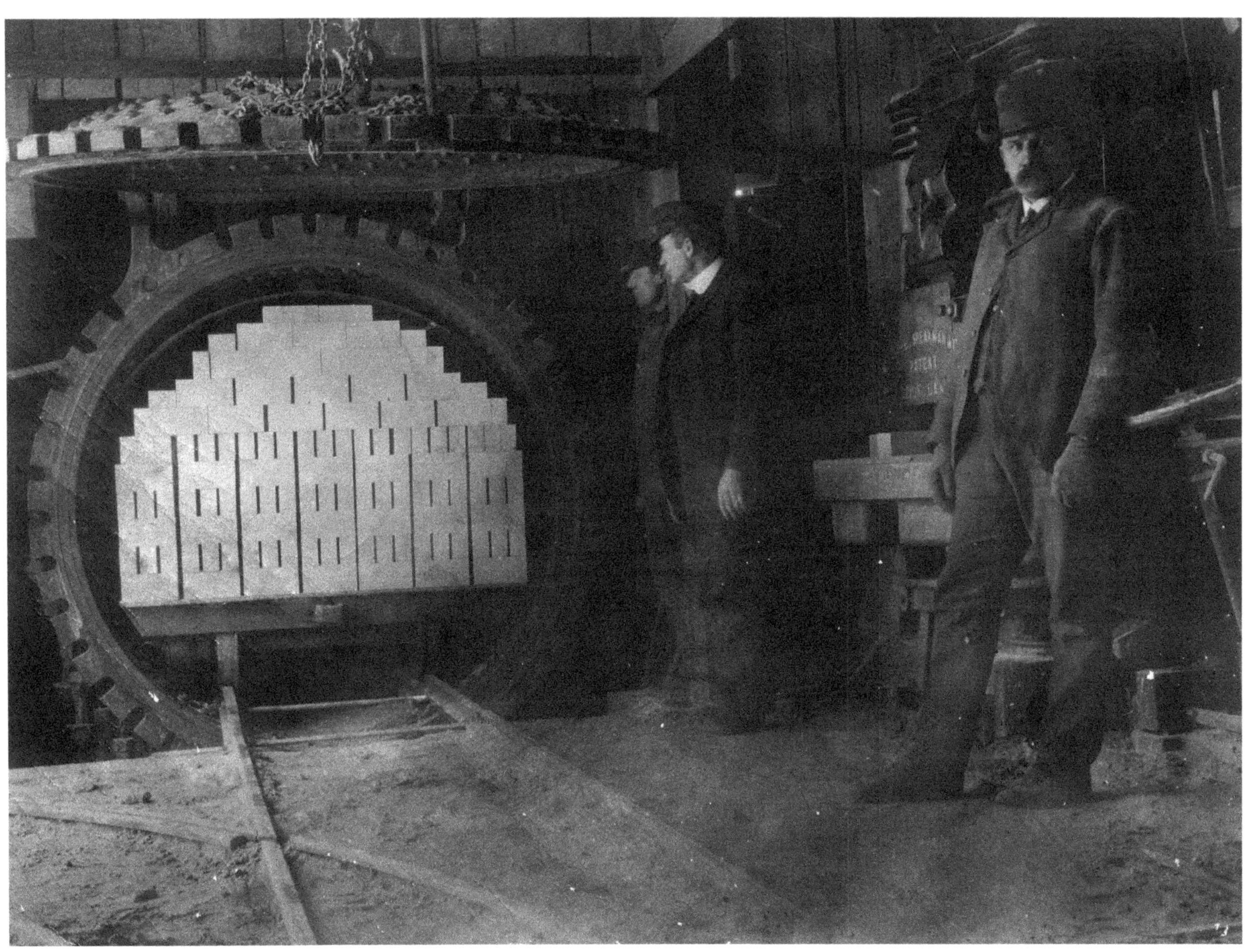

Luther H. Cooper, at far-right, stands before a brick kiln in Manistee, Michigan. More than half the town, a logging mecca boasting more than 20 sawmills, burned on October 8, 1871, the same day the Great Fire of Chicago broke out. The fire prompted a massive enterprise for rebuilding the town with fireproof materials; many of the resulting Victorian-style brick buildings still stand downtown today.

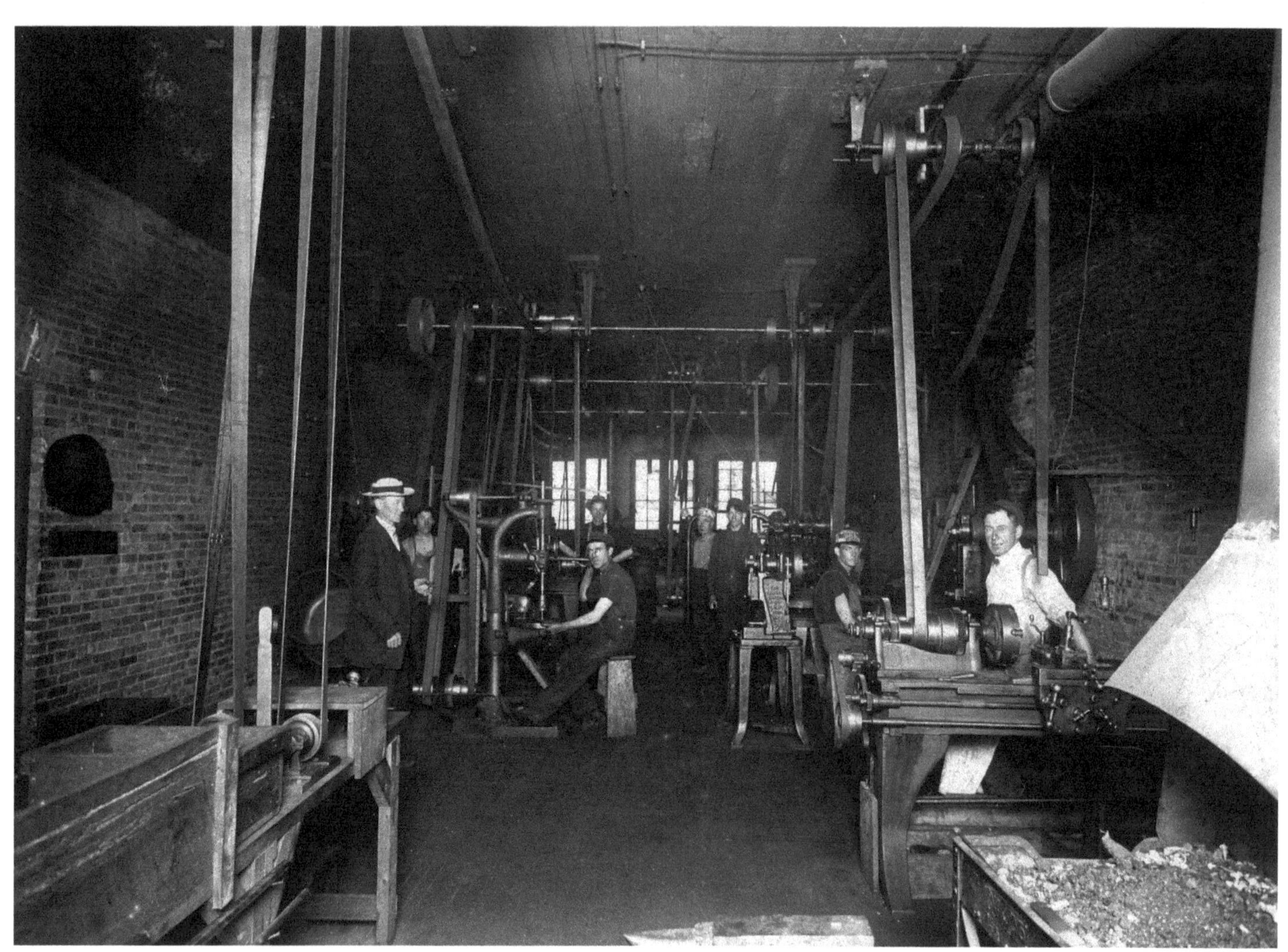

1900s-era laborers inside the Hines Machine Shop in Traverse City, Michigan, take a break.

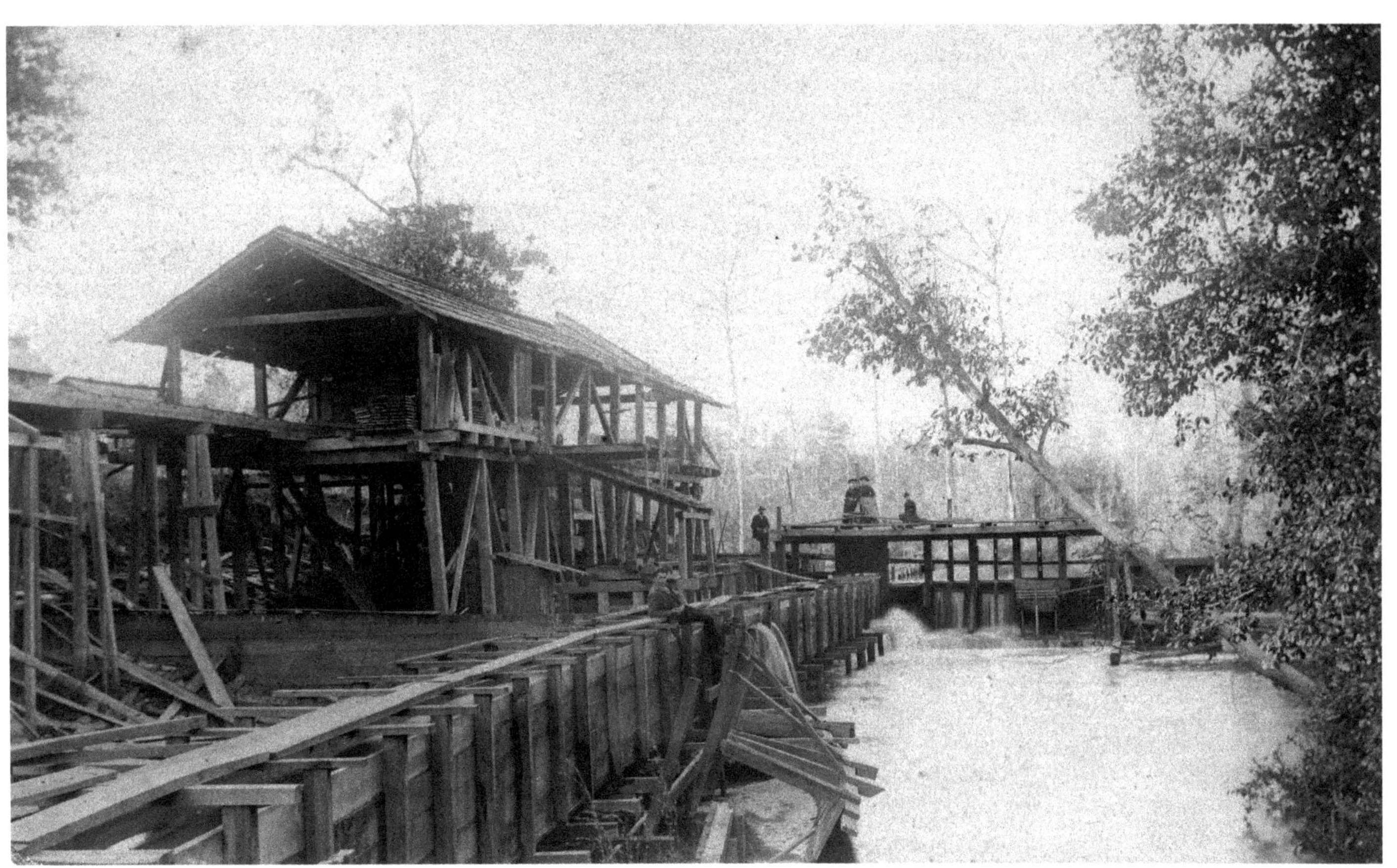

The first sawmill was erected on the Manistee River in Michigan in 1841. By the 1880s, the river's peak lumbering era, dozens more water-powered mills had been constructed along the river, and the city of Manistee boasted more millionaires per capita than anywhere else in the nation.

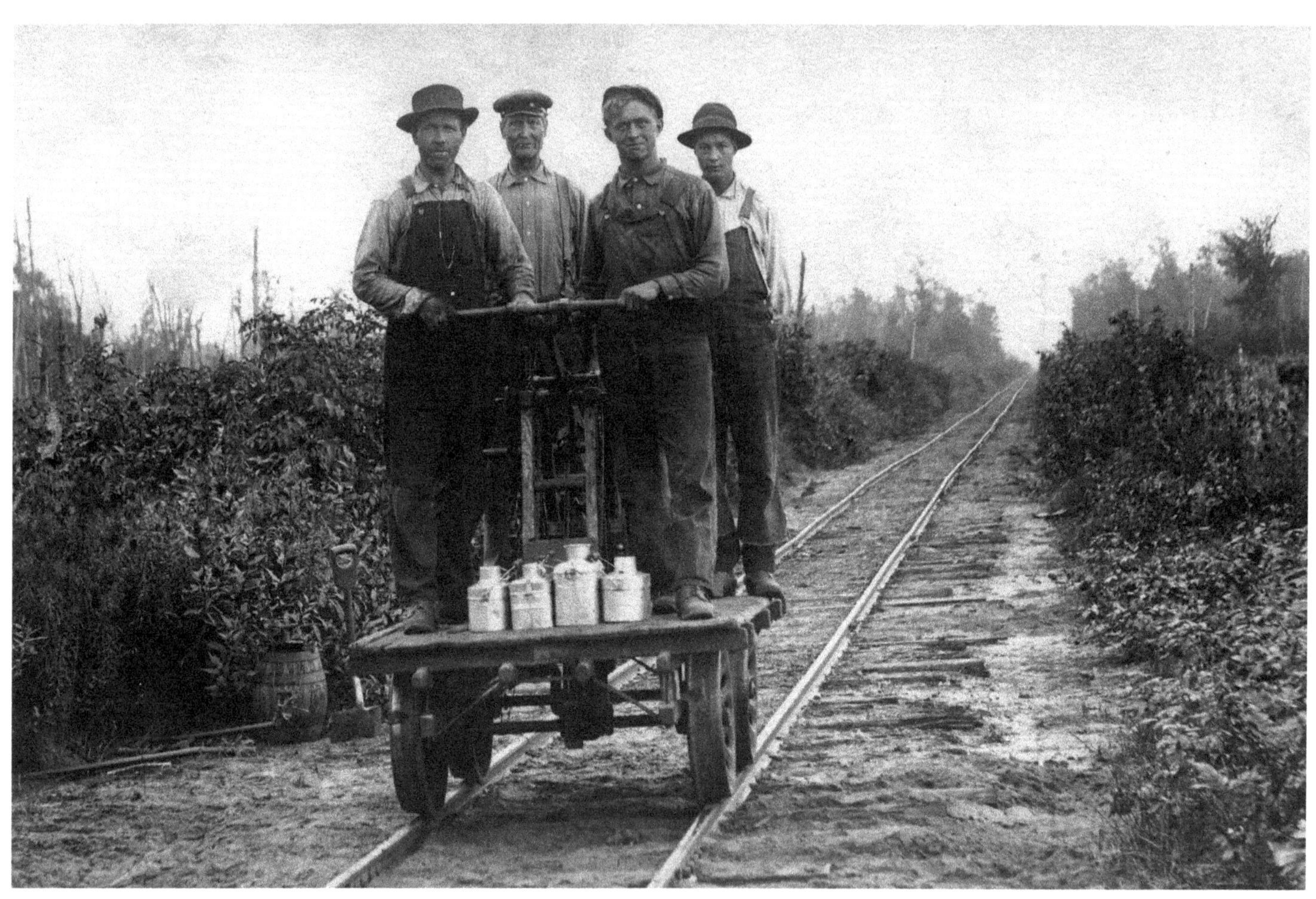

Four men travel by handcar along Michigan's Manistee and Luther Railroad, an 80-mile road that stretched west from Le Roy to East Lake—where lumber baron Richard G. Peters' discovery of vast salt deposits in the early 1880s spurred his second fortune. The Manistee and Luther Railroad remained in operation from 1886 to 1913.

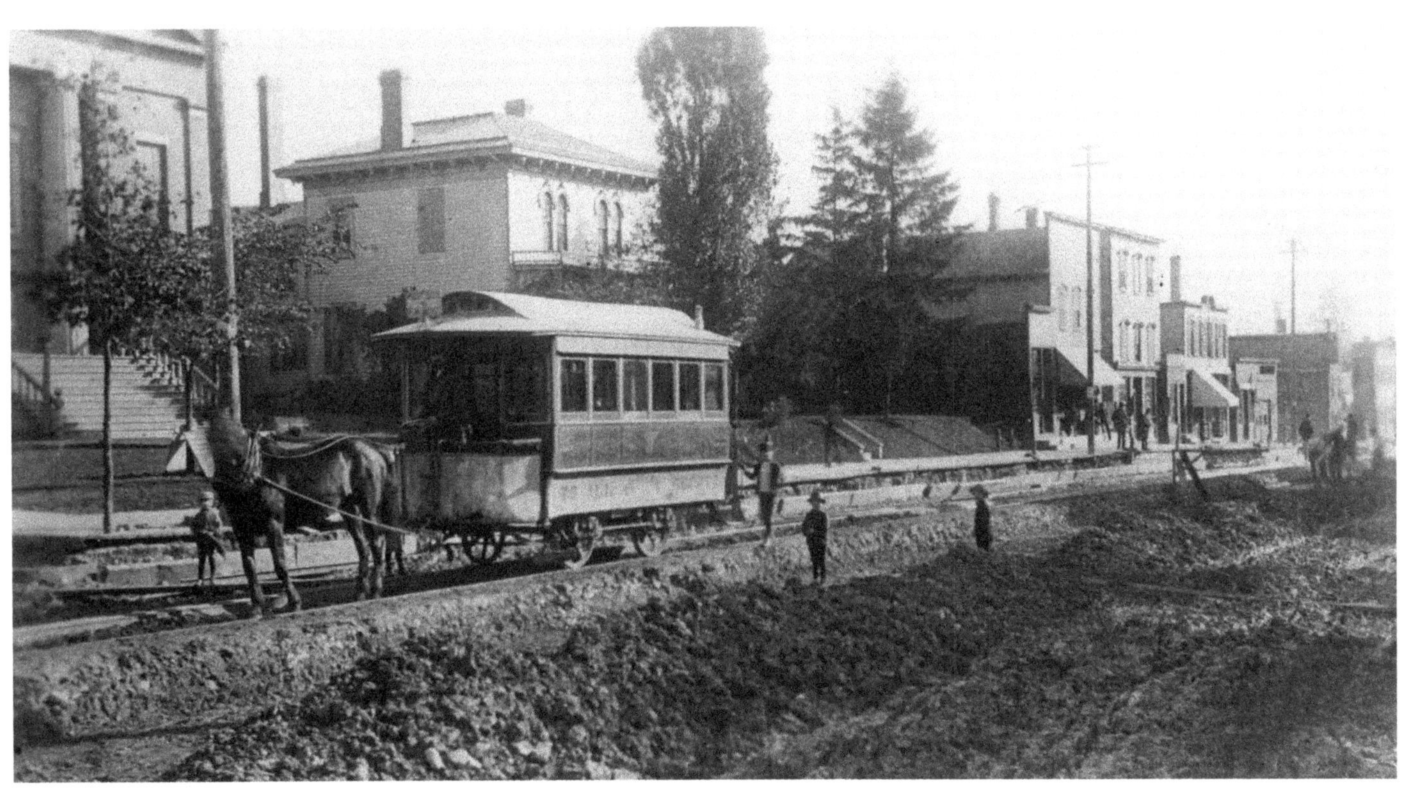

Horse-drawn vehicles, like this trolley, were a common sight in Racine, Wisconsin, in 1891. The city's fire department used a horse-drawn steamer and a horse-drawn hose cart from 1882 to 1918, when a motorized fire engine took over.

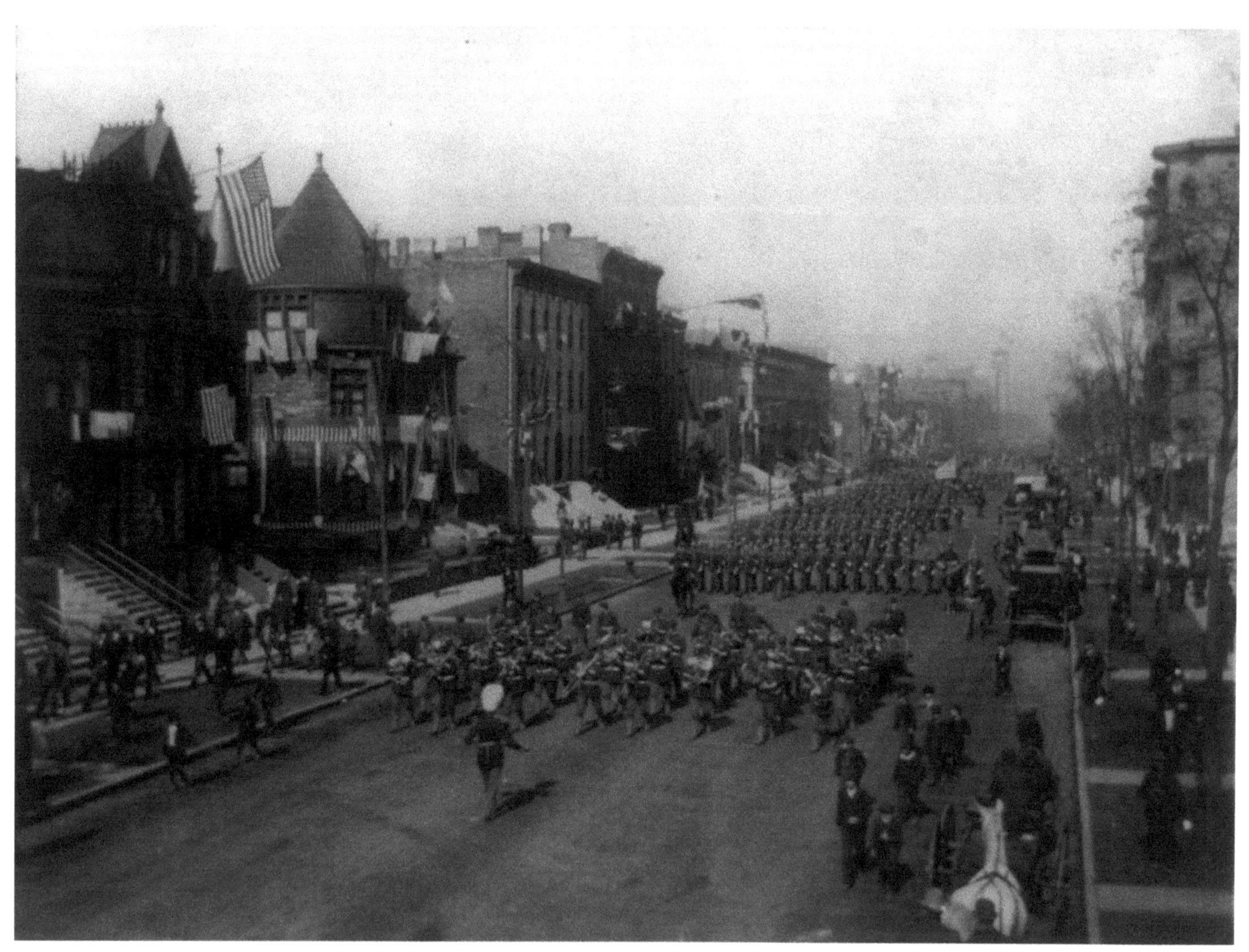

A military outfit marches down Chicago's Michigan Boulevard on October 21, 1892, Dedication Day of the 1893 World's Columbian Exposition—also known as the Chicago World's Fair. A celebration of the 400th anniversary of Christopher Columbus' New World discovery, the exposition was a coup for the city, which beat out New York City, Washington, D.C., and St. Louis for hosting honors. The city underwent massive construction, creating the most elaborate exposition the world had yet seen.

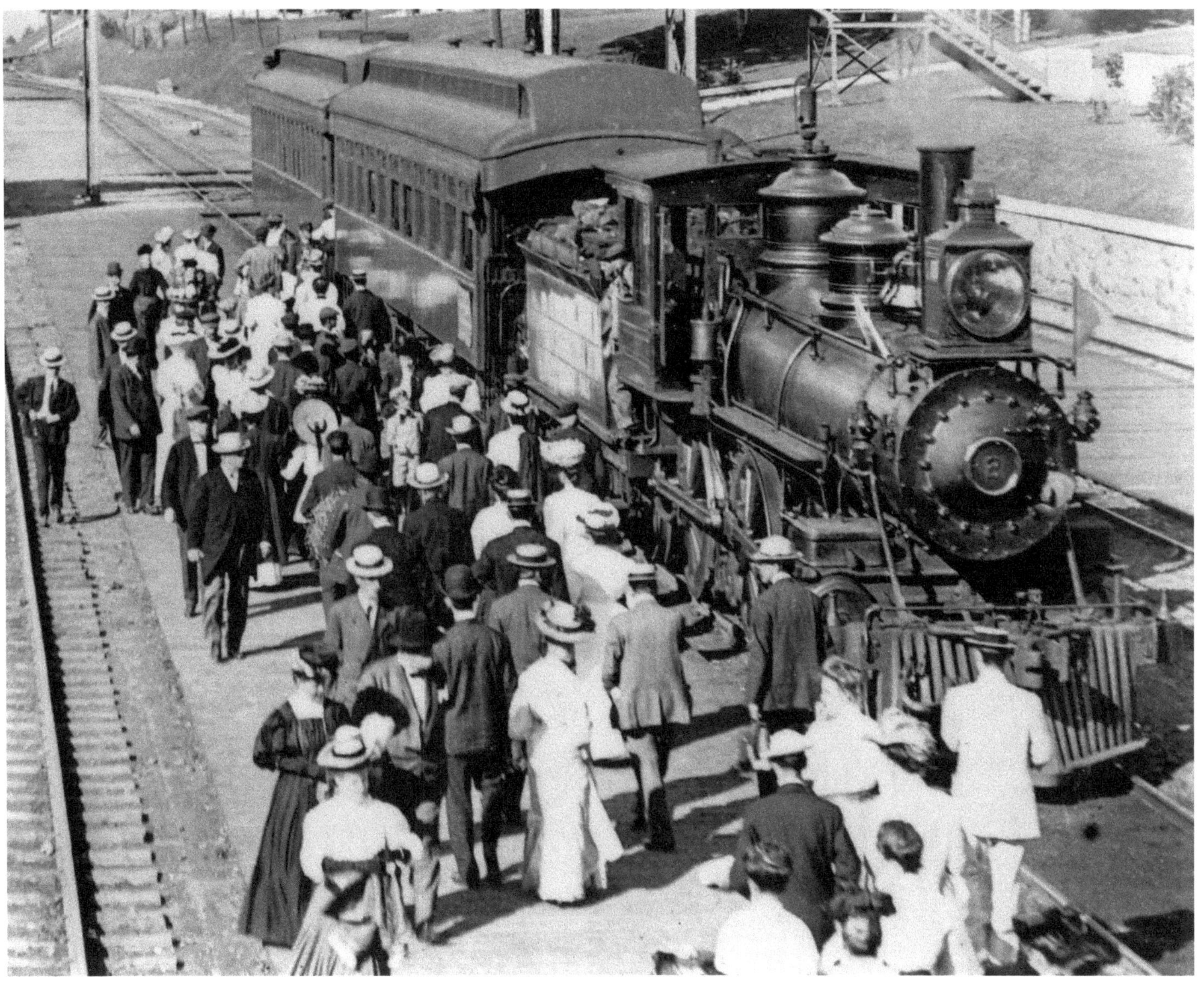

Victorian-era railroad passengers make connections in Petoskey, Michigan. Although the town didn't see its first railroad line, the Grand Rapids & Indiana Railroad, until 1873, the rail company's promotion of Petoskey's healthy northern air, fabulous fishing, and discounted land deals for Civil War veterans lured droves of vacationers and settlers to the Little Traverse Bay city through the turn of the century.

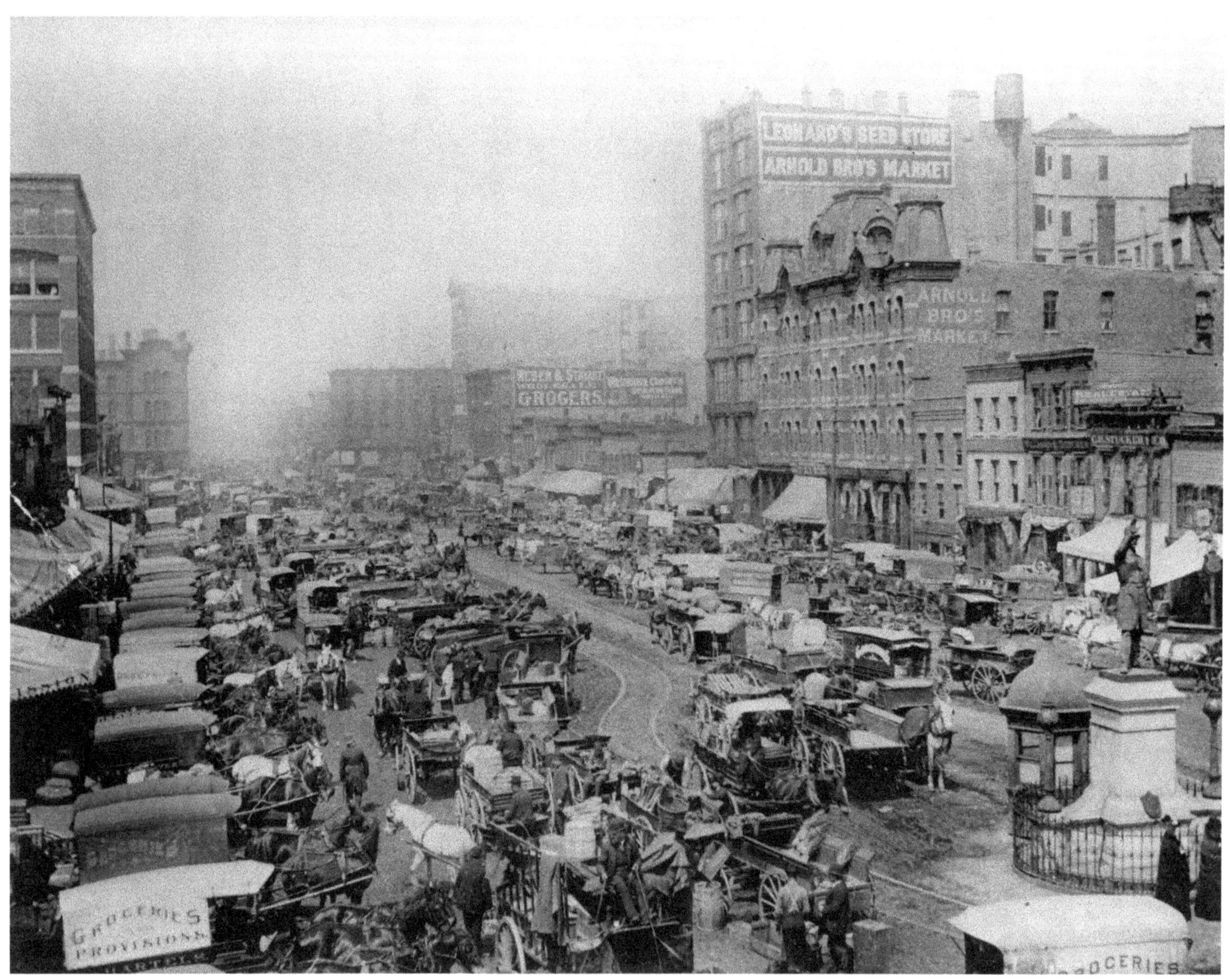

The bustling traffic and commerce of Chicago's Haymarket Square in 1893. Just seven years earlier, the square was the site of the infamous Haymarket Riot, in which more than a thousand laborers protesting police attacks on Union picketers faced off with police. In the aftermath of the violent blast of an anarchist's bomb and the reports of police guns, seven officers and an unknown number of protesters lay dead. Eight anarchists were tried for murder and four of them were hanged.

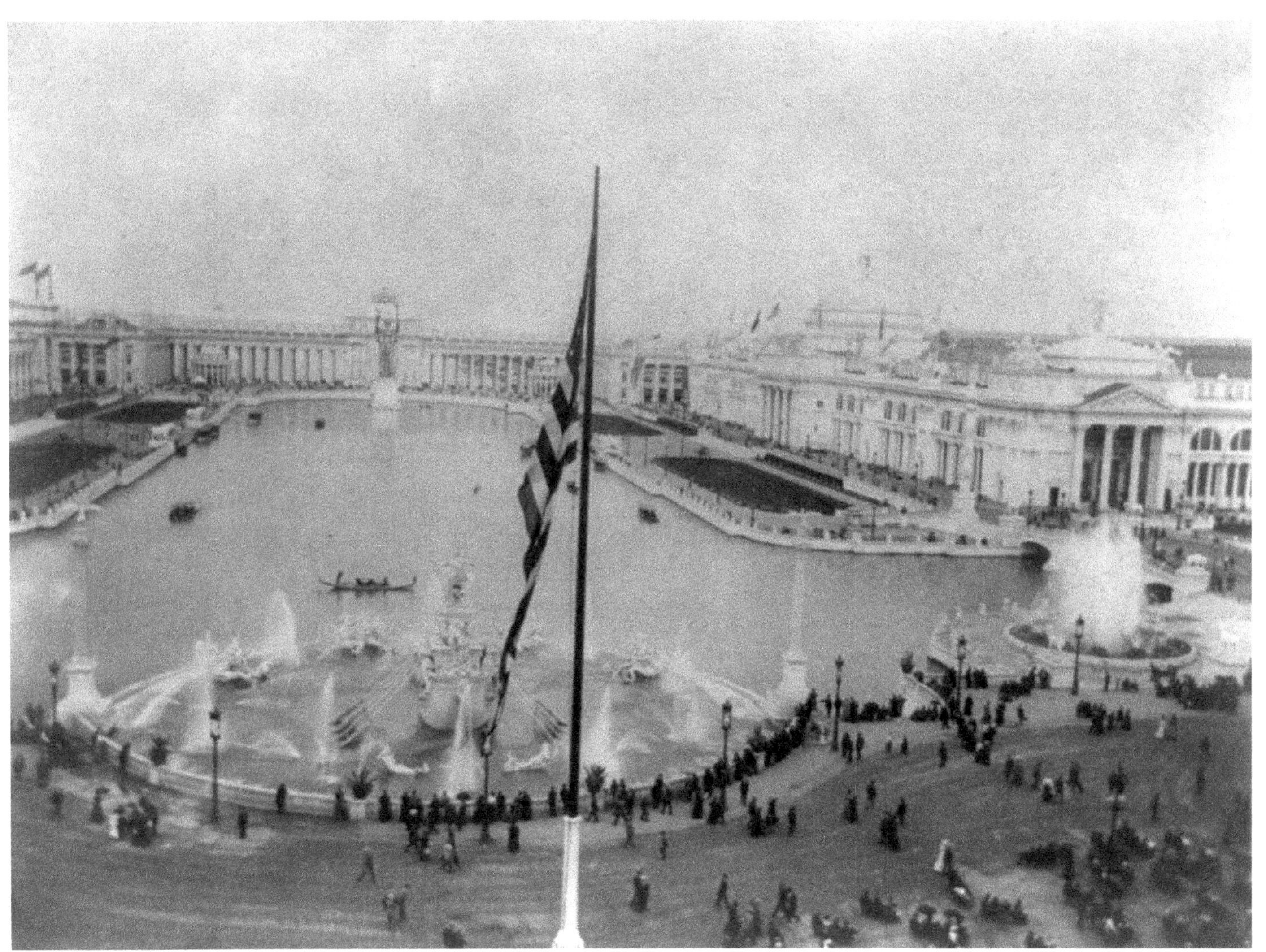

Of the nearly 200 Beaux Arts–style buildings erected for the 1893 World's Columbian Exposition, most famous were the regal white buildings surrounding the Grand Basin at the Court of Honor. Illuminated and glittering a brilliant white, the buildings quickly earned the area the moniker White City, which was said to have inspired L. Frank Baum's Emerald City in his 1900 fantasy novel *The Wonderful Wizard of Oz.*

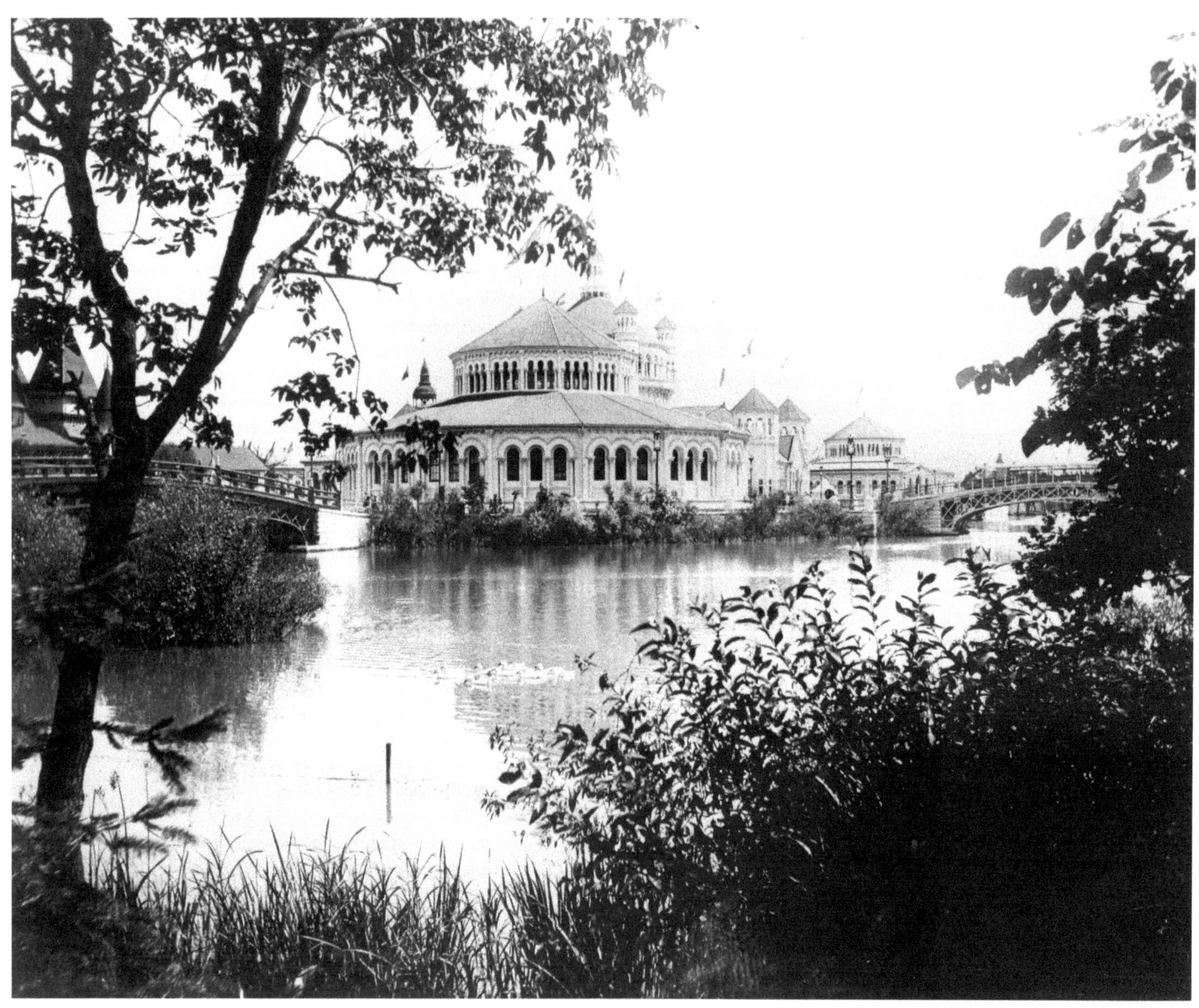

Designed by powerhouse architect Henry Ives Cobb, the Romanesque Fisheries Building at the 1893 Chicago World's Fair sat between Lake Michigan and a giant lagoon built for the occasion. Flanked by polygonal pavilions, topped with a huge circular tower—flanked by polygonal towers itself—and encircled with columns showcasing images of marine life, the building's two acres of exhibition space showcased floor-to-ceiling aquariums filled with hundreds of species of freshwater and saltwater fish.

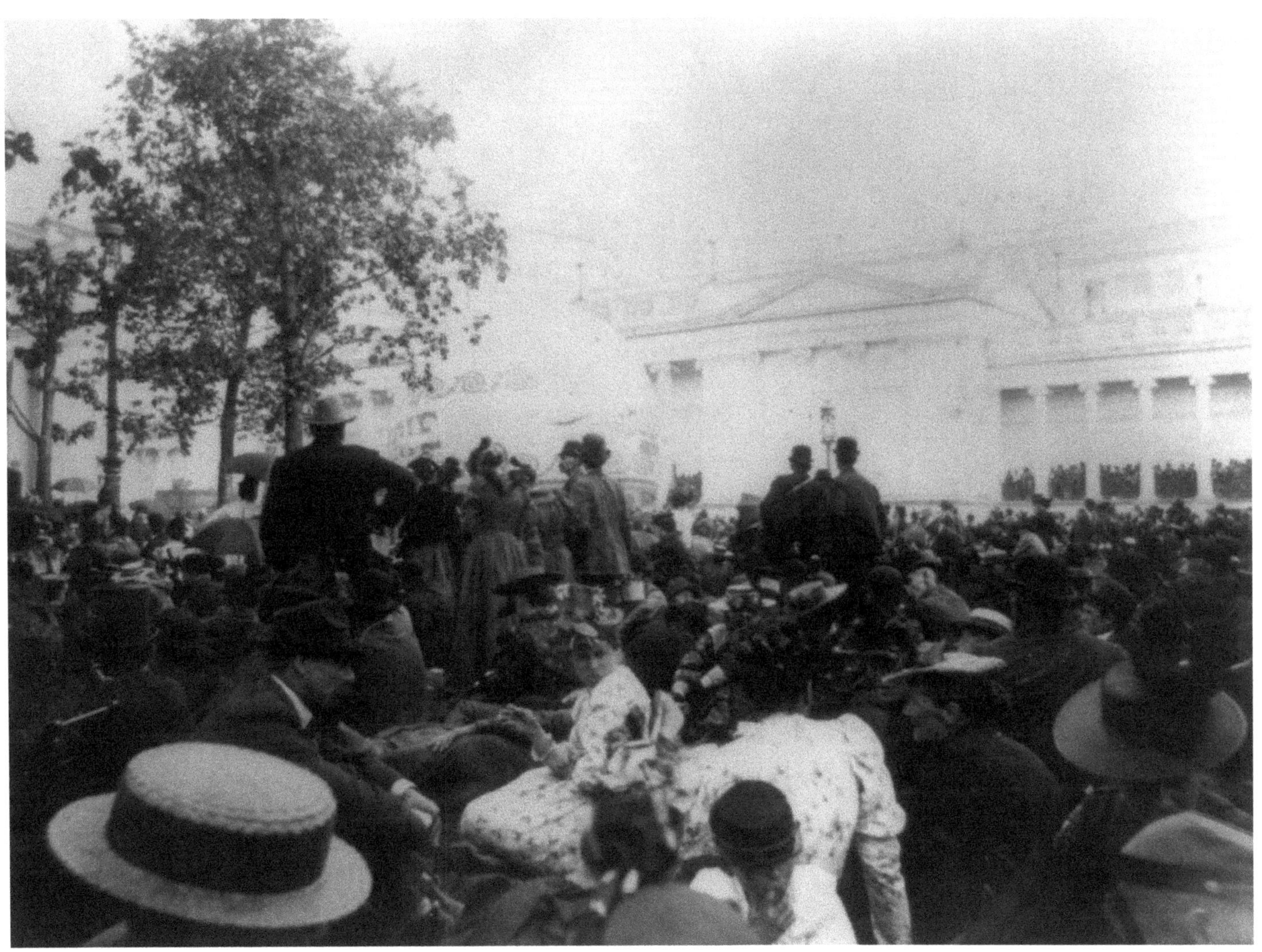

Crowds gather at Chicago's World's Columbian Exposition, home of the world's first midway, waiting for one of the wildest rides to rise: a hot-air balloon. The grand exposition was located along Lake Michigan's south shore, in Jackson Park.

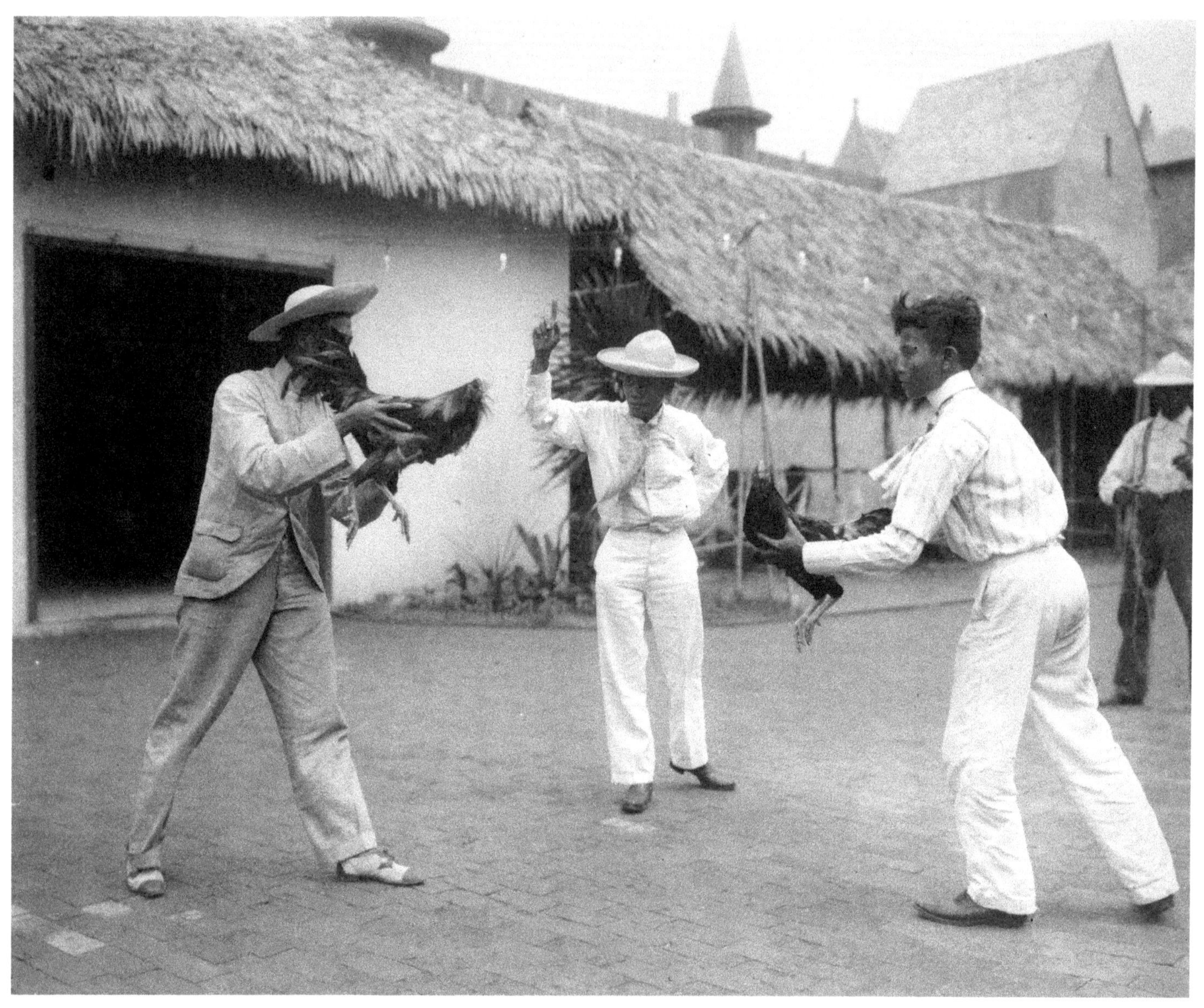

International exhibits were a huge draw at Chicago's 1893 World's Fair. From beer halls and bazaars to belly dancing and cockfighting, American visitors were treated to the culture of nearly 50 other countries.

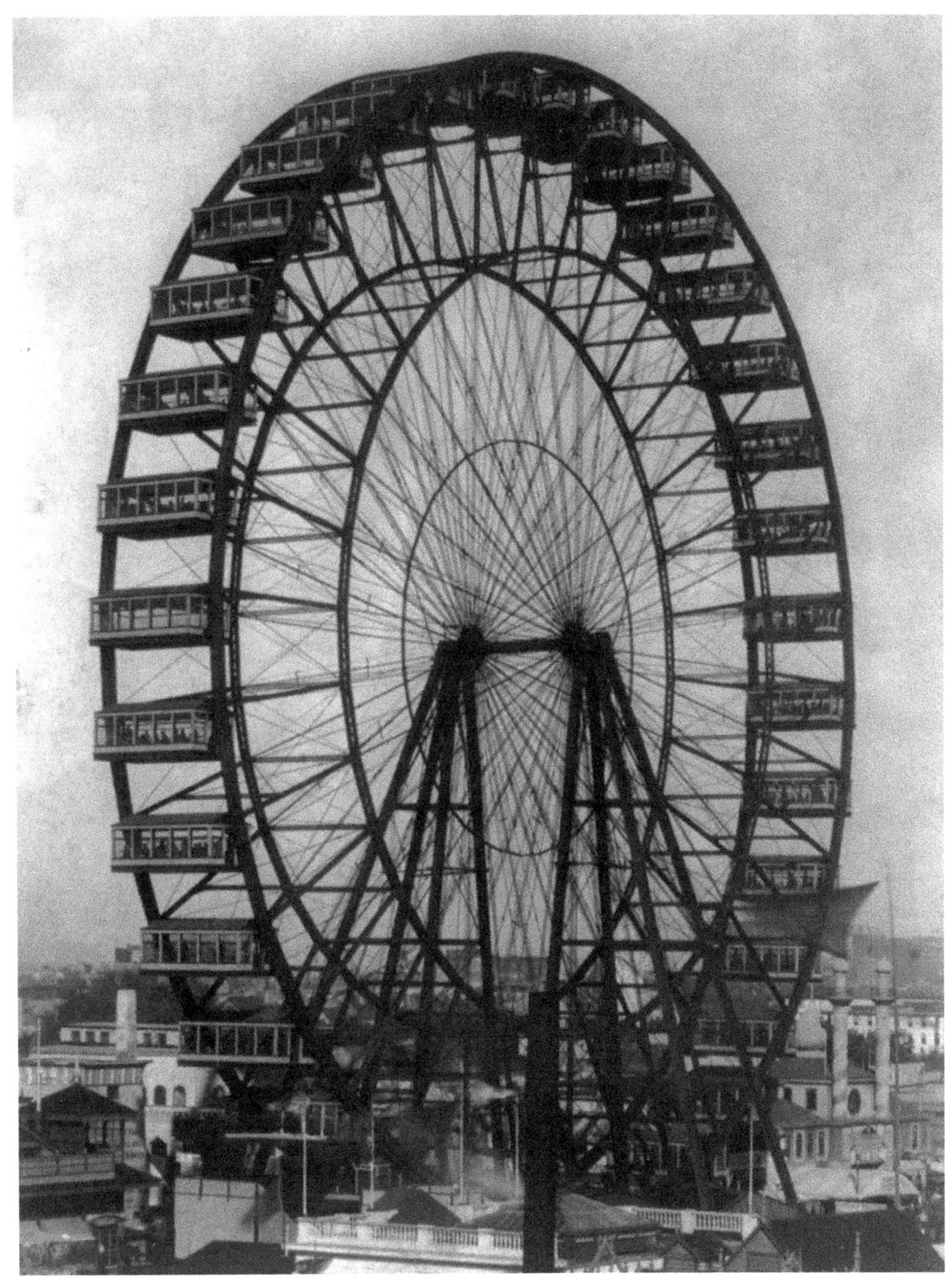

The most remarkable ride at Chicago's 1893 World's Columbian Exposition was a 26-story wheel designed by George Washington Gale Ferris. Meant to outshine the 1889 Paris Exposition's 984-foot Eiffel Tower, the colossal wheel—the world's first Ferris wheel—was a mechanical marvel that could carry 2,160 passengers. By fair's end, more than 1.5 million people had taken their turn. After a disappointing stint at St. Louis' 1904 Louisiana Purchase Exposition, the once-celebrated wheel was dismantled with 200 pounds of dynamite and sold as scrap.

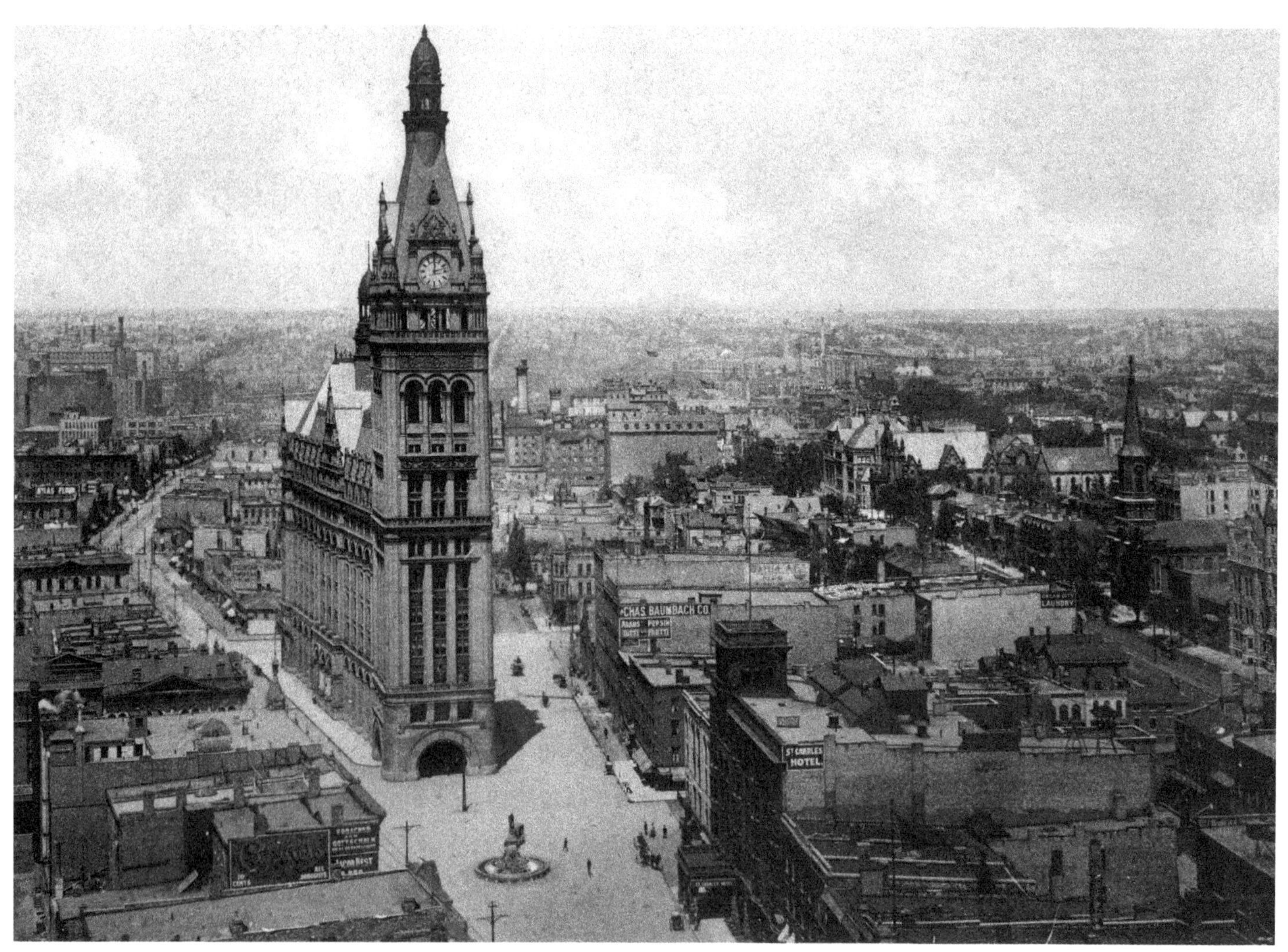

A panorama of Milwaukee and, at upper-right, a sliver of Lake Michigan's western coastline. More than 350 feet above the city's downtown streets towers Milwaukee City Hall's bell tower. When the German Renaissance Revival–style building was erected in 1895, it was the third-tallest structure in the nation after the Washington Monument and Philadelphia City Hall. It still stands today.

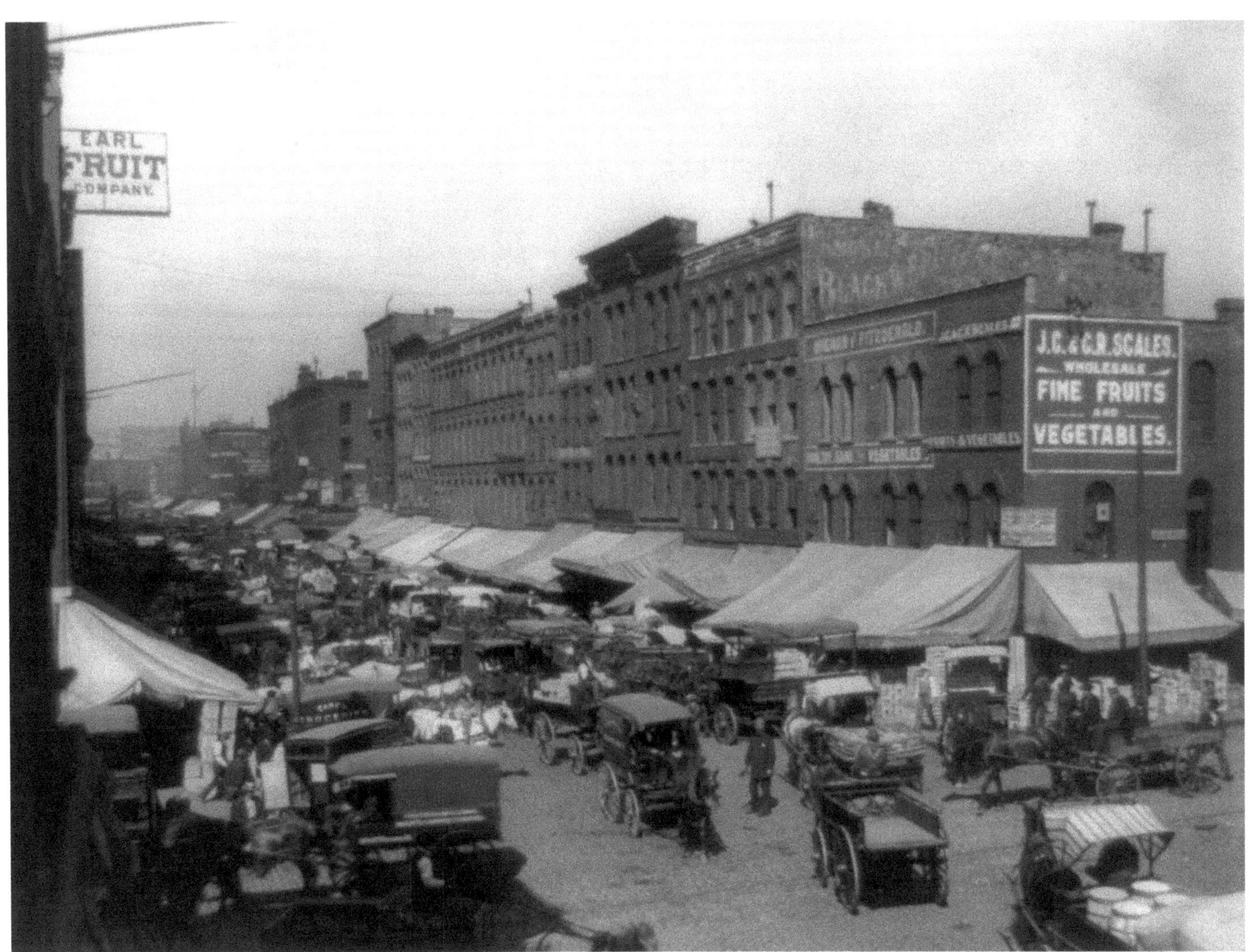

Because of its proximity to Lake Michigan, Chicago's South Water Street was the city's hub for fresh goods arriving from across the Great Lakes. In addition to markets and groceries, the street was also lined with hardware, spice, sugar, and tobacco houses, drawing crowds and earning the street's longtime designation as the busiest in the world. This view is from 1899.

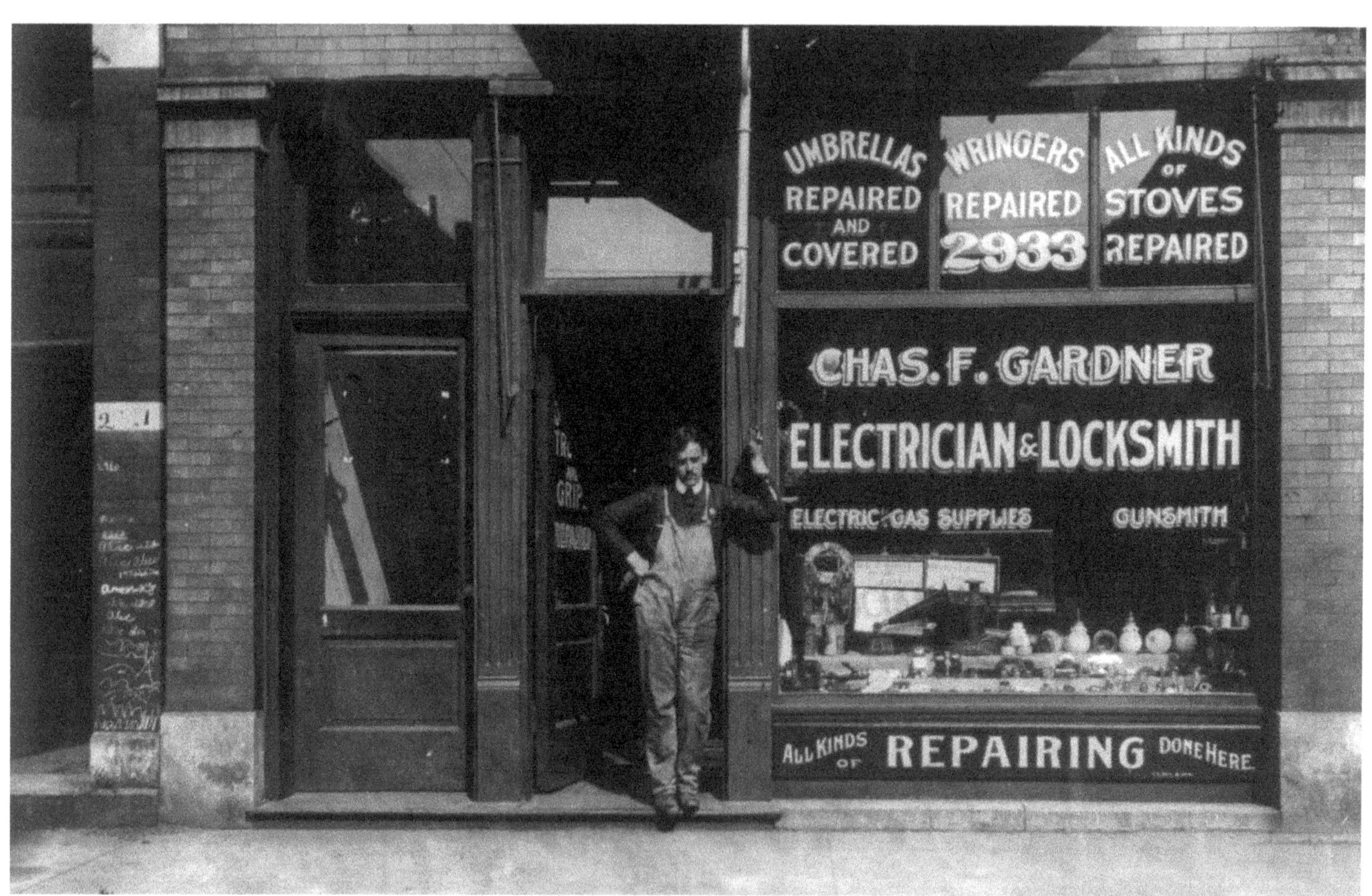

Charles F. Gardner's repair shop at 2933 State Street in Chicago. Windy City merchants have long had good reason to covet a State Street address; not only was it the main route south through the state of Illinois—feeding directly from Lake Michigan's shore at its north end—State Street ran right through the heart of Chicago's downtown.

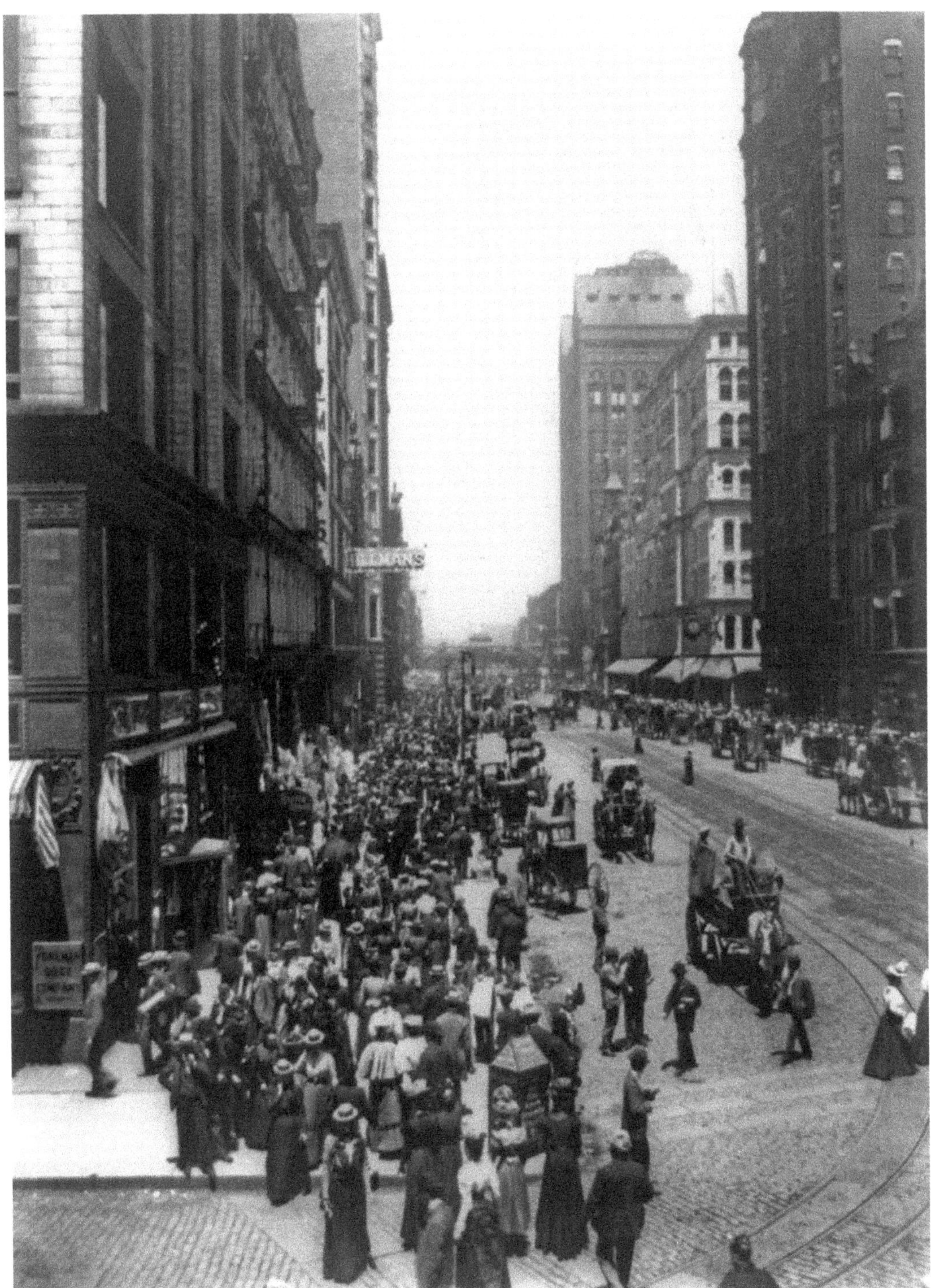

As Chicago's original Main Street, the north-south thoroughfare of State Street bustled in 1899 with pedestrians, streetcars, horse-drawn carts, and carriages. The once-muddy street was transformed into a famous shopping corridor when the Field, Leiter & Company store—the precursor to the now-defunct Marshall Field's stores—moved to the street in 1868, conducting business in a six-story marble edifice with Corinthian columns that was nicknamed the Marble Palace.

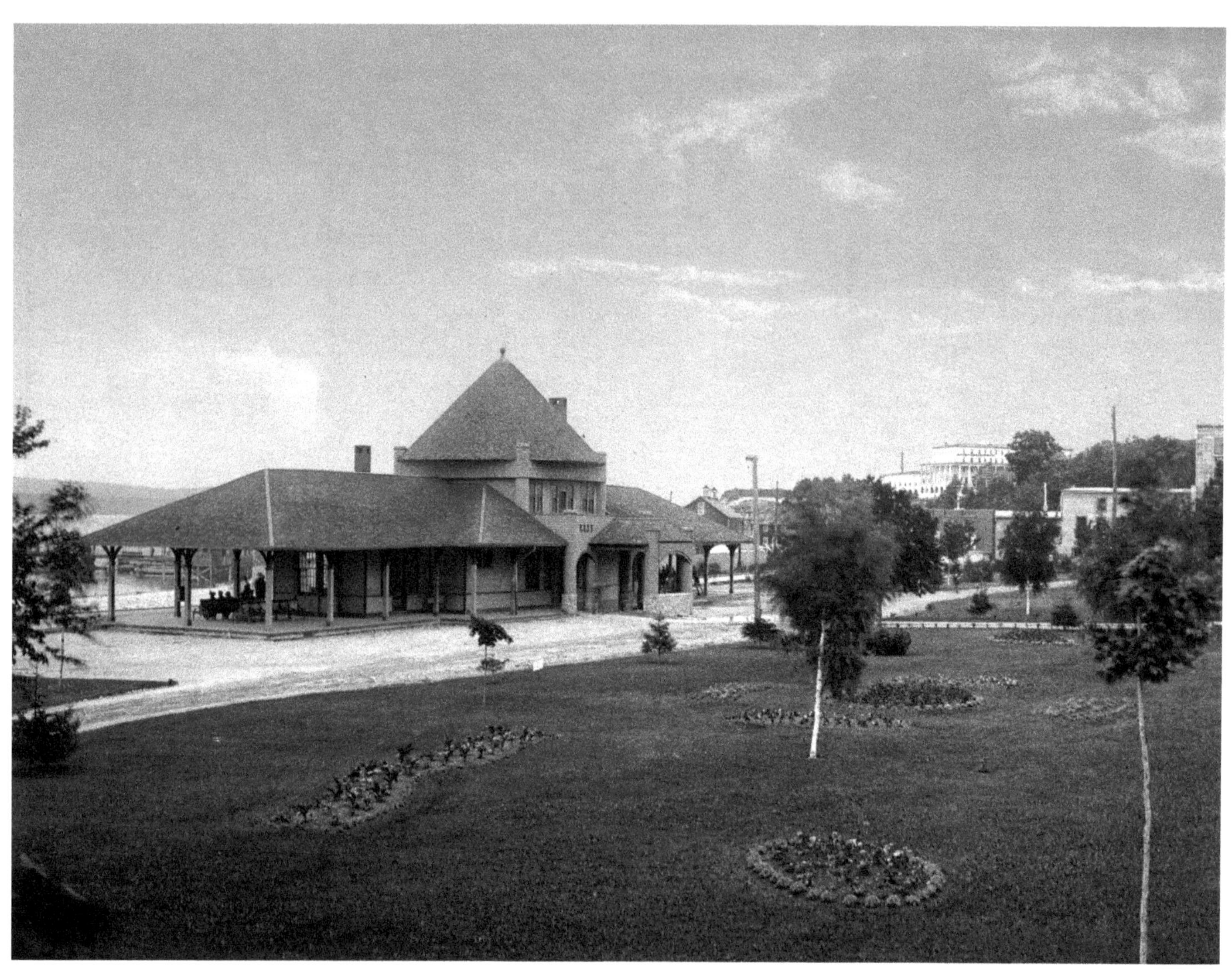

Built in 1892 beside the shore of Little Traverse Bay in Petoskey, Michigan, the picturesque Pere Marquette Depot was later immortalized in "The Indians Moved Away" and "Sepi Jingan"—stories by Earnest Hemingway, who arrived and departed from the station many times as a young man during his numerous summer explorations around Petoskey and Michigan's north.

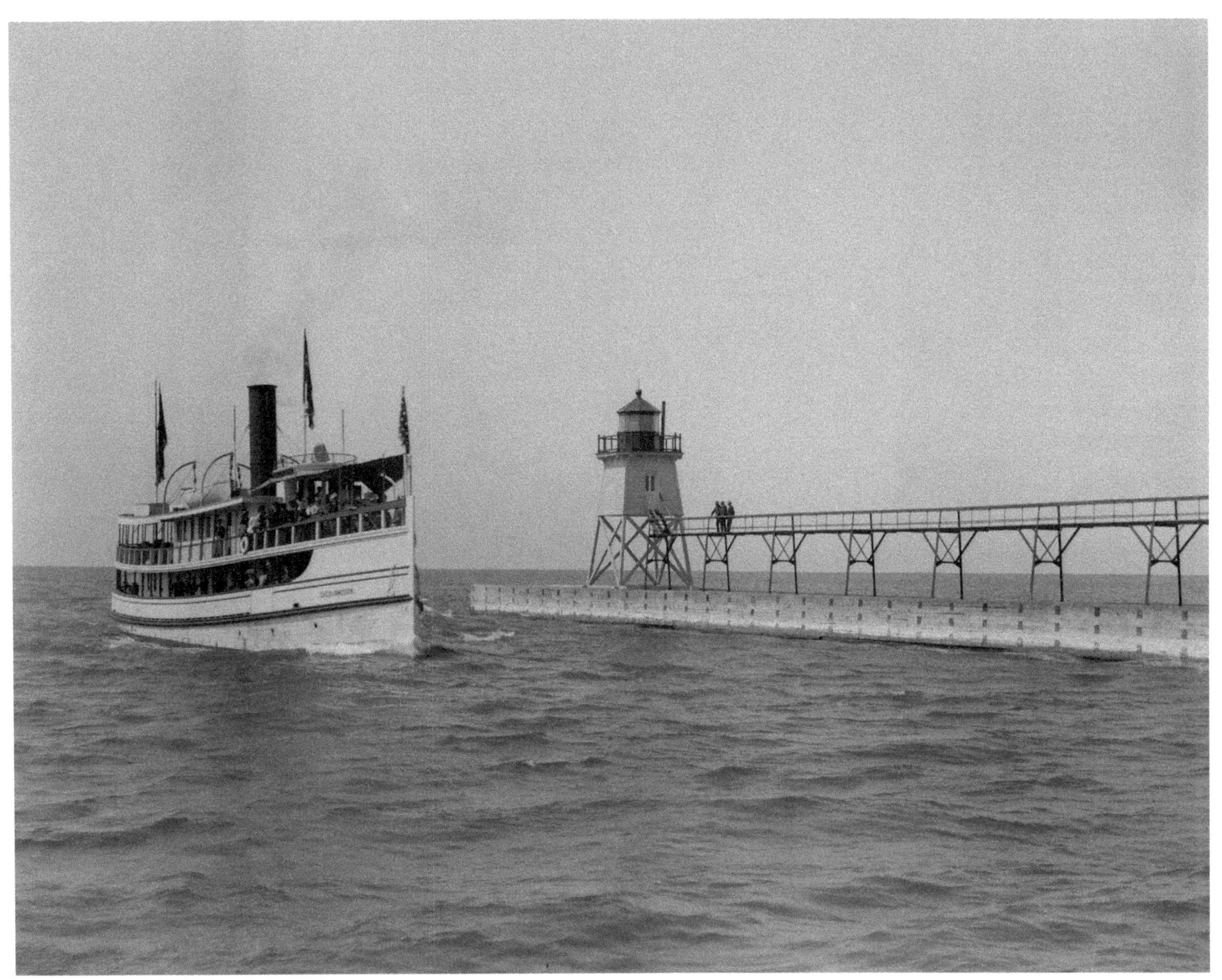

In 1873, Charlevoix needed to stop Lake Michigan's waves from silting up its newly created Pine River Channel. That winter, builders created a pier by erecting giant wooden cribs on the frozen shallows. The cribs cut through the ice, were allowed to sink to the bottom, and then filled with rocks. Little more than a decade later, builders added the elevated timber walk and a light, which was visible beyond nine miles.

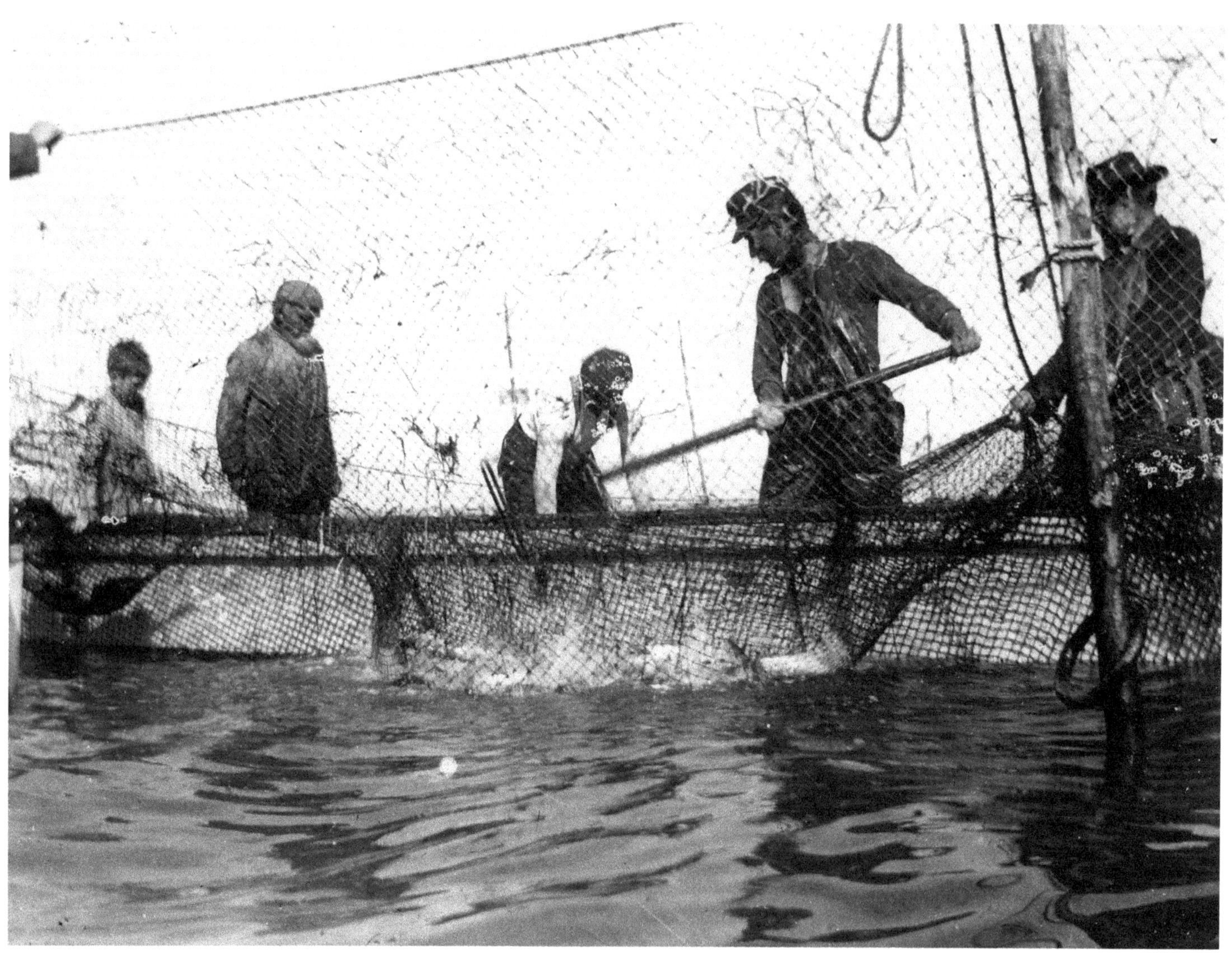

Fishermen empty their nets on an early morning in 1900, just off the coast of Sylvan Beach on White Lake, which flows into Lake Michigan. Dozens of Chicagoans kept summer residences in Sylvan Beach, arriving by steamship each season.

Crests and Troughs

(1901–1929)

For every action there is an equal and opposite reaction, and there exists no better example of this principle in modern times than the first three decades of the twentieth century—and no better showhouse for the rise and fall of those changing times than the nation's communities surrounding Lake Michigan.

Like a building afire, the lumber industry around Lake Michigan completed its collapse during the twentieth century's first decade, reducing many a town and much of the landscape to proverbial ashes. Thanks to the earlier boom, however, some of the dynamic ring of bustling cities and quaint shoreside towns surrounding the Great Lake had accumulated massive wealth and emerged intact—a few stronger than ever before.

The second decade of the new century took the world into war, and thousands of American soldiers hailing from Lake Michigan's coastal regions were lost, never to return to her shores. When the war formally ended in 1919, hope and optimism ruled the region once again.

Despite the Eighteenth Amendment to the Constitution, which gave the nation Prohibition and temporarily put a lid on Milwaukee's brewing industry (while lining the coffers of traffickers in illegal alcohol), the Roaring Twenties were a time of jubilant celebration around the Great Lake. Pleasure seekers plied the waters and rode the rails. Summer resort towns and yacht clubs dotted the coastline from Milwaukee to Chicago to Michigan's Benton Harbor and Harbor Springs. The advent of the automobile and its associated industries brought more freedom and prosperity, and helped turn already strong companies, such as Standard Oil of Indiana, into powerhouses.

The bolstered economy created a new breed of the leisured and the rise of the golden age of sports, when heroes of baseball, boxing, and football loomed larger than life, and spectators packed stadiums and fields around the Lake Michigan coast to watch the likes of boxer Jack Dempsey and baseball player Hack Wilson of the Chicago Cubs. The heyday would end not long after the Cubs' heartbreaking 1929 loss to the Philadelphia Athletics in September 1929. Barely more than a week after the Cubs lost game five of the World Series, the stock market crashed and with it, the nation's economy.

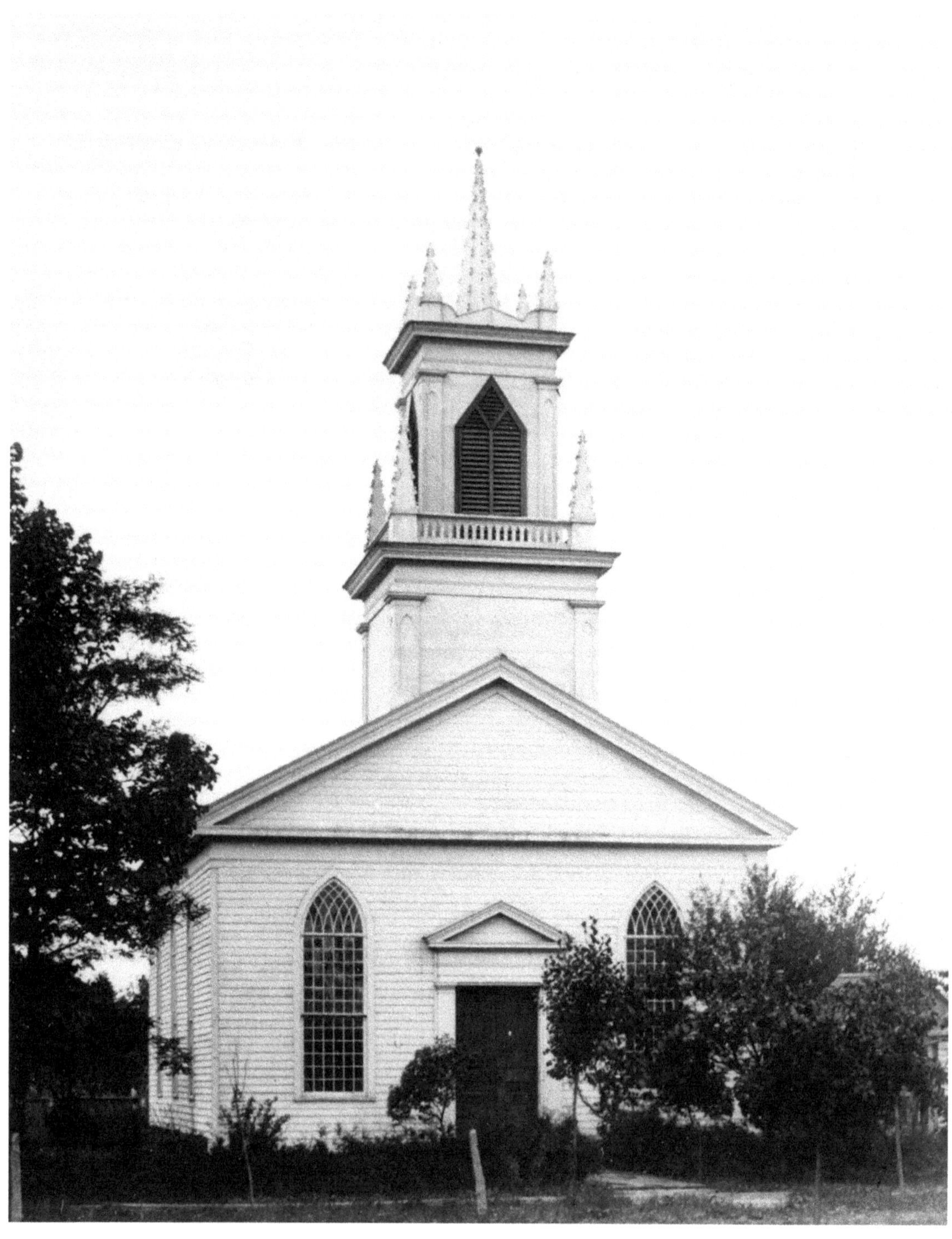

Moravian faithful laid the first cornerstone for their Greek Revival timber-frame church on Moravian Street in downtown Green Bay, Wisconsin, in 1851. It stood there until 1980, when it was moved to Heritage Hill State Historic Park, a 50-acre living-history museum on the banks of Green Bay's Fox River.

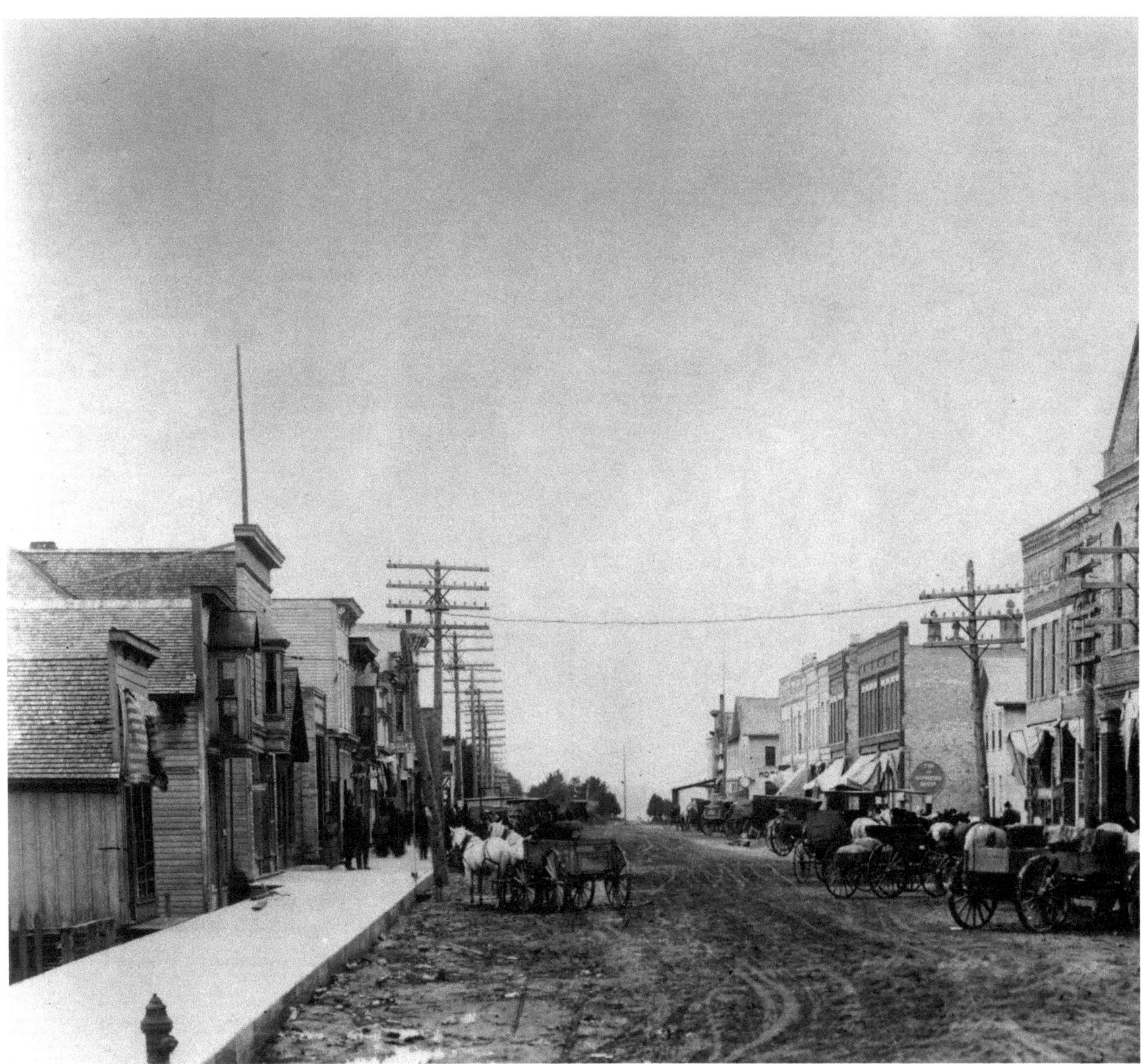

Abram Scranton Wadsworth, the first white settler of Elk Rapids, Michigan, offered village lots for $25 in 1852. The firm Dexter & Noble followed in 1864, building grist and sawmills and a dock on Lake Michigan. By 1900, Elk Rapids was booming, evidence of which is visible on River Street shown here, the town's main thoroughfare. Just ten years later, with the surrounding forests depleted, the village fell into a decline that would last until after the Great Depression.

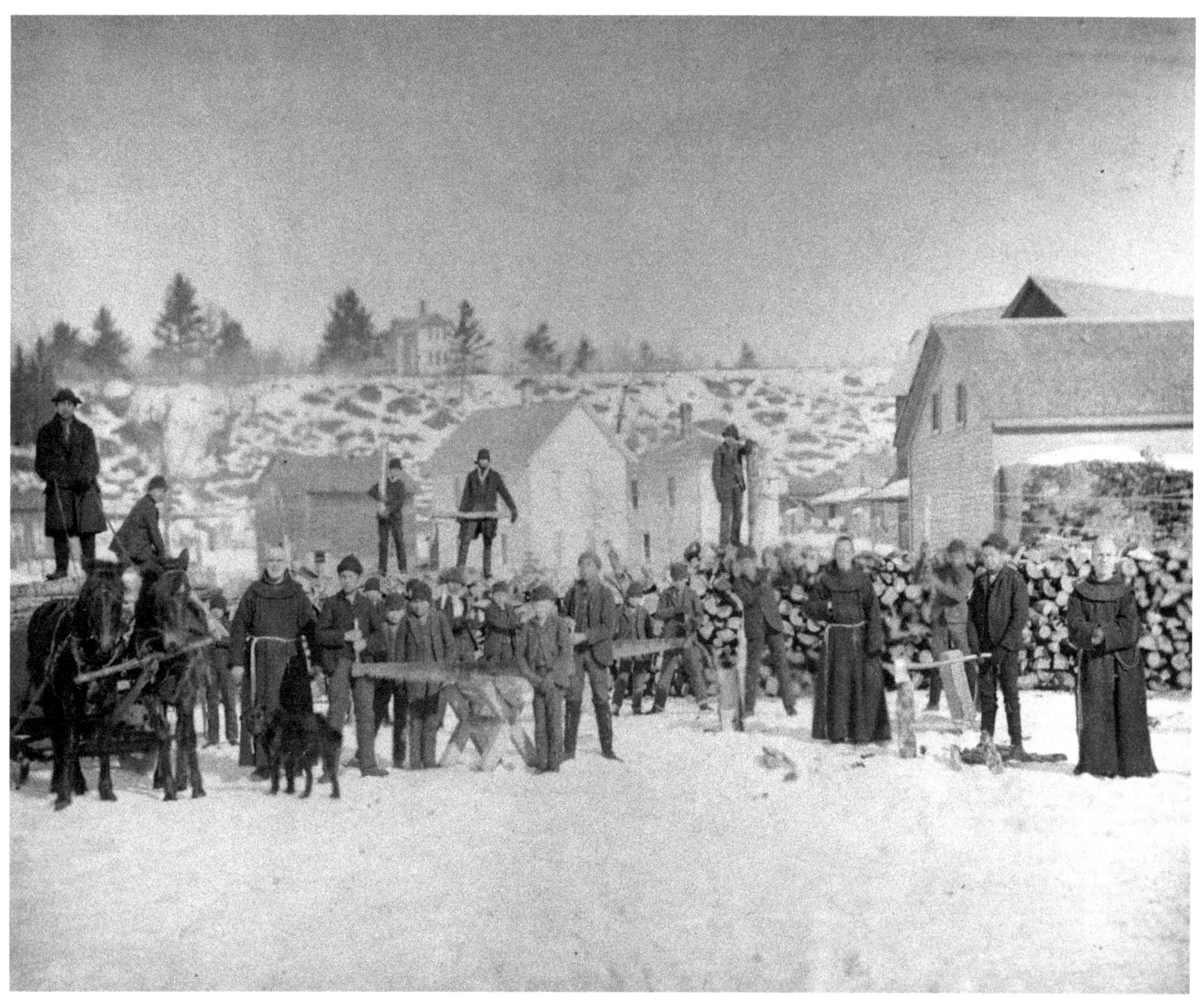

Ottawa Indians and missionaries pose before timber they have cut, split, and stacked at the site of the Holy Childhood Catholic Church and School in Harbor Springs, Michigan. Originally founded by Father Pierre DeJean in 1829 in a simple log structure, the school for Indian children moved to a three-story frame building around 1880, which underwent several additions after 1900. The school building was demolished in 2007.

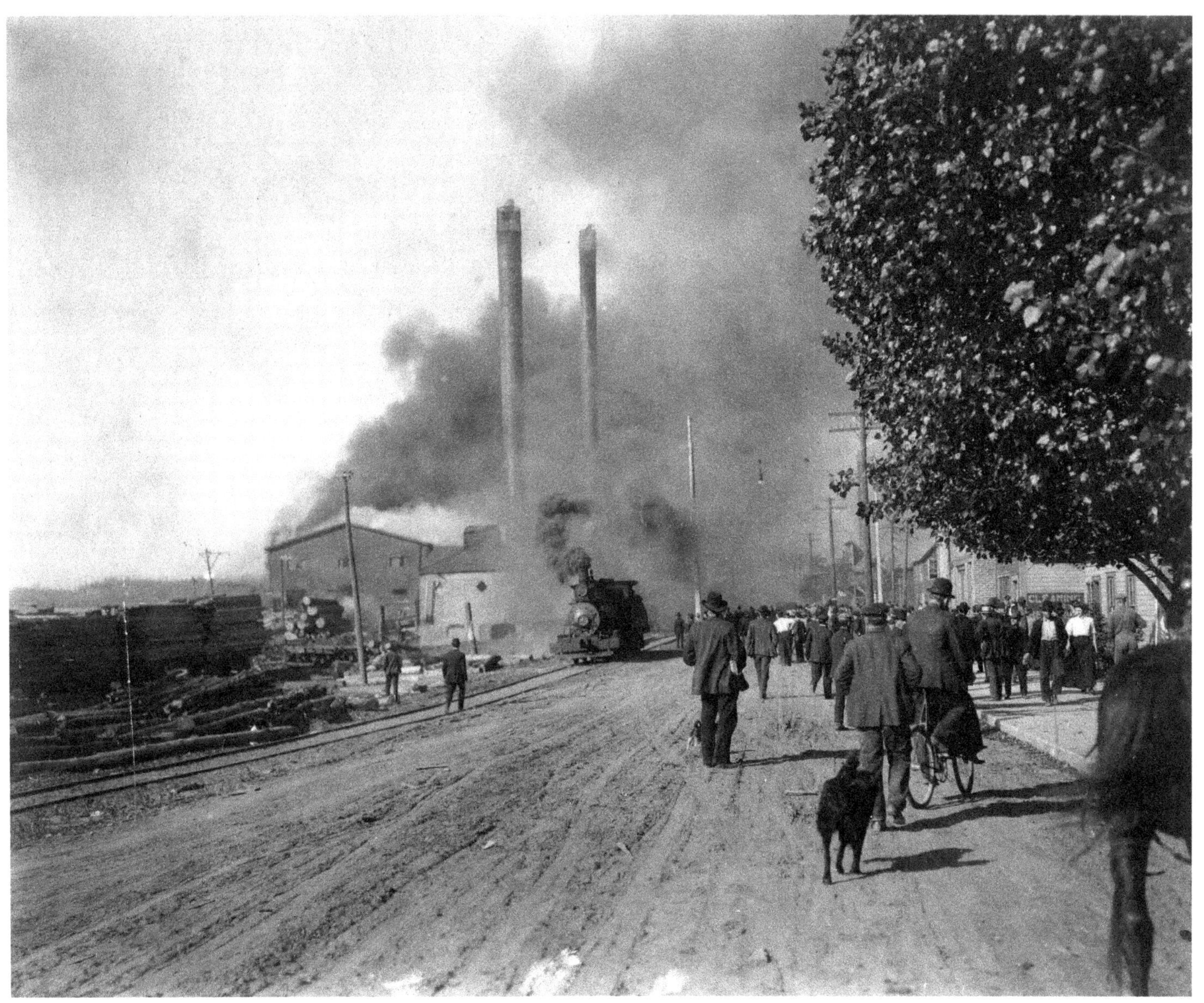

Onlookers watch the fire and smoke of a burning lumber mill in Boyne City, Michigan. Boyne City sits along Lake Charlevoix, which funnels into Lake Michigan through Round Lake and Pine River.

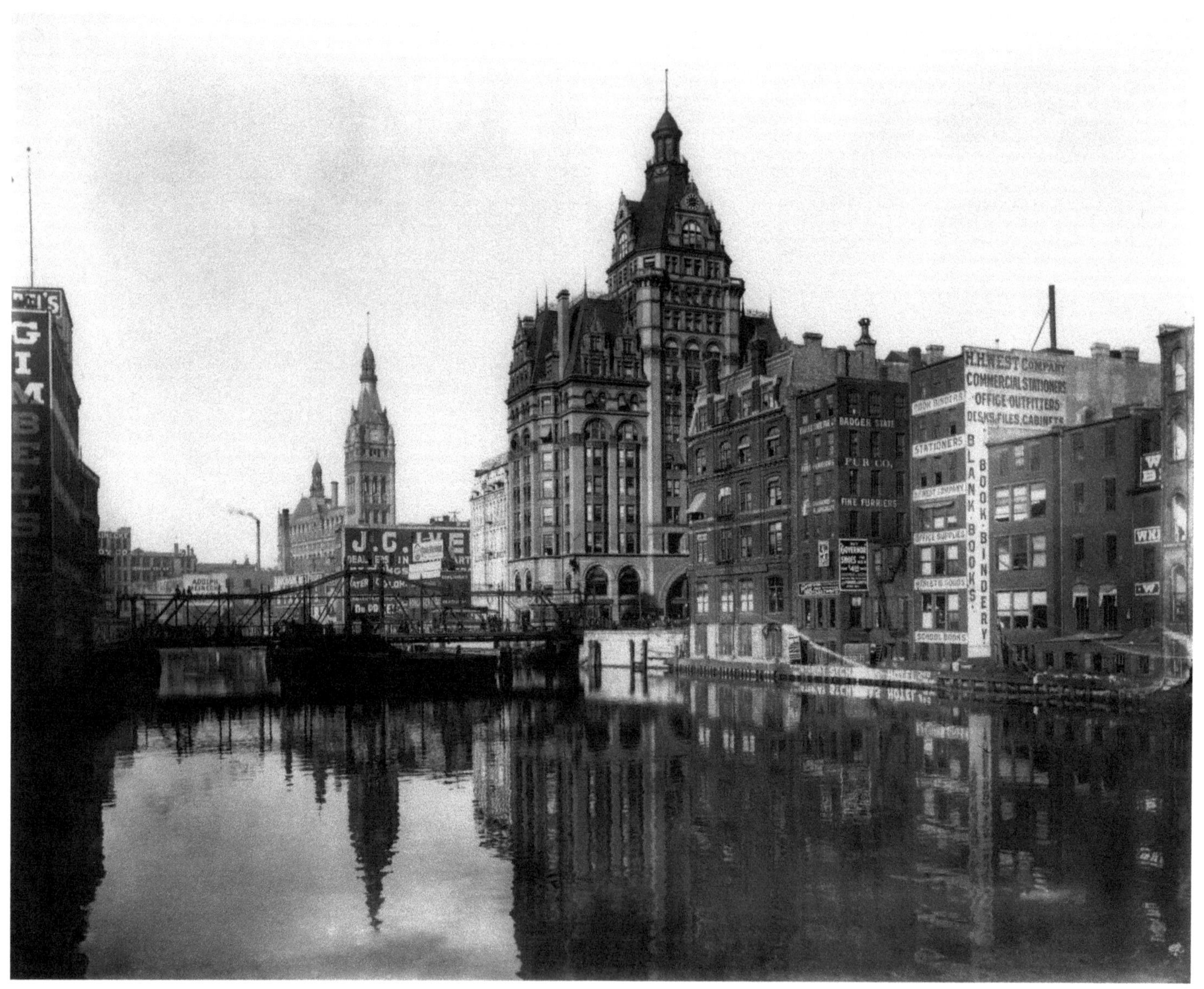

Once a favorite settlement place for Indians and later a conduit for the travels of Jacques Marquette and Louis Jolliet between Lake Michigan and the Fox and Mississippi rivers, the Milwaukee River as seen here from downtown Milwaukee's Sycamore Street was the centerpiece of an urban landscape on the rise. This view dates to the turn of the century.

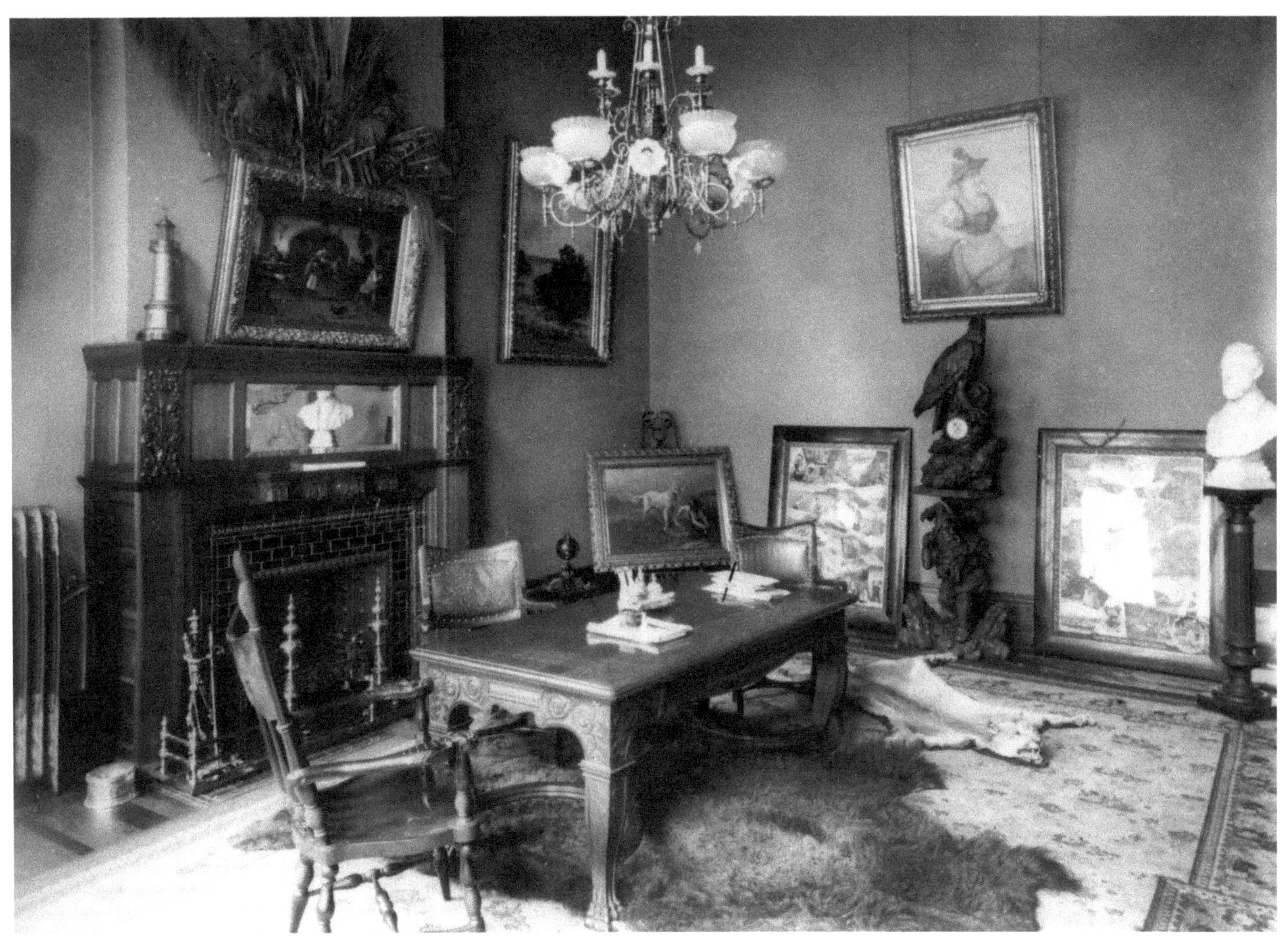

Founded by German-born Joseph Schlitz in Milwaukee in 1856, just six years after he arrived in America, Schlitz beer gained enormous popularity after its maker donated hundreds of barrels of beer to Chicago following the city's Great Fire in 1871. Thereafter known as "the beer that made Milwaukee famous," Schlitz beer went on to sell in excess of one million barrels in 1902, making Schlitz the world's largest brewery. Here, a peek inside Schlitz Brewery's director's room.

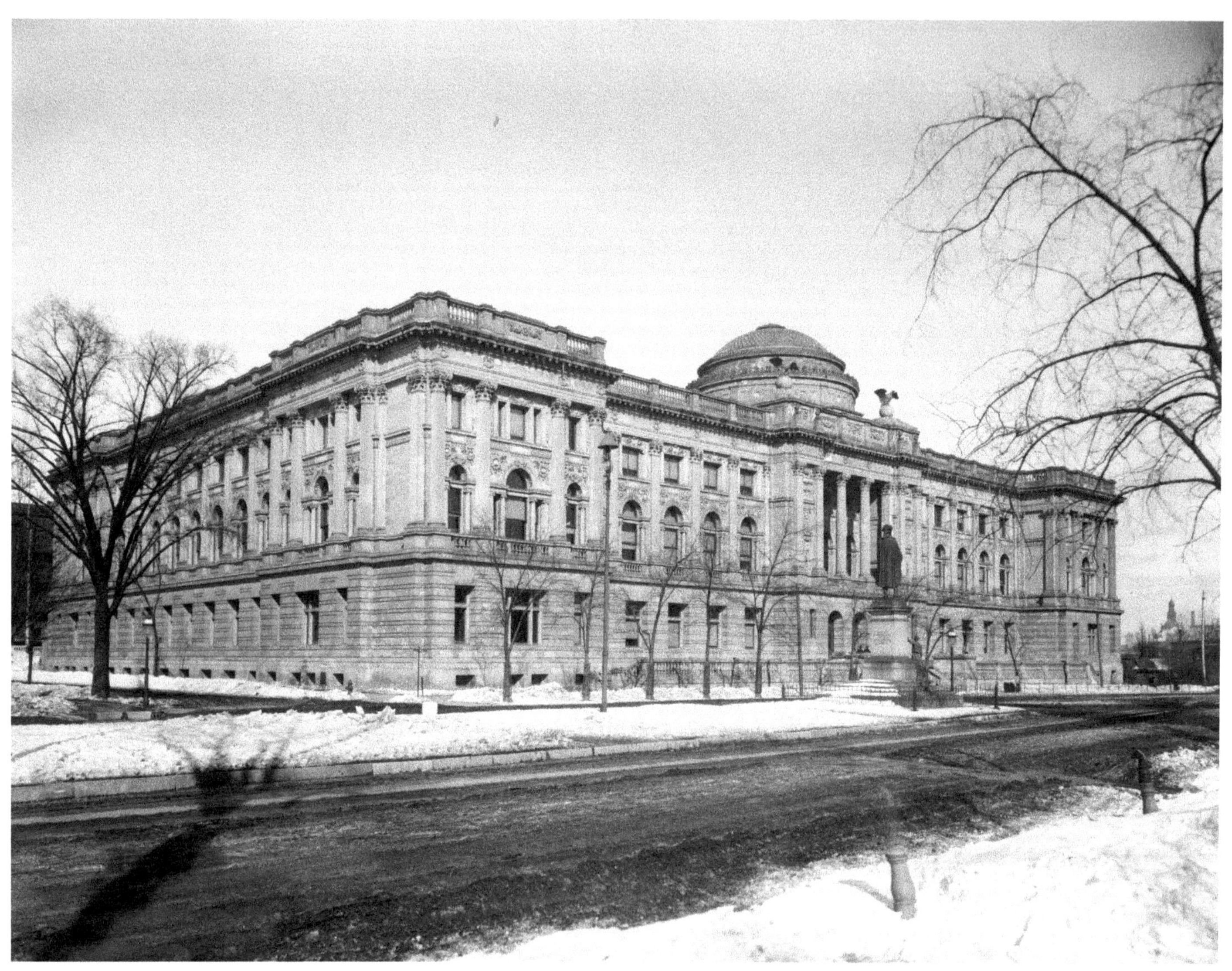

The Milwaukee Public Library was founded in 1878 but moved several times before finding its eventual home on Eighth Street between Wells Street and Wisconsin Avenue. In this locale, in the late 1890s, the city erected the Milwaukee Central Library, a grand French and Italian Renaissance–style structure of Bedford limestone that stretched a full city block. Shown here is the library as it looked in 1901.

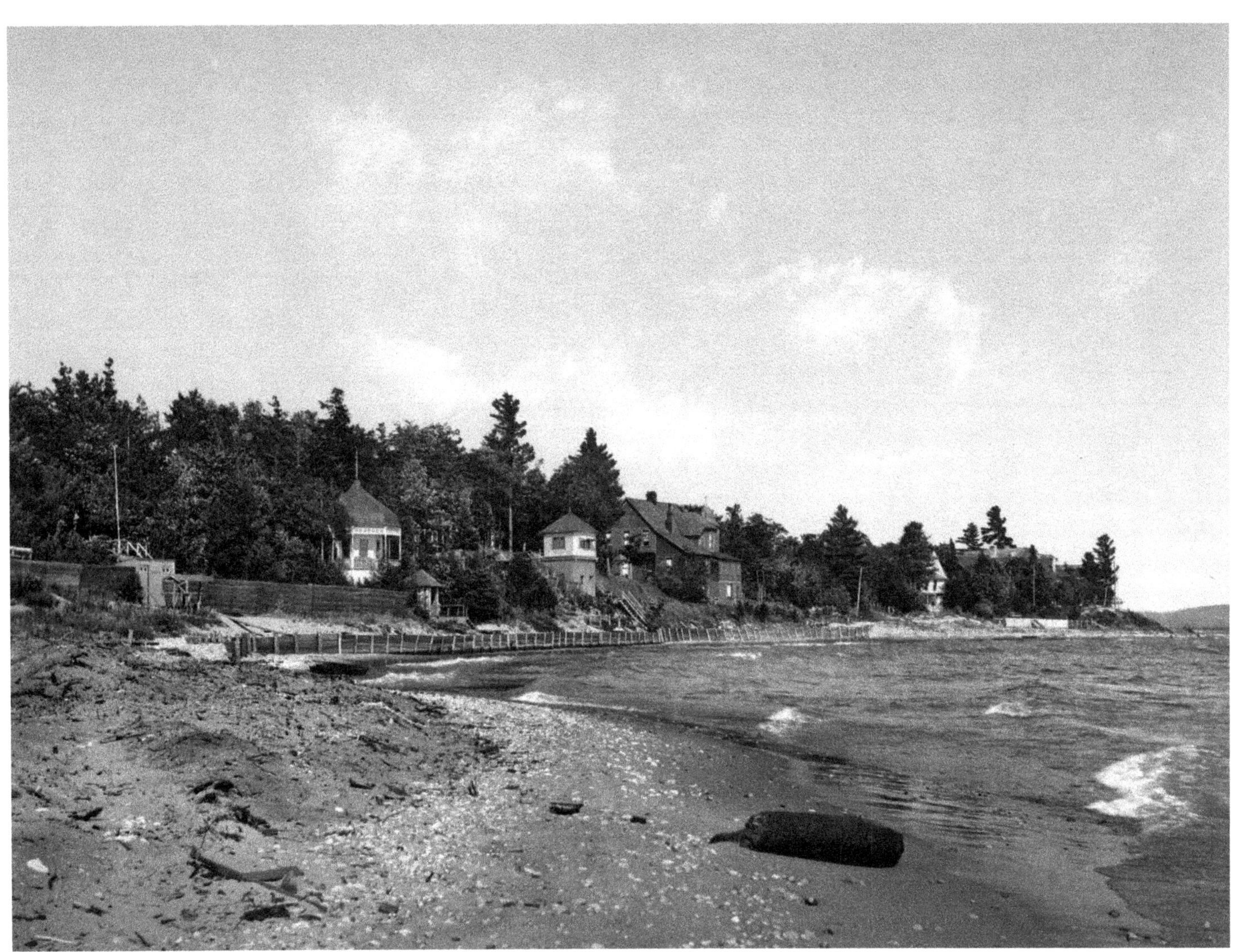

One of the most exclusive enclaves in Michigan, the wee Harbor Point on Little Traverse Bay near Harbor Springs has long been a summer retreat for the families of early century empire builders—the daughter of chewing gum tycoon William Wrigley, Dorothy Wrigley-Offield, and David B. Gamble, son of Procter & Gamble co-founder James Gamble, among them. Though Harbor Point today boasts many more cottages than it did in this 1902 photograph, one thing hasn't changed: transportation here is by foot, bicycle, or horse and buggy only.

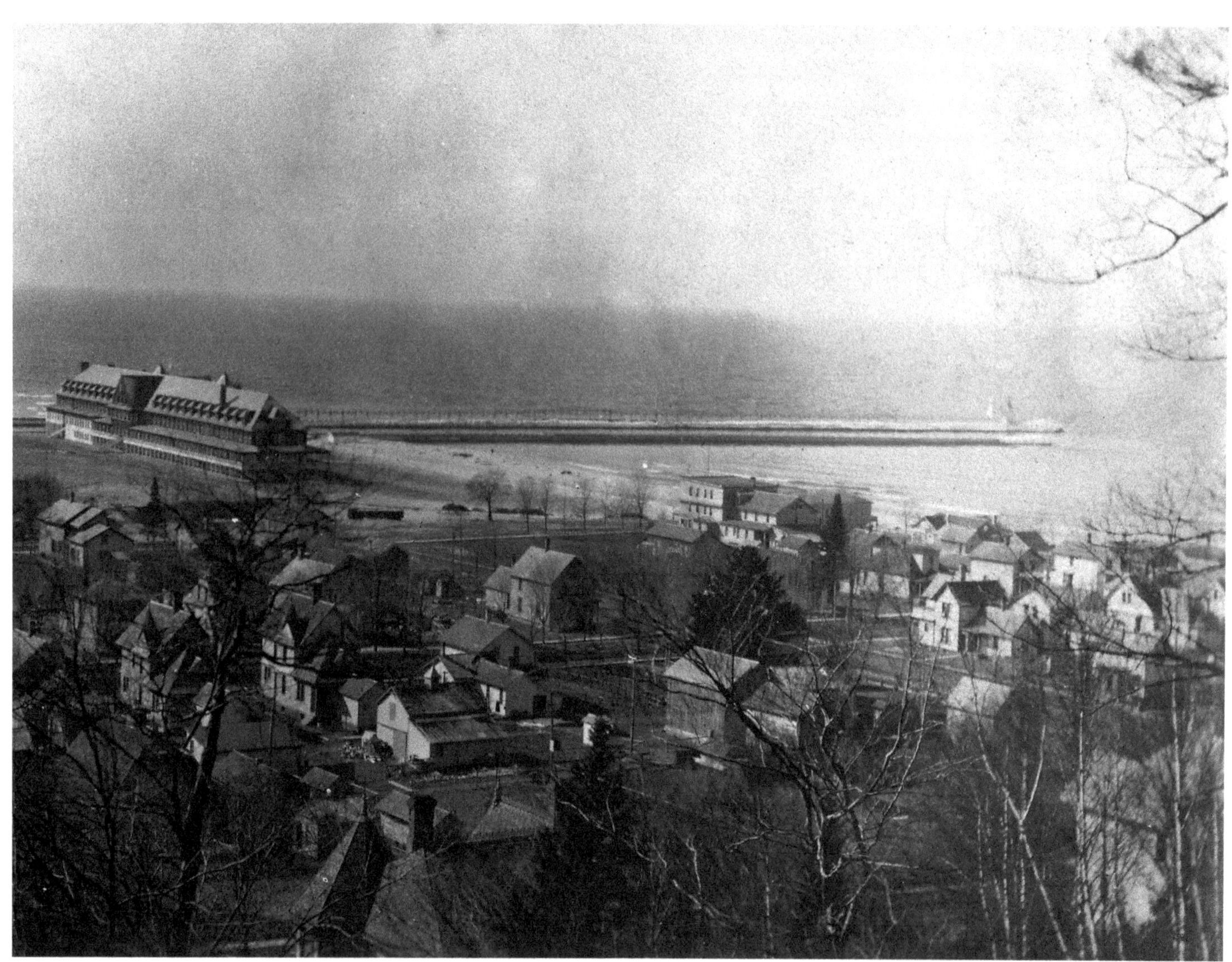

The Ann Arbor Railroad Company opened the Royal Frontenac Hotel in 1902 to lure travelers up its line to the shoreside paradise of Frankfort, Michigan. Intended to rival the Grand Hotel on Mackinac Island, the three-story hotel stretched 500 feet in length and boasted nearly 250 rooms (all with telephones—a rarity in those times), along with a cigar and candy store, game room, and slot machines. The hotel burned down in 1912.

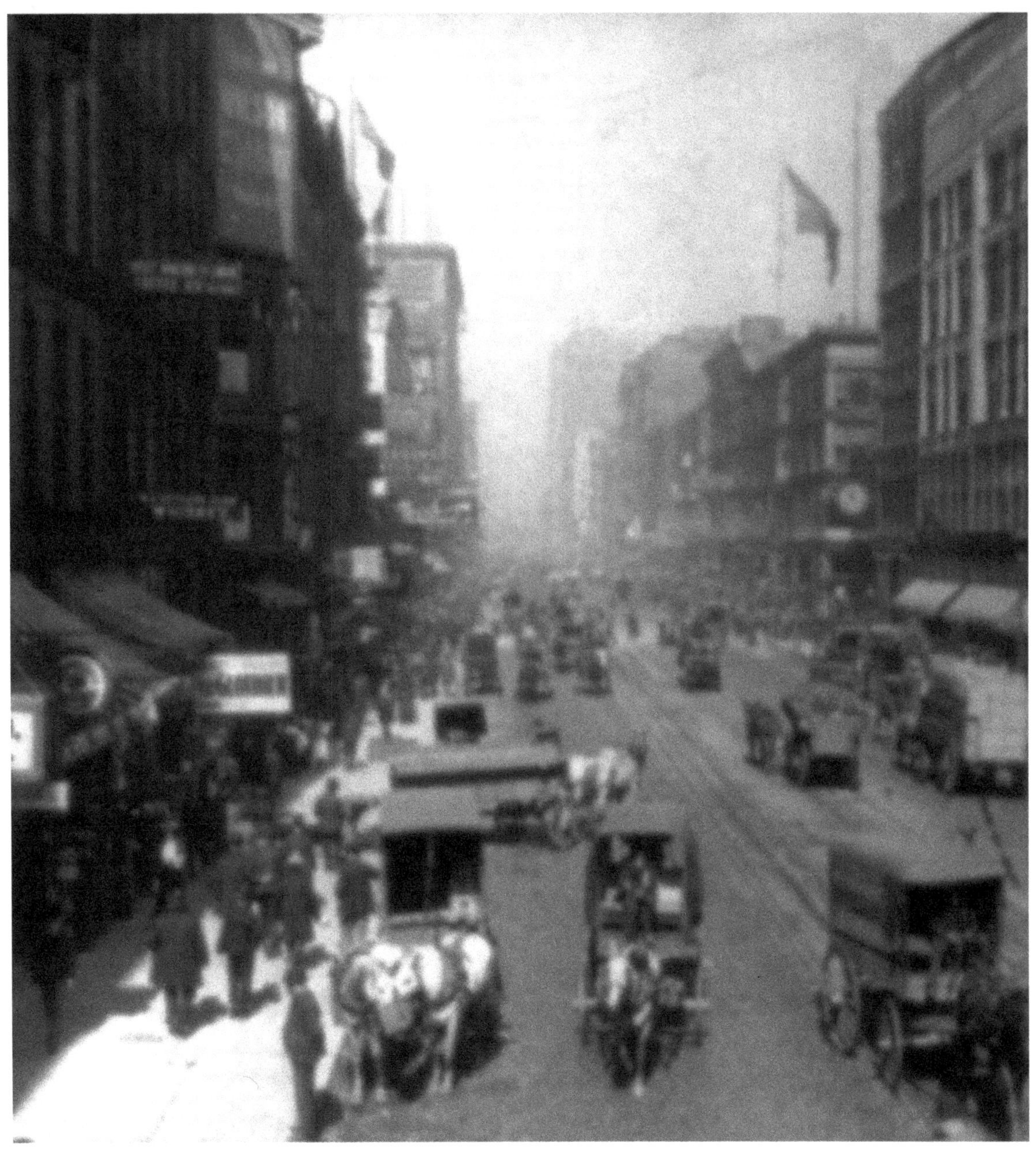

This 1903 stereoscope image of Chicago's greatest thoroughfare, 18-mile-long State Street, faces north toward Lake Michigan.

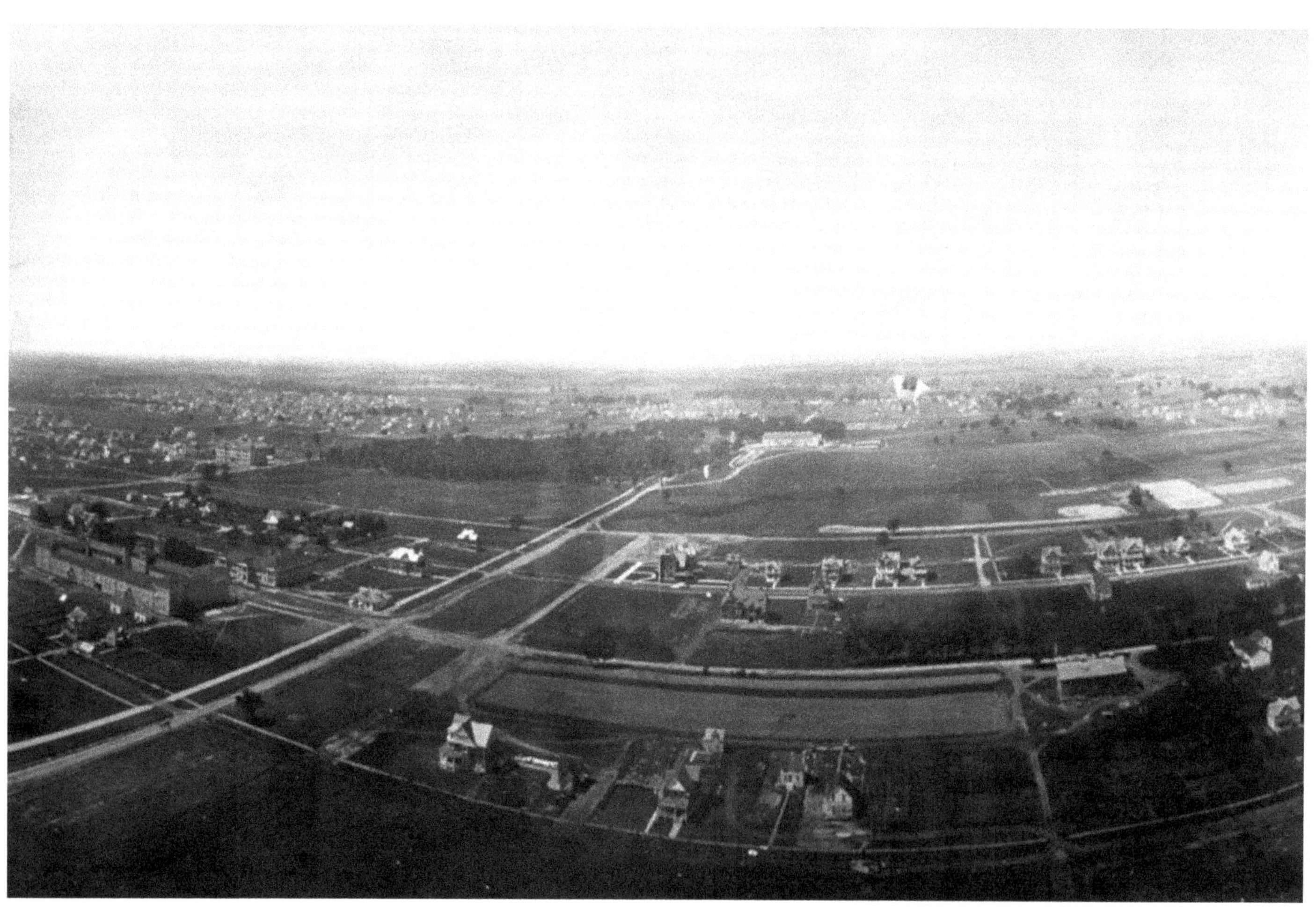

The city of Zion, Illinois. Located between Milwaukee and Chicago off Lake Michigan, Zion was the brainchild of John Alexander Dowie, founder of the International Divine Healing Association. Fully planned before any construction began, Dowie's Zion City was intended as a sanctuary where Dowie would control industries, schools, and recreational facilities, and Dowie's followers would be free from the world's evils and ruled by God.

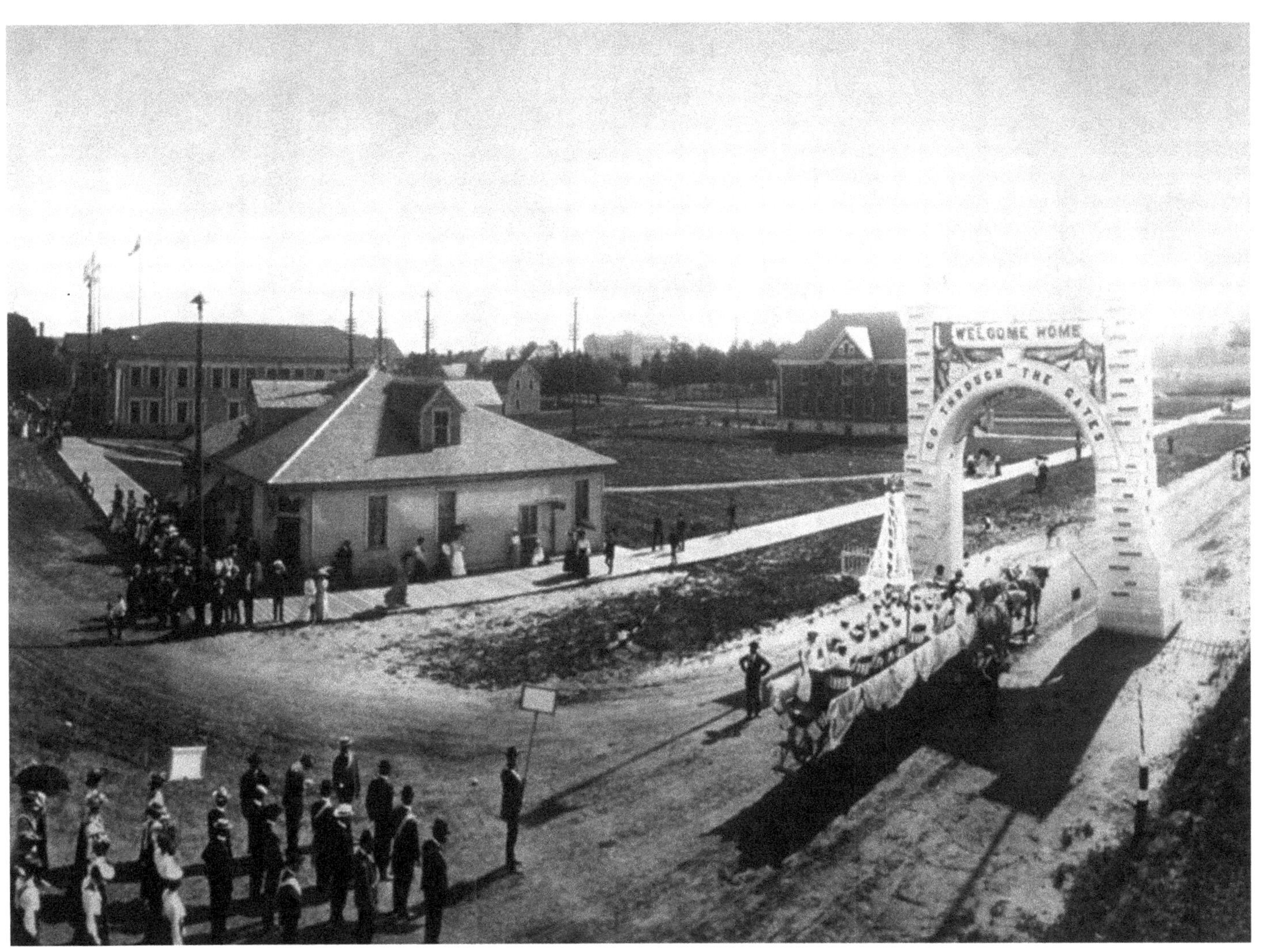

A July 1904 industrial parade makes its way through Zion. One of the city's first industries was the making of lace. Dowie had imported a lace mill from England.

The ornate interior of the Milwaukee Central Library. Credit for the monolithic structure's Neo-renaissance style goes to Milwaukee architects Ferry and Clas, whose design was selected from a pool of 74 entrants—among them a young Frank Lloyd Wright.

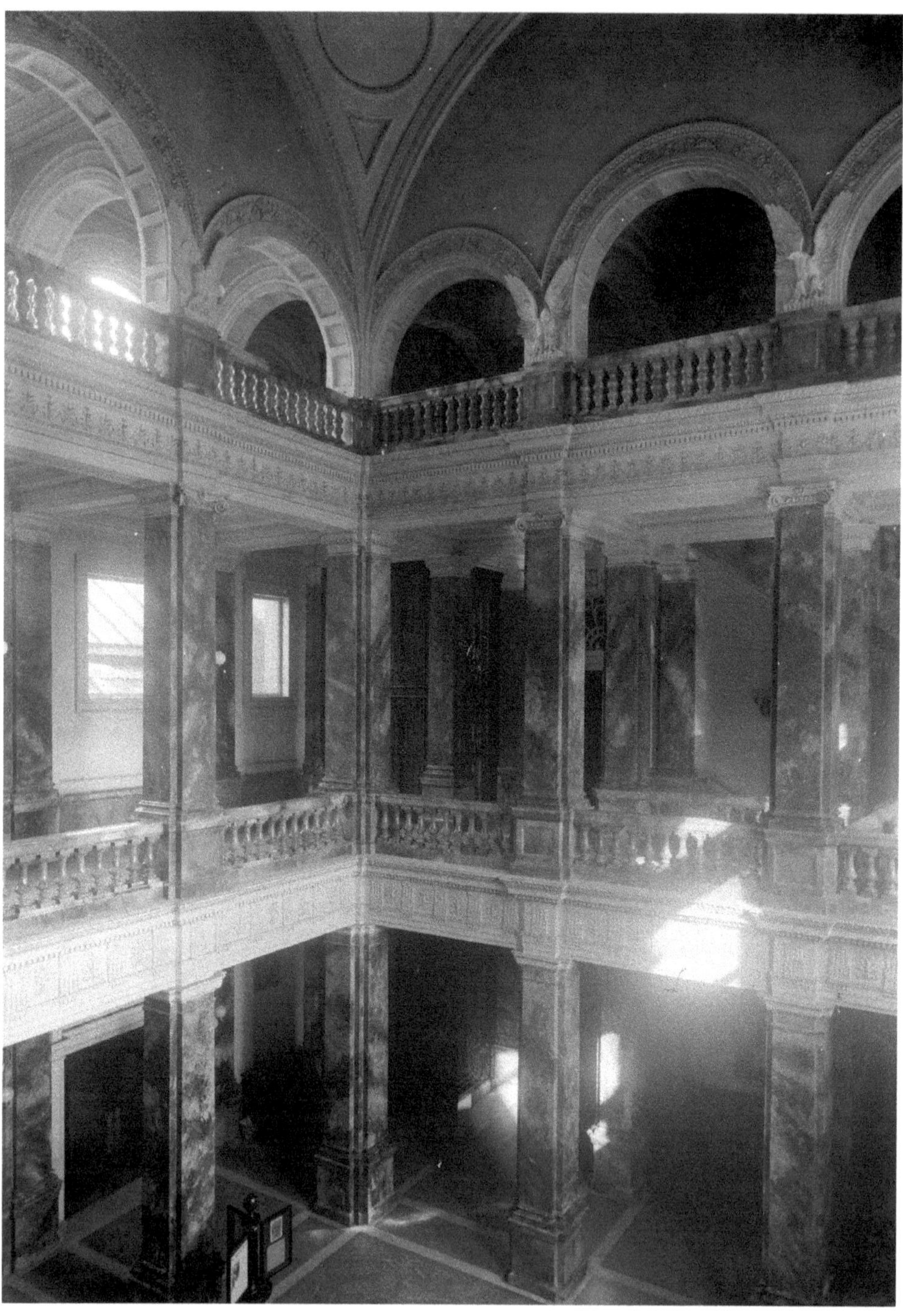

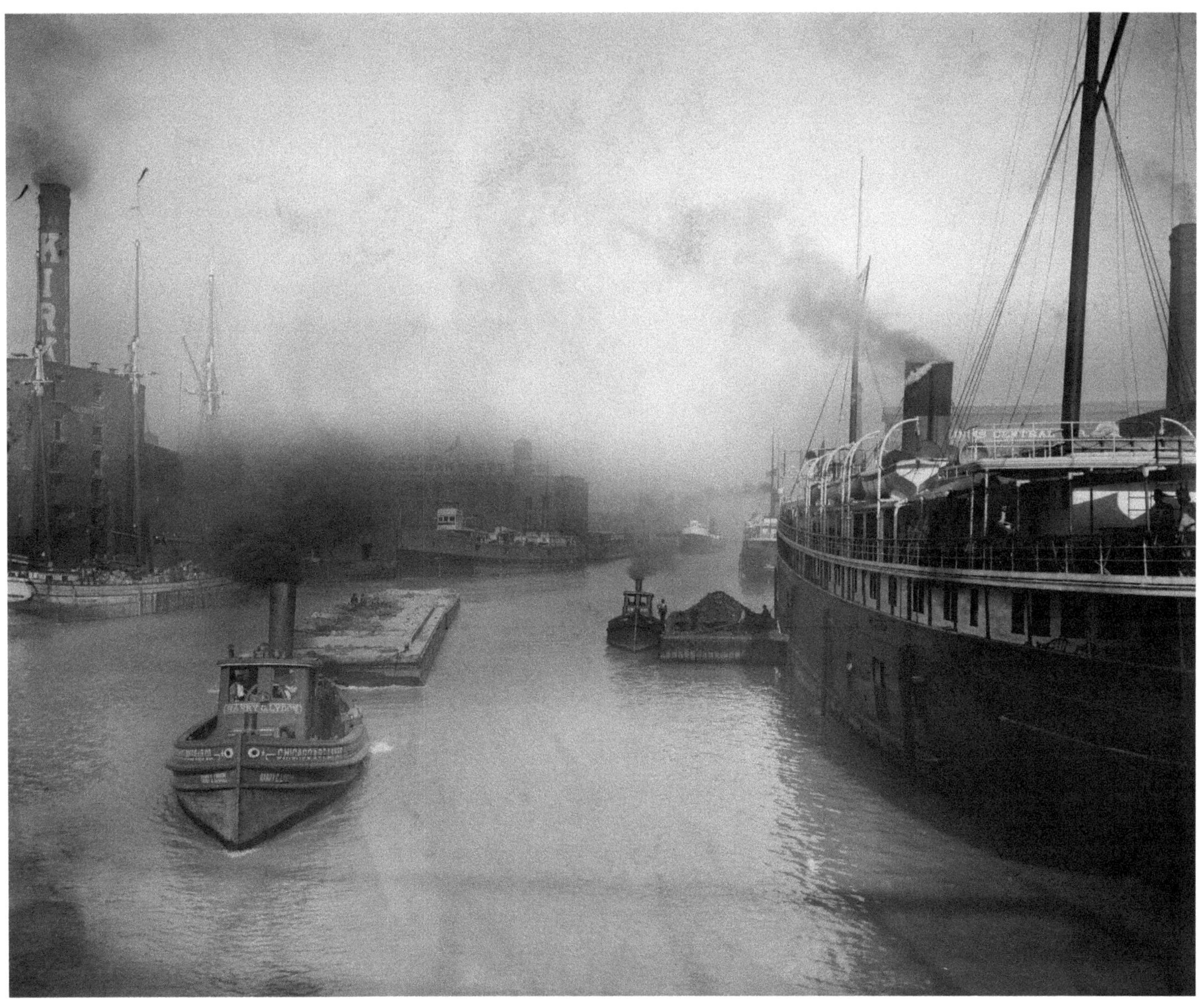

Facing east along Chicago's Chicago River from the Rush Street Bridge around 1904. The 1857 swing bridge was destroyed and rebuilt twice: first after a herd of spooked cattle stampeded over and collapsed it in 1863, and again following the 1871 fire. The bridge met its final fate in 1920, when it was torn down upon completion of nearby Michigan Avenue Bridge.

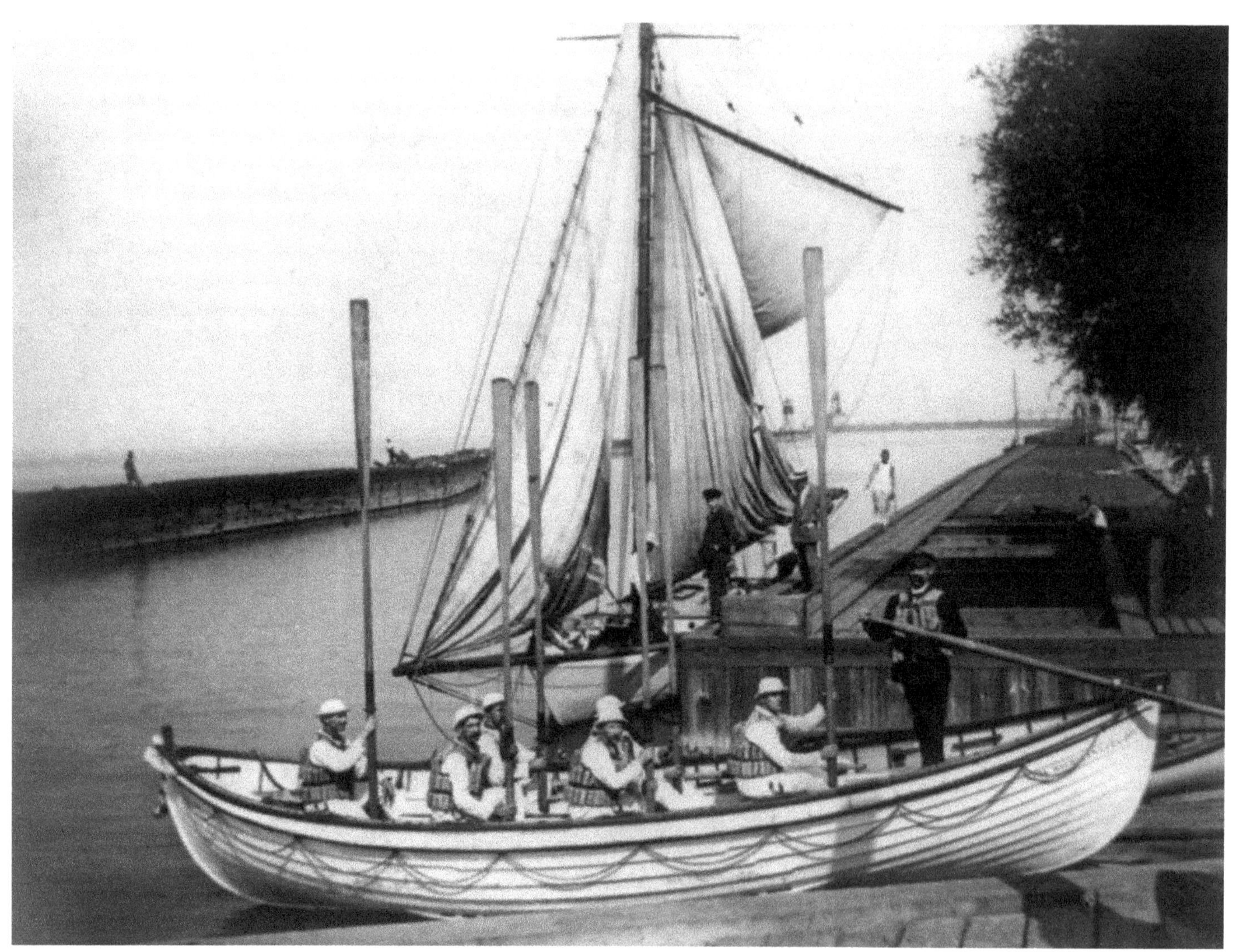

Equipped with paddles and life vests, a crew shoves off from the U.S. Lifesaving Station in Michigan City in 1905. The only lifesaving station on Indiana's Lake Michigan coast, Station Michigan City has been in operation since 1888.

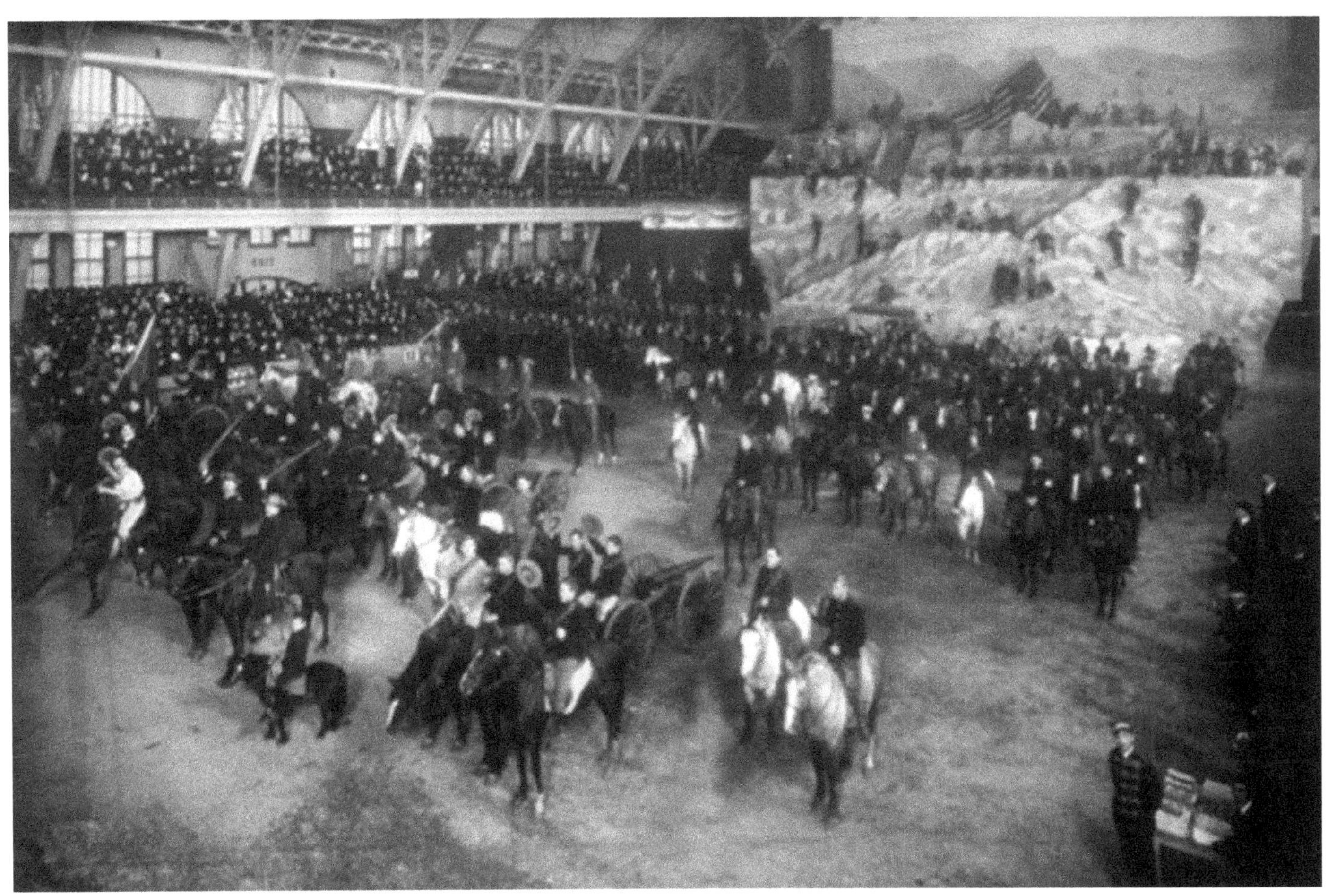

The finale of a 1905 theatrical production about the recent Boer War in Africa, on the floor of the Chicago Coliseum. Over the next several decades the Coliseum on Wabash Avenue would host several Republican National Conventions; a Progressive Party Convention; several early Chicago sports teams—including the NHL's Blackhawks, Cardinals, and Shamrocks; and rock concerts—the Grateful Dead, Cream, and Jimi Hendrix among them—before it was demolished in 1982.

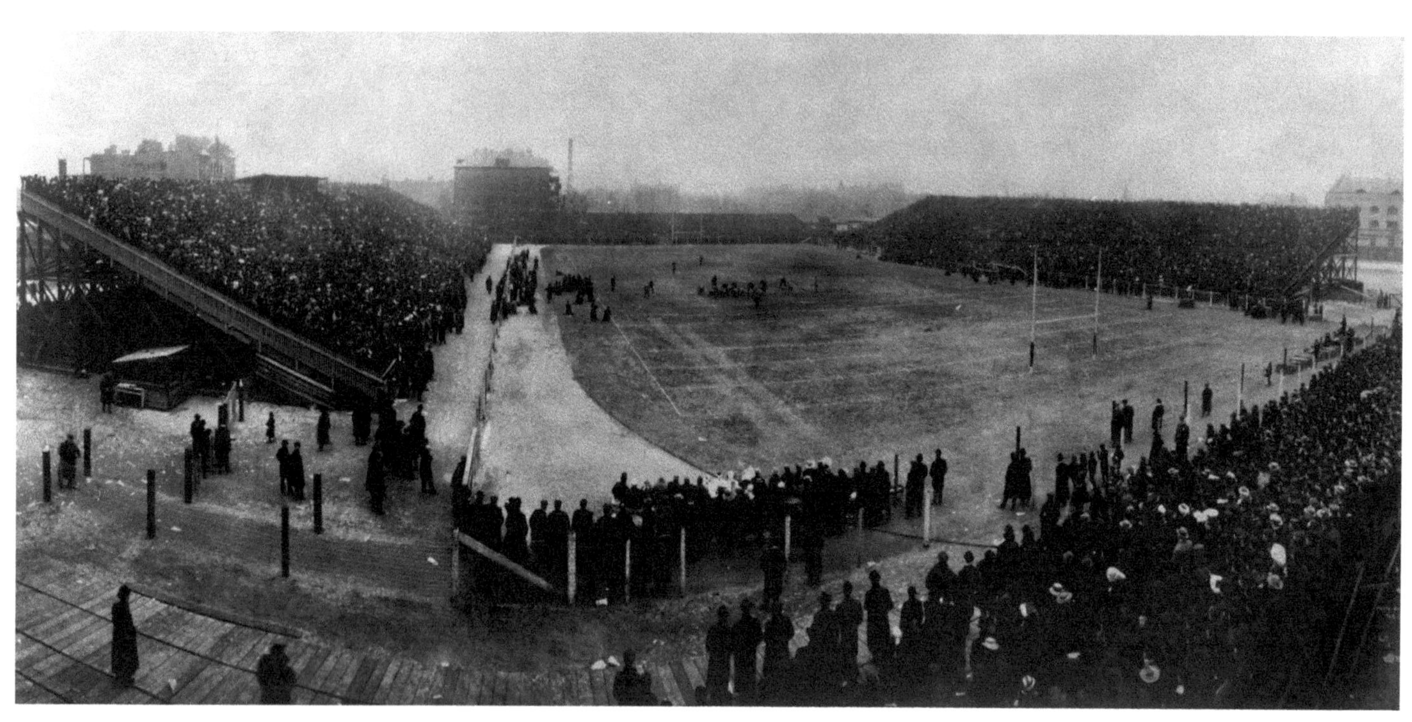

In its final Thanksgiving Day game in 1905, the University of Chicago Maroons football team dominates the University of Michigan 2-0—nabbing its first perfect record on the way to its second Big Ten title—before a crowd of 27,000 spectators at Marshall Field.

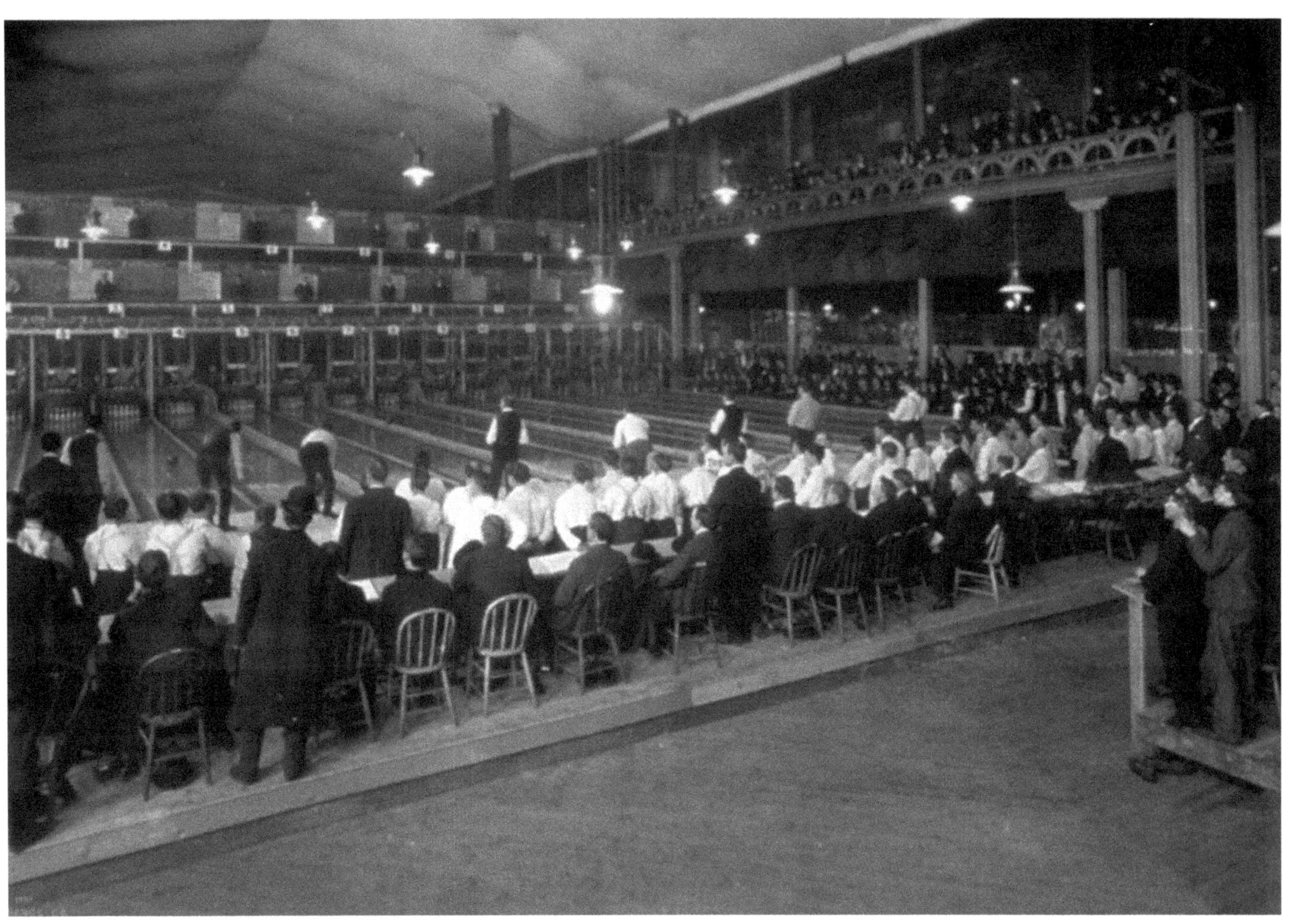

Spectators watch the 1905 American Bowling Congress Bowling Tournament in Milwaukee. The ABC, the first official governing body of bowling, was founded in New York City in 1905 but its headquarters were moved to Milwaukee in 1906. In 2005, ABC merged with other bowling organizations to become the United States Bowling Congress, and in 2008, its headquarters were moved from the Milwaukee suburb of Greendale to Arlington, Texas.

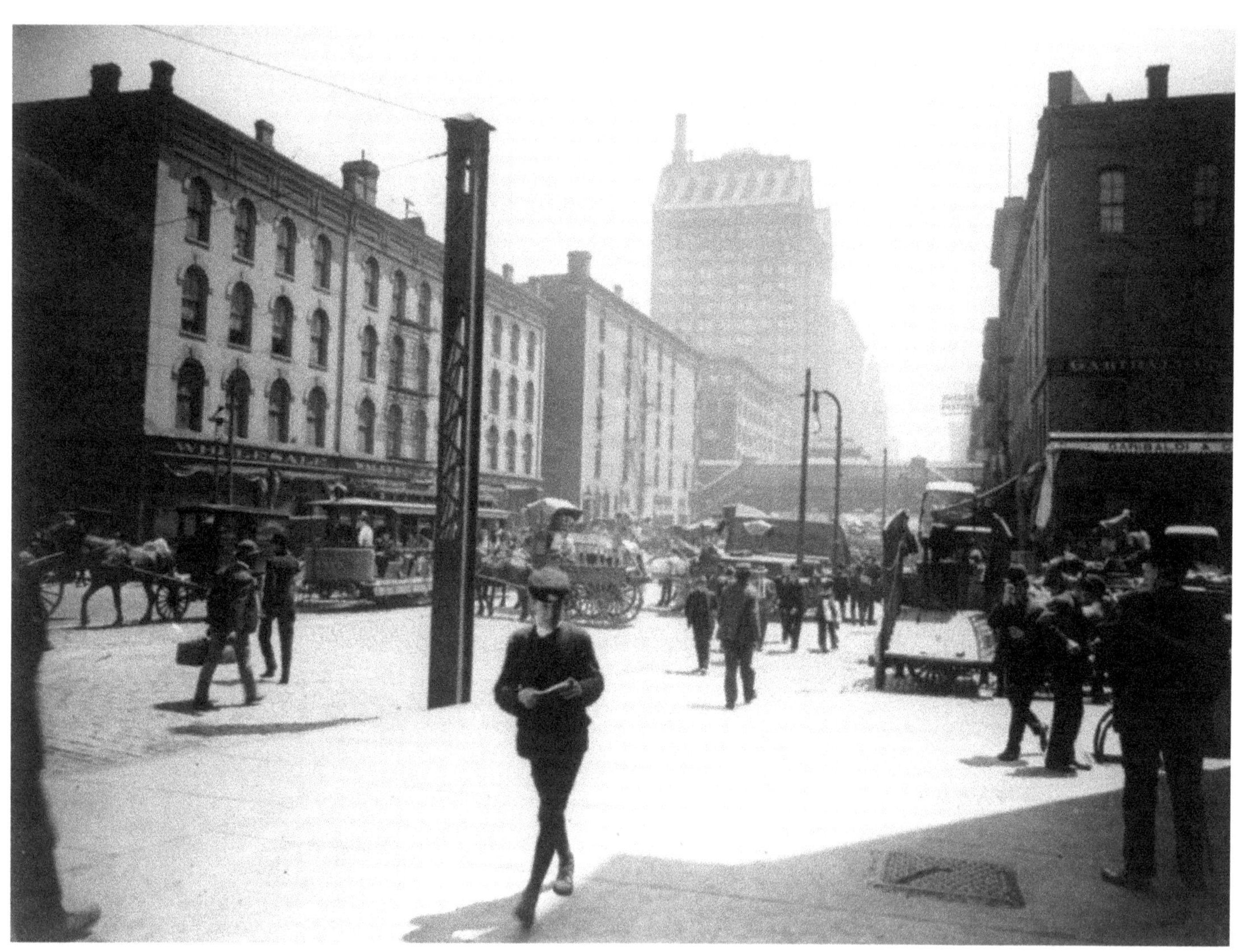

Chicago's State Street, as viewed from South Water Street, as it appeared on a day in 1906.

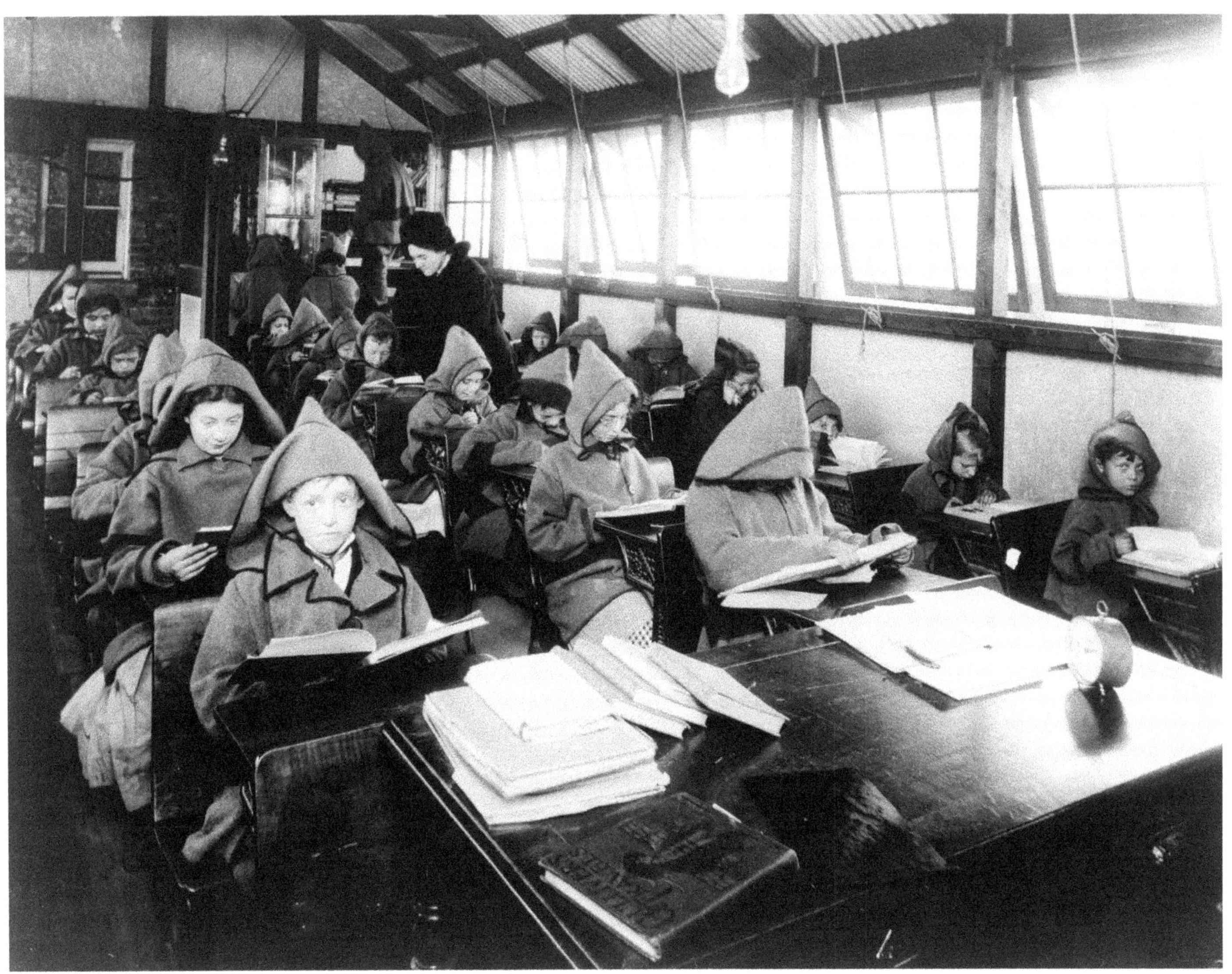

One product of the Society for the Prevention of Tuberculosis' efforts? Open-air schools. Despite Chicago's notoriously brutal winters, the city embraced the open-air movement of the early twentieth century, incorporating its tenets of fresh air, ventilation, and sunlight into public and private schools. In evidence at this open-air school on the rooftop of Mary Crane Nursery in Chicago, dressing for the school day required dressing for the elements. A copy of *Gulliver's Travels* rests on the front desk

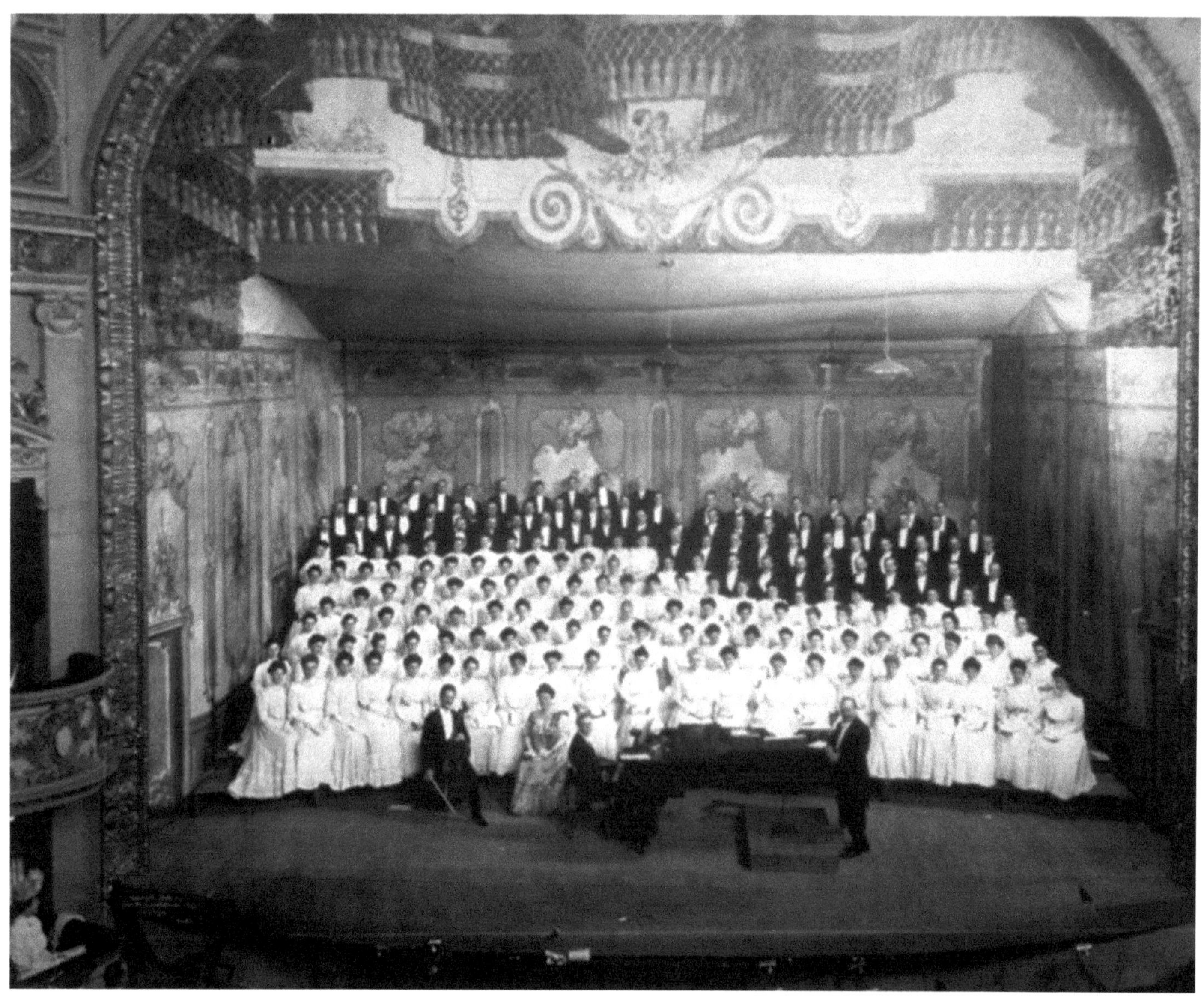

Considered the country's foremost producer of major choral works at the end of the nineteenth century, Milwaukee's Arion Musical Club is shown here at a performance in the Pabst Theatre on November 23, 1906, under the direction of one of its most famous conductors, Daniel Protherone, who began with the club in 1899.

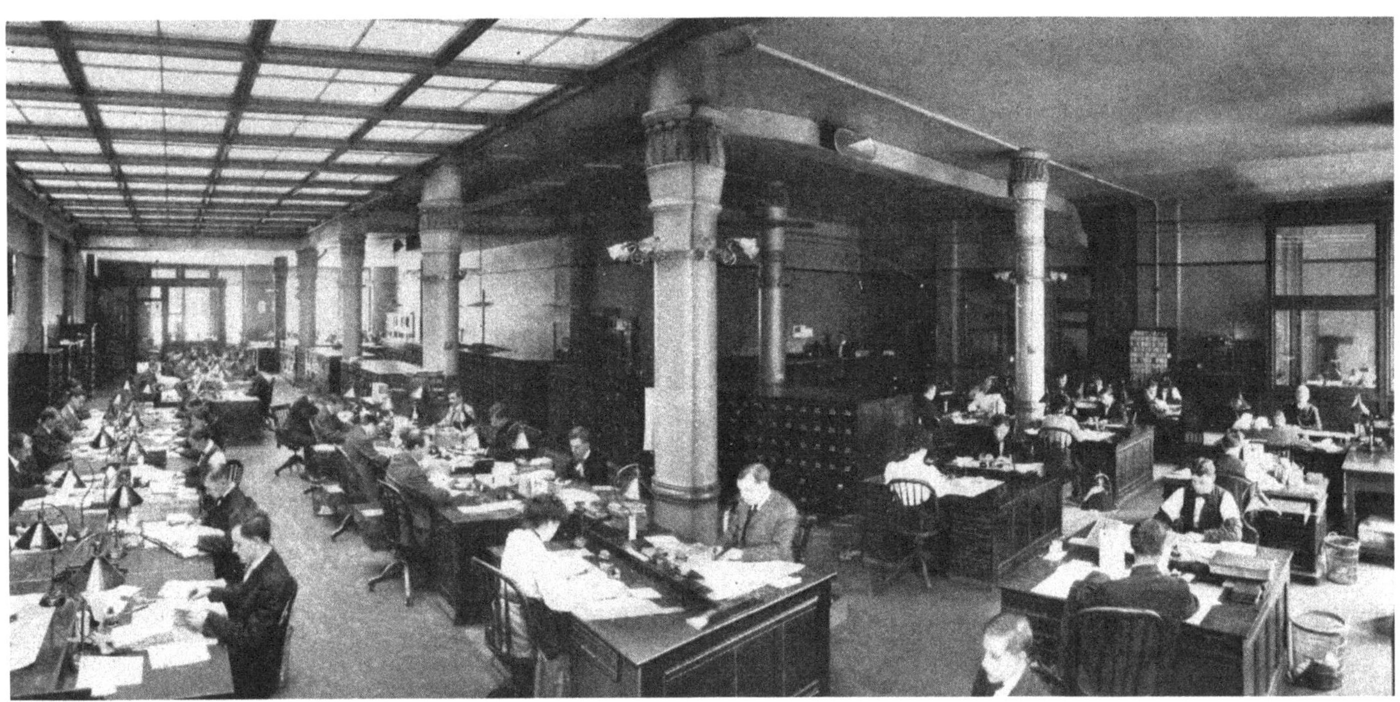

Founded in Janesville, Wisconsin, in 1857, Northwestern Mutual Insurance Company moved shortly thereafter to Milwaukee, first occupying two small rooms in a building at Main (now Broadway) and Wisconsin streets. The company expanded and moved four times before 1886, when it erected and occupied the six-story Richardsonian Romanesque–style building (at Broadway and Michigan streets) in which this photograph of the Main Room of the Secretary's department was taken.

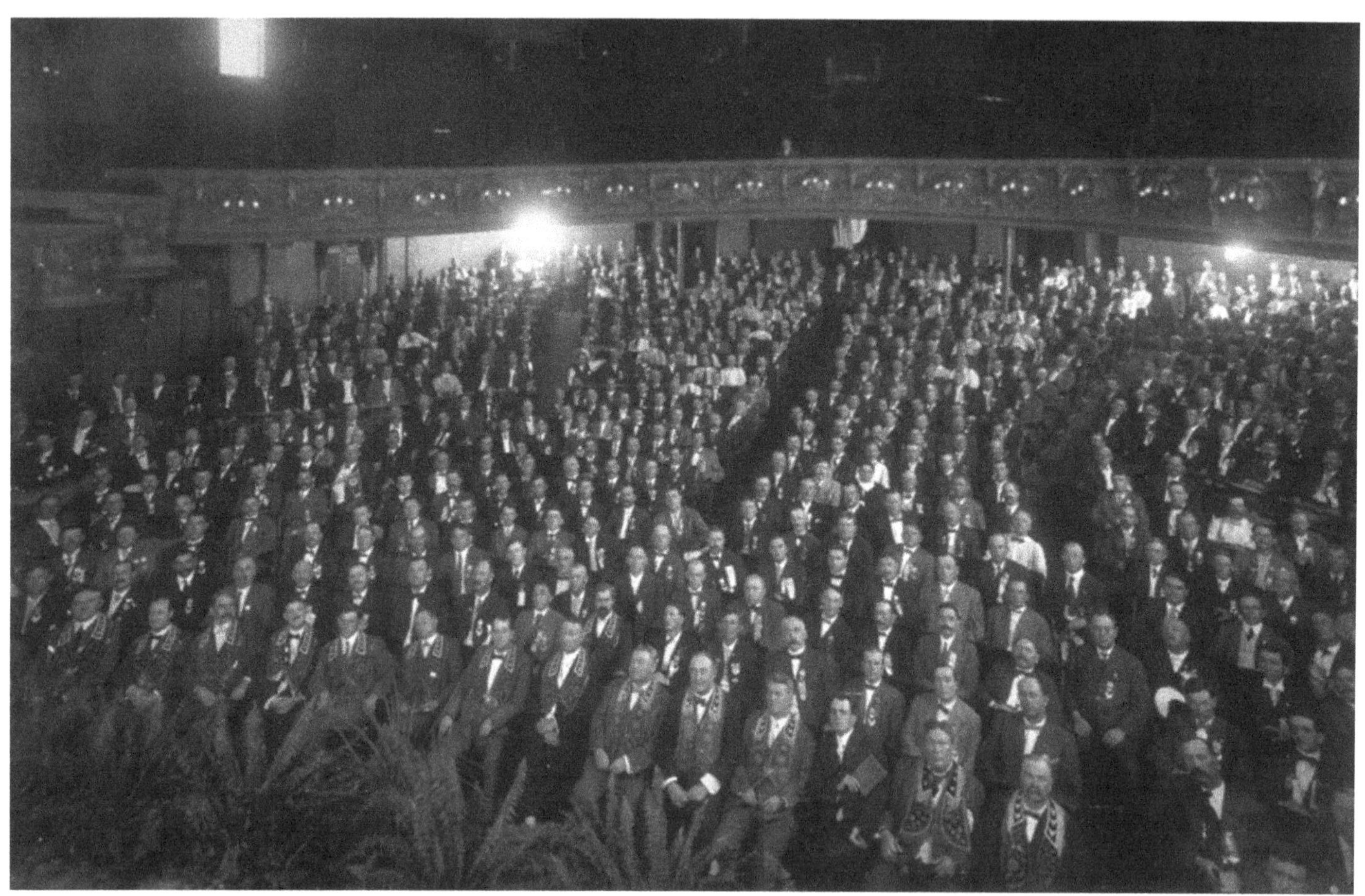

The convention of the Fraternal Order of Eagles assembles in Milwaukee in August 1906. Membership in the F.O.E., originally founded by a group of theater owners in Seattle, Washington, in 1898, grew exponentially around the turn of the century, thanks to its many members who toured with theater troupes and spread the Eagles' story. The Eagles supported the founding of Mother's Day and Social Security, among other activities.

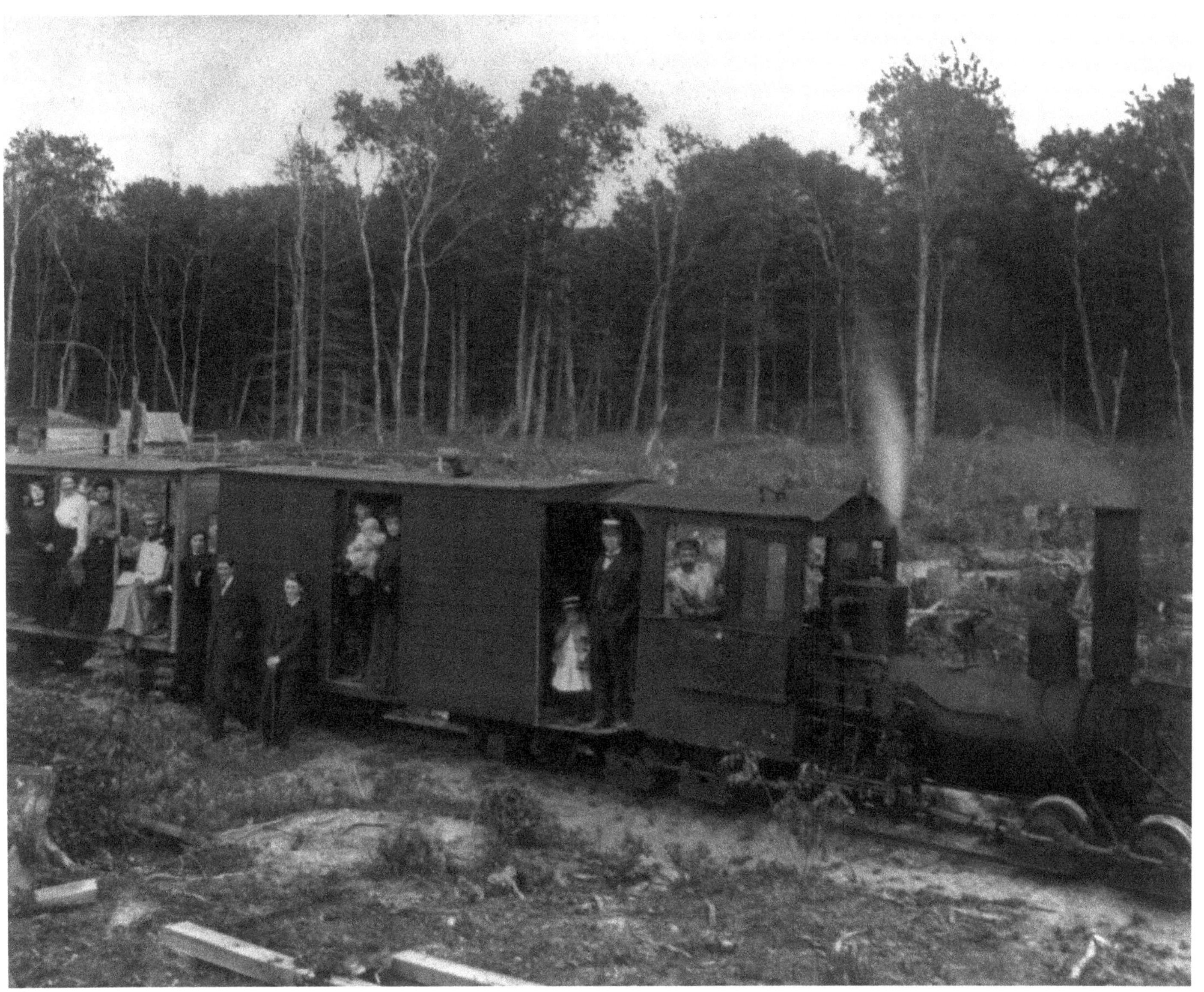

Many vacationers, like these trundling through Harbor Springs, Michigan, in 1906, were drawn not only to the fresh air and the beauty of Little Traverse Bay but also to the nation-changing logging operations in the state that helped build (and in some cases, rebuild) the cities from which the vacationers hailed. As such, excursions on logging trains were often a coveted activity on resorters' touring schedules.

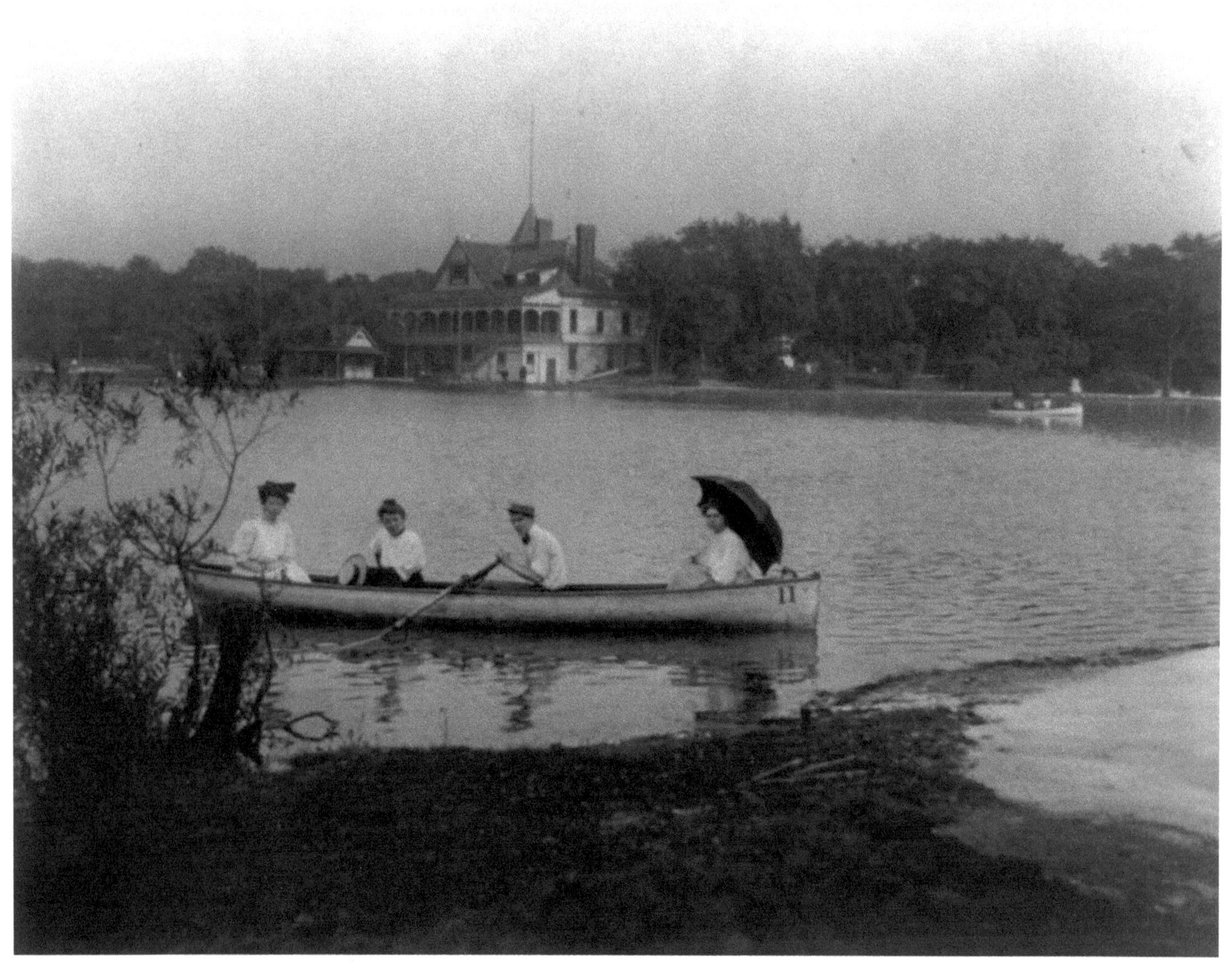

This large lagoon was one of the most remarkable features of Chicago's Central Park. Used for boating in summer and ice-skating in winter, in spring it fulfilled an entirely practical purpose: draining the parkland.

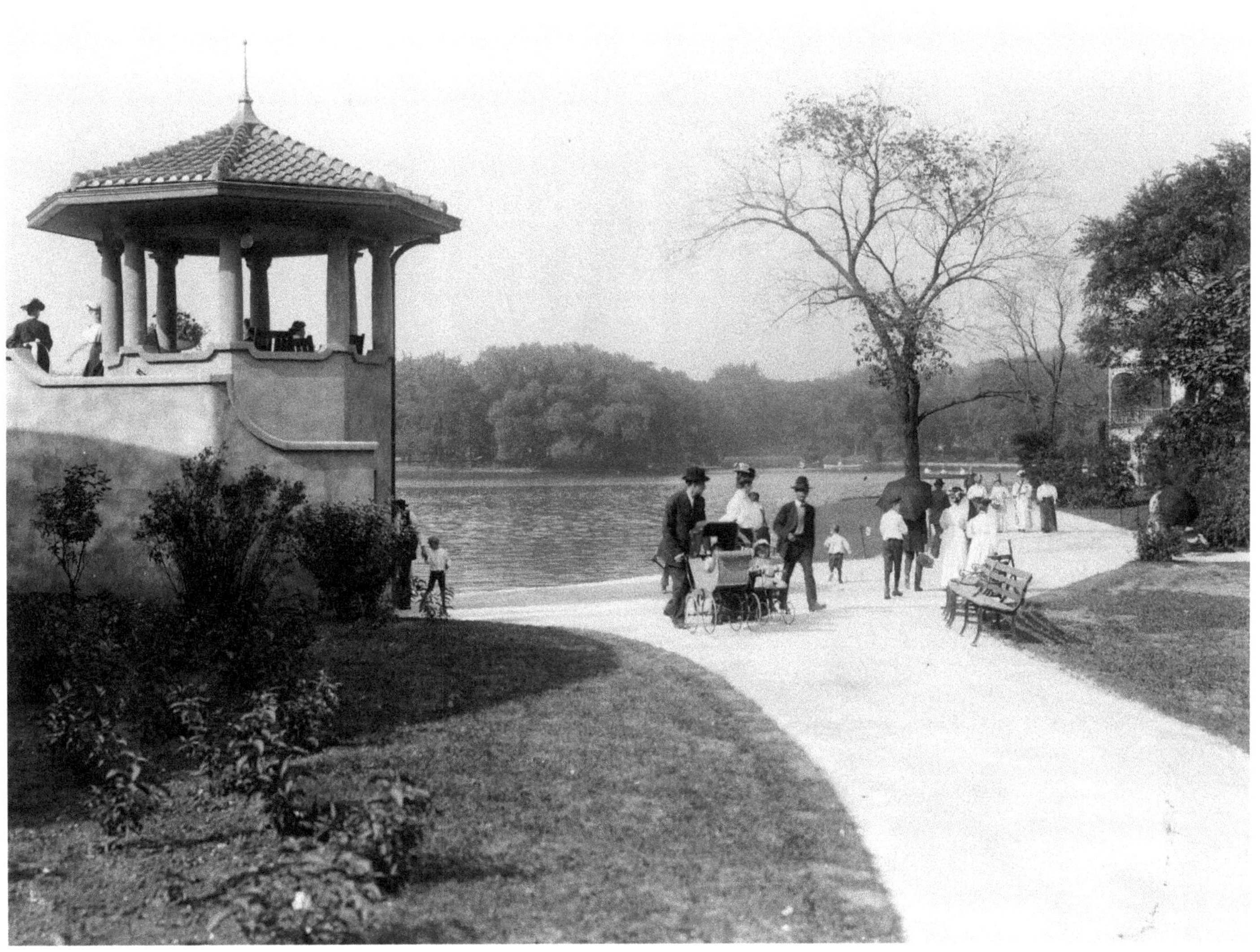

People stroll in Chicago's Garfield Park in 1907. Originally known as Central Park, the 184-acre pleasure grounds was the first of the three parks created on Chicago's West Side in the 1870s. After the assassination of President James A. Garfield in 1881, it was renamed Garfield Park. Credit for the design of all three parks and their interlinking boulevards goes to William Le Baron Jenney, who is most widely known as father of the American skyscraper.

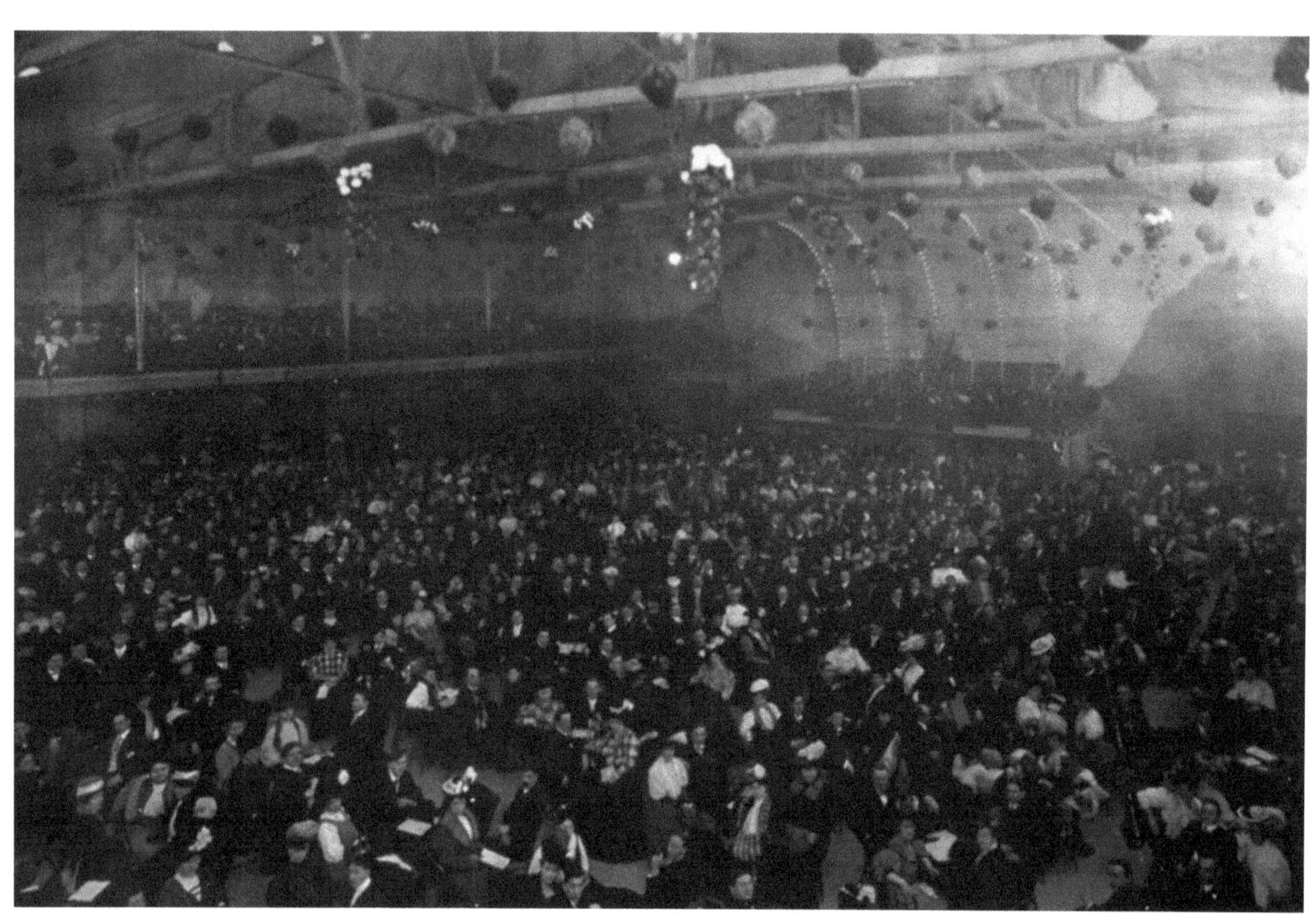

Crowds gather inside Milwaukee's Hippodrome in 1907, an immense exposition hall that counted among its most famous showcases the first annual Automobile and Motor Show of the Milwaukee Automotive Club.

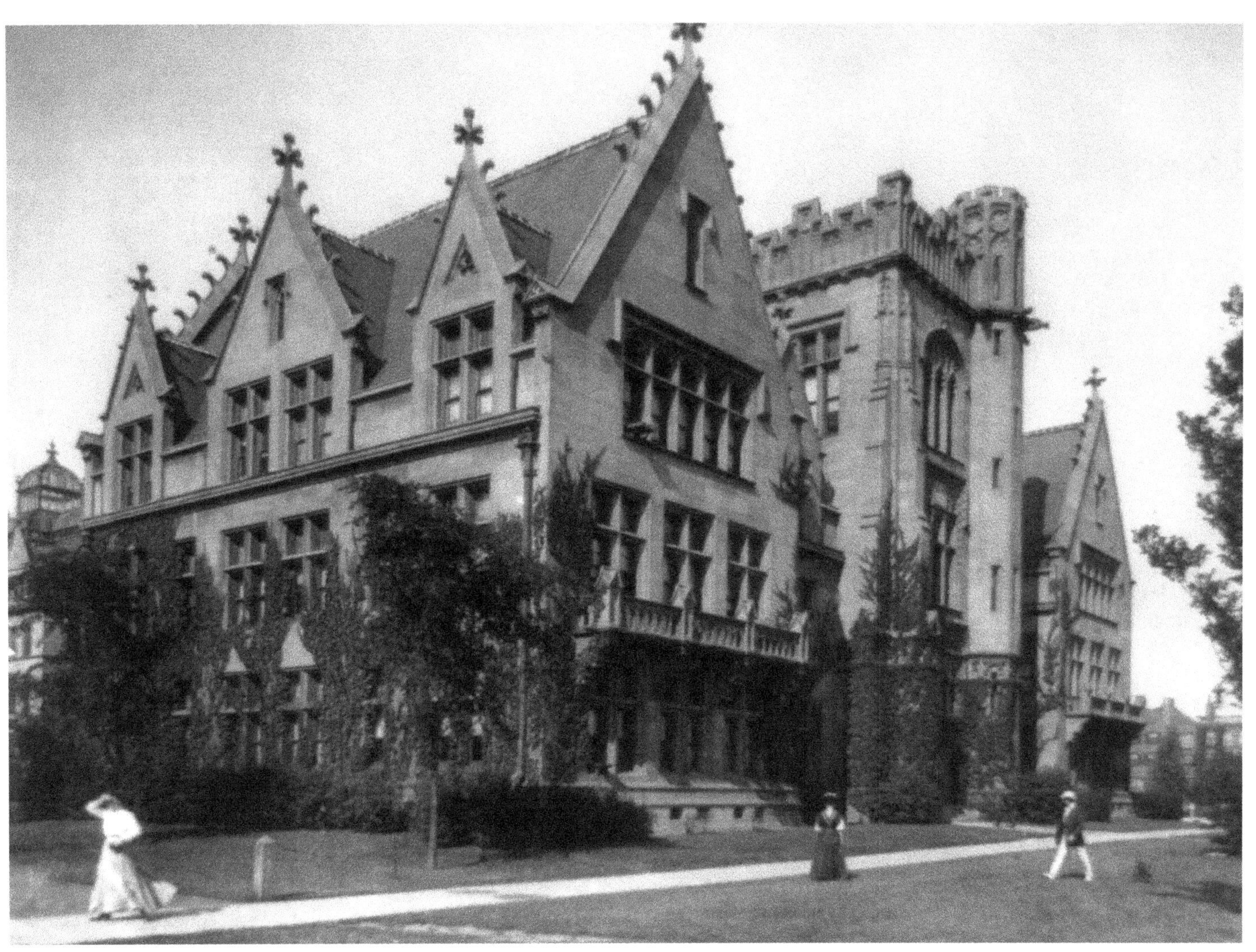

Dedicated in 1894, the neo-Gothic grandeur of the University of Chicago's Ryerson Physical Laboratory—captured here in 1907—suited the many advances in physical science made within its walls. Several Nobel prize winners, not to mention the Manhattan Project, have occupied its hallowed spaces.

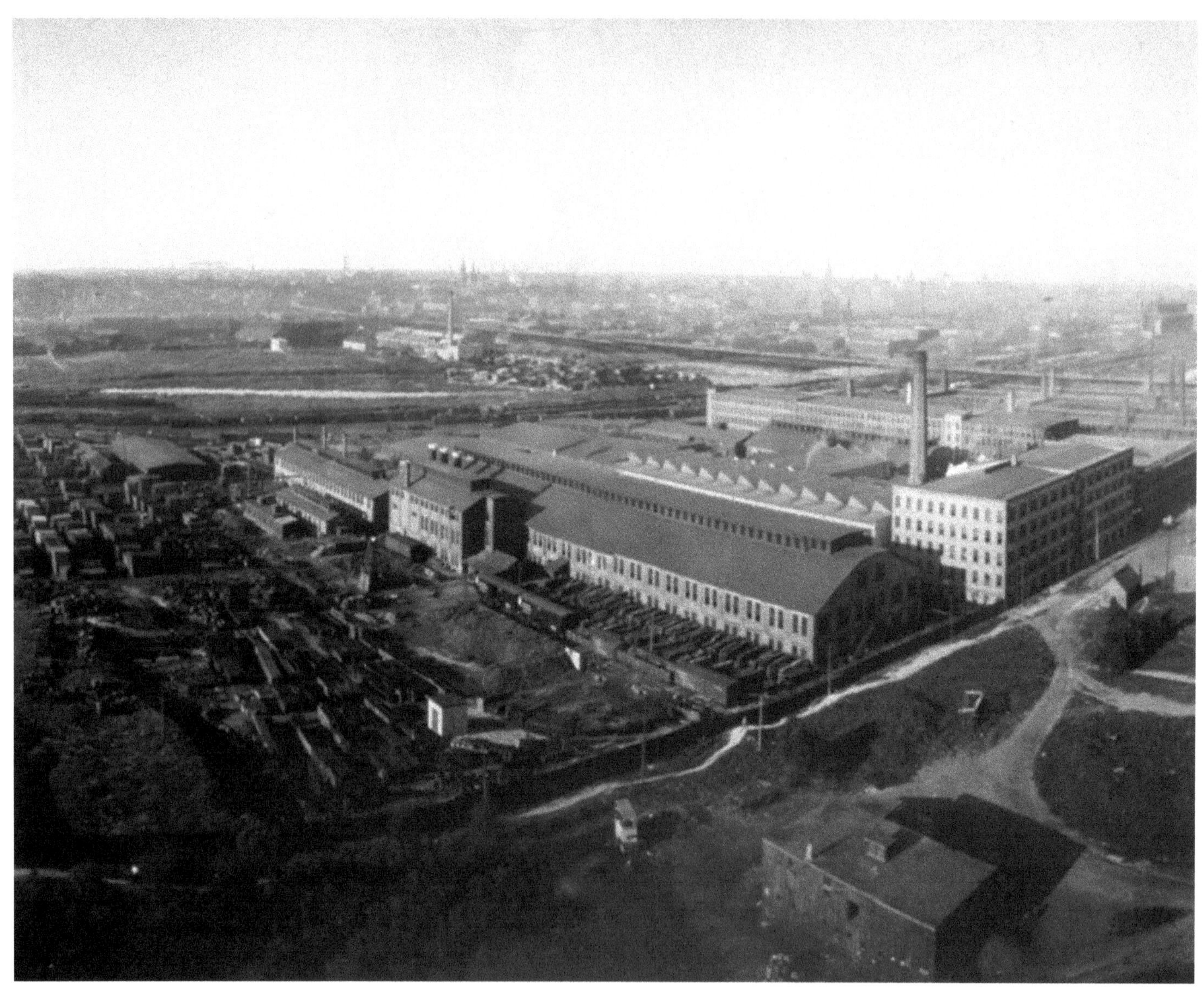

Shortly after patenting his horse-drawn reaper, Virginian inventor Cyrus Hall McCormick launched the McCormick Harvesting Machine Company in Chicago in the late 1840s. In 1902, J. P. Morgan bought McCormick's company, as well as other agricultural machinery companies, merging them into one: the International Harvester Company, pictured here in the city in 1907.

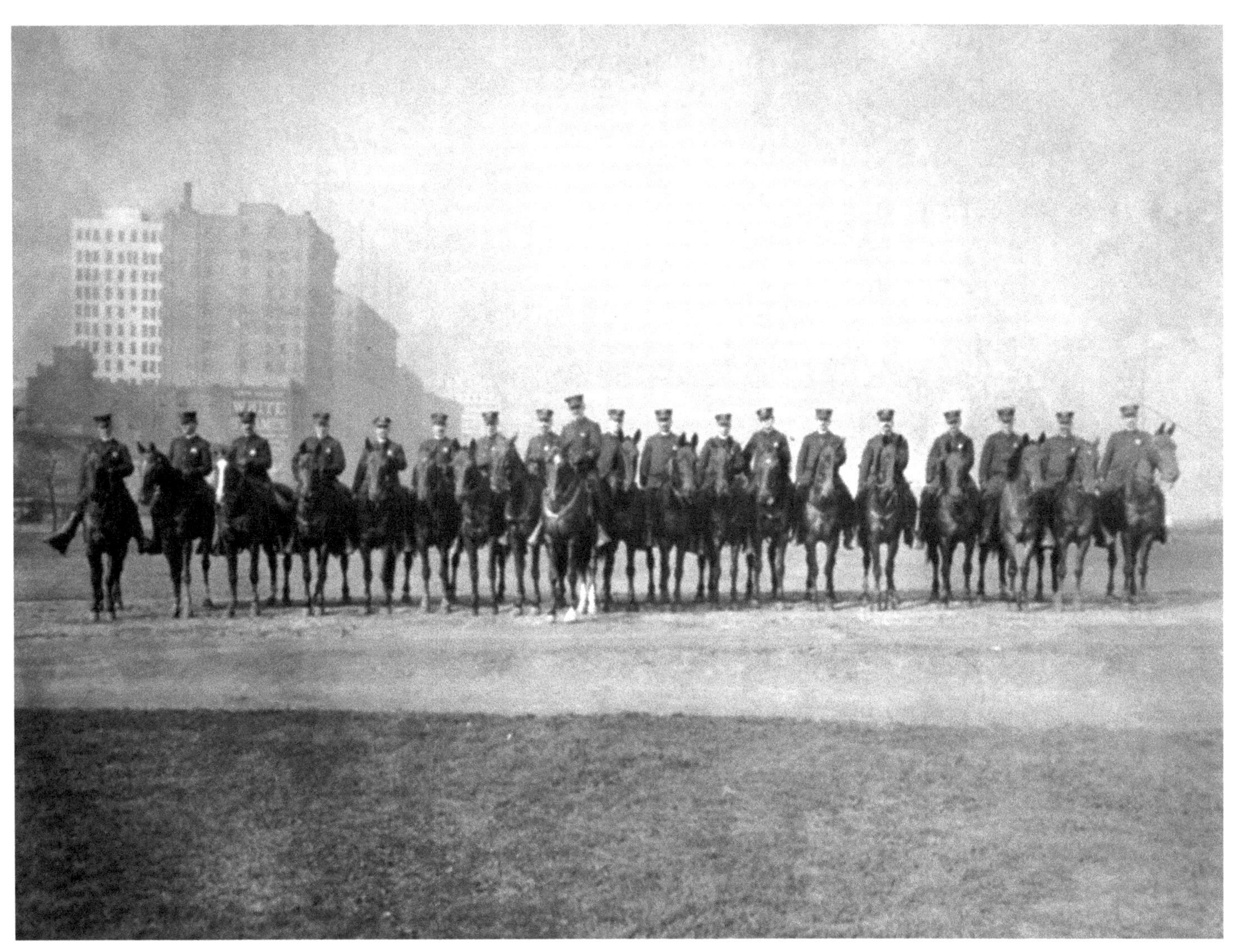

With the Chicago cityscape in the background, a squad of Chicago's mounted police line up for duty. Except for a 25-year hiatus between 1949 and 1974, mounted police have been a tradition in the city for more than a century.

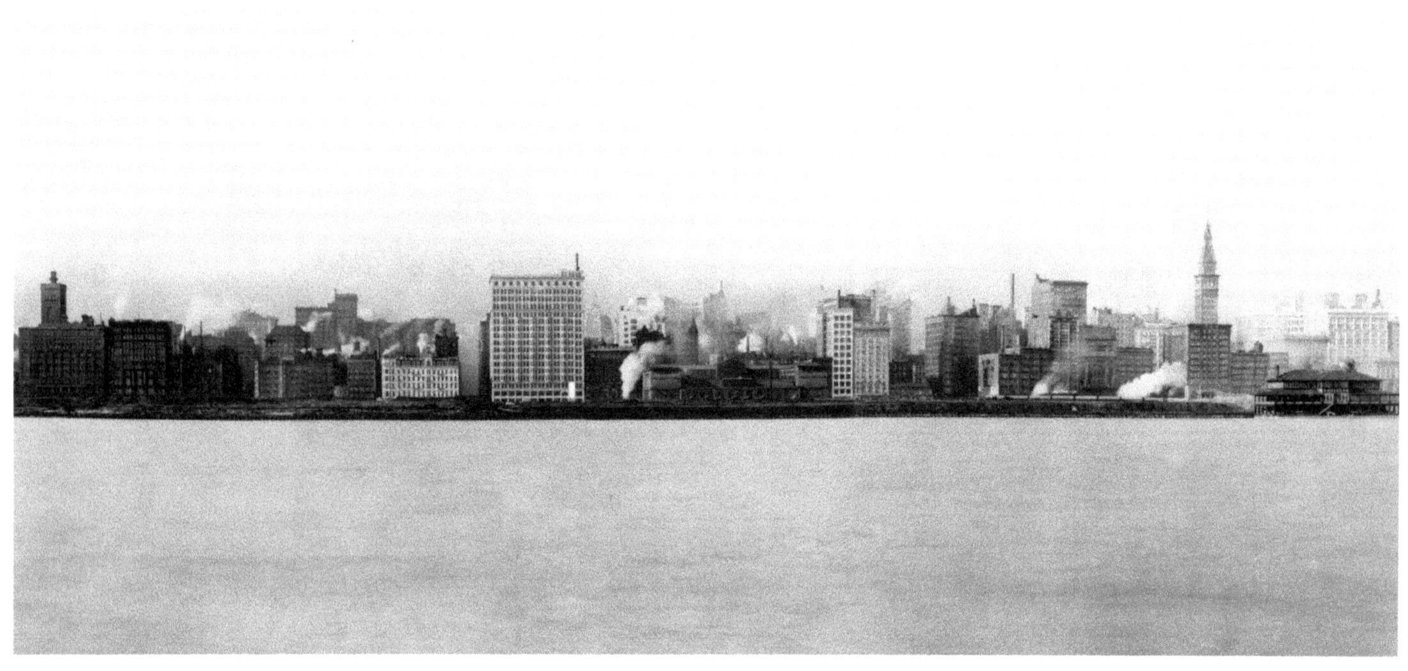

This panorama of Chicago's waterfront from a boat on Lake Michigan was recorded in 1907.

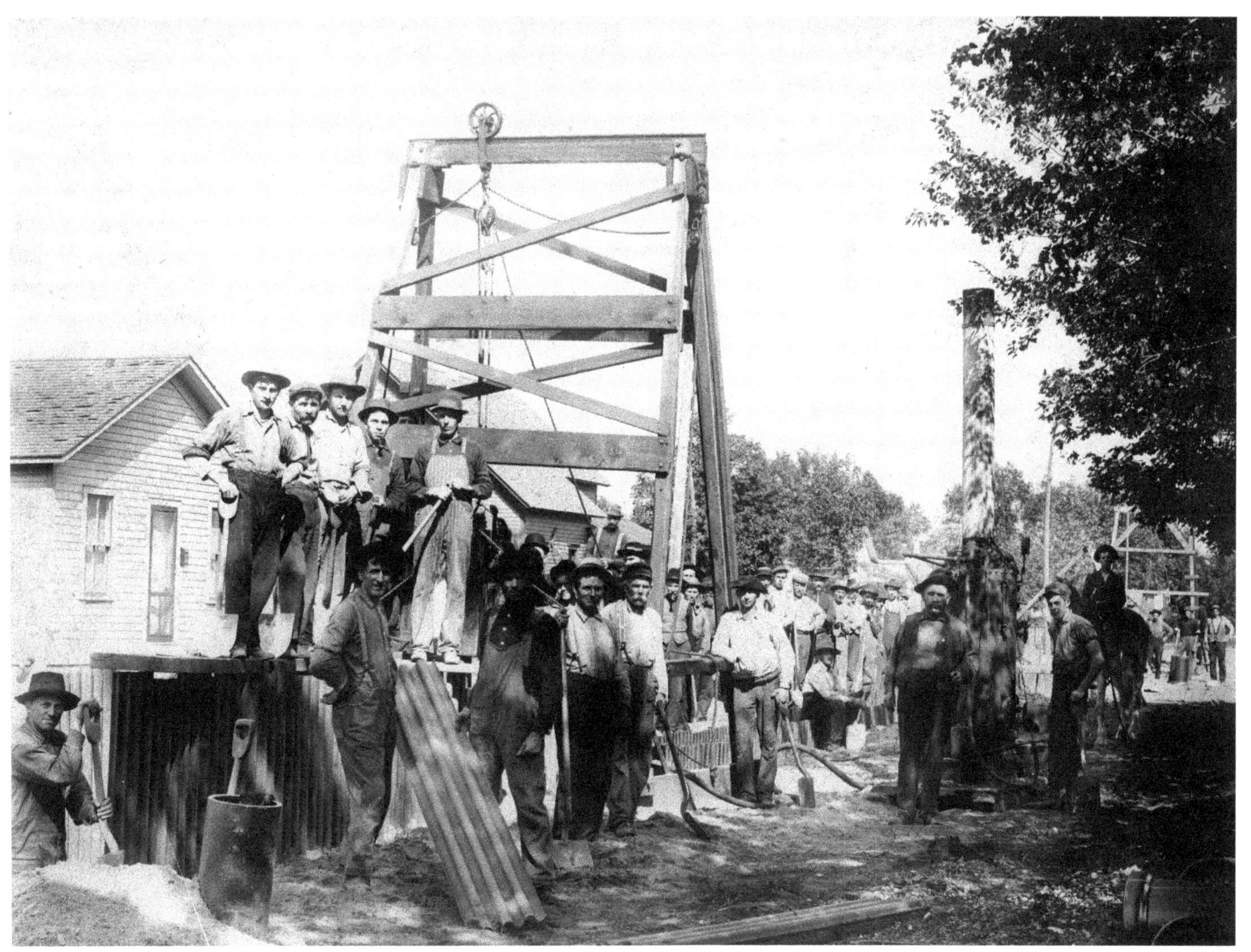

Although sewers existed in the city of Muskegon from before the late 1880s, following the turn of the century, the city rushed to accommodate its growth by adding sewer districts. Here, sometime before 1910, laborers equipped with wooden-handled shovels take a break from digging.

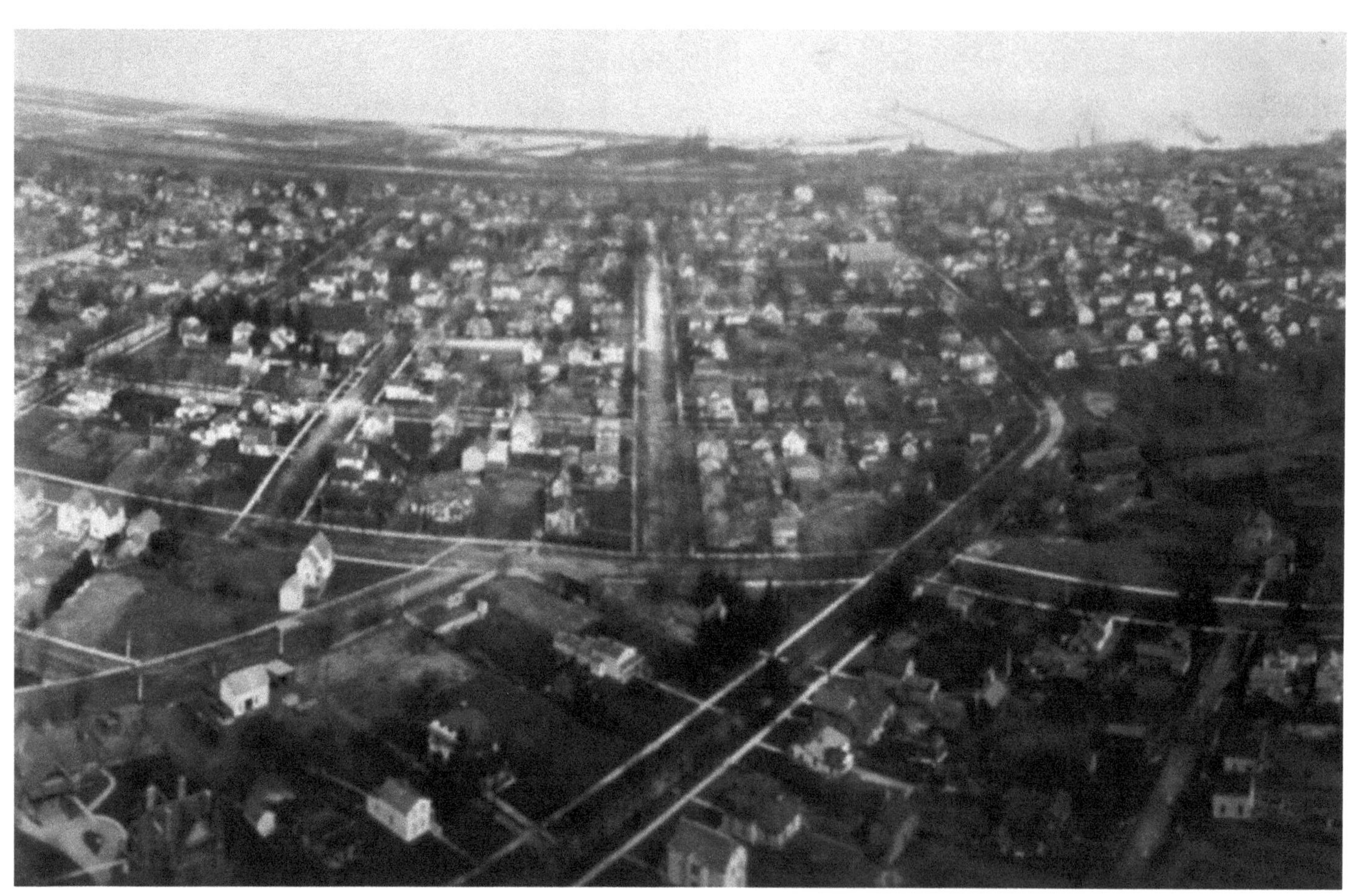

Proclaiming "The Hitherto Impossible in Photography Is Our Specialty," early twentieth century photographer George Lawrence's specially designed kites and cameras—a contraption he referred to as the Lawrence Captive Airship—captured the largest negative images ever from an airborne vehicle. Shown here is a 1908 bird's-eye view of Waukegan, Illinois, from a Lawrence airship at 1,000 feet. Lake Michigan appears at top in the distance.

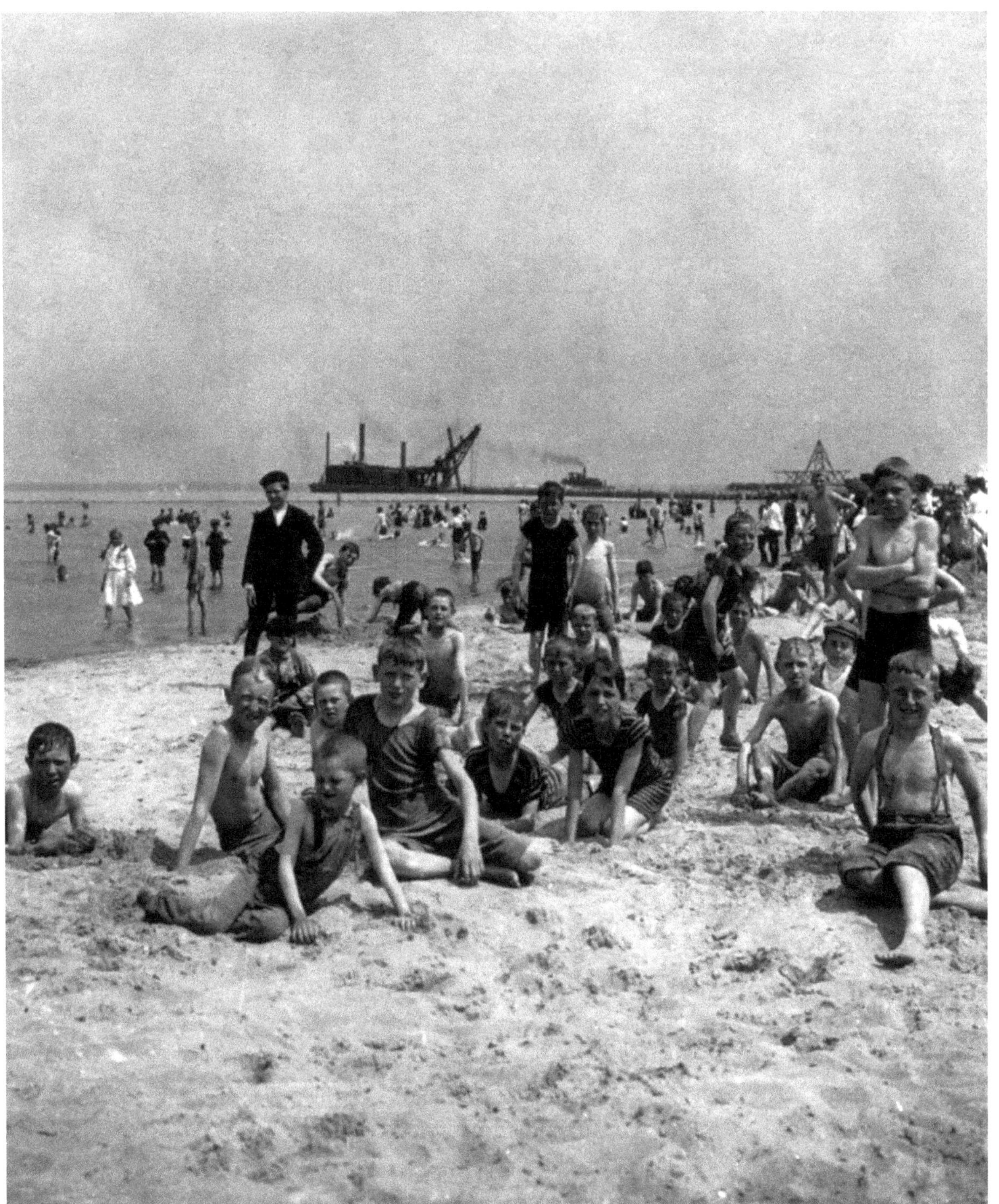

Much as it is now, the Chicago shore at Lake Michigan was a popular summer escape for beach lovers the year these boys paused for a group shot.

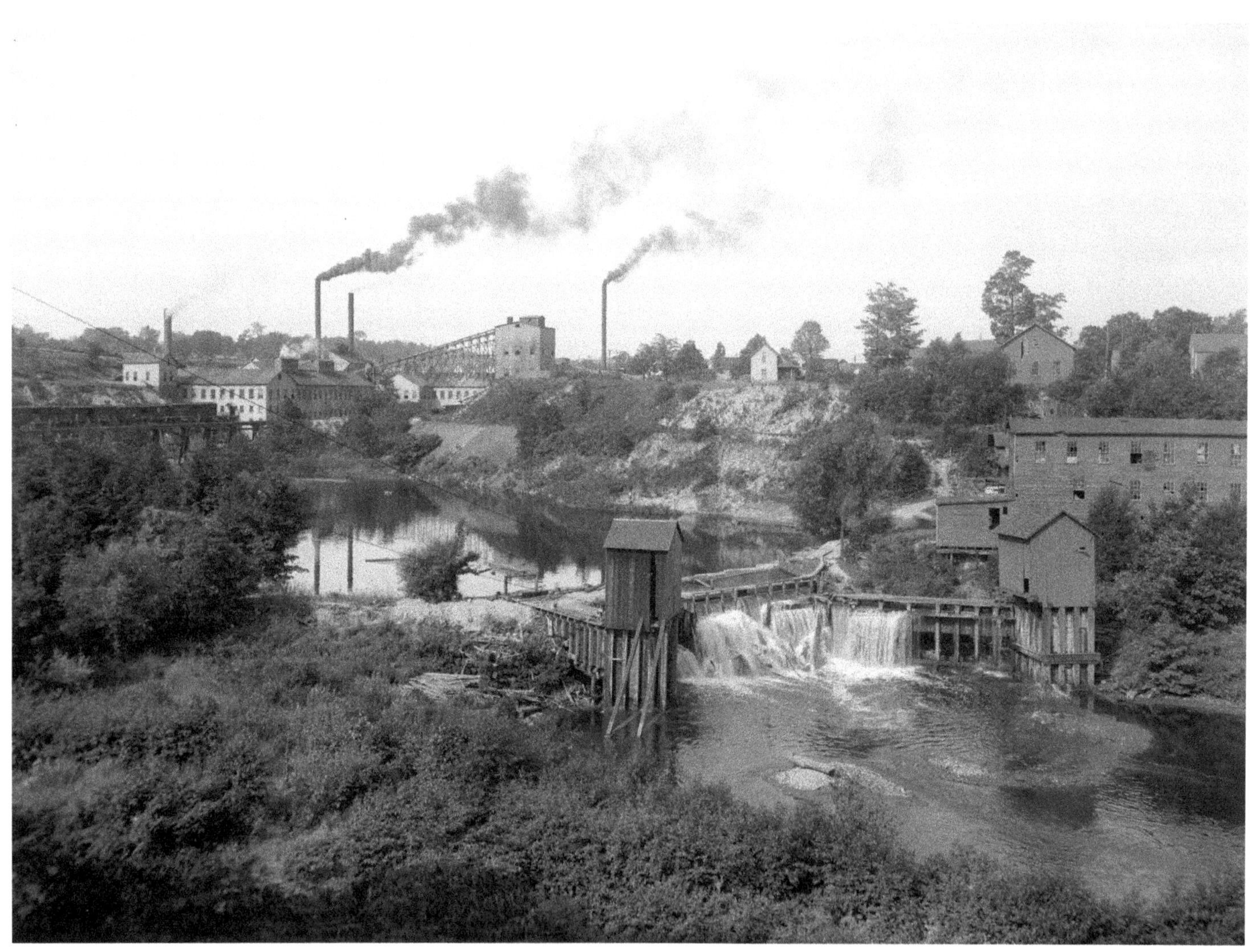

The Petoskey, Michigan, skyline in 1908. Smoke from the pipes of a paper mill, probably the Petoskey Paper Fibre Company's sulphite mill, curls into the sky beside the Bear River, which flows into Lake Michigan's Little Traverse Bay.

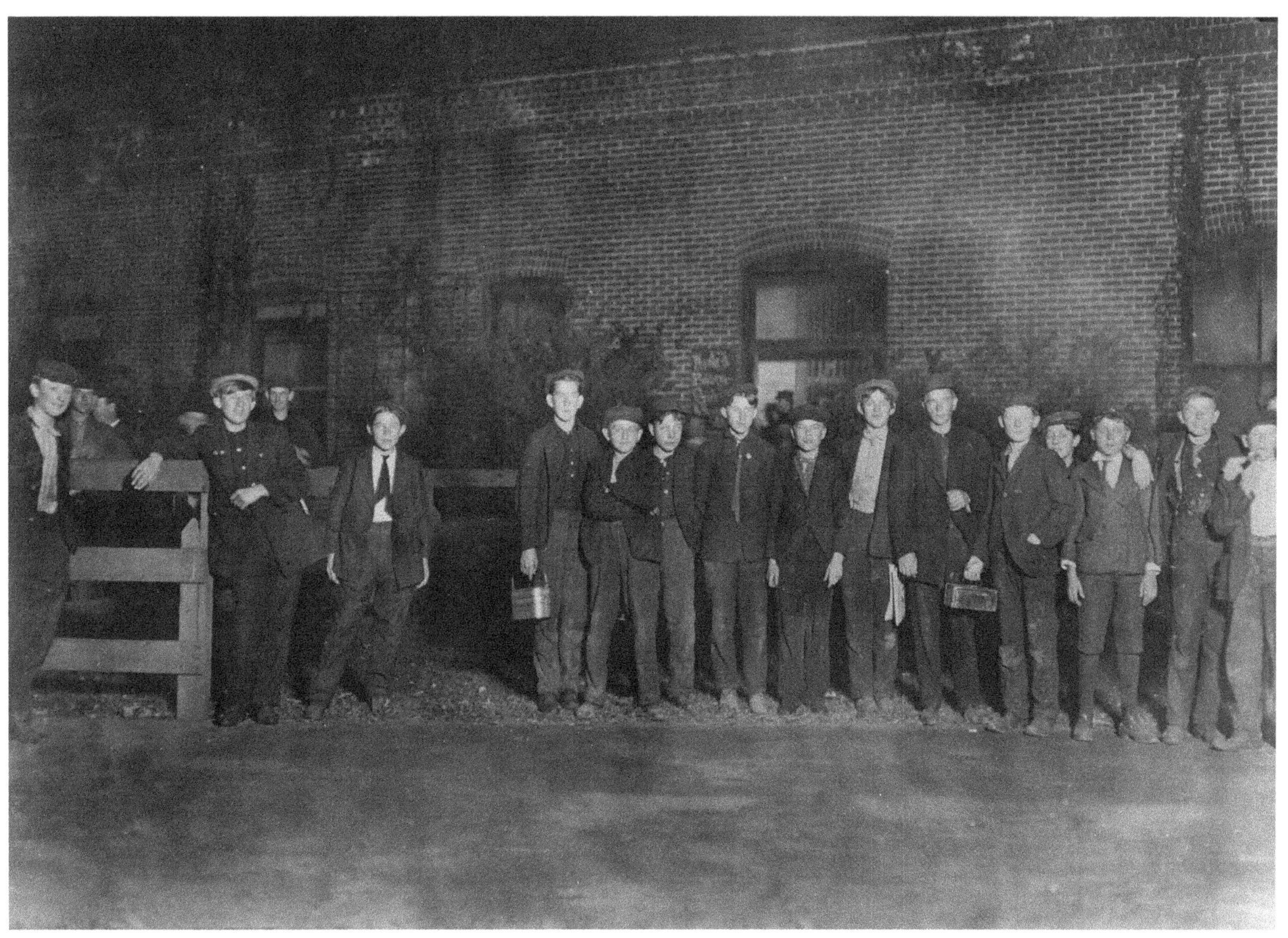

A group of boys line up outside the W. B. Conkey printing plant in Hammond, Indiana, at the end of the workday in 1908. (Girls exited from another door.) Hammond is located off Lake Michigan, near its southernmost extremity. The Conkey printing and publishing company, whose plant was the largest in the world the year this image was recorded, began producing the Sears Roebuck catalog in 1898, its first year of operation.

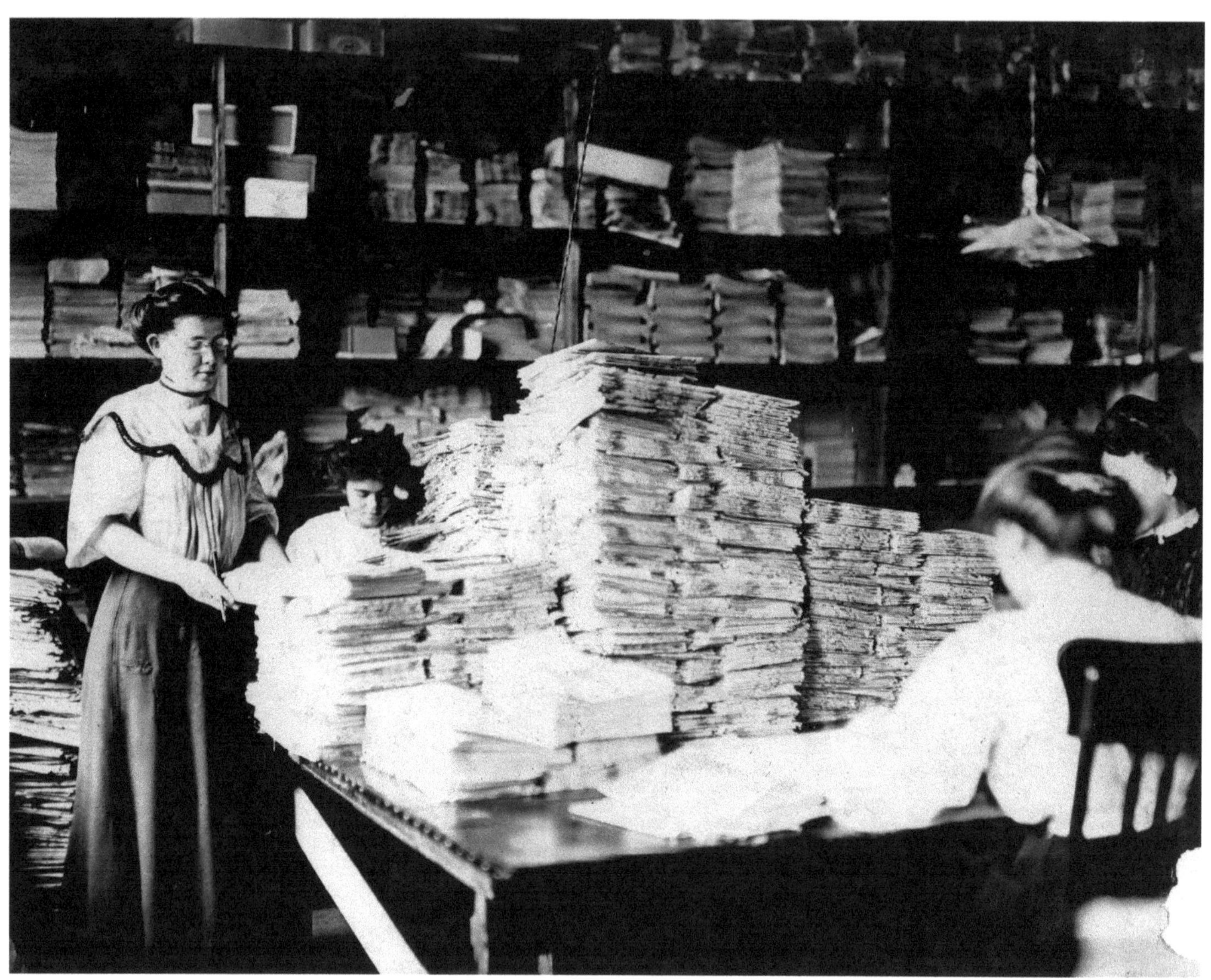

With only $25 capital, Frank S. Betz cut out the middleman and began his surgical supply company in a 120-square-foot space in Chicago in 1895. By 1908, the Frank S. Betz Company had moved to Hammond, Indiana, where it occupied 84,600 square feet of space in a brick factory building and reportedly filled orders directly to physicians, surgeons, dentists, veterinarians, and more than 2,200 hospitals at the rate of one every 20 seconds.

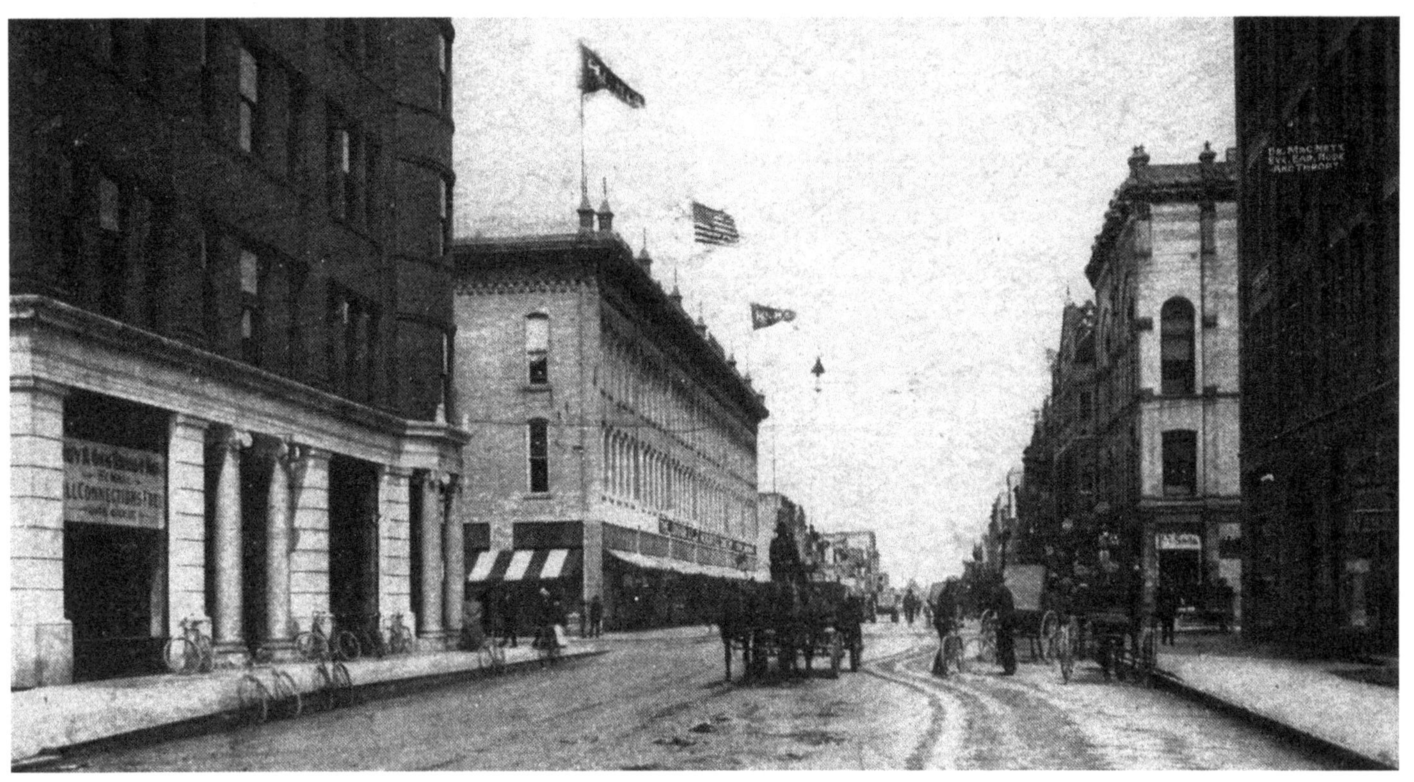

Facing east on Front Street in Traverse City, Michigan, 1908. Located at the southern end of the peninsula that separates the eastern and western channels of the lake's Grand Traverse Bay, Traverse City straddles the land between these waters.

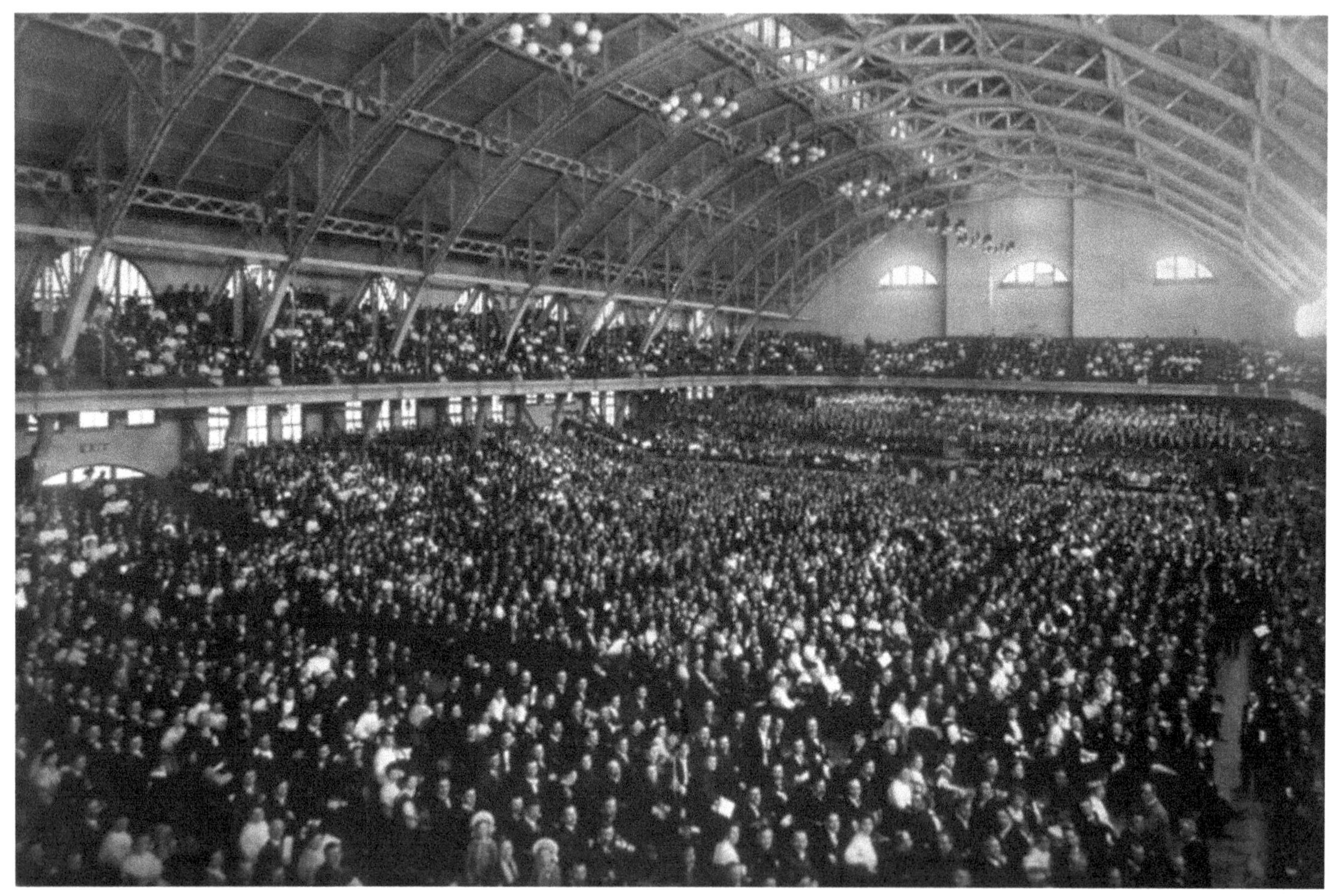

Crowds gather inside Chicago's Coliseum on May 24, 1908, for a Silver Jubilee, celebrating the 25th anniversary of the founding of the Catholic Order of Foresters, a fraternal society that began with just 42 members at Holy Family Parish in Chicago, Illinois, to help families beset by tragedy with money for burial expenses, as well as food for the surviving family members.

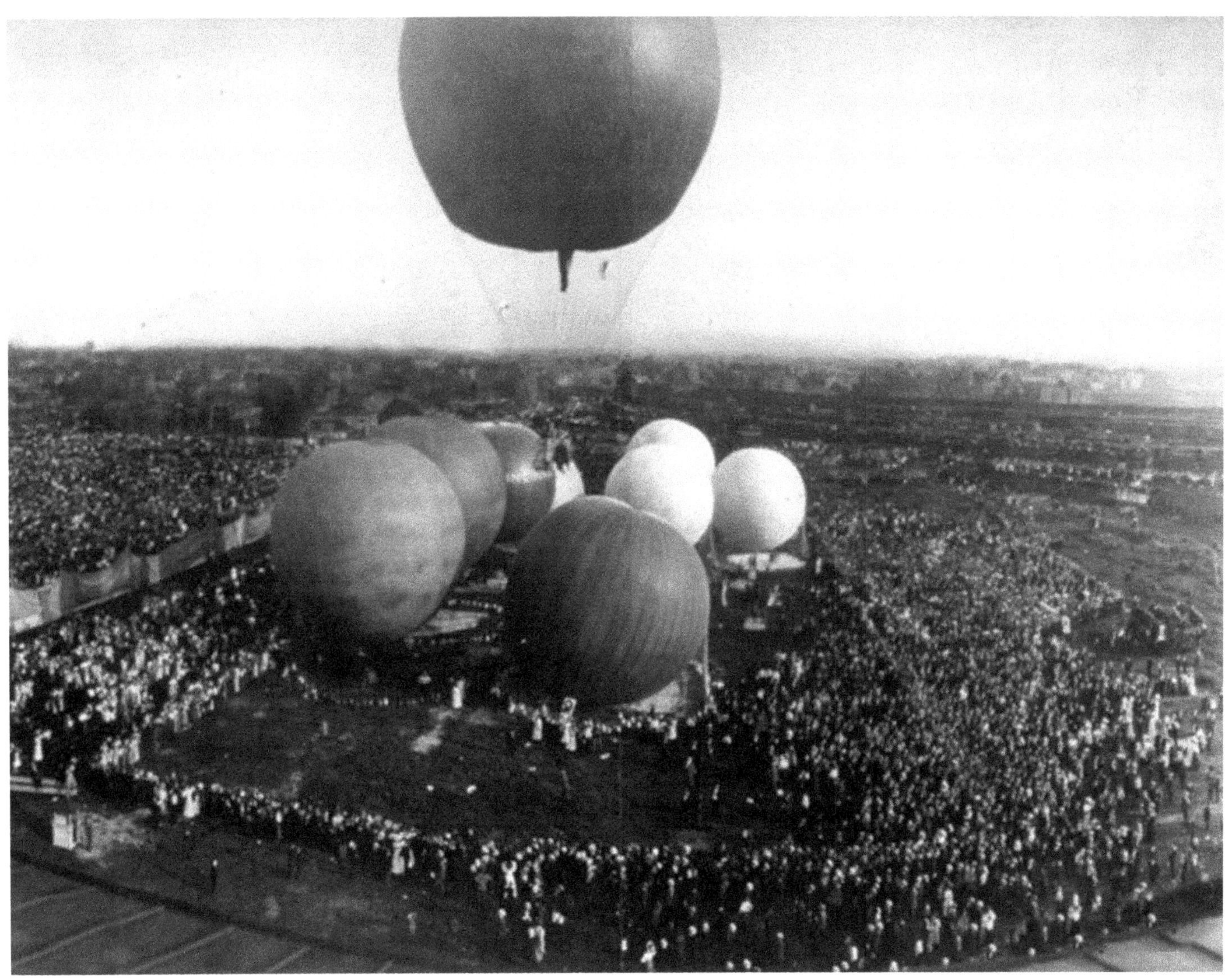

Chicago was long a lift-off site for balloonists: Silas M. Brooks' gas balloon *Eclipse,* likely the first ever to fly over the city, ascended July 4, 1855. The 1893 World's Columbian Exposition featured a giant hydrogen balloon named *Chicago,* which hoisted hundreds of fair visitors a thousand feet into the air. No balloon event held before 1908, however, compared to this one: the International Ballooning Contest, held in Chicago on the 4th of July 1908, drew more than 150,000 spectators.

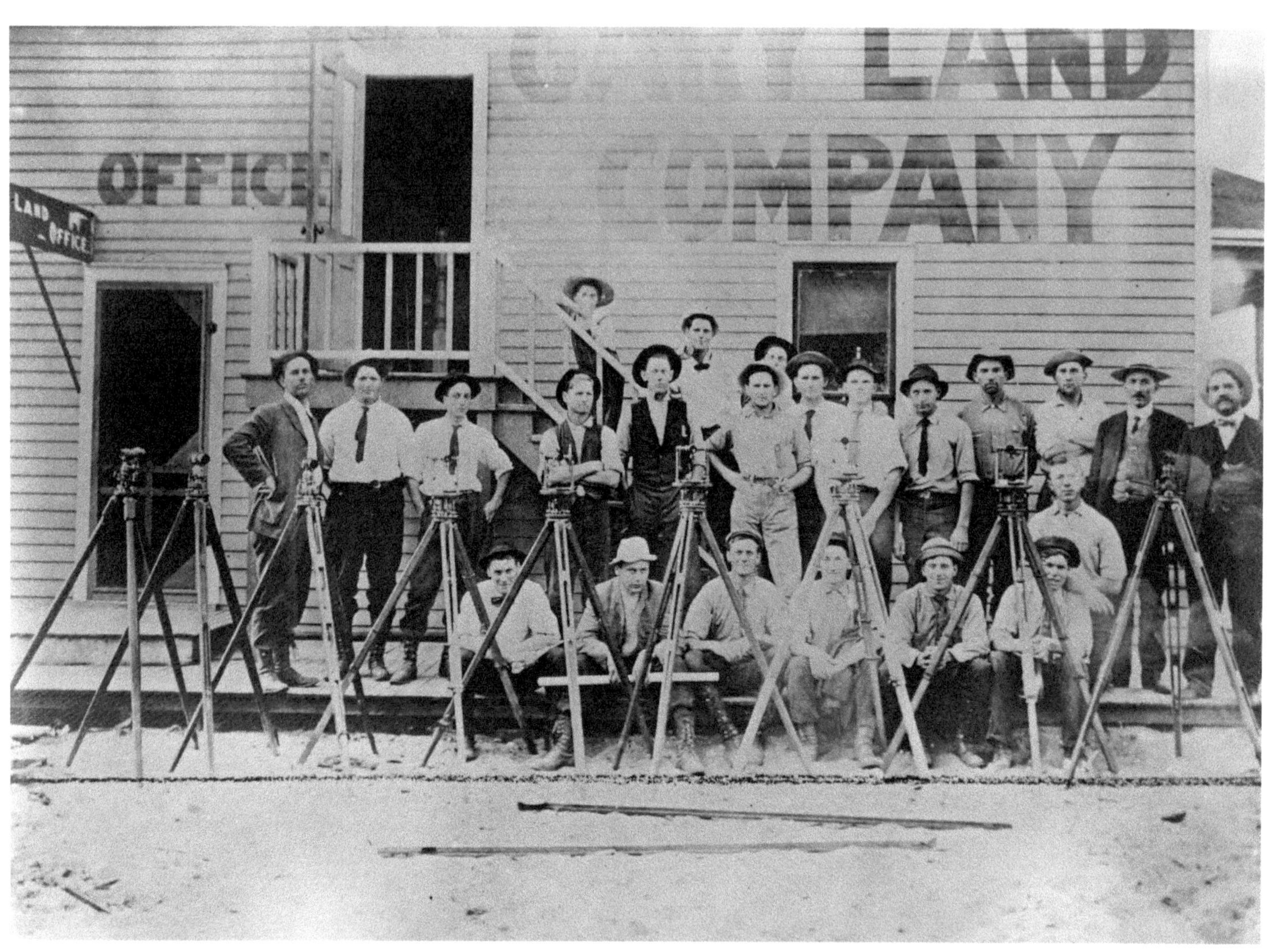

Envisioning a company town befitting its state-of-the-art steel manufacturing operations, U.S. Steel Corporation in 1906 created a subsidiary, the Gary Land Company, to design the town of Gary in Indiana. Gary's aptly named First Subdivision, on the north side of town, was an 800-acre grid of paved streets and sidewalks bordering 4,000 platted lots, well-manicured yards, and a downtown business district—centered on 5th and Broadway—of two-story stone and brick buildings. Gary was founded off the southernmost extremity of Lake Michigan, just east of Hammond.

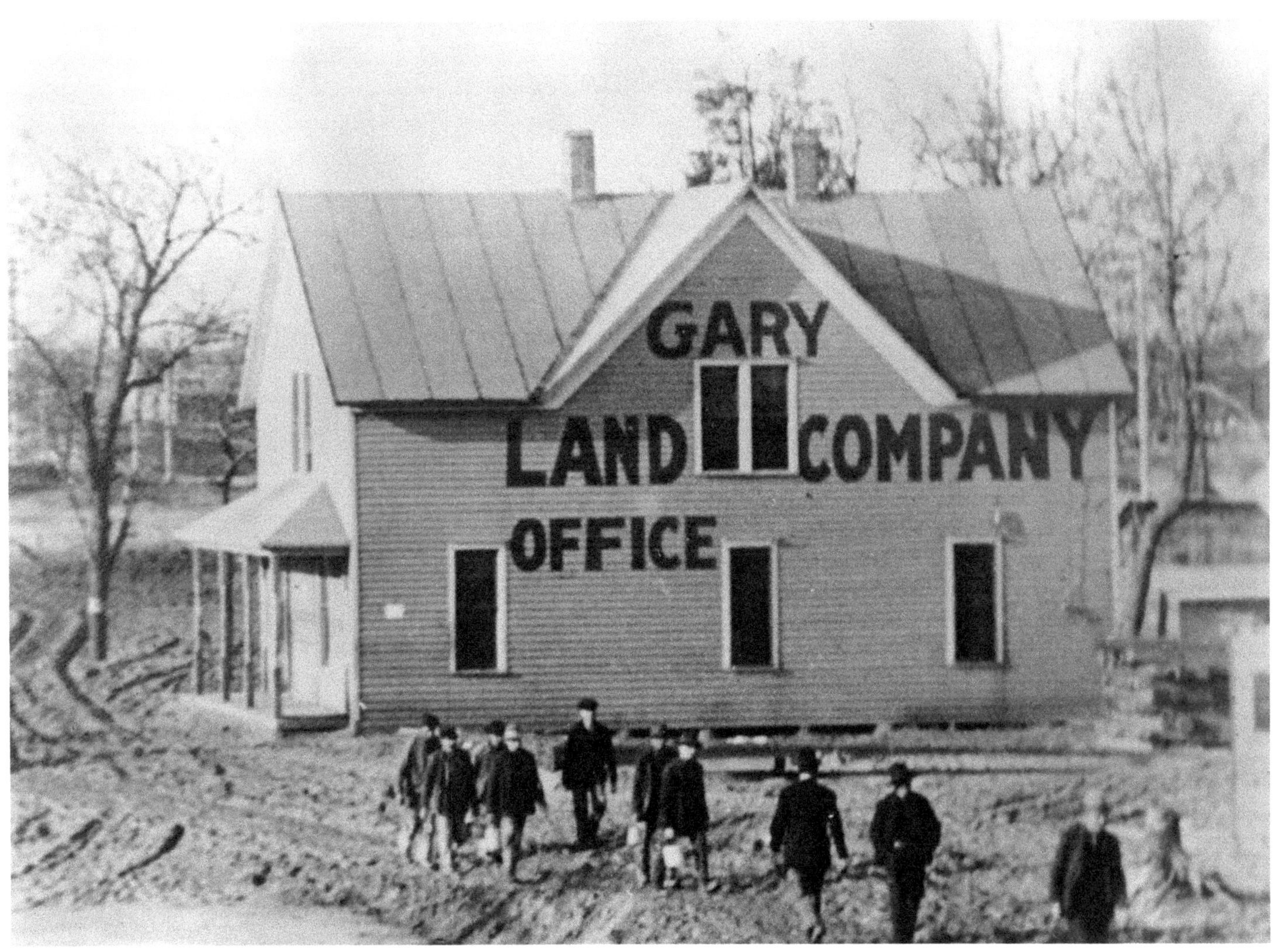

By the time this photograph was taken in 1908, two years after construction began on U.S. Steel's mill and town of Gary—often referred to as the "City of the Century"—U.S. Steel had spent more than $42 million on their creation.

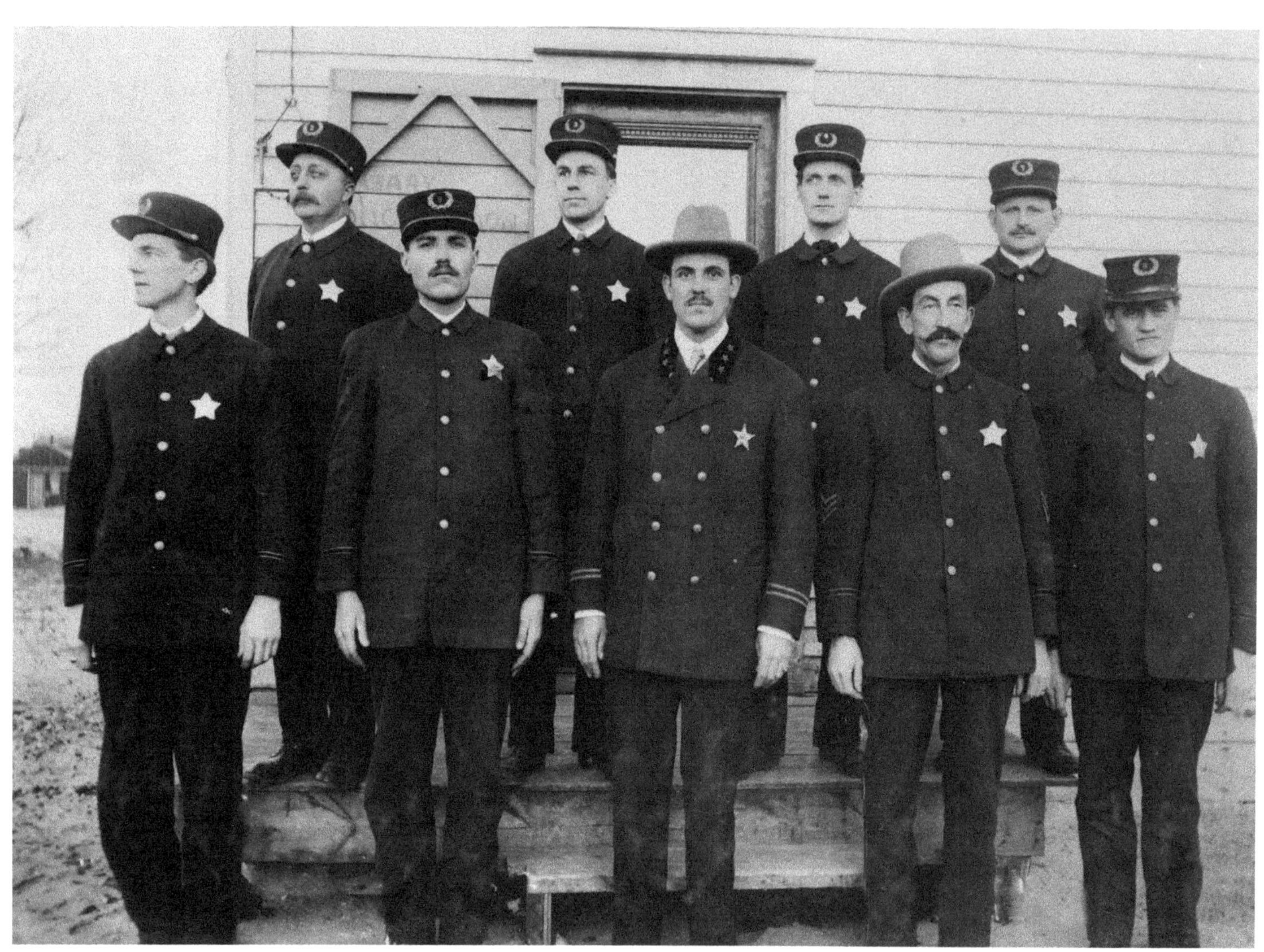

The nine-man Gary Police Force, photographed in 1908, just two years after the founding of the city of Gary, Indiana.

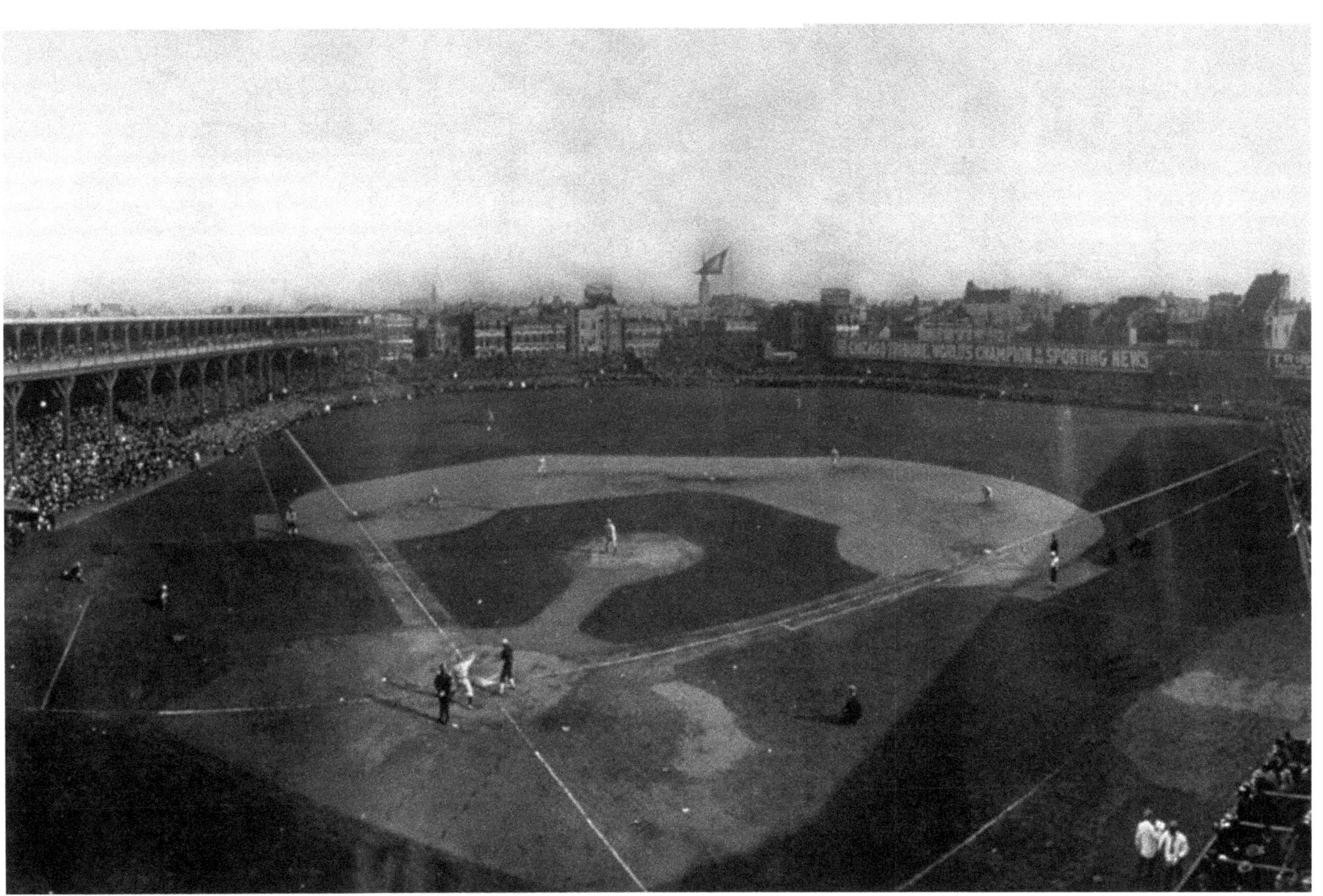

The City Championship series between the Cubs, Chicago's National League baseball team, and the White Sox, the city's American League team, didn't affect either team's league rankings. It did, however, add fire to the rivalry between the two and drew a giant crowd, in evidence here by the throngs in the stands of the Cubs' first home field, West Side Park, during a series game in 1909.

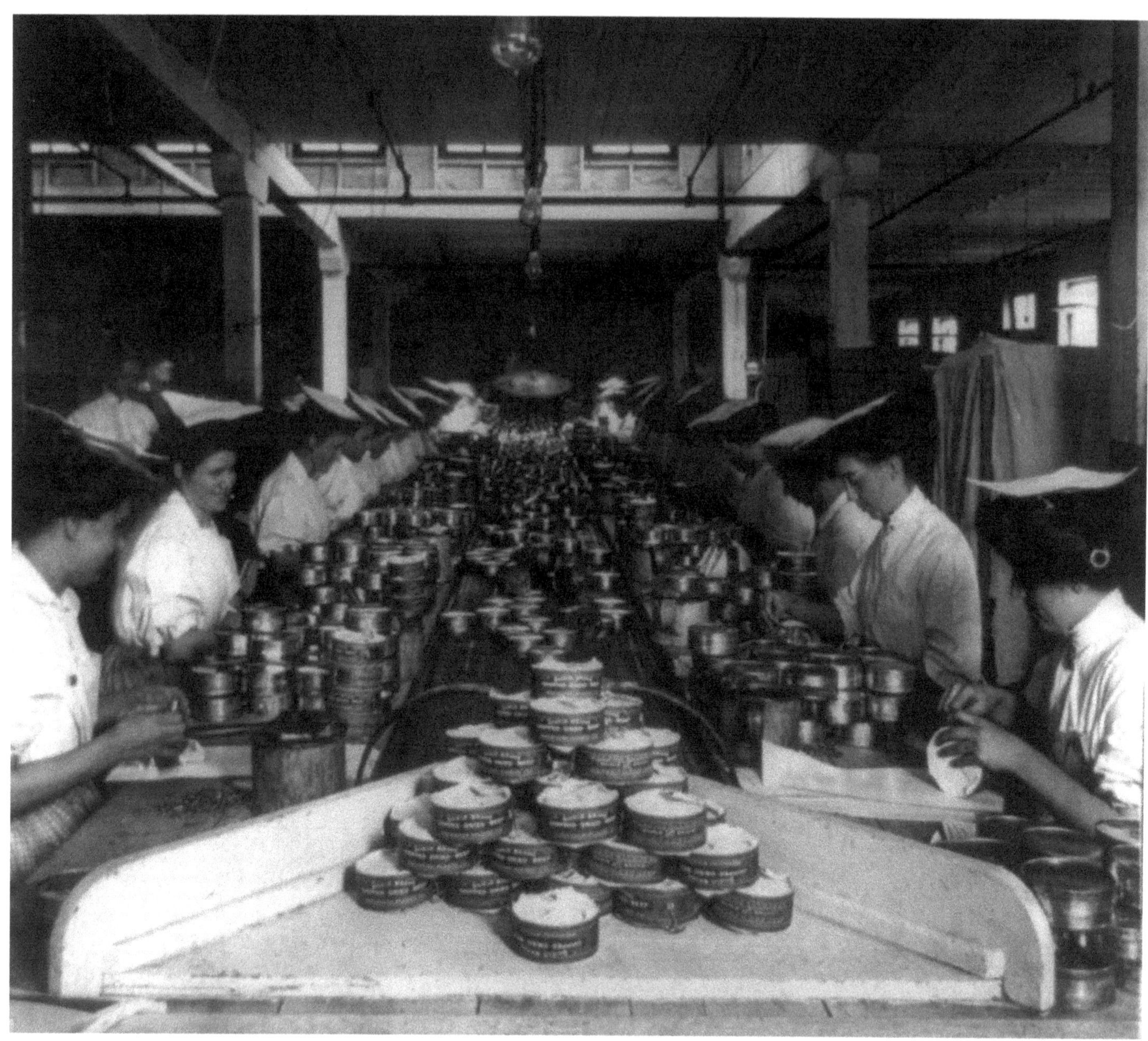

Chicago's Armour & Company, one of the largest meat producers in the world at the time of this 1909 photograph, also carried a full product line of groceries—from canned meat and shrimp to peanut butter and grape juice—under the trademark Veribest. In this view, an assembly line of women label scads of Veribest cans inside Armour's Packing Plant.

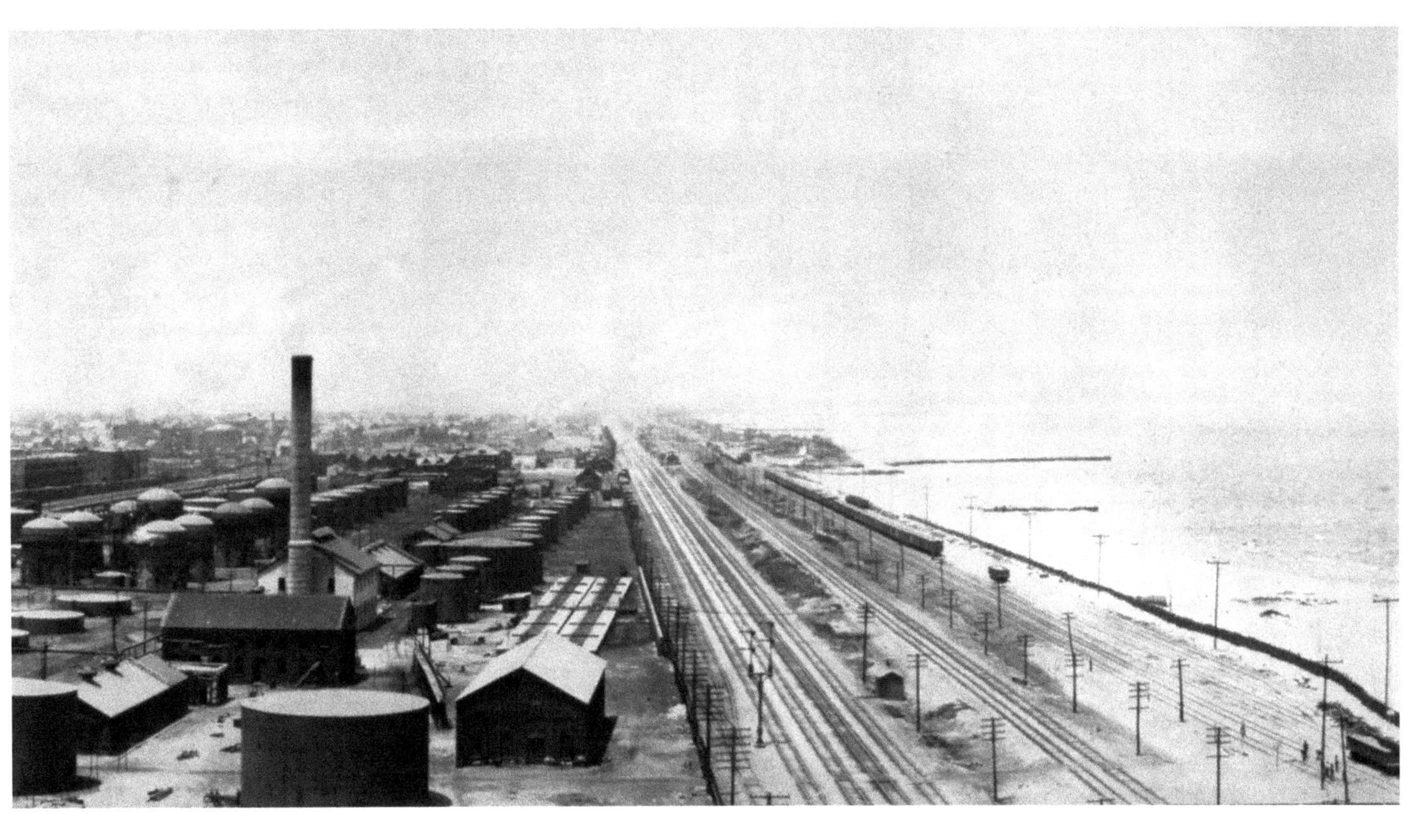

Erected in 1889, John D. Rockefeller's Standard Oil refinery in Whiting, Indiana, was the largest refinery in the United States by the mid-1890s. By 1910, when this photograph was taken, pipelines linked the Whiting refinery to oil fields in Kansas, Oklahoma, Ohio, and Indiana. The federal government forced Rockefeller to break up his oil monopoly in 1911; Rockefeller responded by making his Indiana refining operations an independent company: Standard of Indiana.

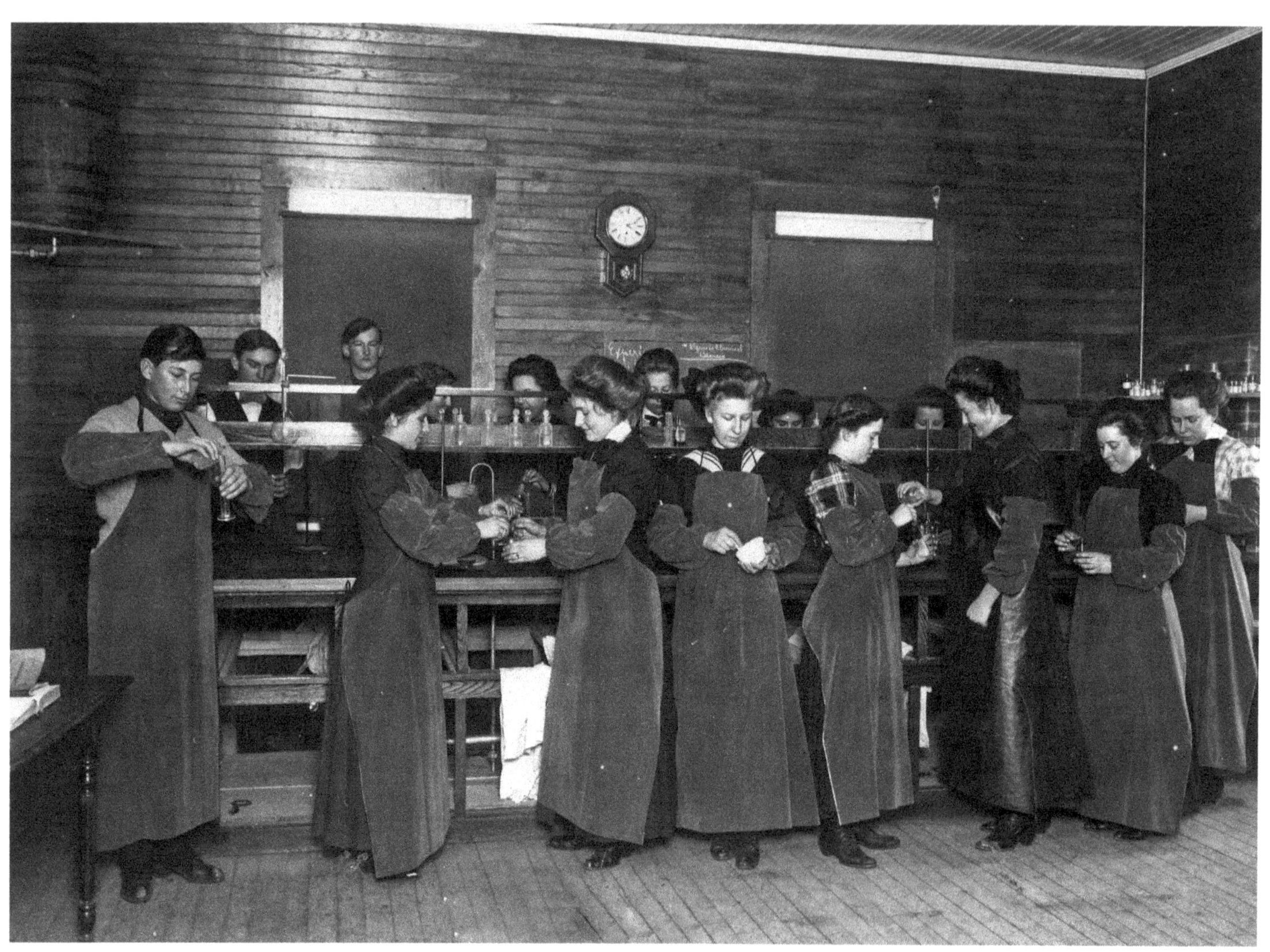

Northport Public School chemistry class pupils are shown at work in 1910. Northport is a village on the Leelanau Peninsula, situated on the northwest coast of Michigan's Lower Peninsula.

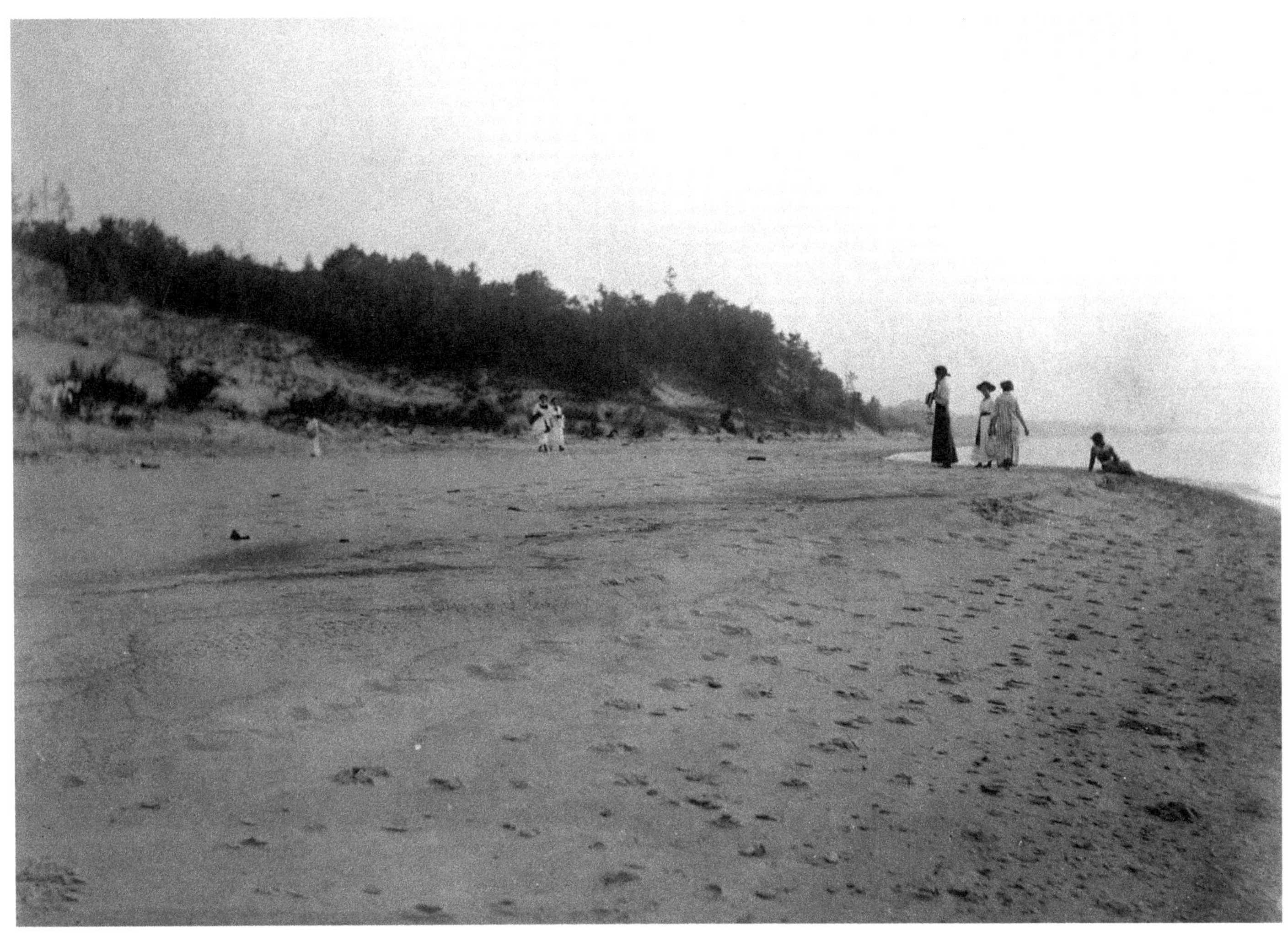

Progressive-era ladies stroll the Lake Michigan shoreline at the Great Warren Dunes, near Sawyer, Michigan, in 1910. The area looks much the same today as it did then, thanks to the dunes' namesake, Edward K. Warren. Ahead of his time and exceptionally wealthy, Warren purchased this land—then considered worthless—around the turn of the century in order to preserve it. Warren Dunes was designated a state park in 1930.

Following Spread: The city that U.S. Steel Built—Gary, Indiana, shown here in 1910—was named after Elbert H. Gary, who cofounded the corporation with J. P. Morgan.

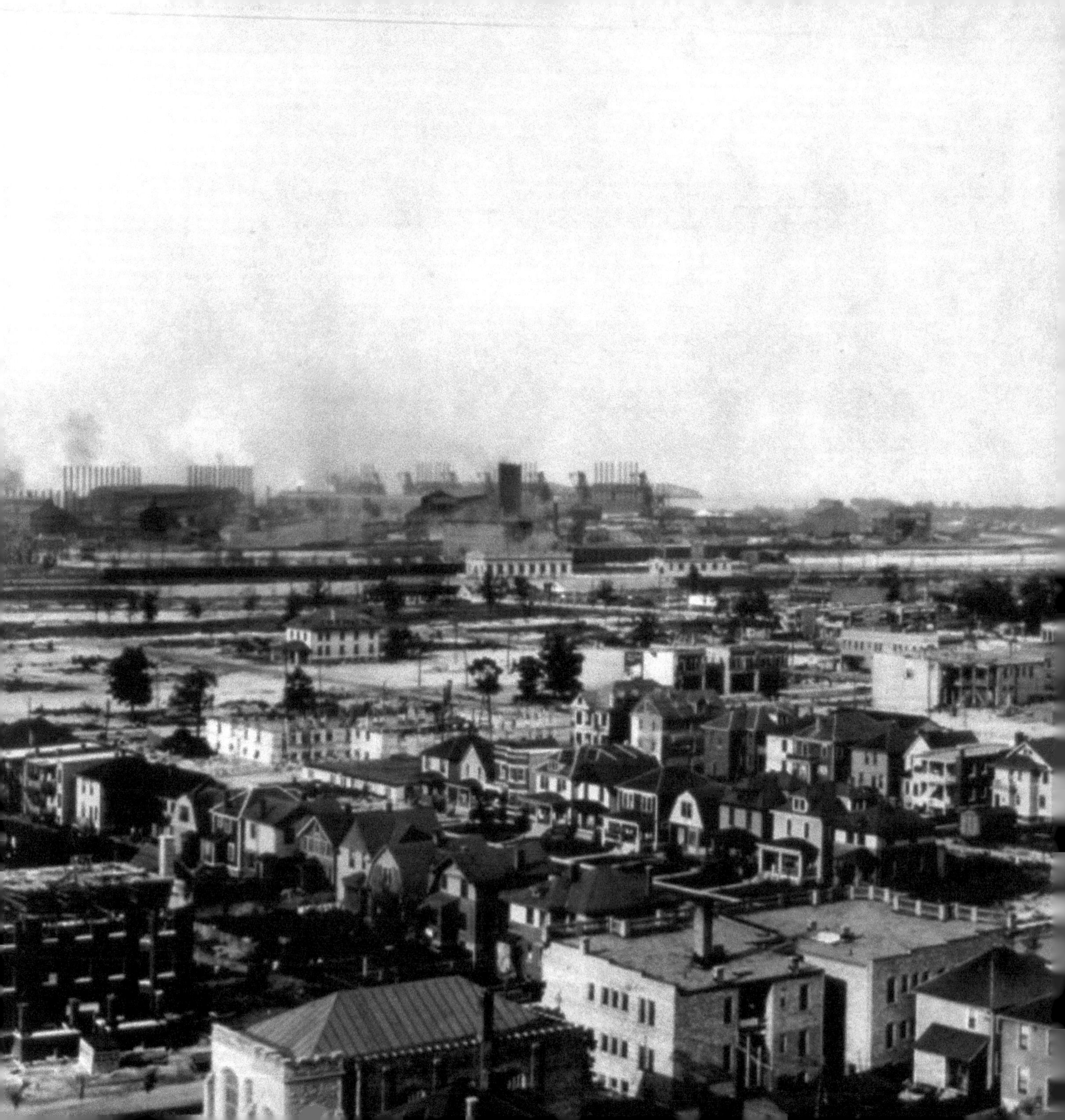

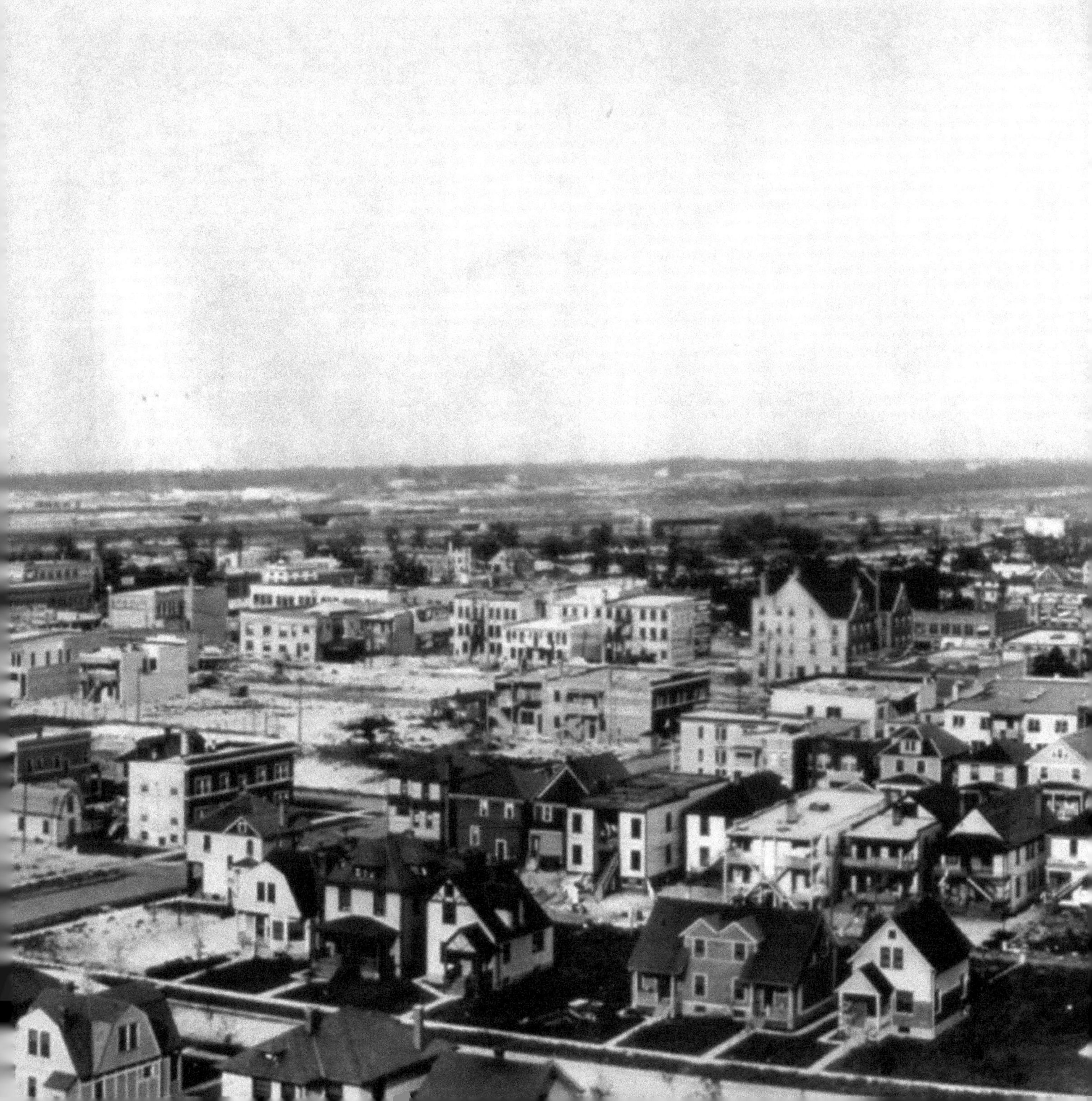

A train crosses the railroad bridge on the Belt Line across the Sheboygan River in Sheboygan, Wisconsin, in 1910. Sheboygan was founded along Lake Michigan in 1818 as a fur trading post and was incorporated in 1846. When the railroads arrived in the late 1850s, the population of the village quickly rose from a handful of citizens to several thousand.

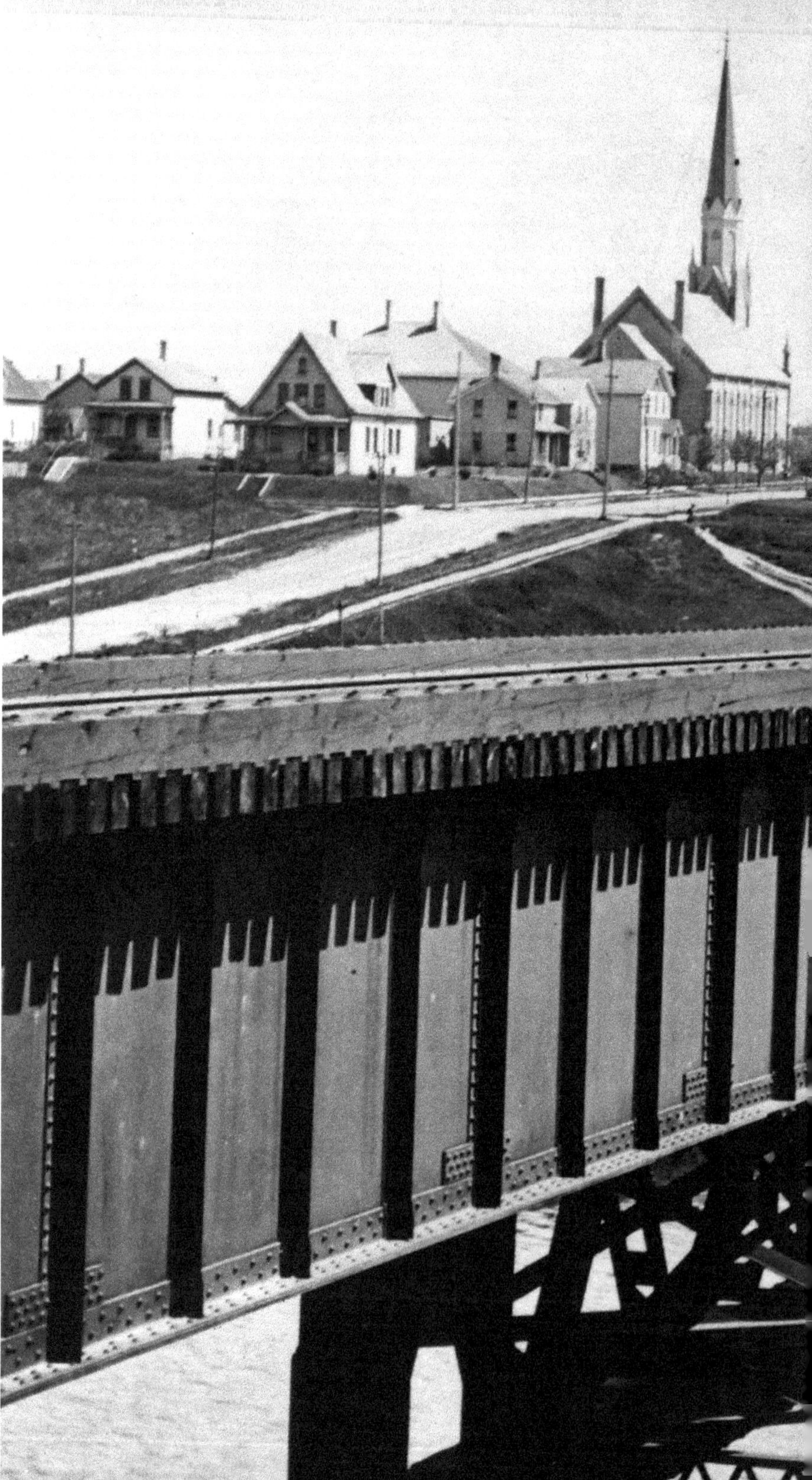

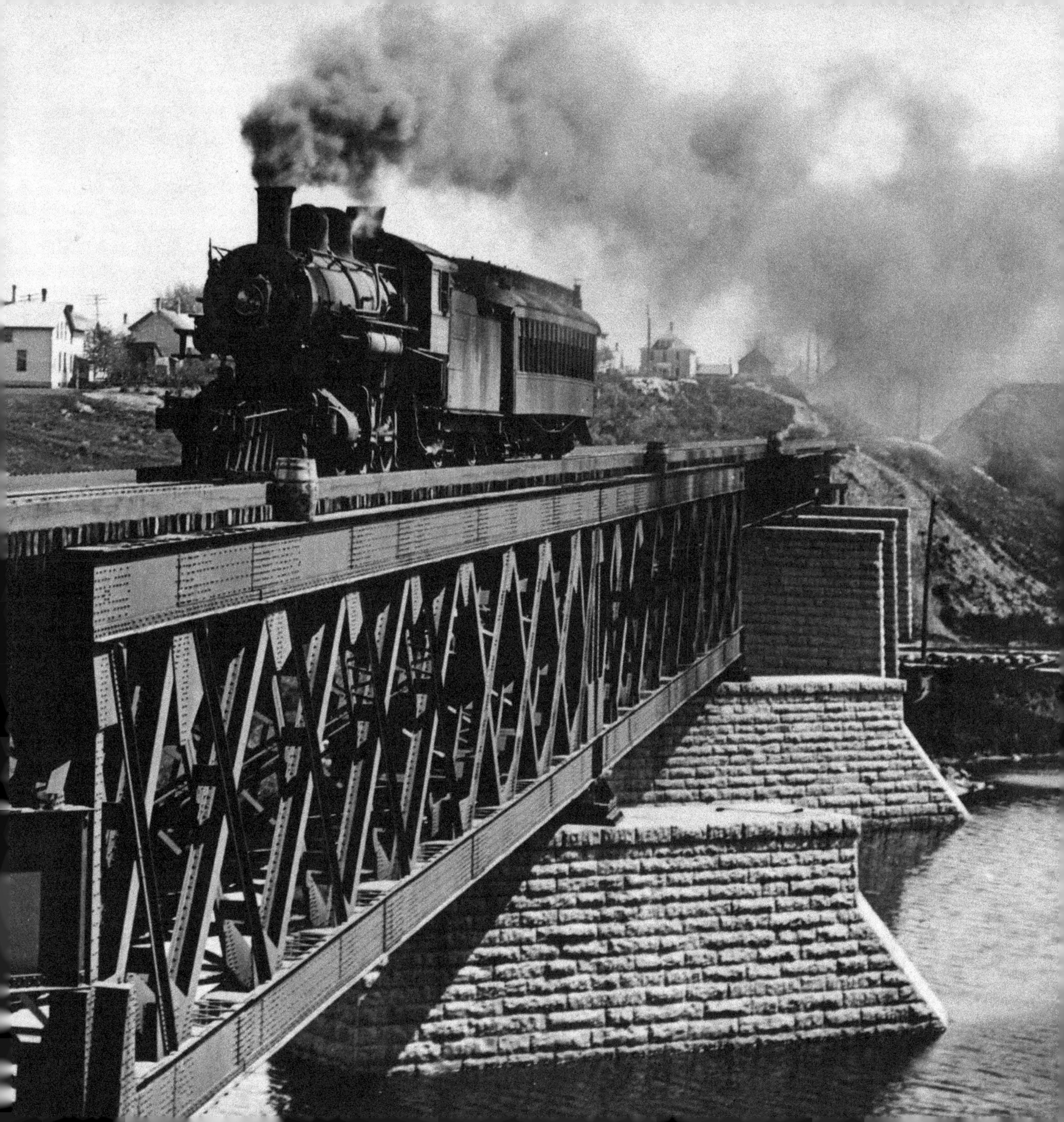

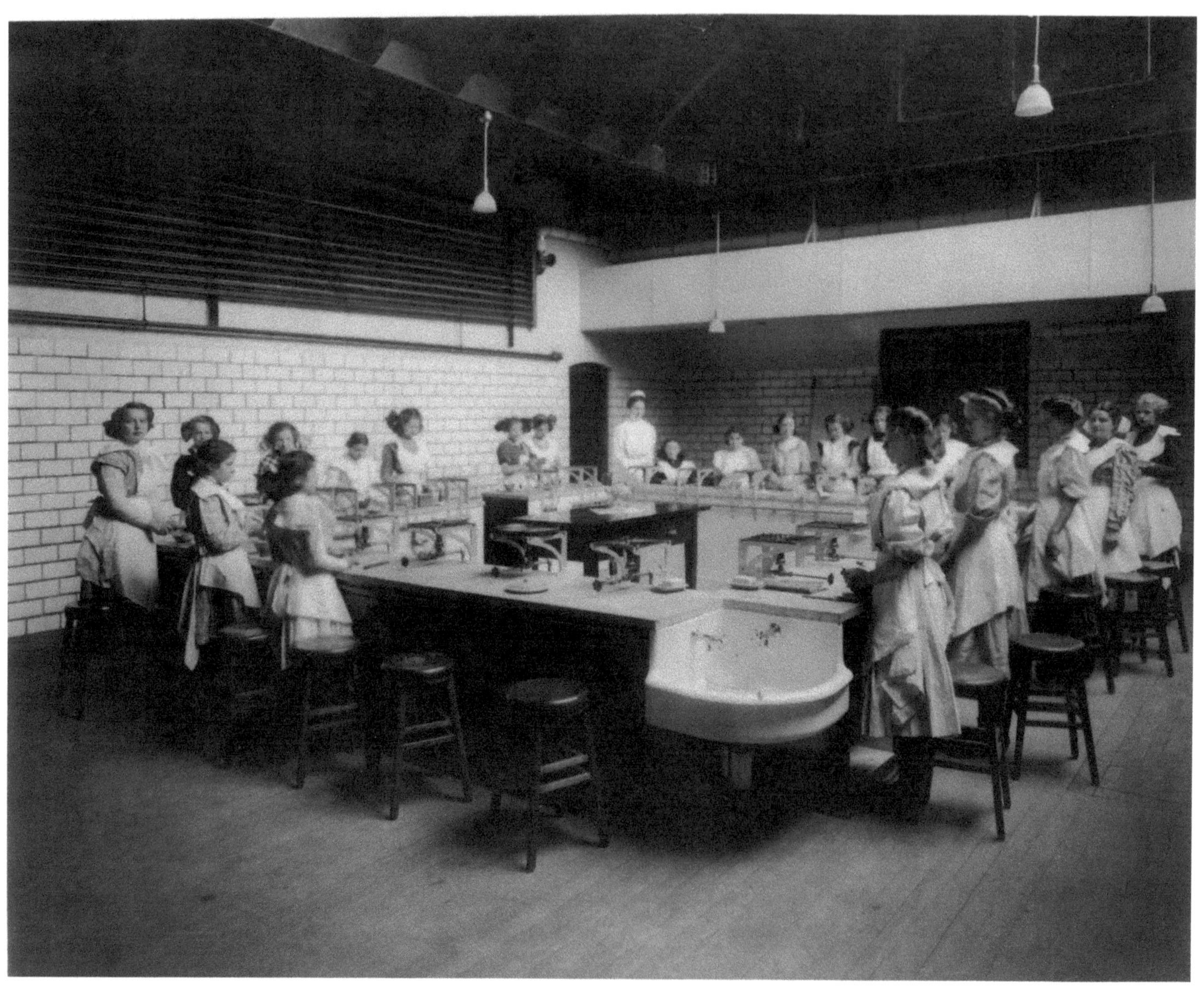

A domestic science class is at work in 1910 inside Emerson School in Gary, Indiana. Founded as a middle school in 1908, Emerson, named for the writer Ralph Waldo Emerson, went on to become a high school. Considered the most prestigious in the Midwest, the school boasted the state's first swimming pool and first school-run zoo. It closed in the early 1980s but reopened a few years later as Emerson School for Visual and Performing Arts.

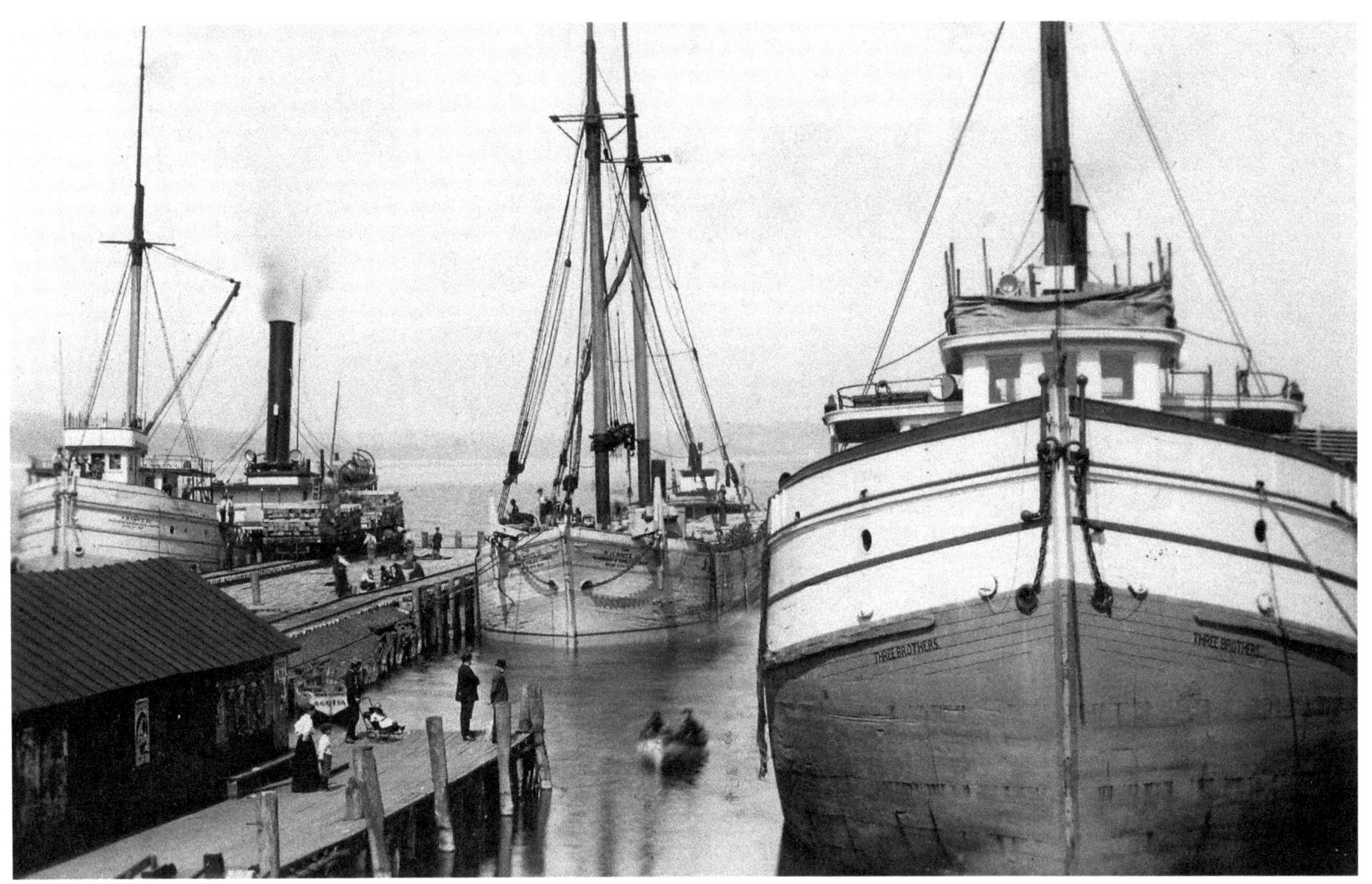

Despite the miles of track running in and around Michigan's Boyne City, the booming lumber town's link to Lake Michigan by way of Lake Charlevoix and Round Lake proved too tempting for lumber industrialist W. H. White, who maintained a fleet of White Company ships to ply the waters leading to and from the city.

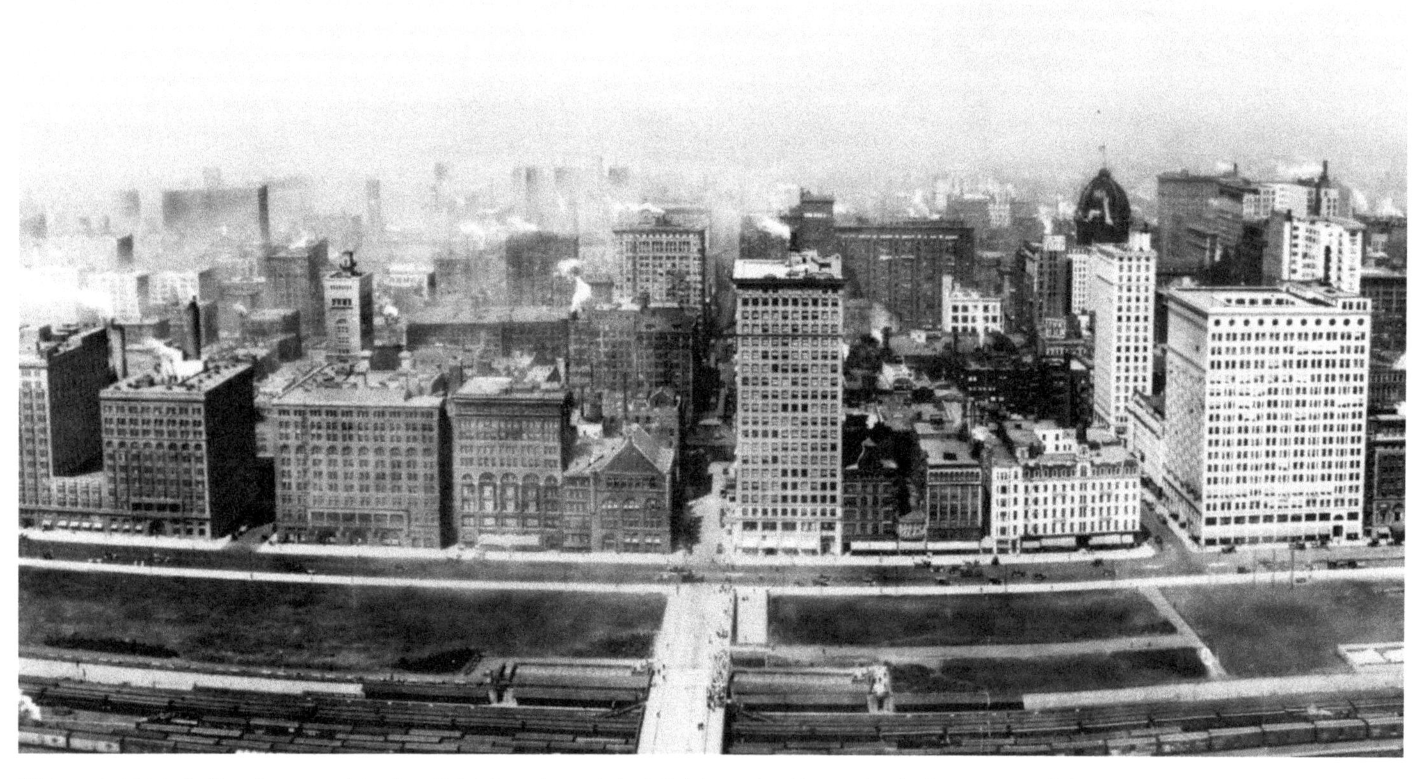

Chicago's 1911 skyline from an altitude of 700 feet above Lake Michigan. At Chicago's Blackstone Hotel that year, during a dinner attended by civic leaders, the proposal was made that Chicago host an international aviation meet. The meet took place in August.

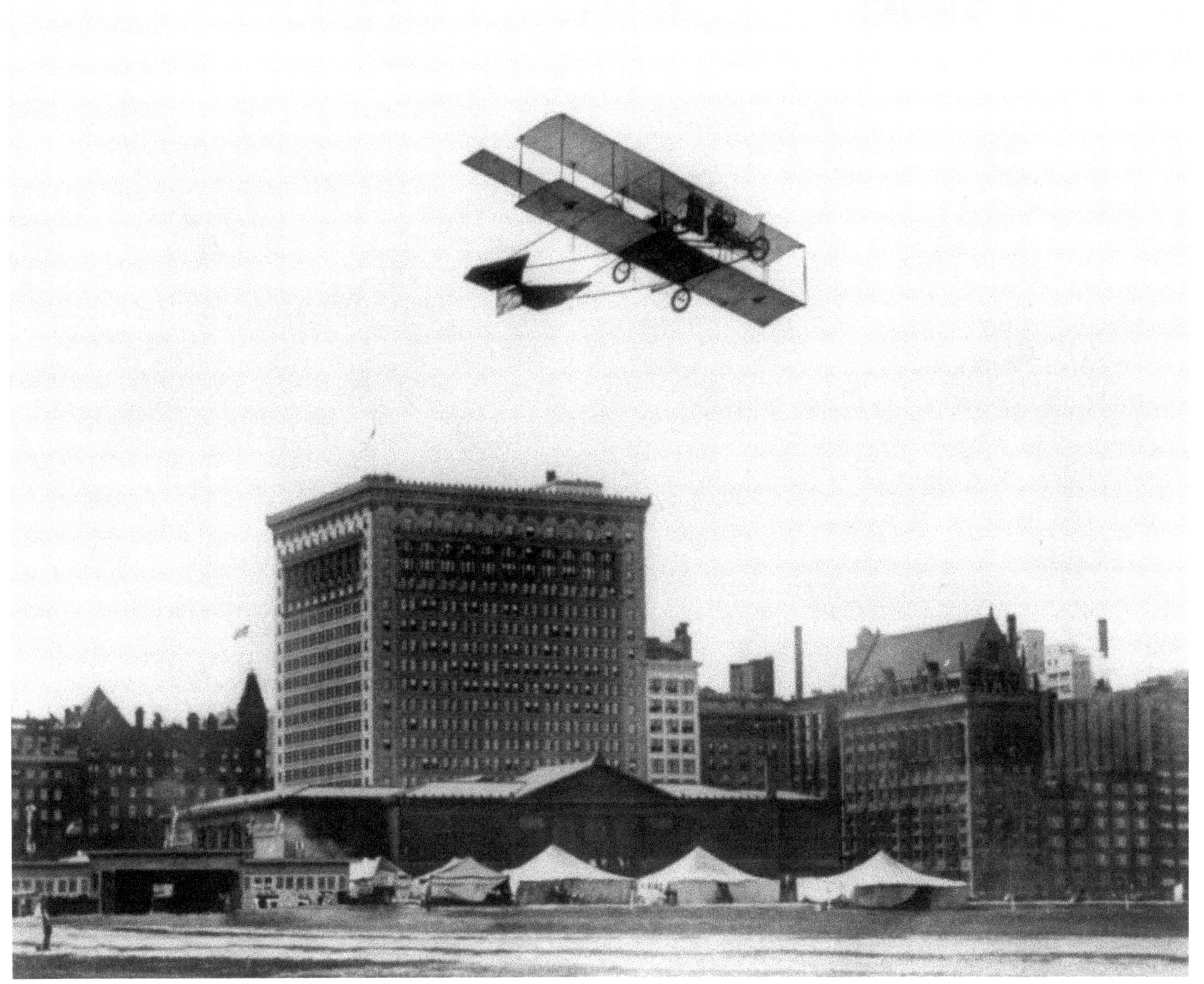

"The Man Who Owns the Sky," Lincoln Beachey, was considered the greatest aviator in history, owing in part to his record-breaking performances during the 1911 Chicago International Aviation Meet. While crowds of 75,000 watched from Grant Park, Beachey set a new altitude record, flying two miles straight up (before running out of fuel and gliding back to earth), and a new speed record, flying 20 miles in 23 minutes and 12 seconds.

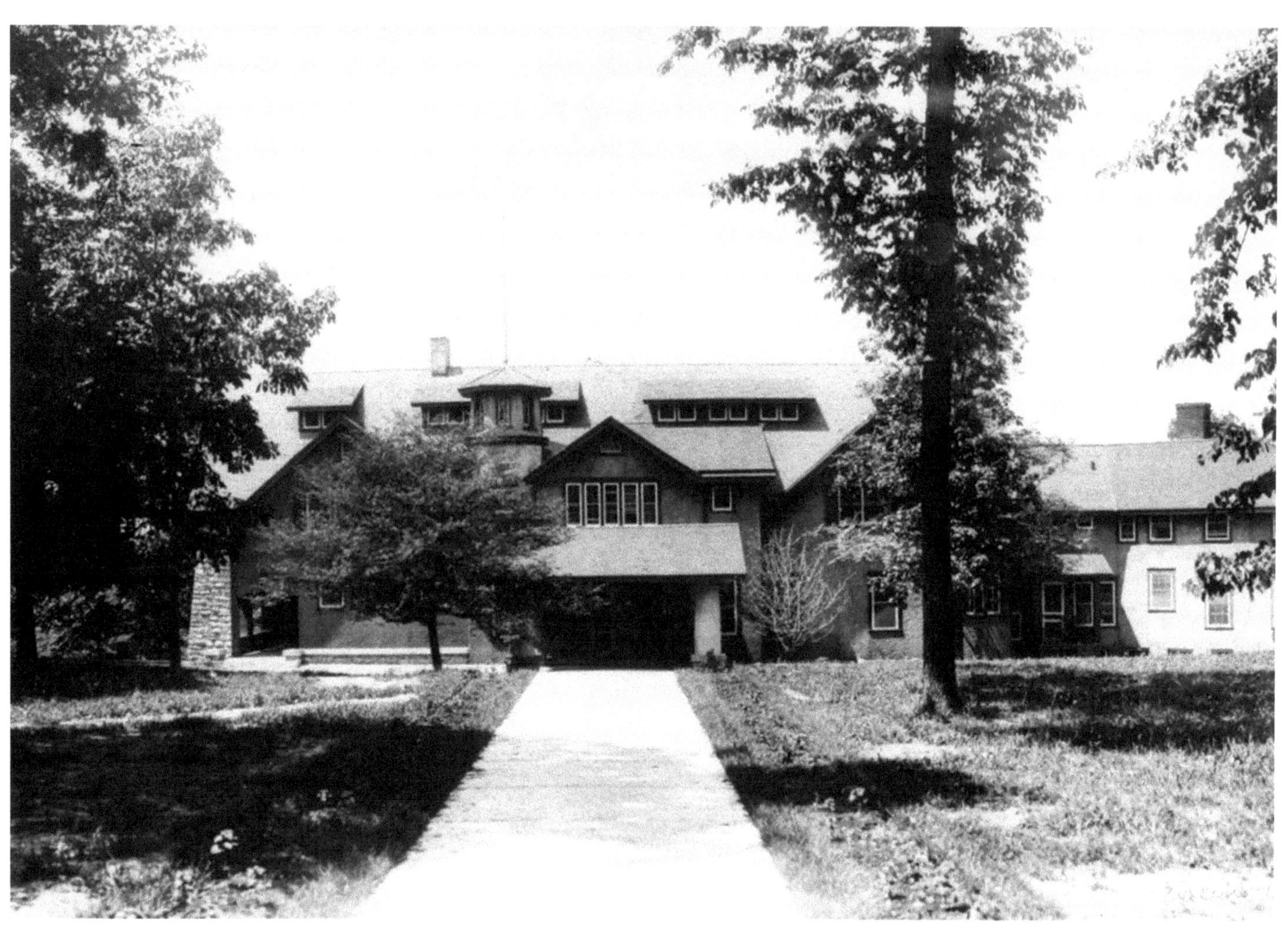

Founded around the turn of the century, the Racine Country Club built a new course and clubhouse in 1909, shown here as it appeared in 1911, on what was formerly the Charles Wustum Farm. The clubhouse, built by Andy Kappel, provided a dining area, open porches, and second- and third-floor rooms to accommodate overnight guests.

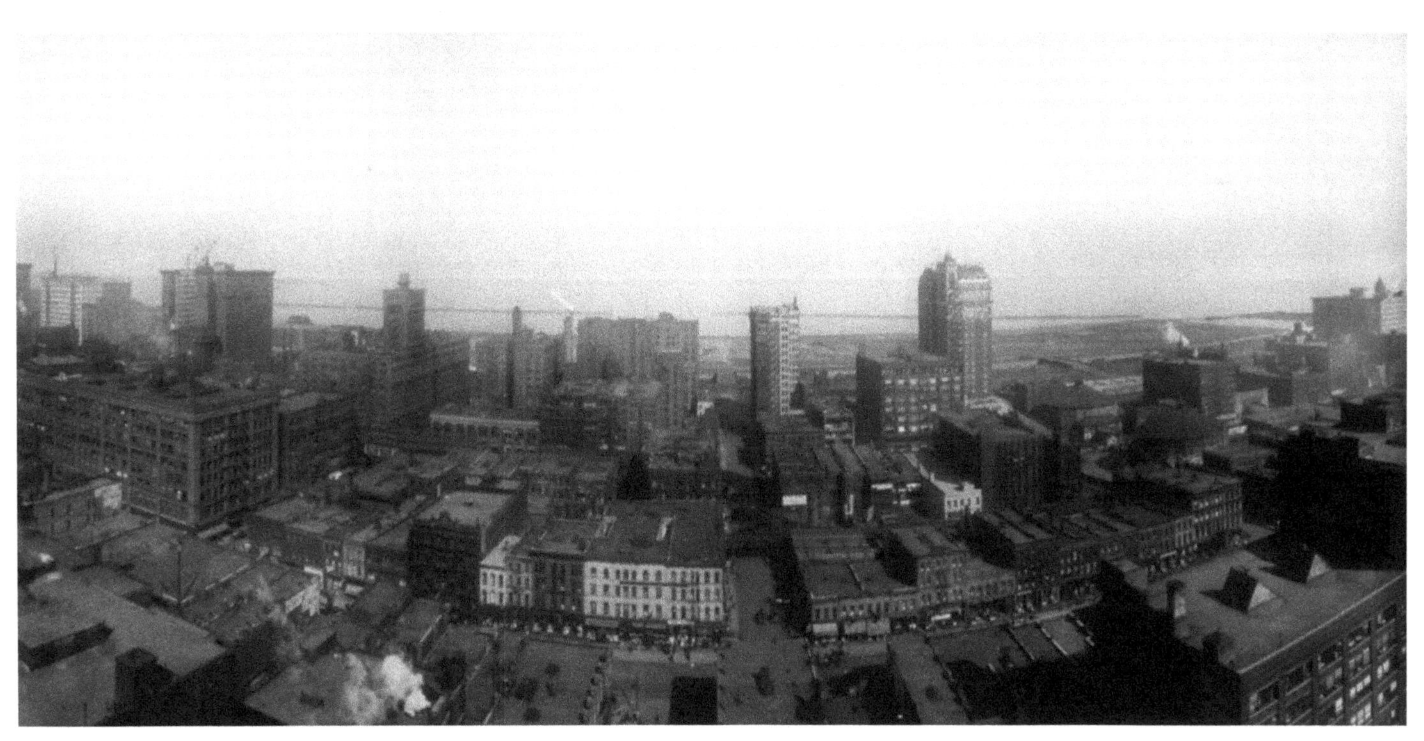

A bird's-eye view of Chicago and its Lake Michigan shoreline as they appeared in April 1912.

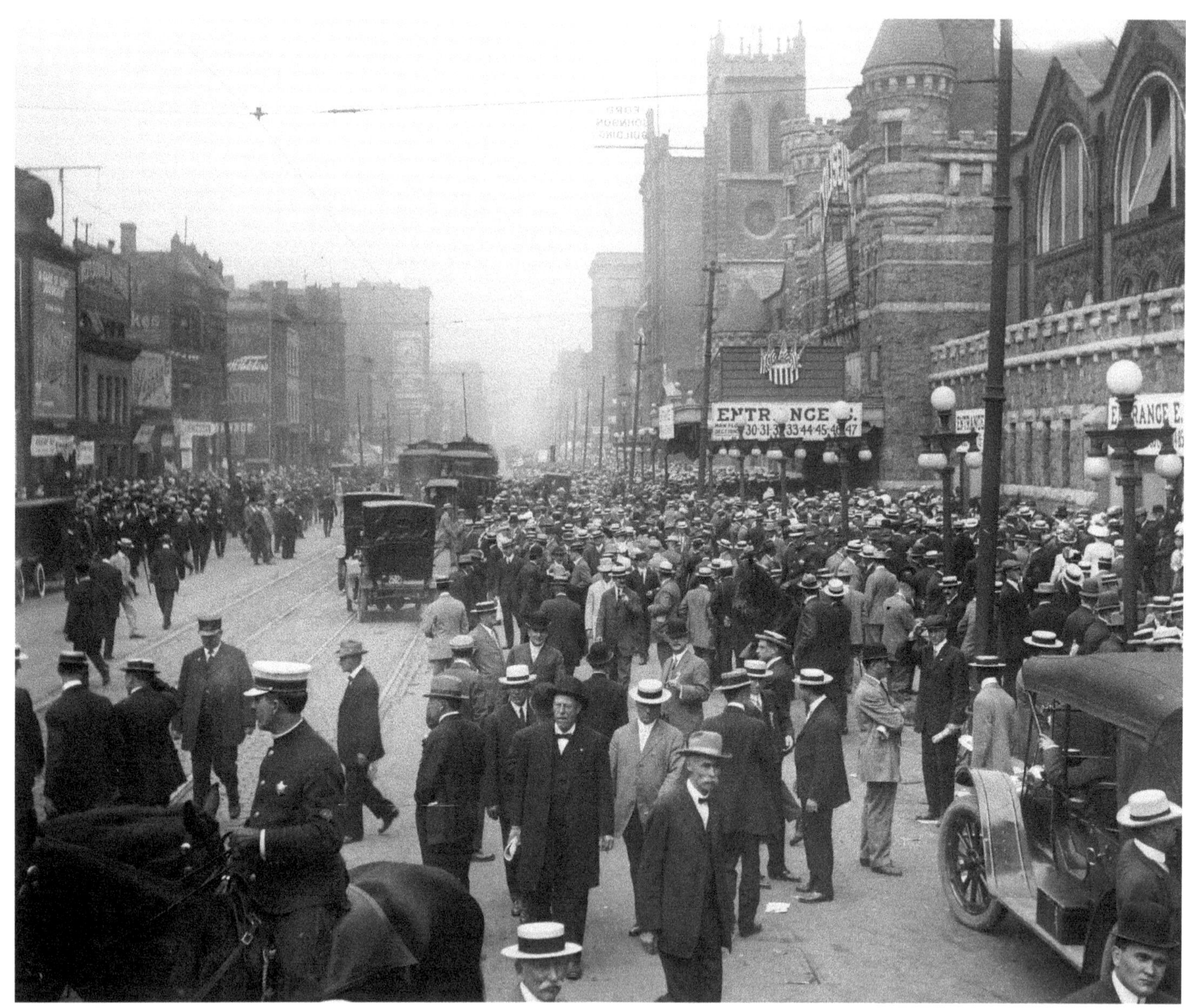

Crowds gather outside the 1912 Republican National Convention, held at the Chicago Coliseum. Four years before, President Theodore Roosevelt had nominated his successor, William Howard Taft of Ohio, to run on the ticket. Taft won the presidency, but by 1912 a rift had formed between incumbent Taft and former president Roosevelt, which led to a struggle for the party's nomination. In control of the Republican National Committee, Taft won the day, which spurred Roosevelt to form a third party to challenge both the Republican and Democratic tickets. Roosevelt's continuing popularity among Americans split the Republican vote, giving the election to the Democratic nominee Woodrow Wilson.

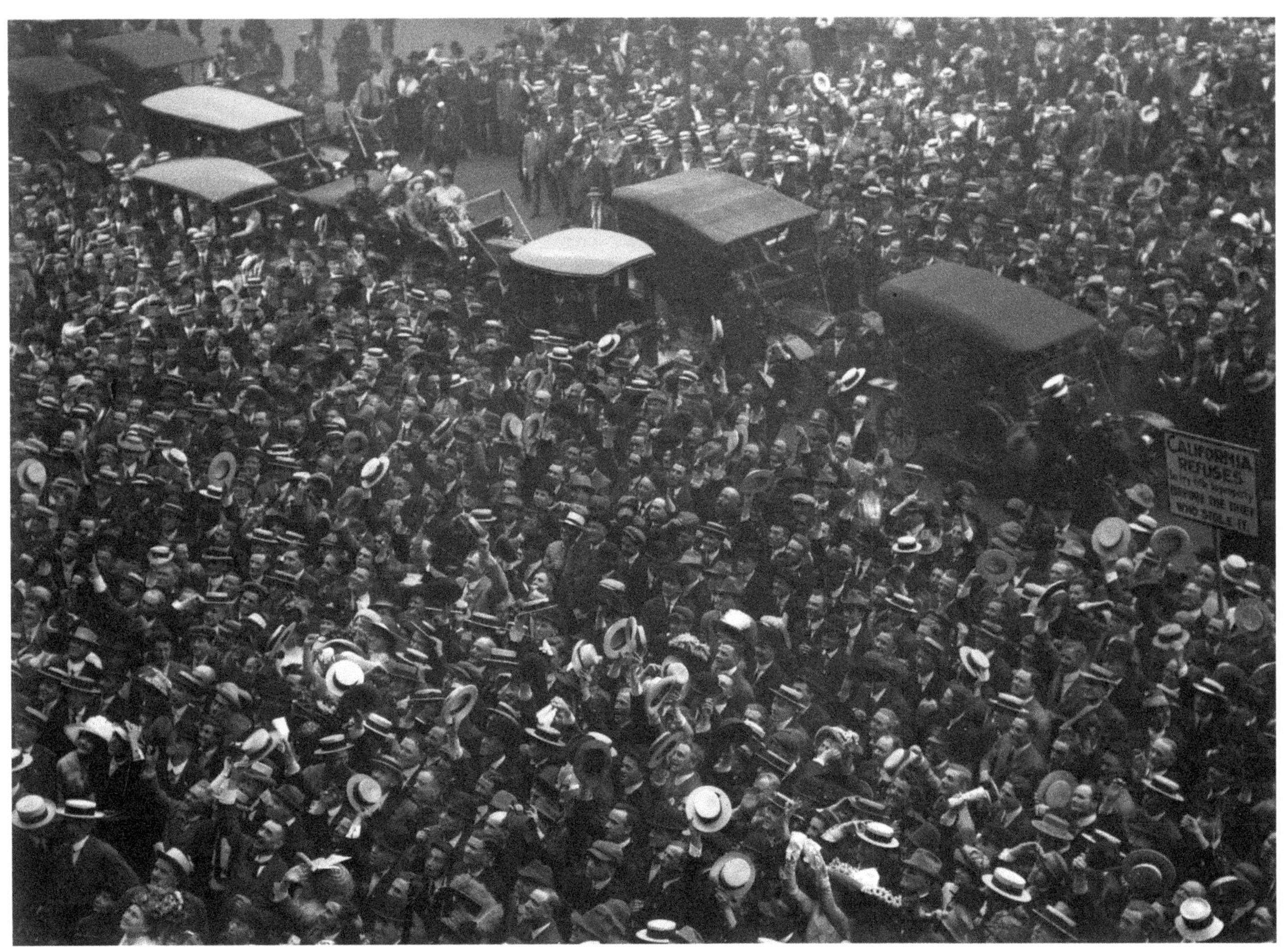

A note scrawled along the edge of this 1912 photograph read, "Crowds Listening to T. R. Speaking, Chic." It is likely that this photograph was taken as Theodore Roosevelt's speech at the Republican National Convention was being piped over speakers to the throng of citizens clamoring outside.

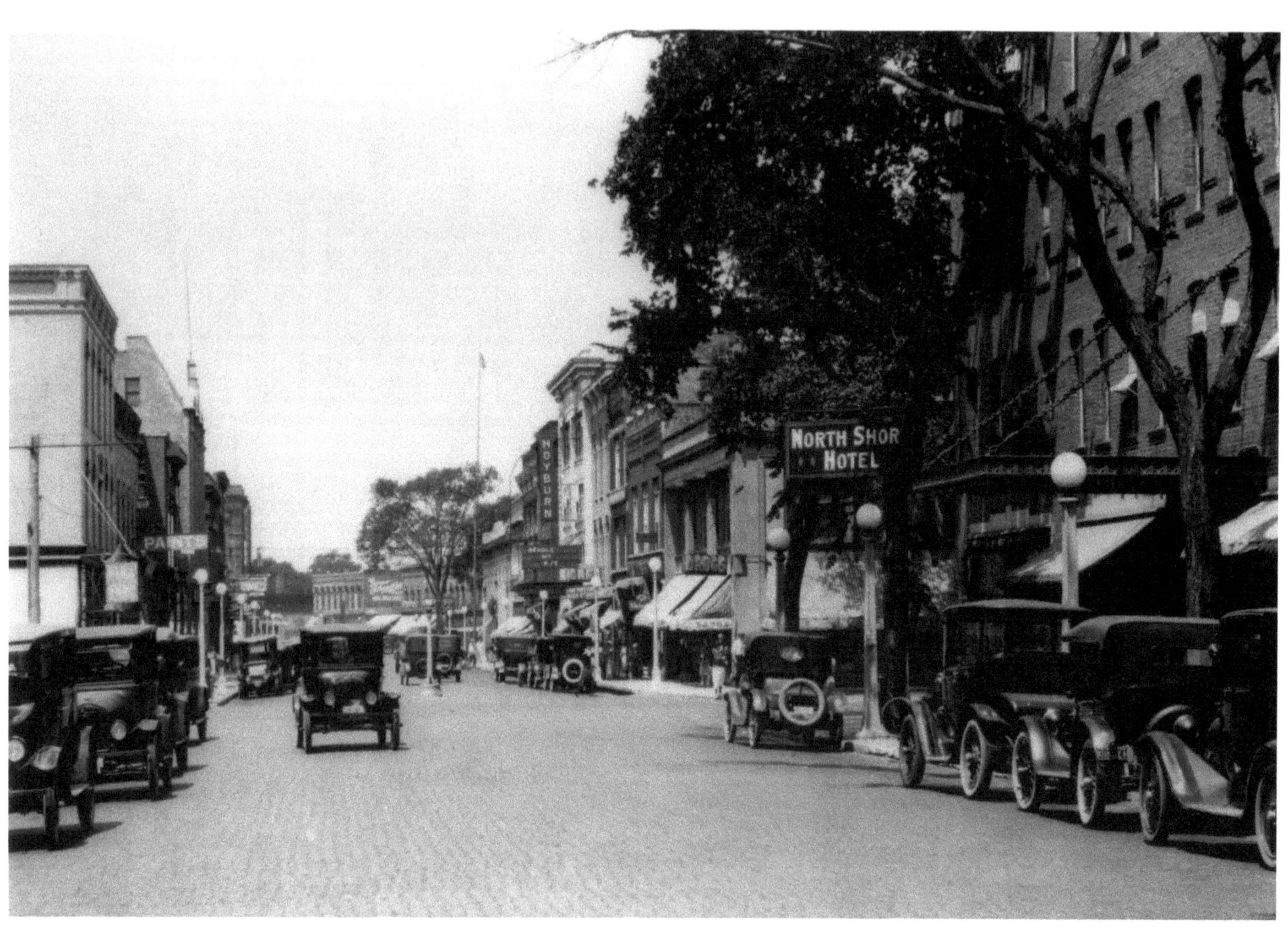

An early twentieth century street scene in Evanston, Illinois, located just north of Chicago on the Lake Michigan coast.

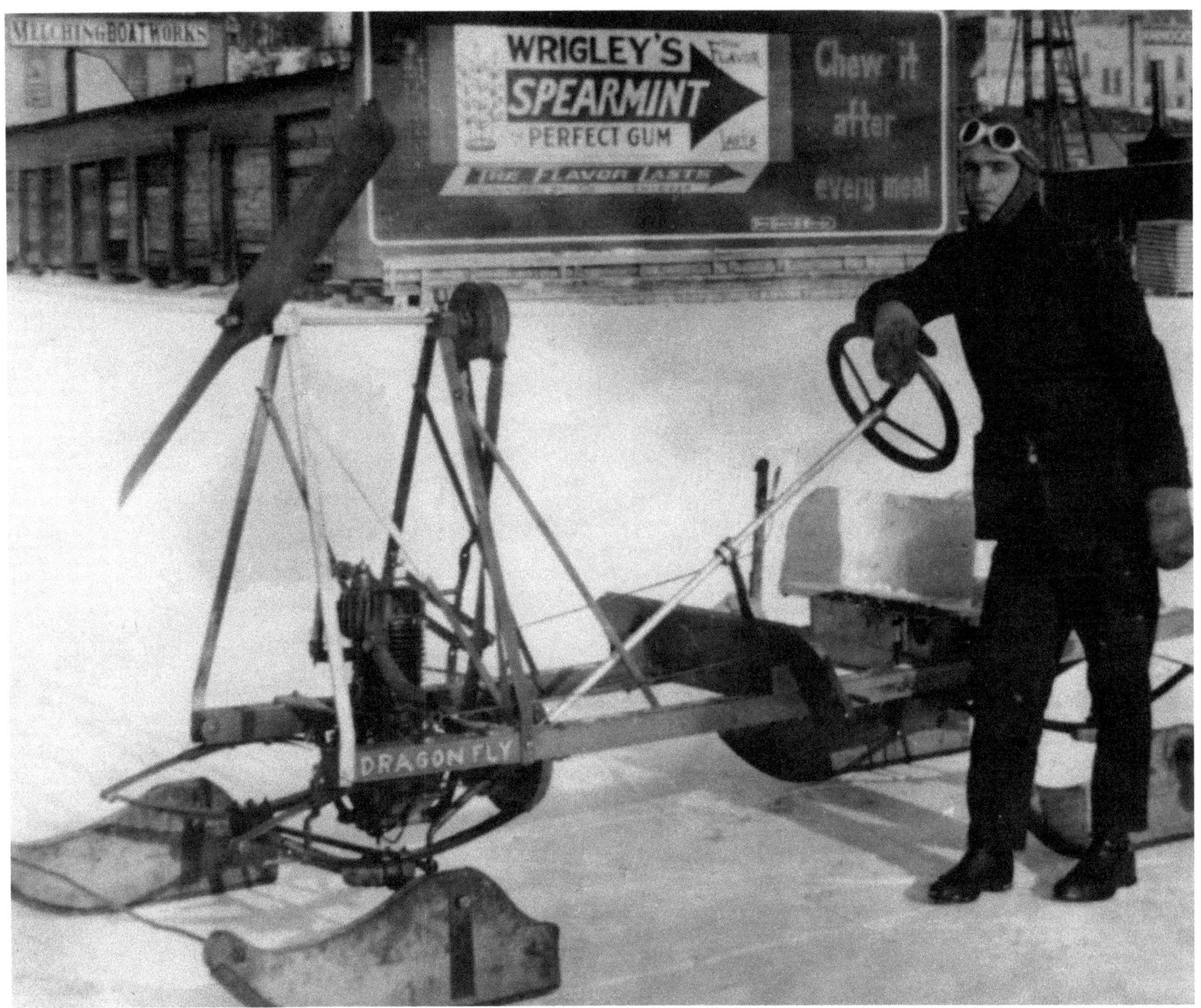

Like many residents of Northern Michigan, Ray Freeland of Harbor Springs, pictured here at Little Traverse Bay with his homemade ice sled called *Dragonfly*, devised means of transportation that wouldn't be stymied by the region's notoriously wicked winters.

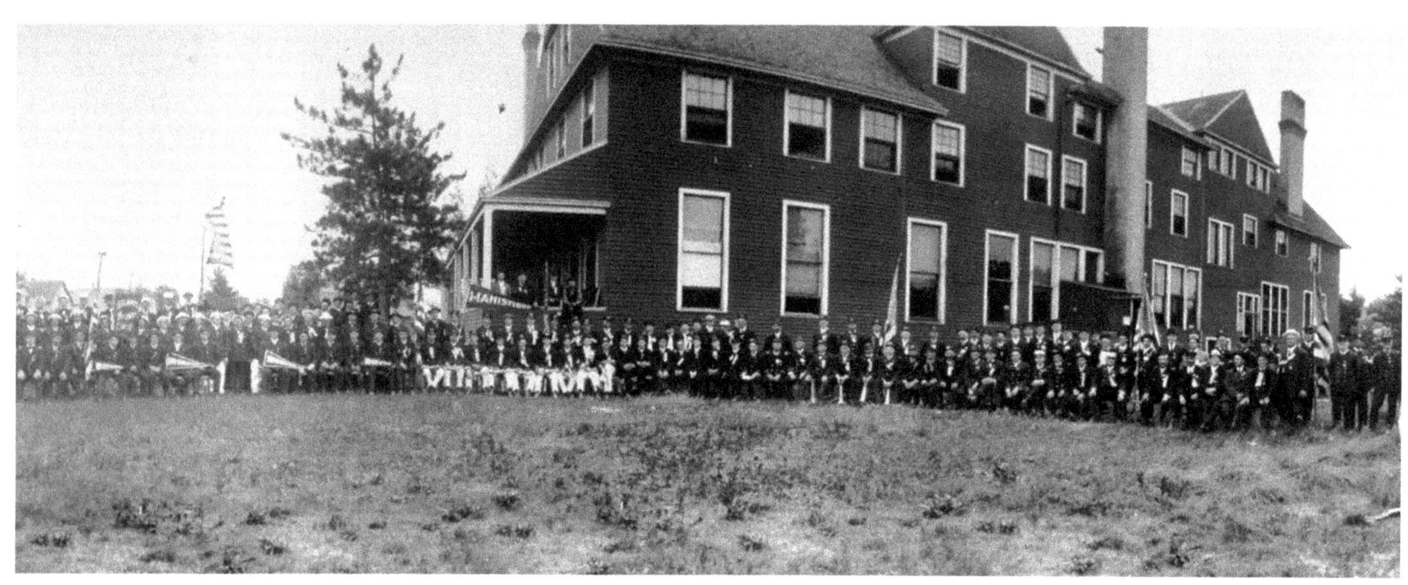

Since 1894, fire fighters from all around Michigan's Upper Peninsula have gathered for an annual tournament and celebration featuring bands, a parade, a ball, and most important, contests—from hose connecting to ladder climbing. This photograph showcases the many fire fighters in attendance at the 1912 tournament in Gladstone in which the Wells Fire Department took first prize.

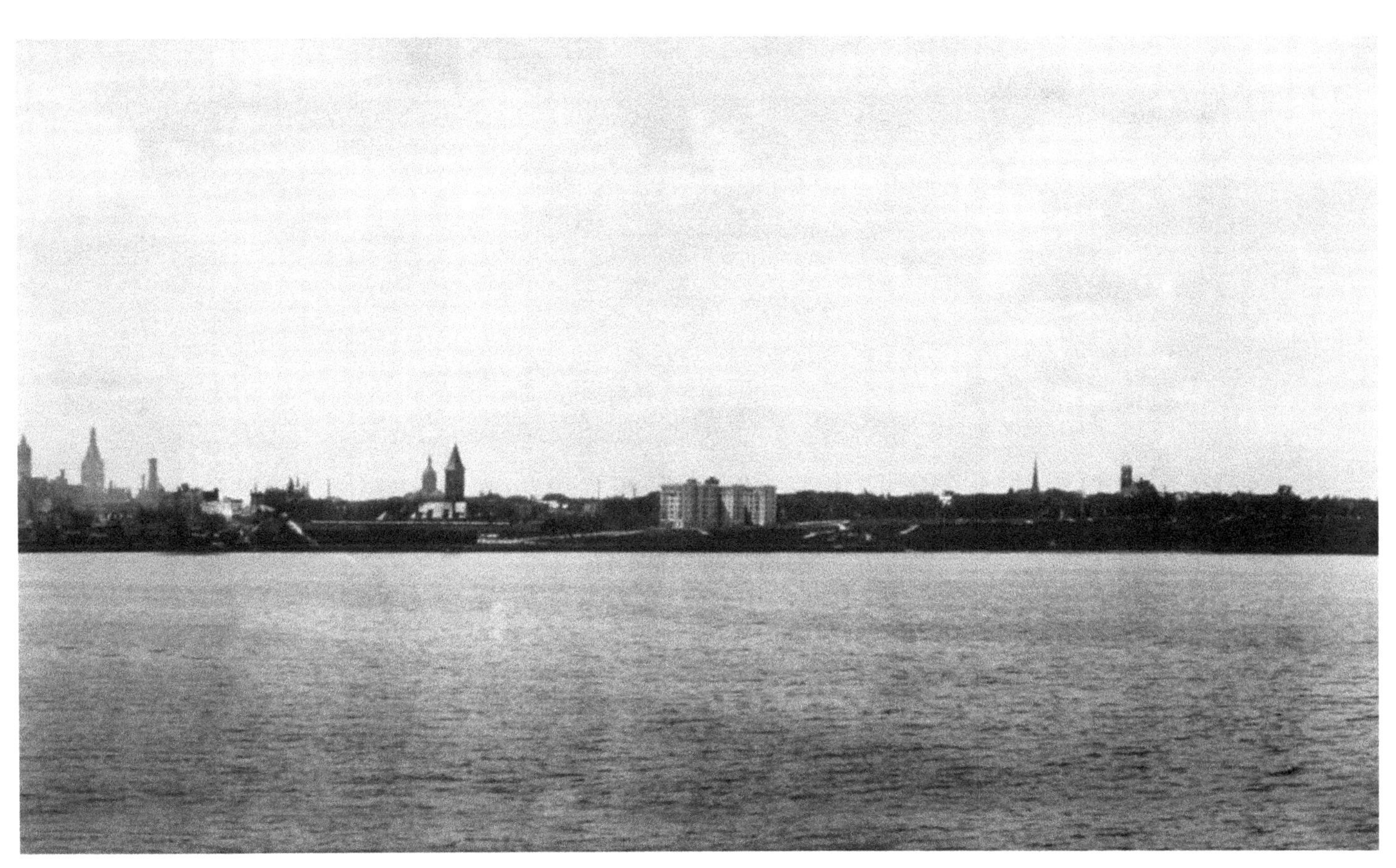

Milwaukee as seen from the bay in 1912.

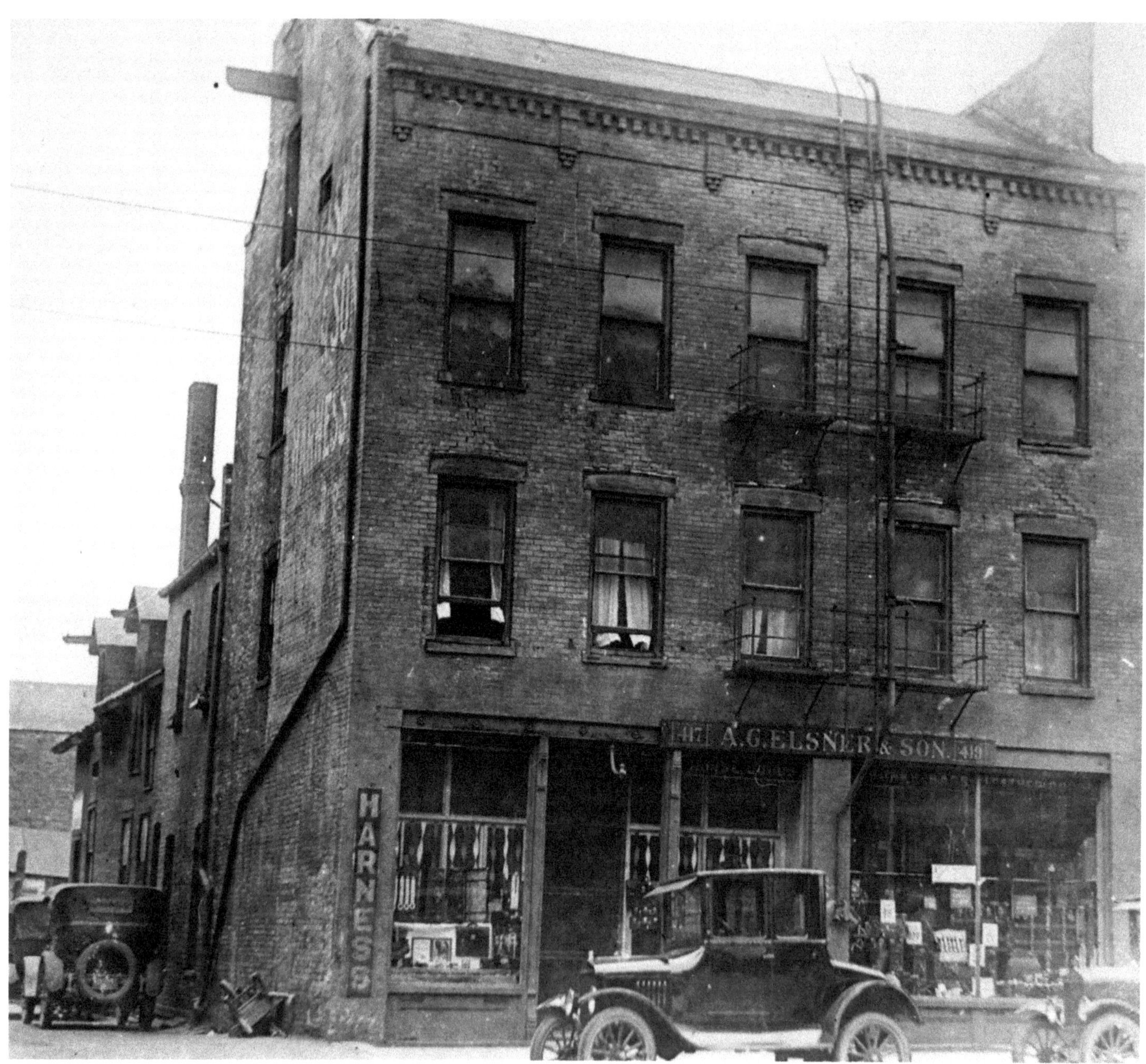

The Gipfel Union Brewery building, located on West Juneau Avenue for 154 years, housed the longest-lived independent brewery in Milwaukee. The late Federal-style brick structure, which the brewery occupied from the early 1850s until competition from brewing industry giants forced closure in the 1890s, is one of the oldest commercial buildings in the city. It was moved one block east of its original location in 2007 for restoration purposes.

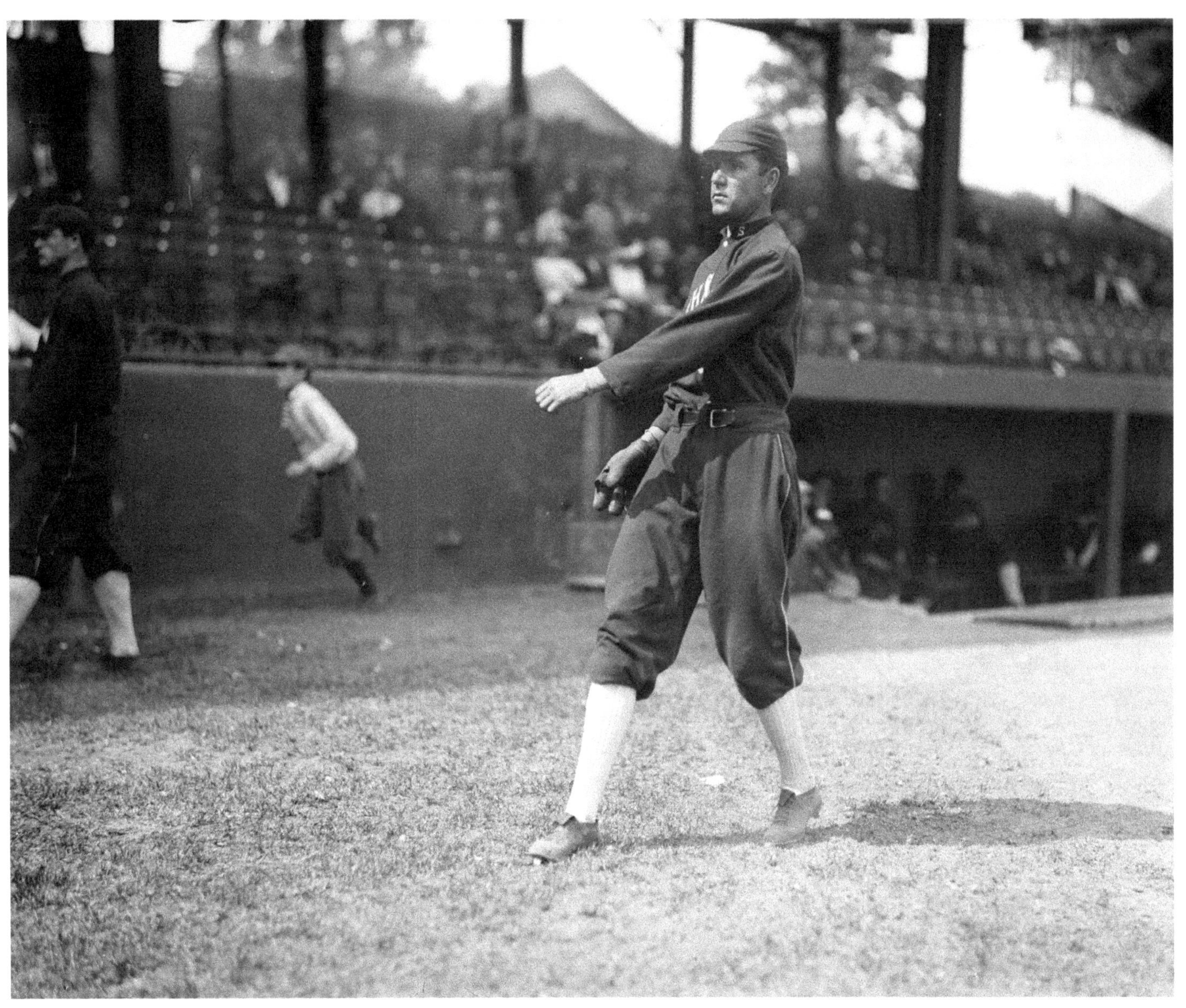

Guy Harris White, more commonly known as Doc White, played for the American League's Chicago White Stockings (later White Sox) from 1903 until 1913. A lefty, White's pitching led the league with a 1.52 ERA in 1906 and 27 wins in 1907.

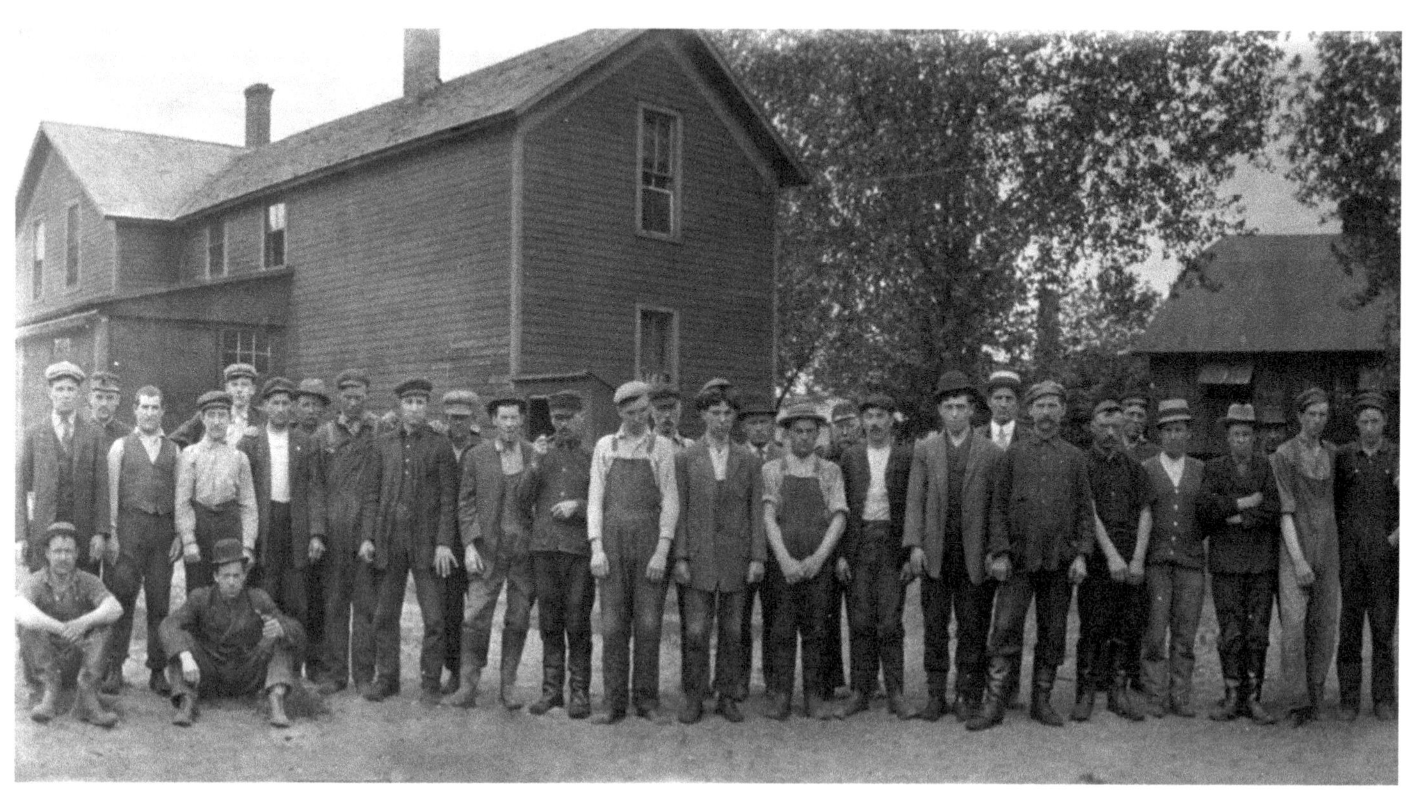

Workers in 1913 stand outside the W. W. Rice Leather Company, a tannery on Little Traverse Bay at Petoskey, Michigan, which began as a producer of dry-hide hemlock sole leather for shoes in the late 1880s. The land had previously been deeded to the region's Ottawa Indians by an 1855 treaty. Today, the land is the site of the Petoskey State Park.

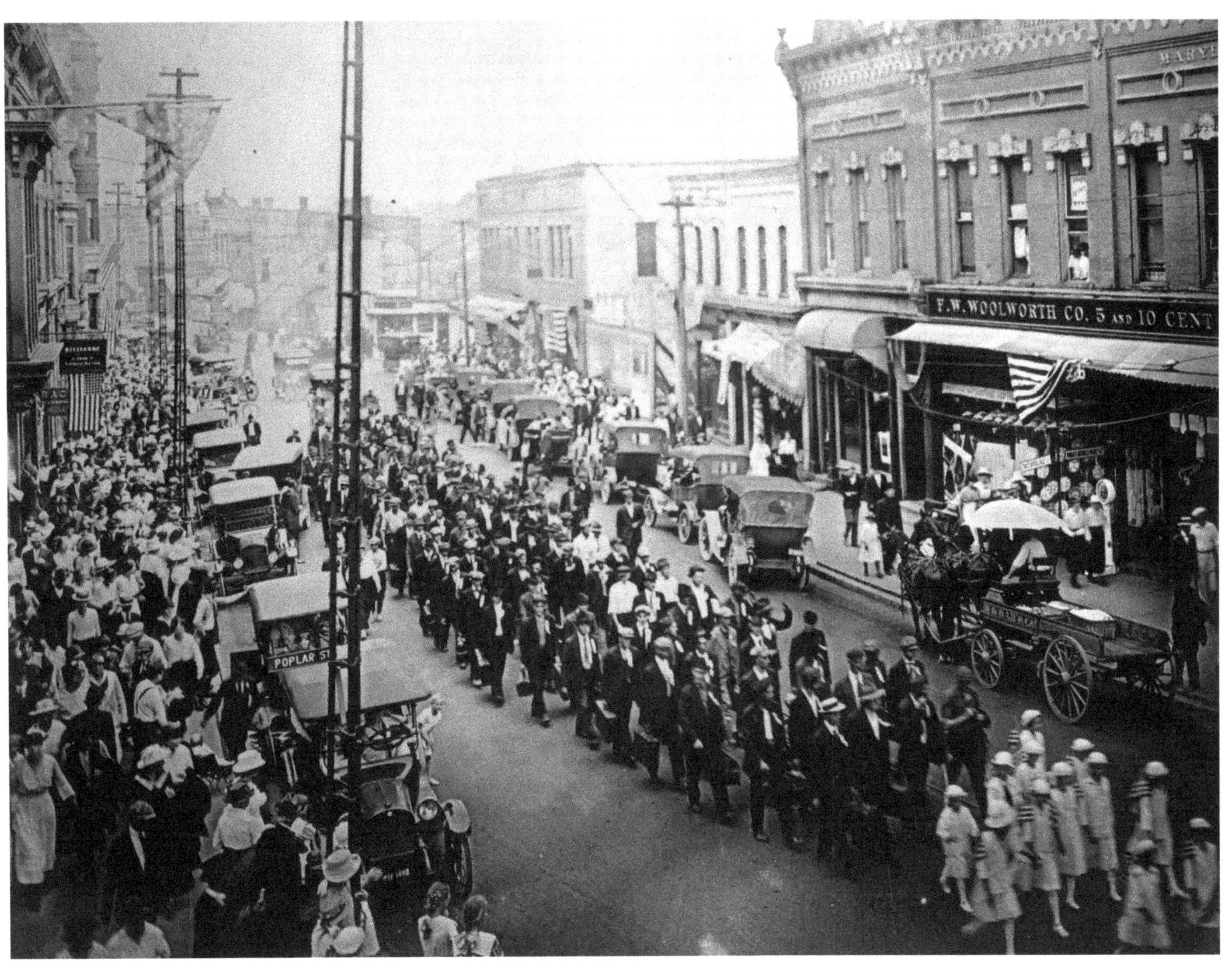

A July 4 parade through the port city of Manistee, Michigan, in 1914 passes the Woolworth store at Poplar Street.

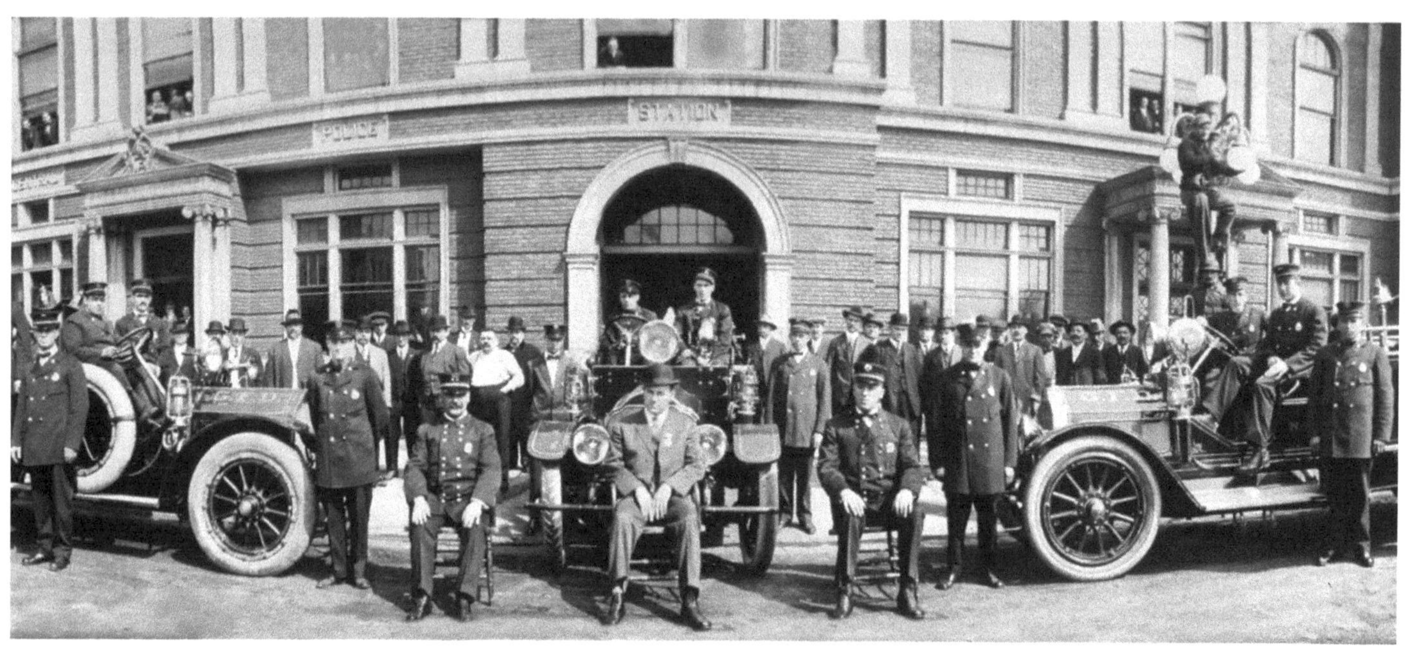

The firefighting brigade of Gary, Indiana, assembles for a group shot outside the Central Police Station in 1914.

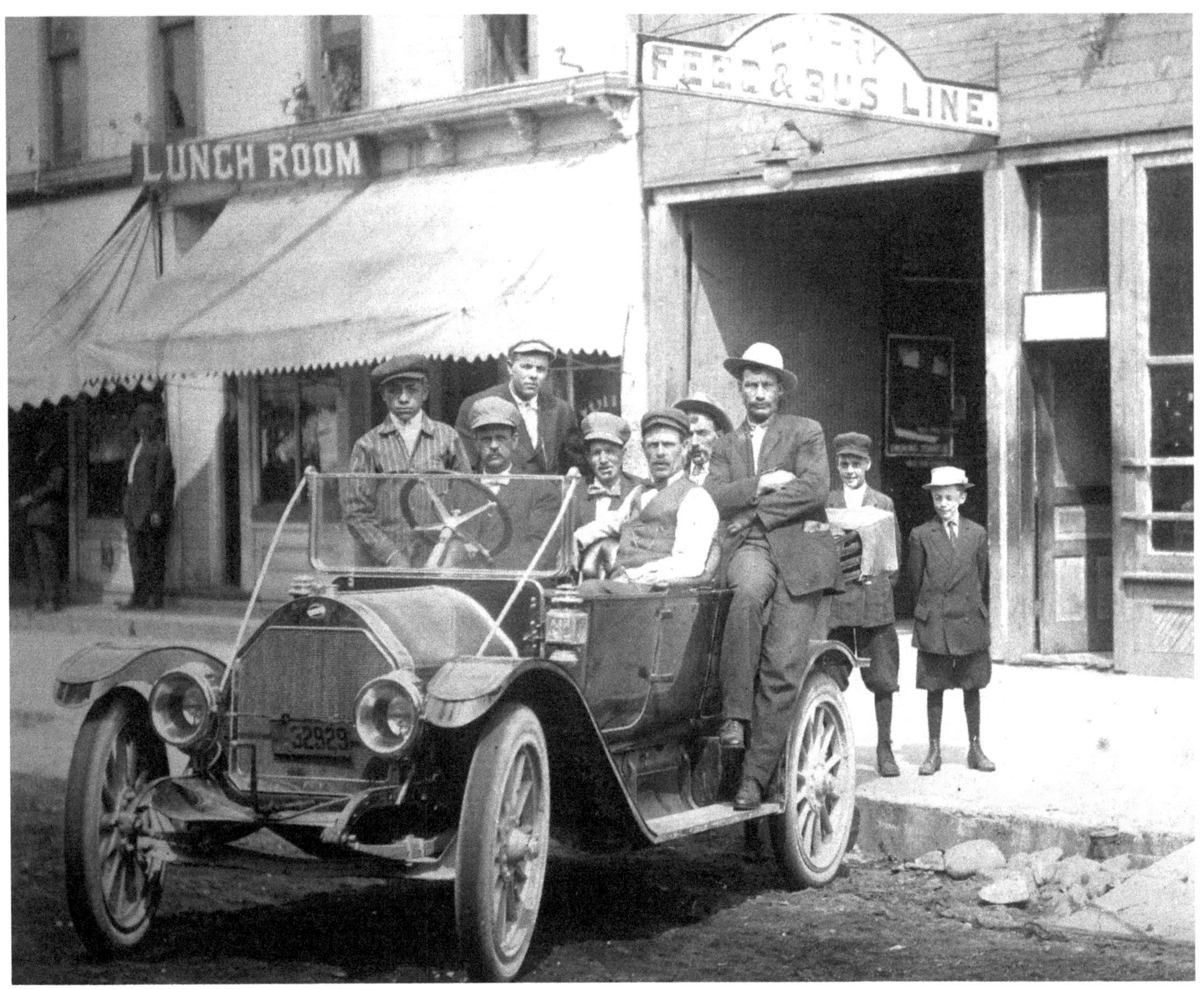

In 1914, a group of men crowd into and gather around an Overland automobile in downtown Harbor Springs, Michigan, in front of a sign that reads, "Livery Feed and Bus Line." Evidently, the feed tank of the four-legged "bus" was on empty.

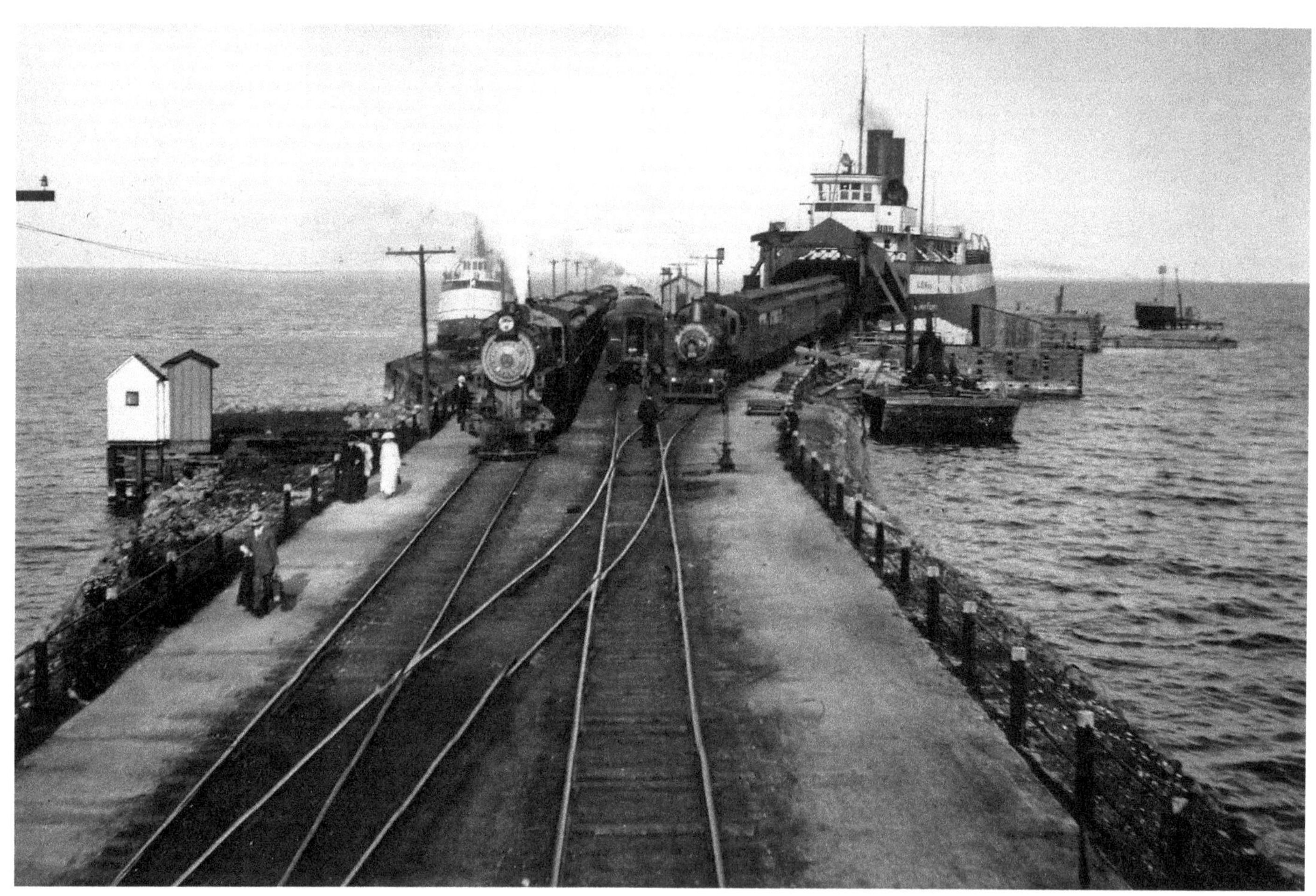

In 1915, a train car is loaded onto the railway ferry and icebreaker *Chief Wawatum,* at Mackinaw City, Michigan's northernmost city on the Lower Peninsula. The ferry's name honors the Chippewa Indian Wawatum, who helped English trader and friend Alexander Henry evade the danger of a 1763 Indian revolt against British soldiers by taking him across the water to hide in Mackinac Island's Skull Cave.

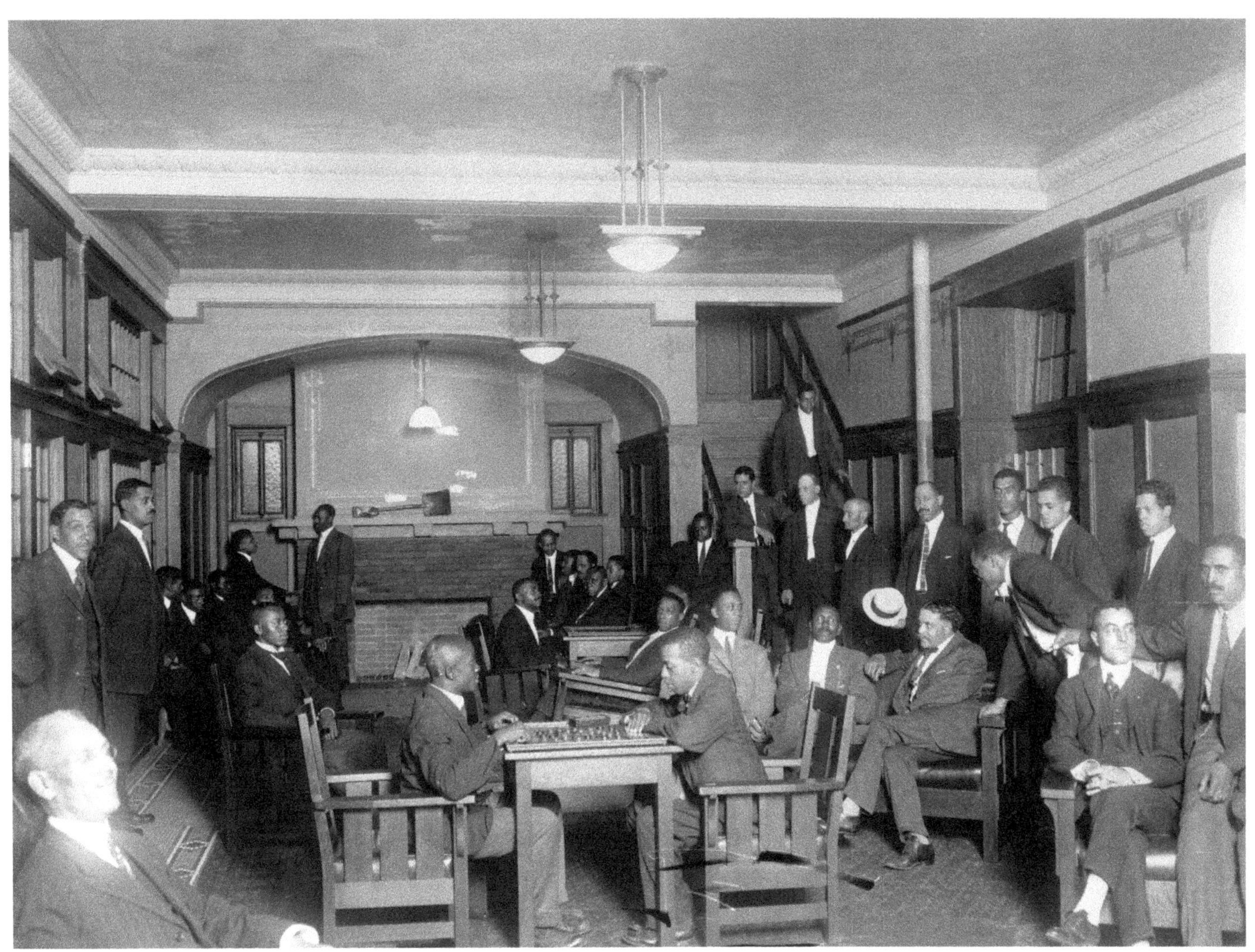

A group of men lounge in the lobby of the Chicago colored Y.M.C.A. in 1915. Twenty-five Y.M.C.A. buildings were made possible for African-Americans around the nation owing in part to the financial incentive of Julius Rosenwald, the businessman credited with managing the massive growth of Sears in the early twentieth century. In 1910, the wealthy philanthropist offered $25,000 toward the cost of a Y.M.C.A. building for African-American men in any city that would raise $75,000 toward the cause.

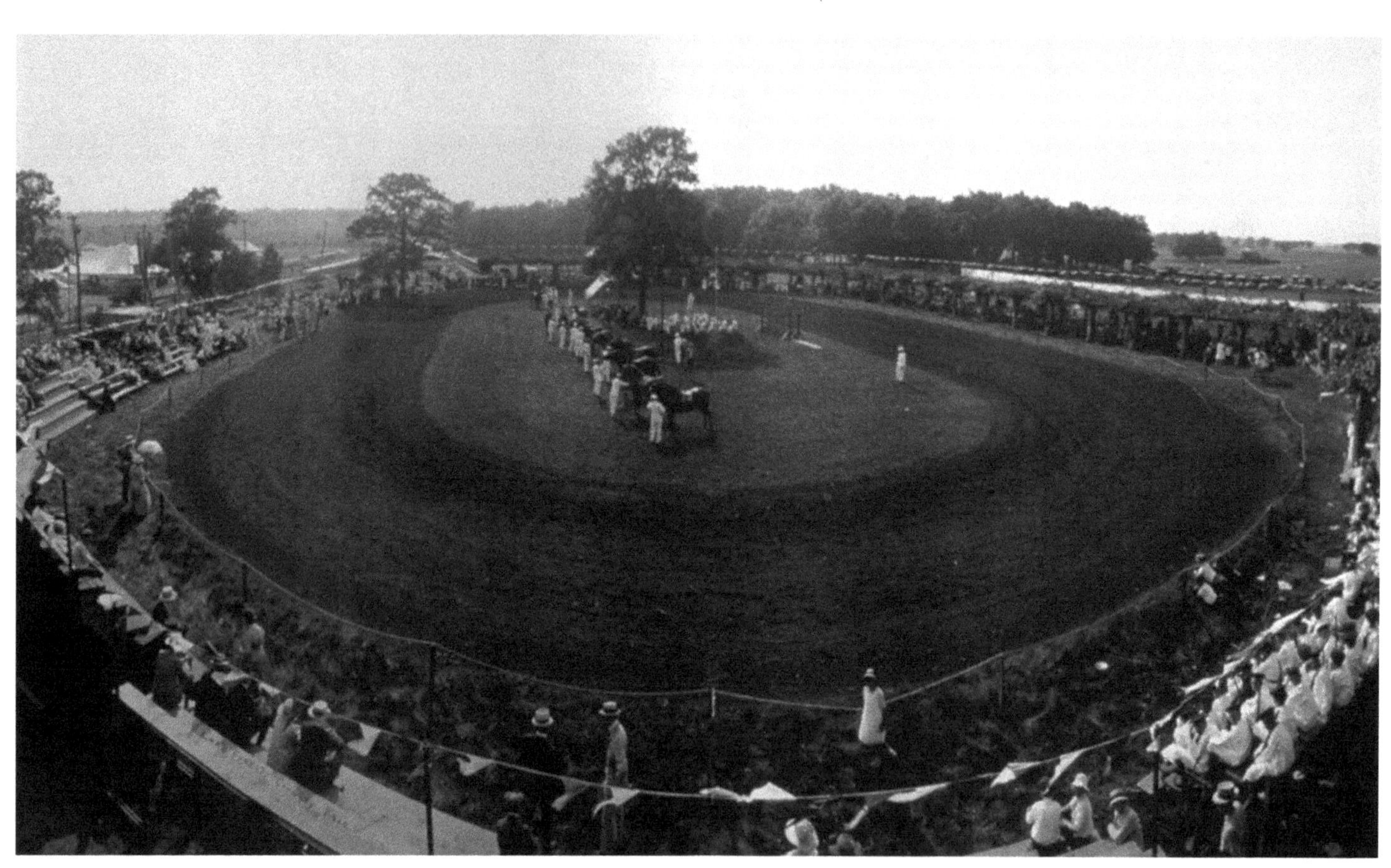

Platted lakeside in 1857 by landscape architect Almerin Hotchkiss, Lake Forest, Illinois, was one of the nation's first towns designed utilizing principles of aesthetics that call to mind those of English gardens. Instead of a formal grid, streets were laid out according to the land's natural contours and features like ravines and lake bluffs. The Lake Forest community is shown here gathered at the Lake Forest Country Fair in 1916.

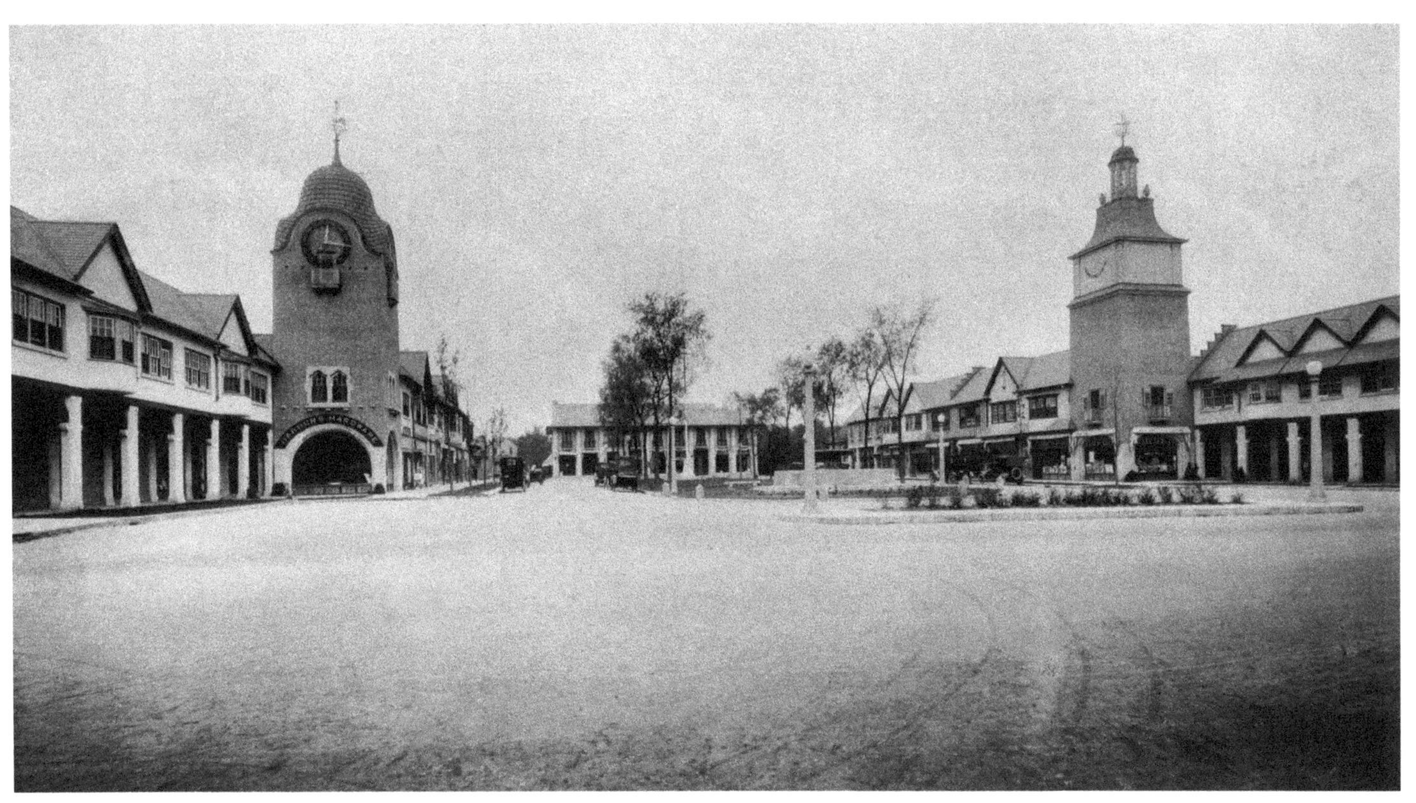

Architect Howard Shaw designed Lake Forest's Market Square in 1916. Known as the "first artfully designed shopping center in the country," the square was intended to resemble a small European county market. Featuring two Tyrolean towers, an Italian Renaissance–style central building, and arcades in the eastern corners, Shaw's Market Square cost $750,000 to build—an astonishingly large sum for the time.

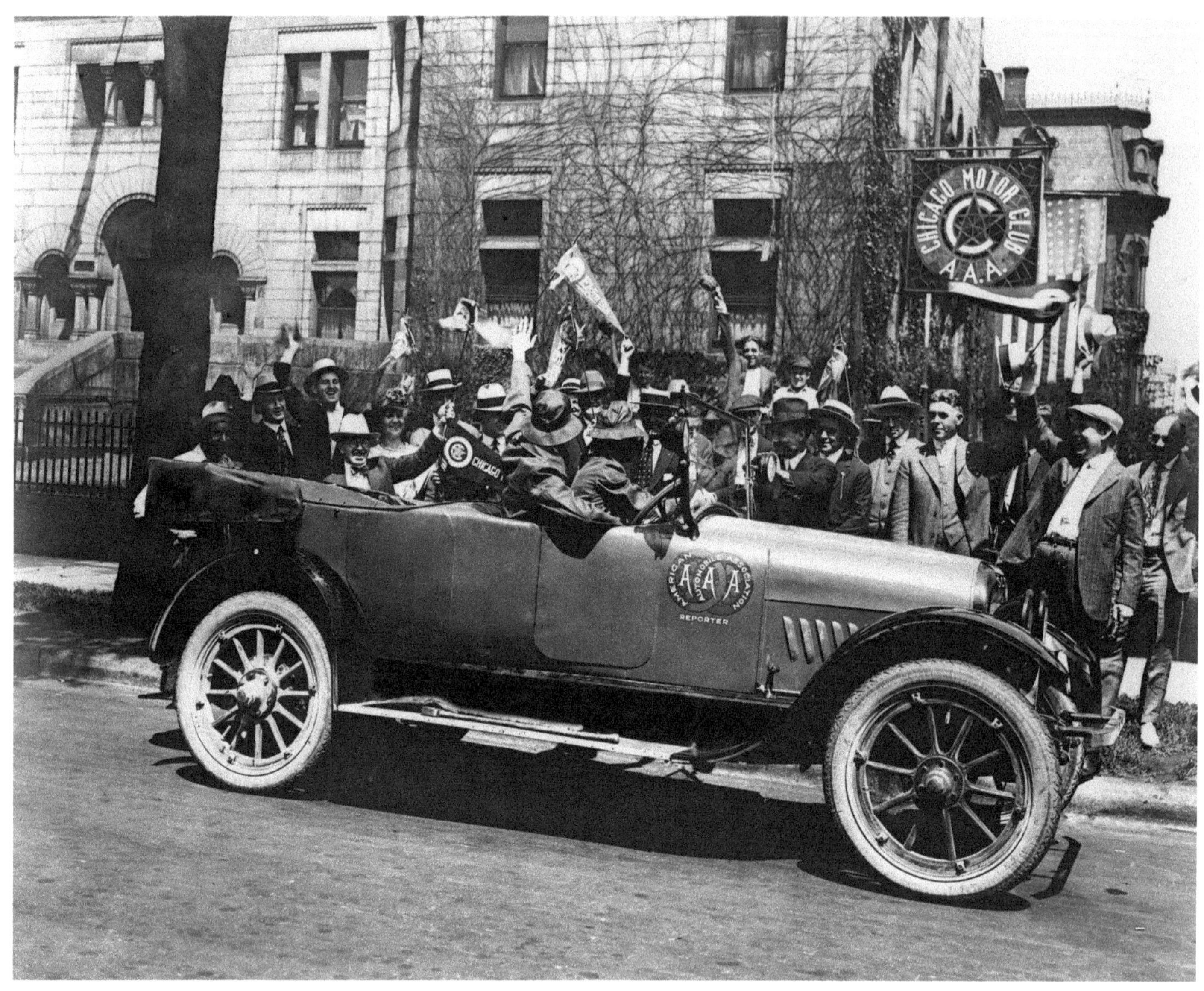

A 1917 shot of Elgin Motor Car Corporation's Elgin Six National All Trails Scout Car on its way through Chicago. The company, which priced the car at $985 that year, attracted public interest while performing what was billed as a public service: touring the country on a nonstop run of more than 6,000 miles and reporting road conditions to various national automotive and touring associations, clubs, and newspapers for the benefit of tourists.

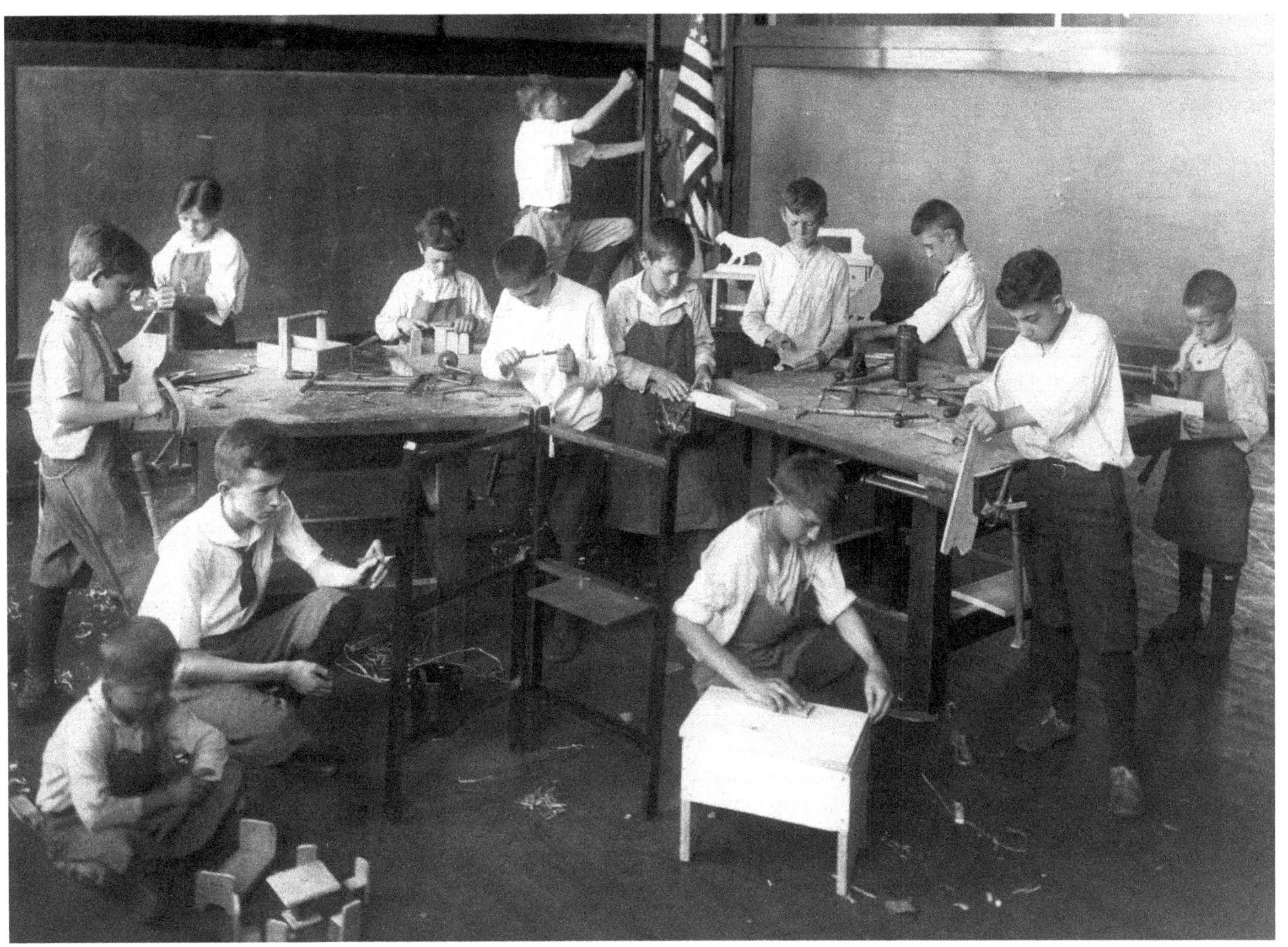

Students are at work in the manual training class at the Franklin School, a "low temperature–open window" school in Chicago's 21st ward. The school was one of many that were part of the nation's open-air movement, which espoused the therapeutic powers of fresh air to ward off tuberculosis and other illness among children.

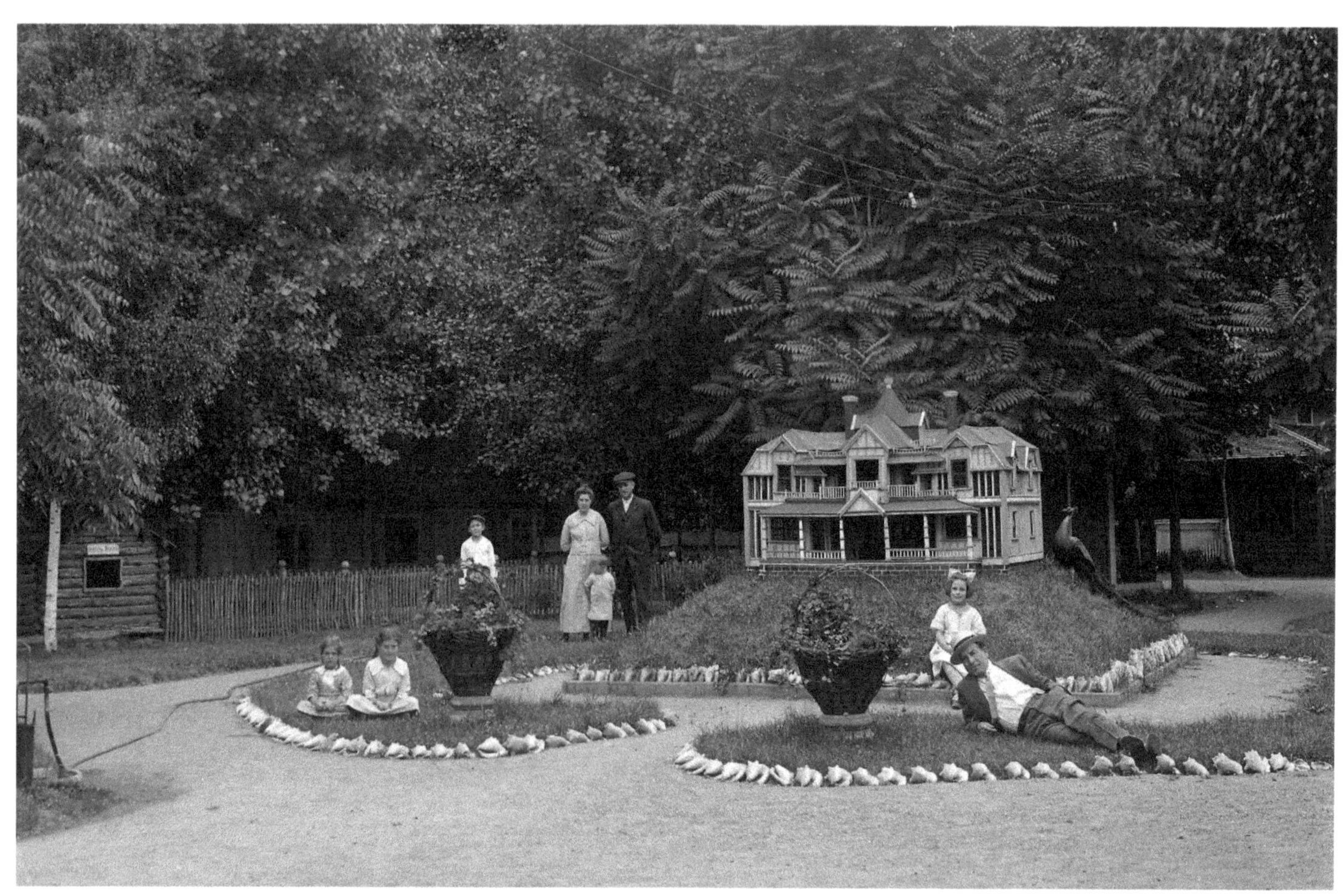

Following his claim that he had received a revelation that he was the seventh messenger described in the book of Revelation, former roving preacher Benjamin Purnell established the Israelite House of David at Benton Harbor, Michigan, in 1903. By the 1920s, his colony—which boasted commercial ventures that included a restaurant, gift shop, hotel, amusement park, and zoo (shown here)—counted more than 900 members.

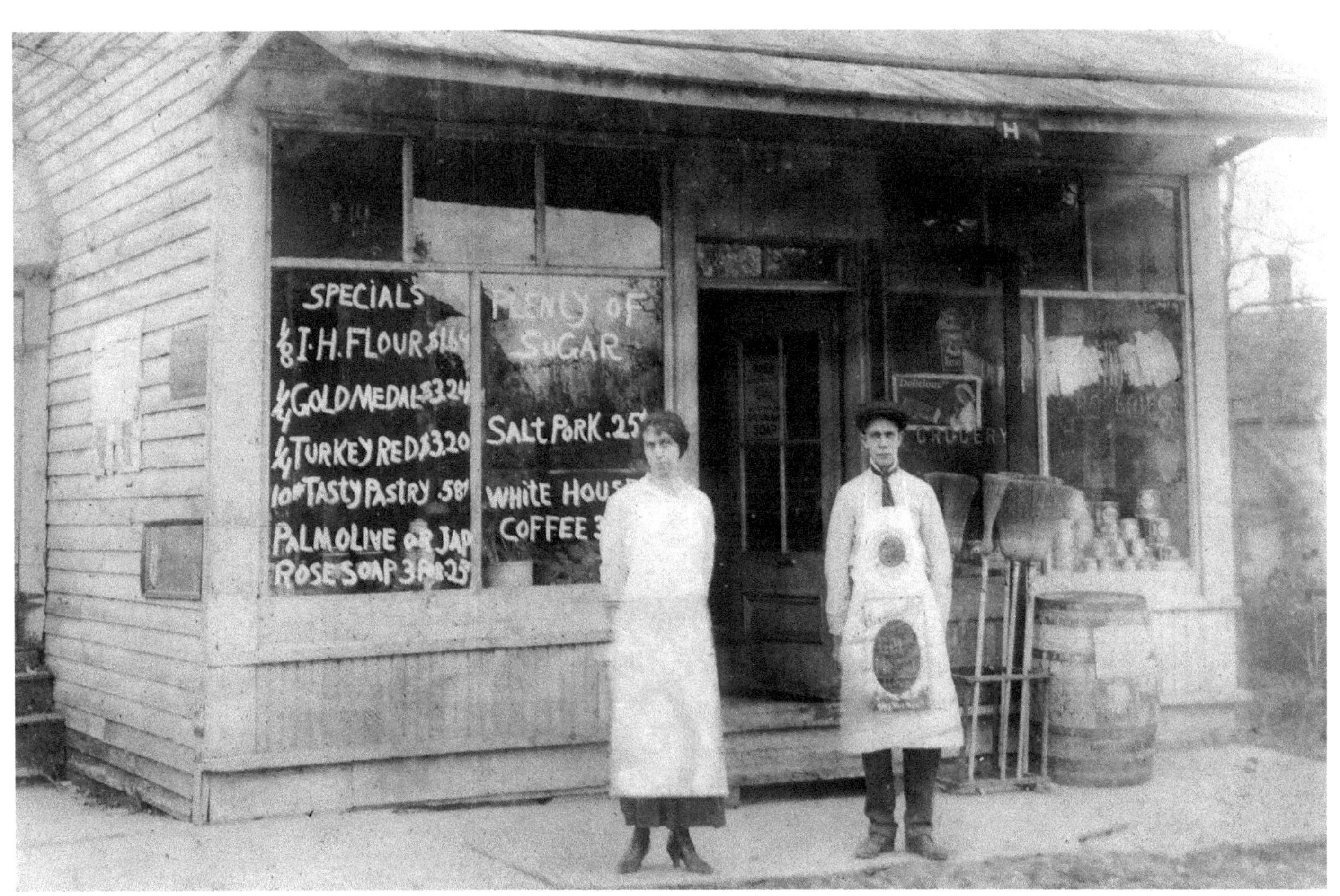

A storefront in Traverse City, Michigan, in 1919, advertises brand names available then and still familiar today.

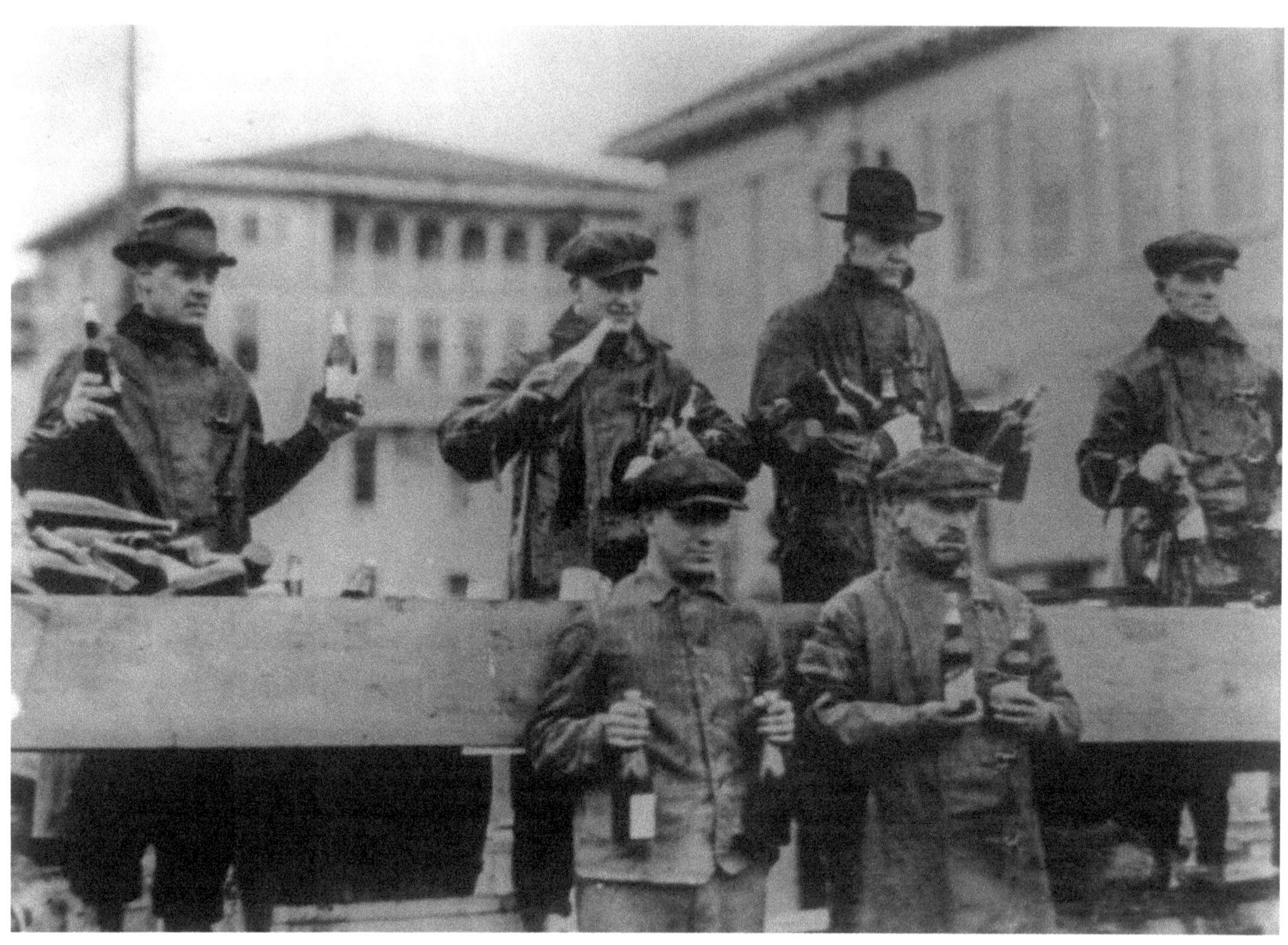

In November 1919, as the first year of Illinois state prohibition got under way, a group of vigilantes in Zion, Illinois, intercepted a truck sneaking a load of beer out of Chicago. The *New York Times* reported public dumping of nearly 139,000 seized bottles into a trough that ran into a sewer. Others estimate the number at closer to 80,000.

Following the seizure of illegal beer being transported through Zion from Chicago during Prohibition, Zion City mayor W. Hurd Clendein is the first to dump beer into the trough running to the city sewer. The Chief of Police, Theodore Becker, would be the second.

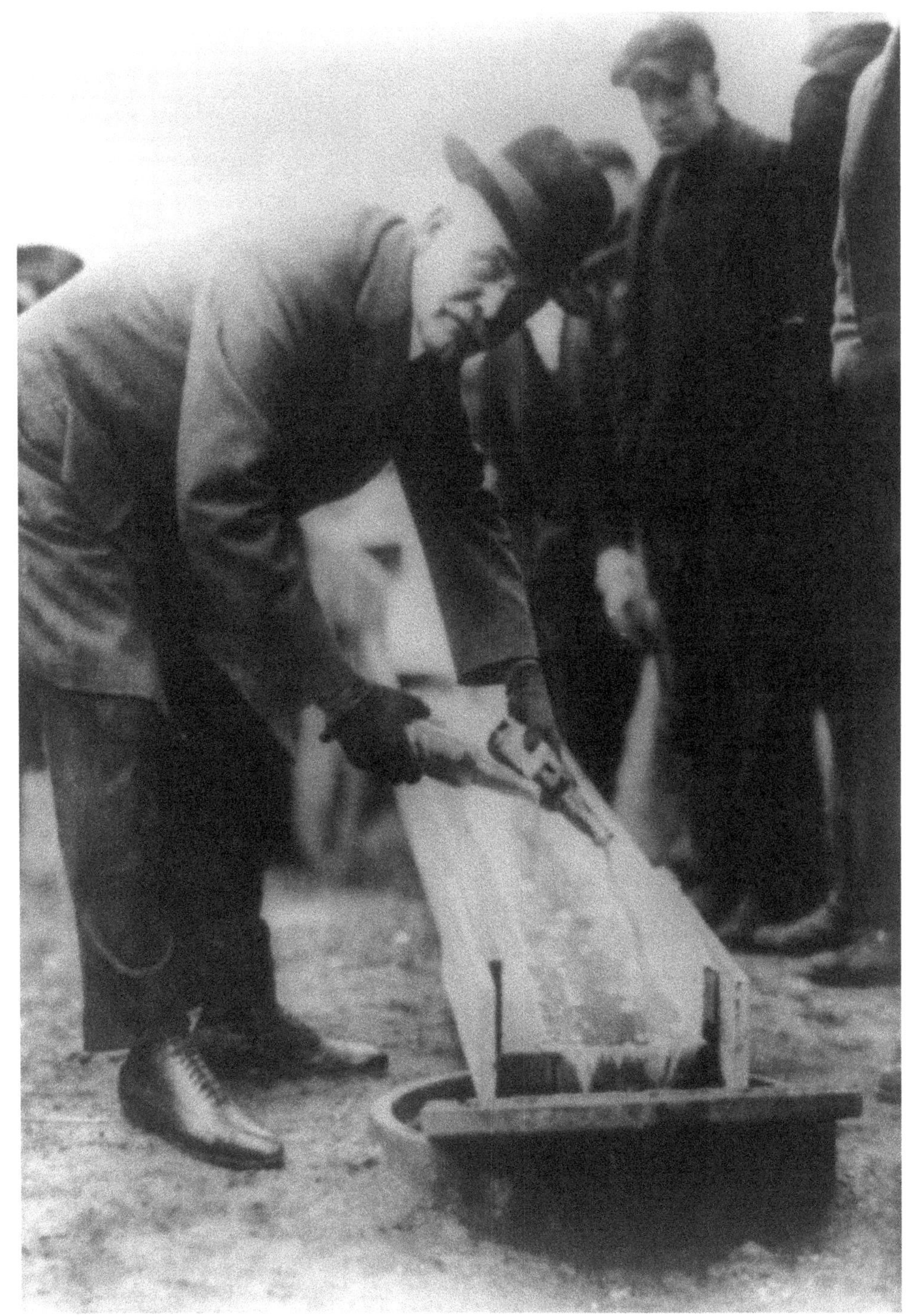

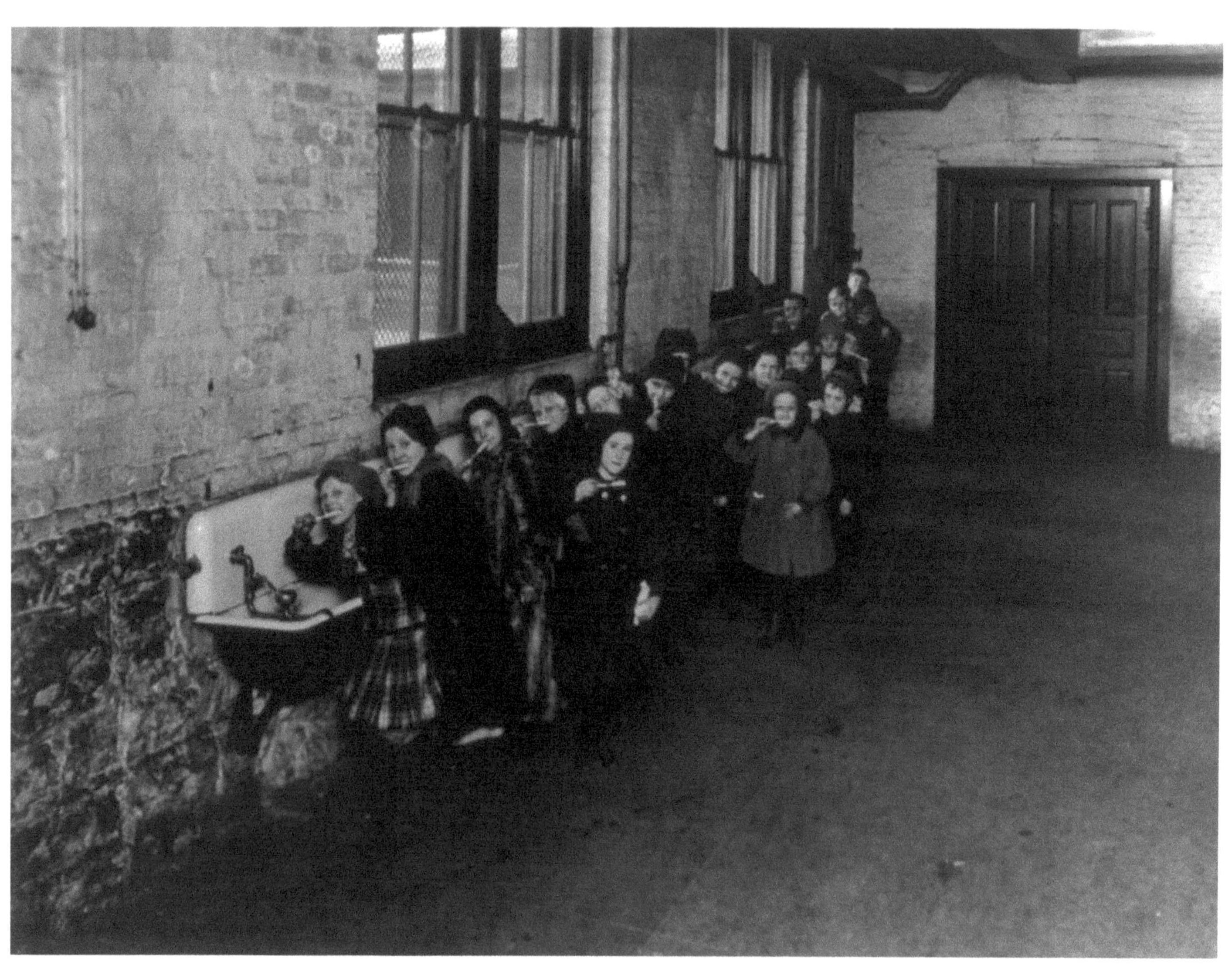

The "Open-Air Crusaders," those behind the movement toward better ventilation and open-air schools for children, believed there could be no good health without good hygiene. This 1920s-era photograph shows children in line for a toothbrush drill at Chicago's Franklin School—a low-temperature, open-window school that supported the open-air movement.

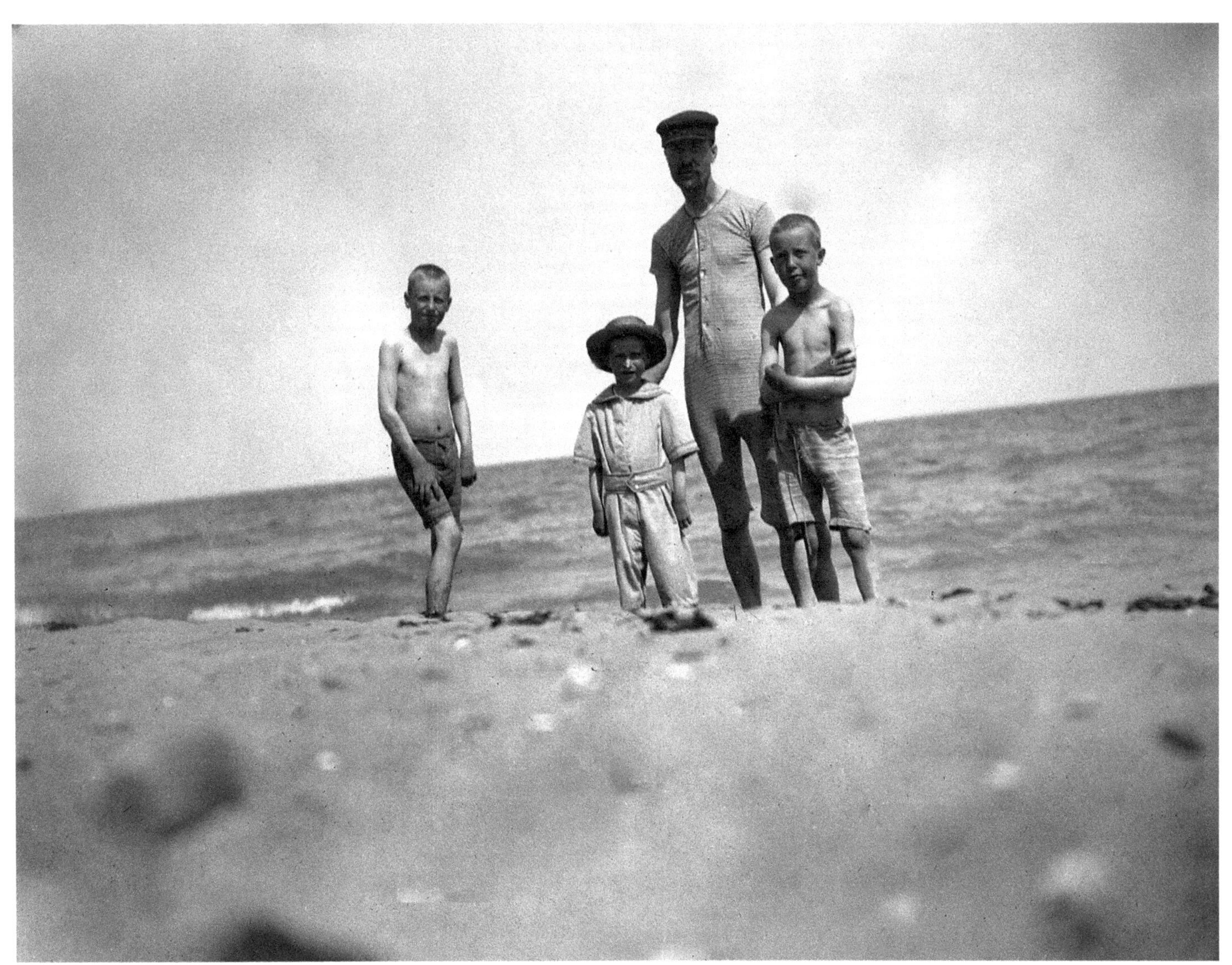

A man and his three sons pose on the Lake Michigan beach at Sturgeon Bay, Wisconsin.

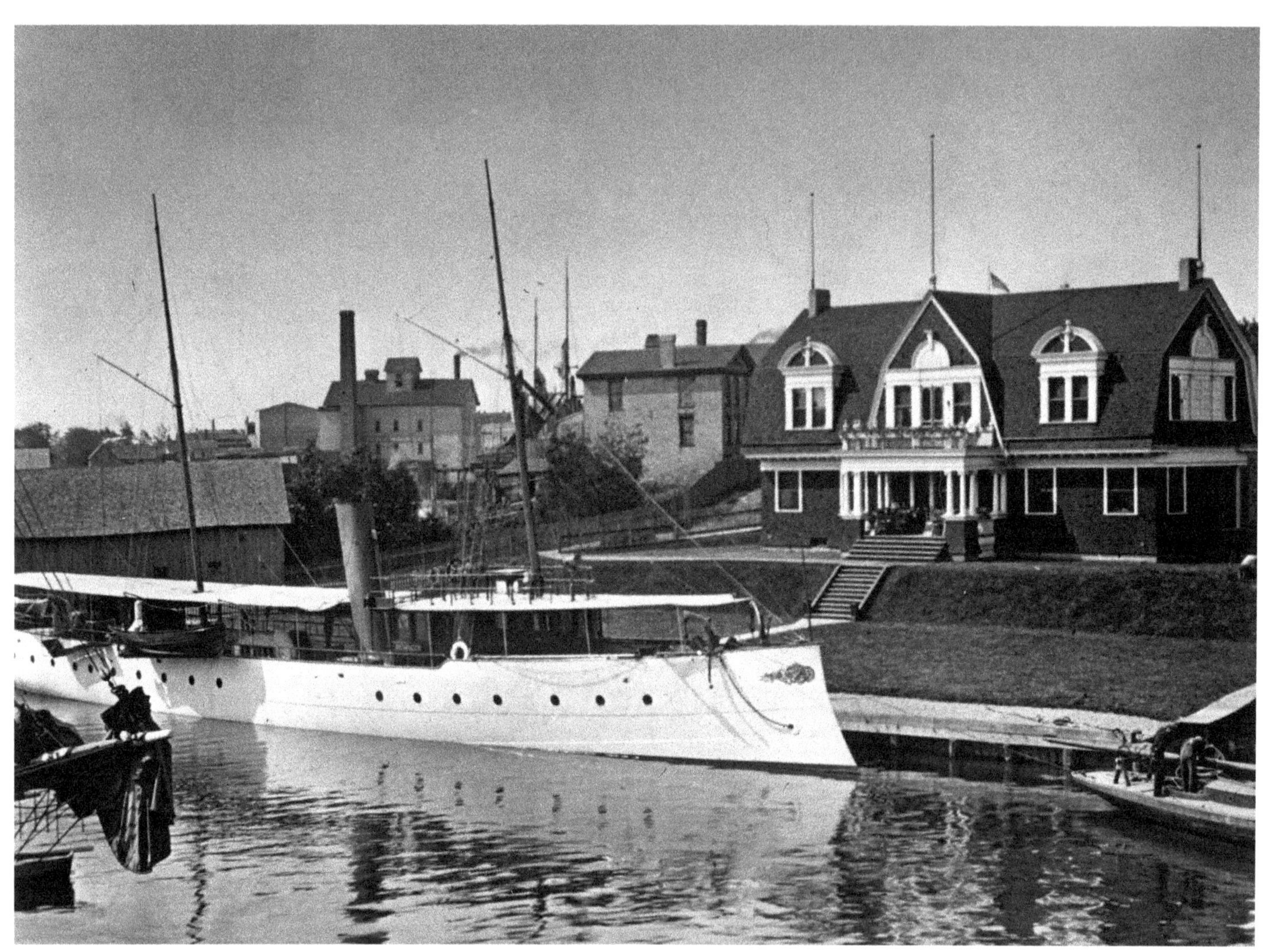

A 1920 shot of the Morgan Club House in Kenosha, Wisconsin. Built around the turn of the century by F. W. Morgan, commodore of the Chicago Yacht Club, the two-story Colonial-style building sat on Morgan's riverfront property. Morgan used it as a place to entertain his fellow yachtsmen in summer and, in winter, as a laying up station.

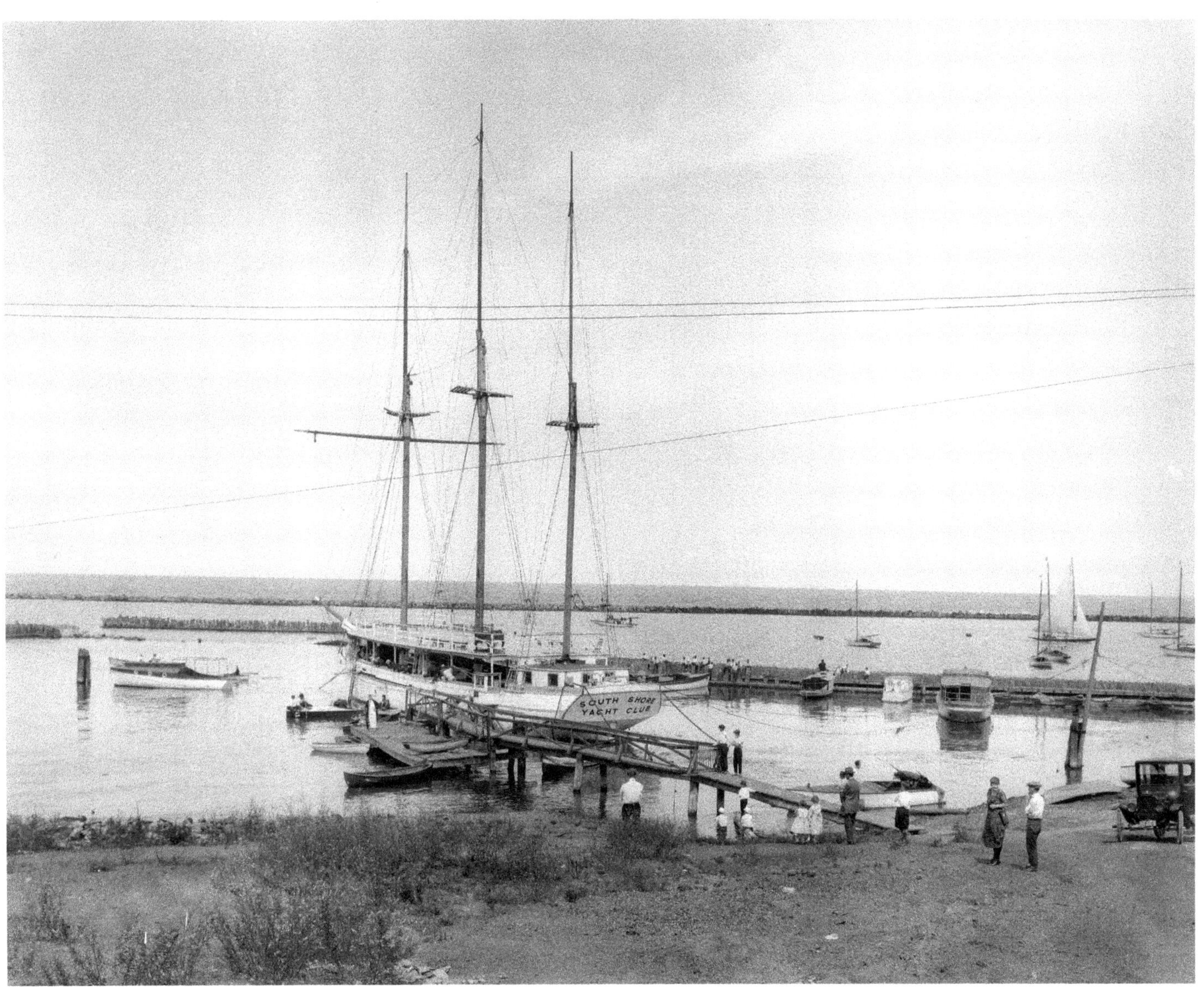

In her career as a lumber schooner, the 1869-built *Lily E.* (formerly the *Louisa McDonald*) suffered storms, beaching, and leaks. It seemed her spot in the muddy boneyard near Sturgeon Bay, Wisconsin, would be her final resting place. That is, until the South Shore Yacht Club, formed in tandem with the beautifying of Milwaukee's lakefront in 1913, purchased and converted the old schooner into a floating clubhouse, which the S.S.Y.C. used until 1921.

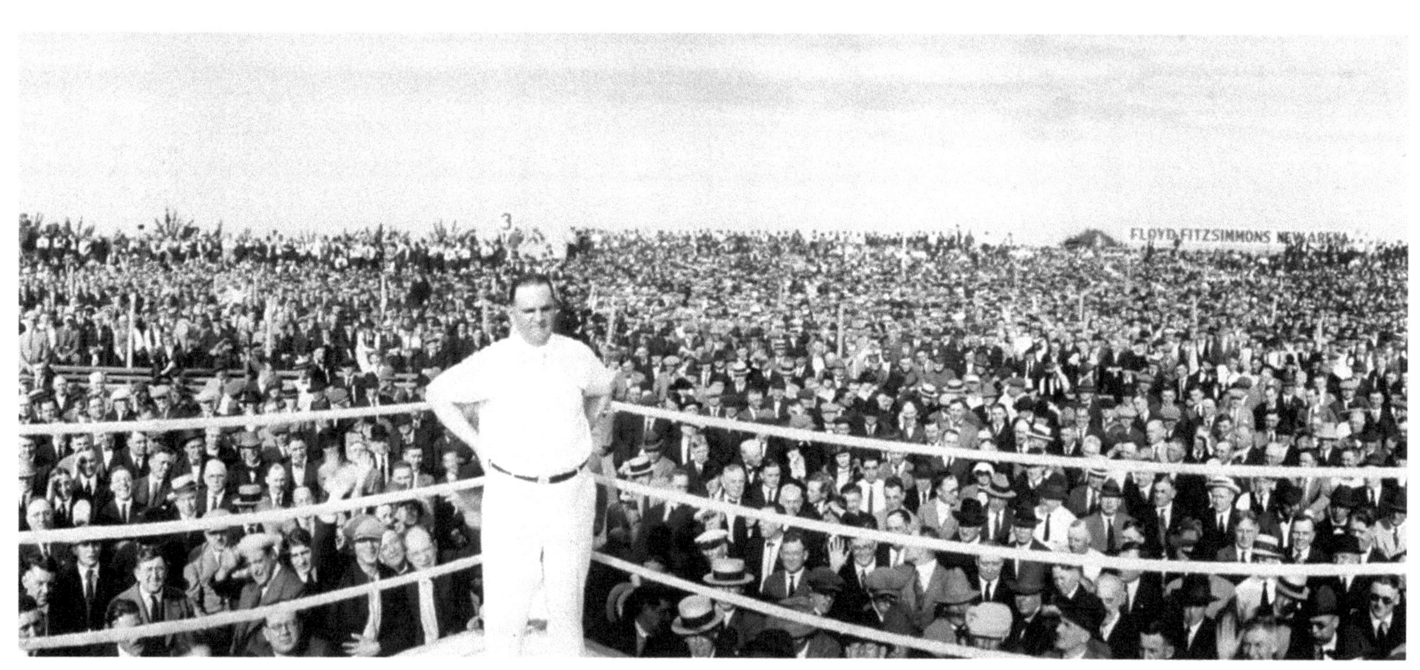

One year after brutally beating the defending world heavyweight champion Jess Willard, Jack Dempsey—the Manassa Mauler—successfully defended his championship title in Benton Harbor, Michigan. On that Labor Day in 1920, he knocked out Billy Miske—the St. Paul Thunderbolt—in the third round. It was the only time Billy Miske had ever been knocked out.

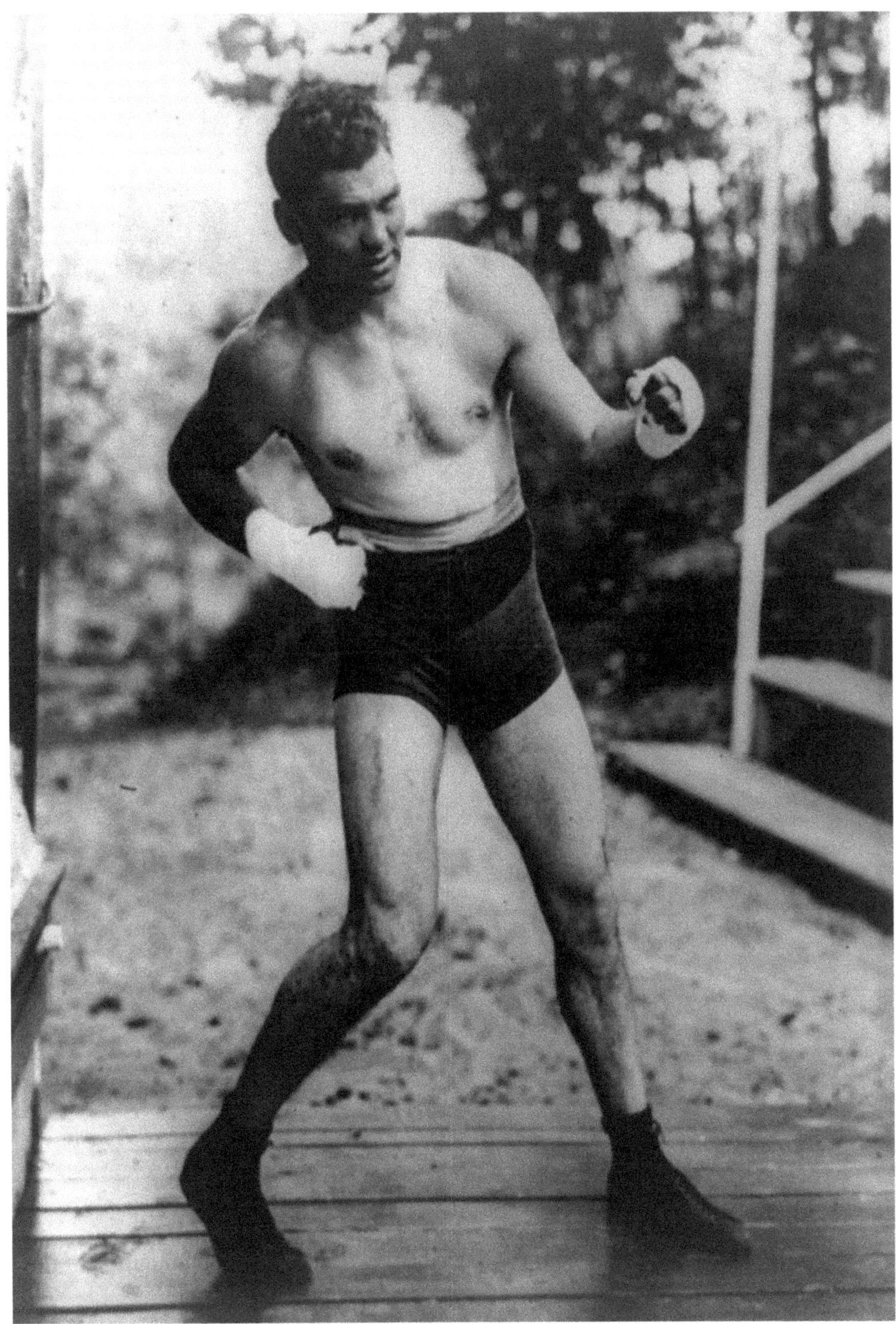

A 1922 photograph of boxer Jack Dempsey taken in Michigan City, Indiana, while he was heavyweight champion of the world. The title, first won in Toledo, Ohio, in 1919, when Dempsey defeated Jess Willard, and successfully defended against Georges Carpentier in 1921, would be lost to Gene Tunney in 1926.

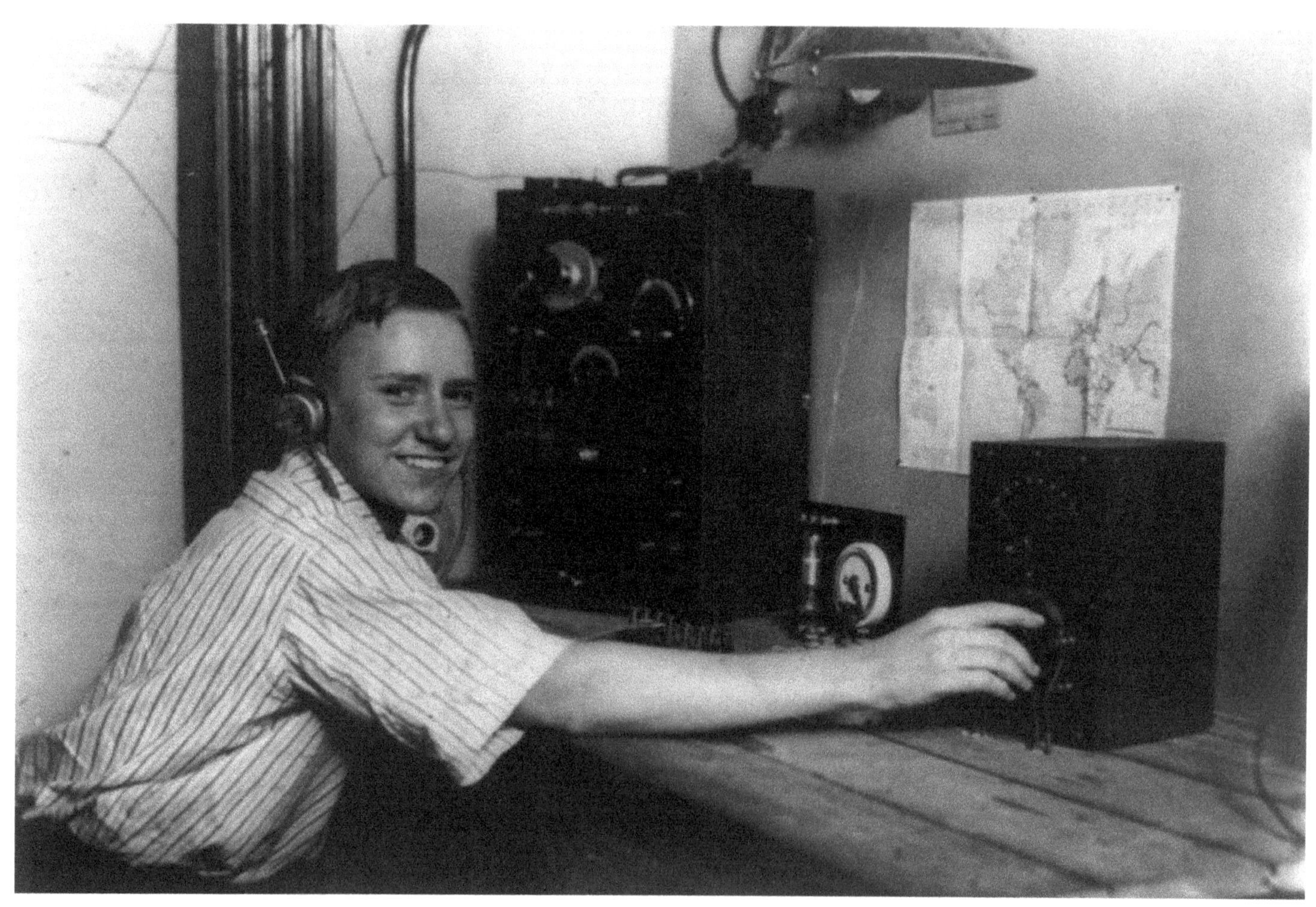

Following the end of World War I and its civilian radio restrictions, amateur radio hobbyists, like 14-year-old John Iringle of Chicago shown here in 1922, built radio outfits to receive and sometimes transmit broadcasts of their own.

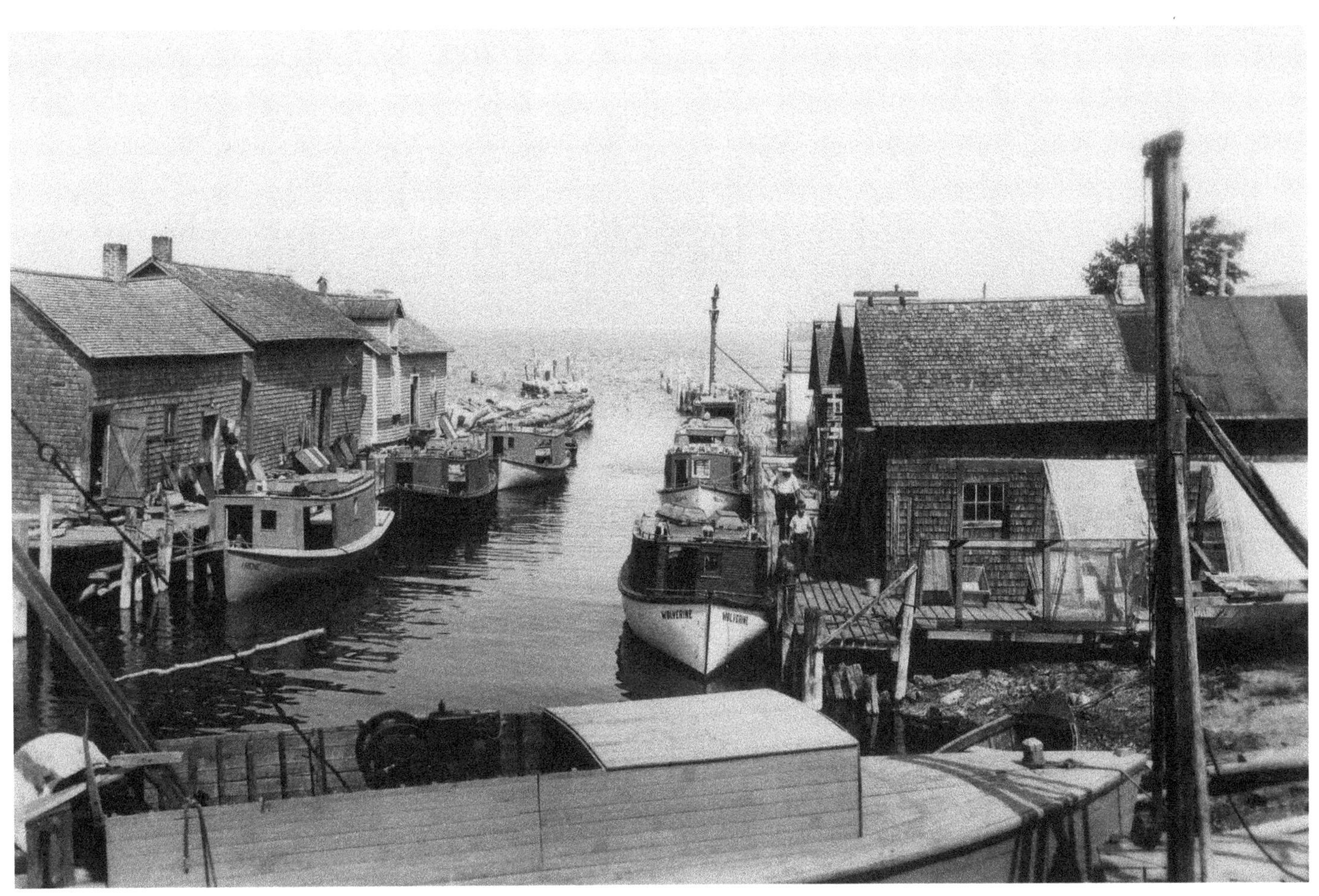

A photograph of the harbor at Leland, Michigan, taken sometime after 1920. Leland's commercial fishing village began taking shape along the Leland River and Lake Michigan in the late 1800s. Known as historic "Fishtown" today, the village looks much the same as it does in this photograph, thanks to the excellent preservation of its weathered shanties, smokehouses, and docks.

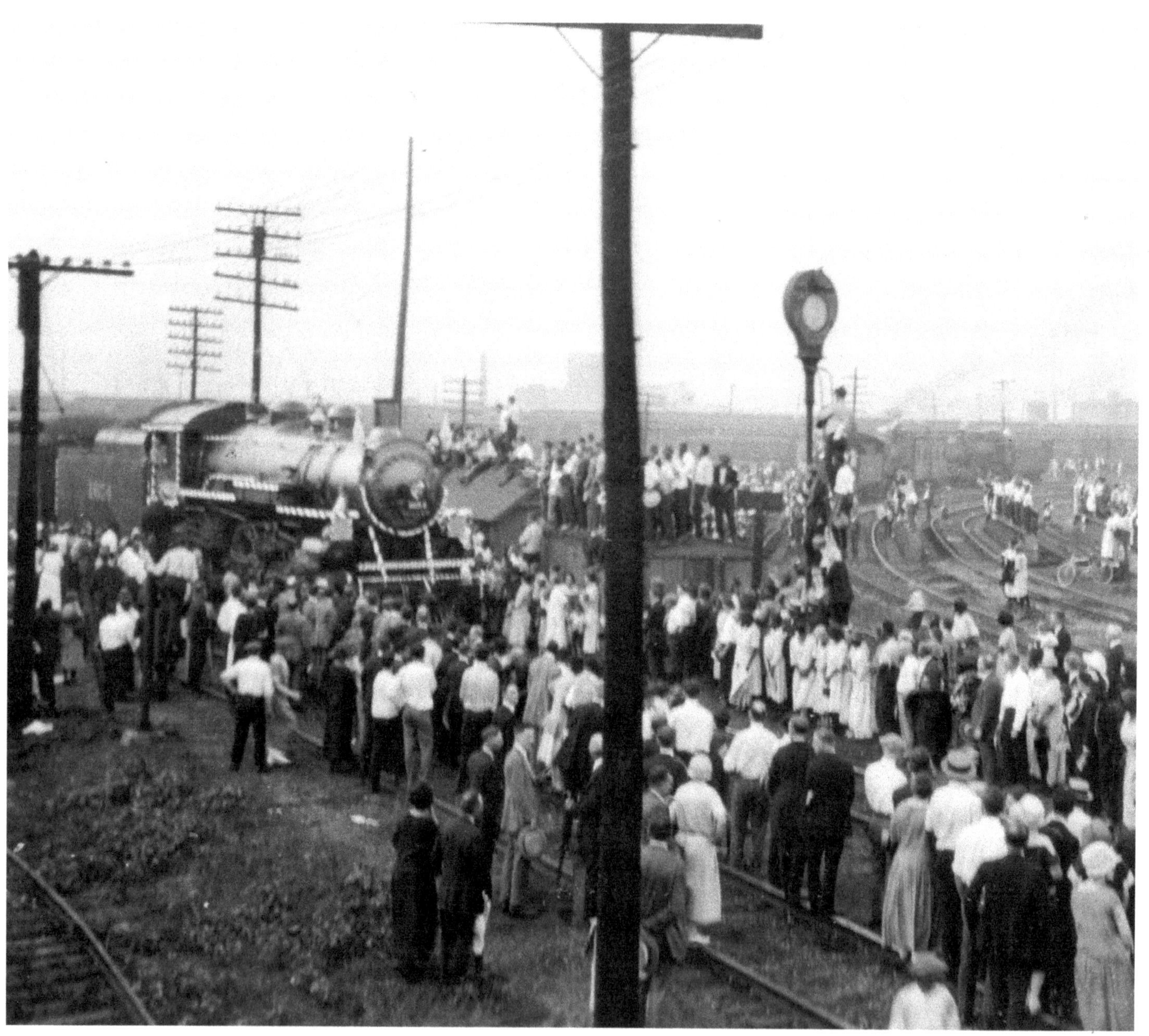

Warren G. Harding was considered by many to be the worst president in American history up to that time, thanks to his cabinet's involvement in the Teapot Dome scandal and corruption in the Veterans Bureau and the Justice Department. He died in 1923, the second year of his presidency, while visiting San Francisco. Here, the funeral train carrying his body rolls into Chicago.

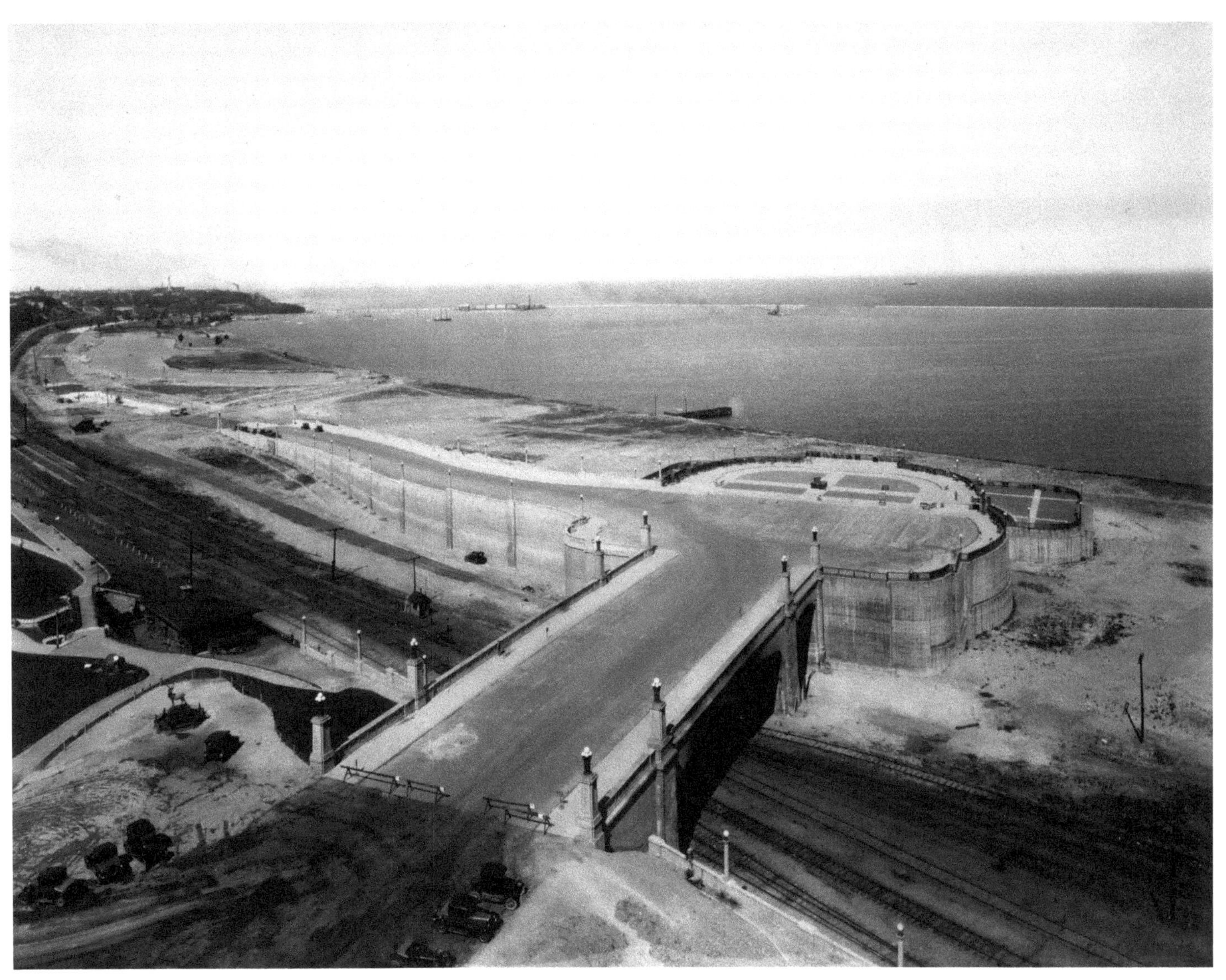

A bird's-eye view of the lakeside intersection of Lincoln Memorial Drive and Wisconsin Avenue in Milwaukee. The site, still serene in this pre-1930 photograph, is now occupied by the Milwaukee County War Memorial Center.

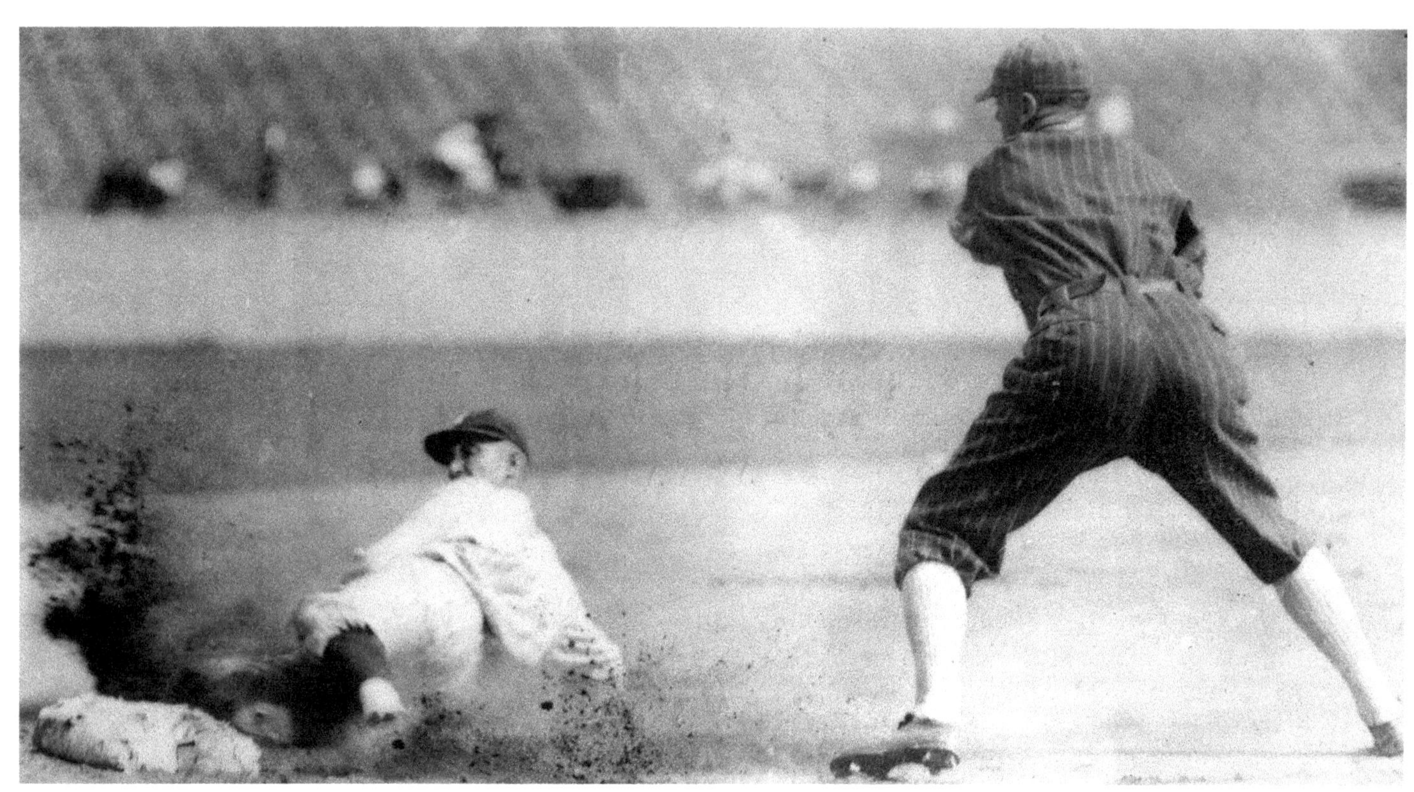

The Washington Nationals' Sam Rice slides into third base during a baseball game against the Chicago White Sox in 1925. Rice, widely regarded as the greatest hitter ever to play for Washington, was safe.

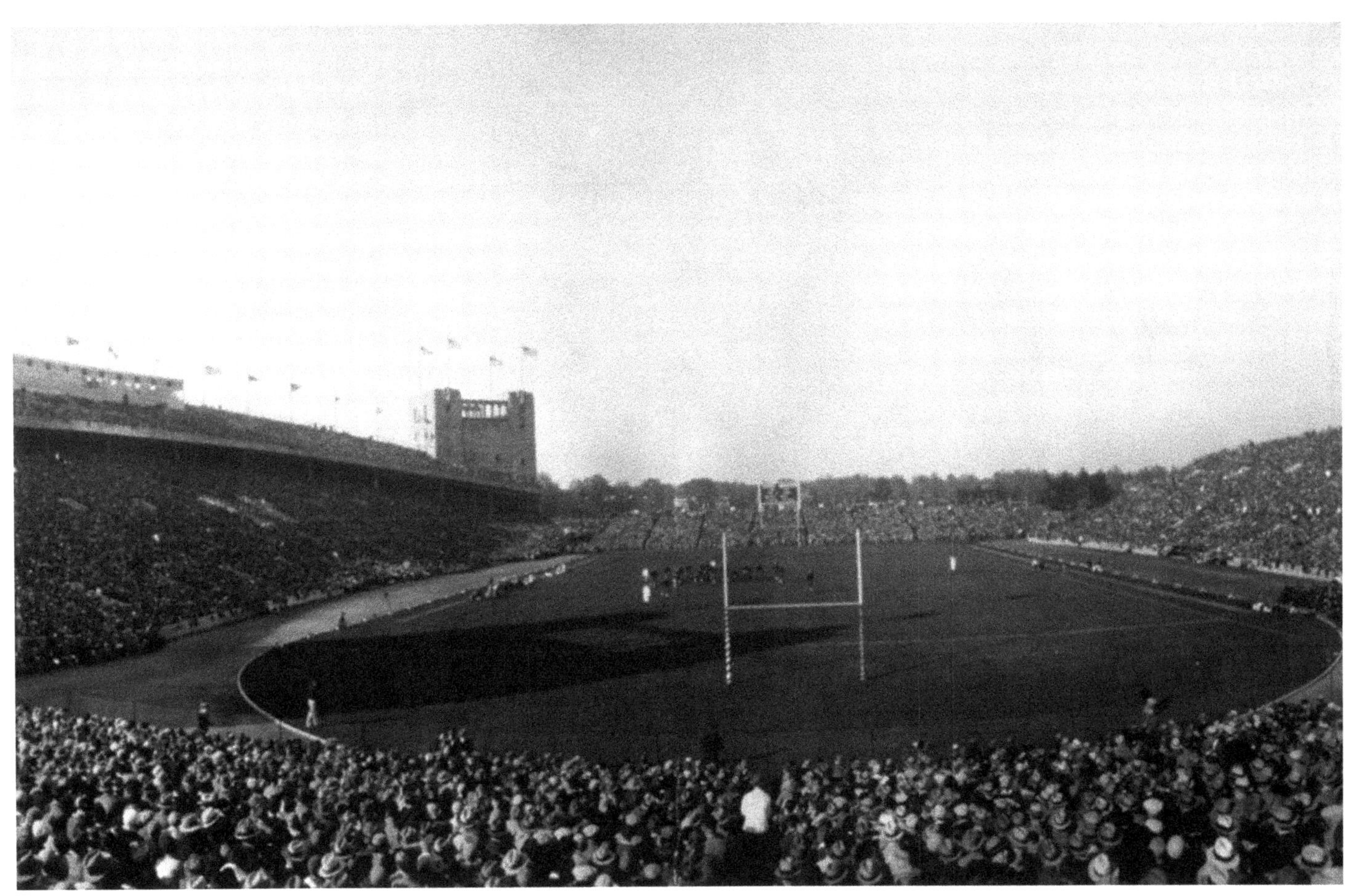

Although the Northwestern football team—the 1926 conference champions—launched the 1927 season with two cool victories over South Dakota and Utah, and one hard-fought win over Ohio, the tide turned at this game against Illinois at Dyche Stadium in Evanston on October 22, 1927. Northwestern lost the game, as well as its next three, rising at last with a 12-0 win over Iowa at season's end. As for Illinois? The team wound up conference champions of 1927. The Northwestern University campus is located in Evanston, Illinois, along Lake Michigan.

President and First Lady Coolidge make a stop in Hammond, Indiana, on June 14, 1927, to dedicate Wicker Memorial Park to war veterans. In the president's arms is six-year-old Loretta Jablowski, a resident of the city.

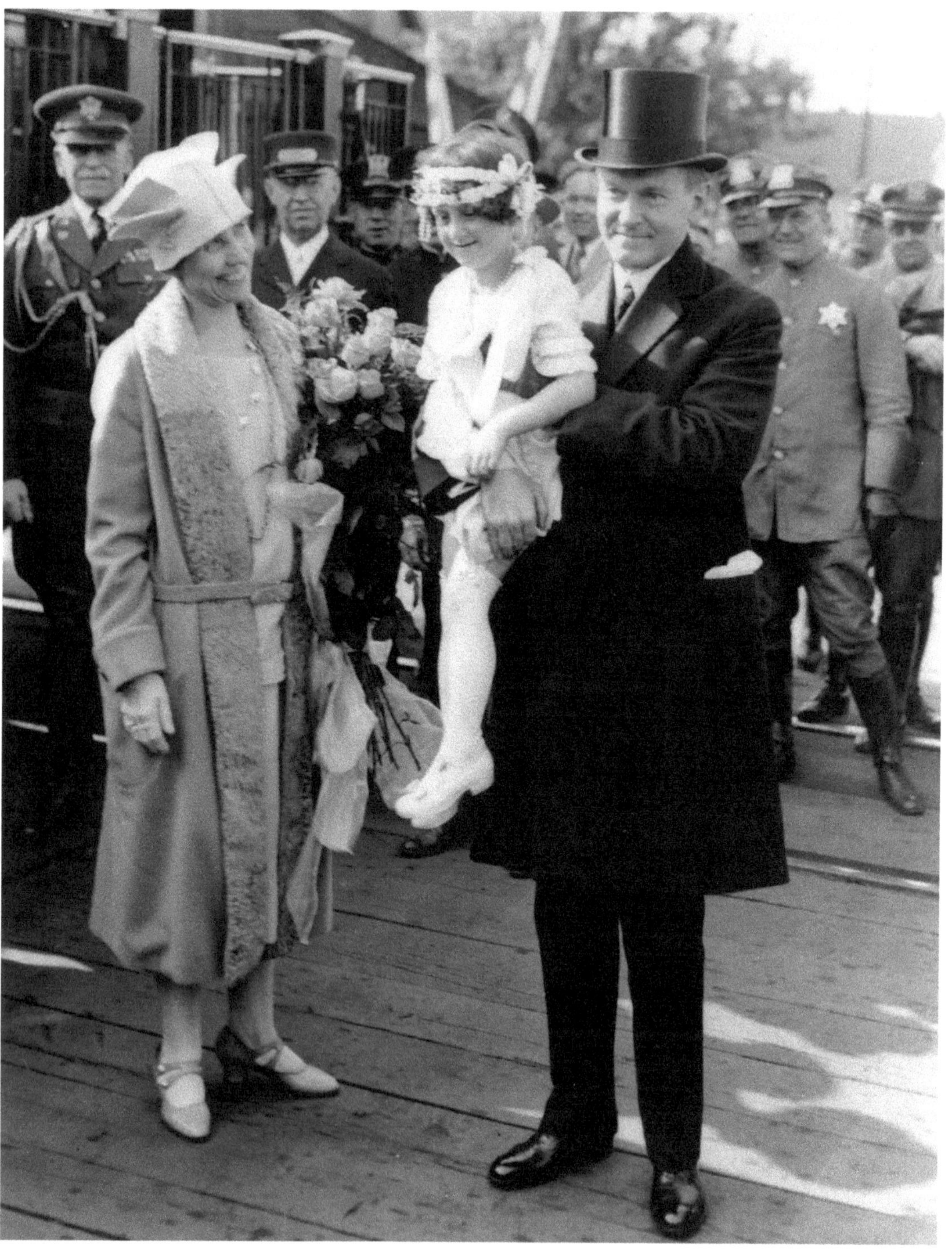

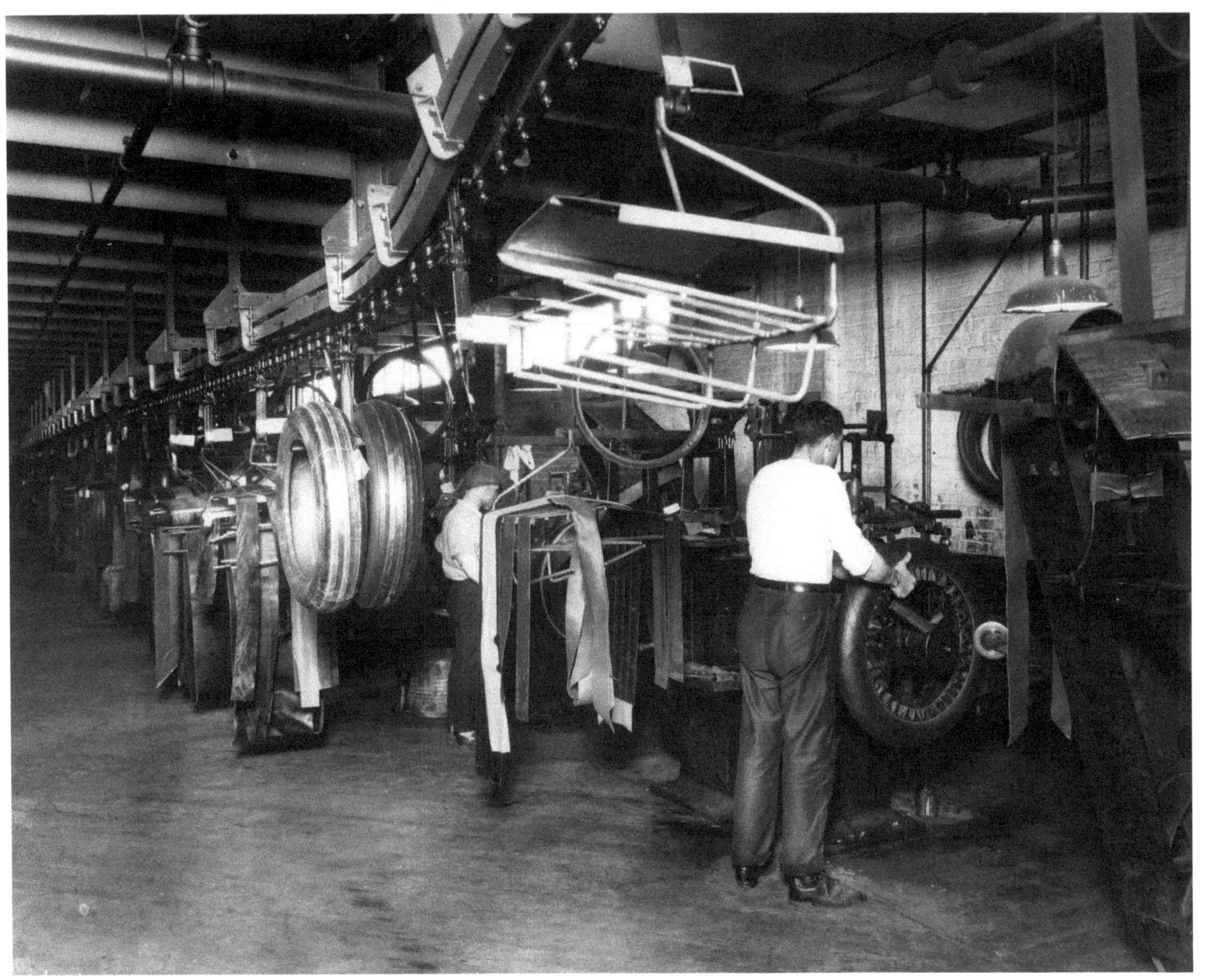

Laborers crank out tires on the line at the Ajax Rubber Company plant in Racine, Wisconsin, in 1928, one year after the Racine company consolidated with the McClaren Rubber Company of Charlotte, North Carolina.

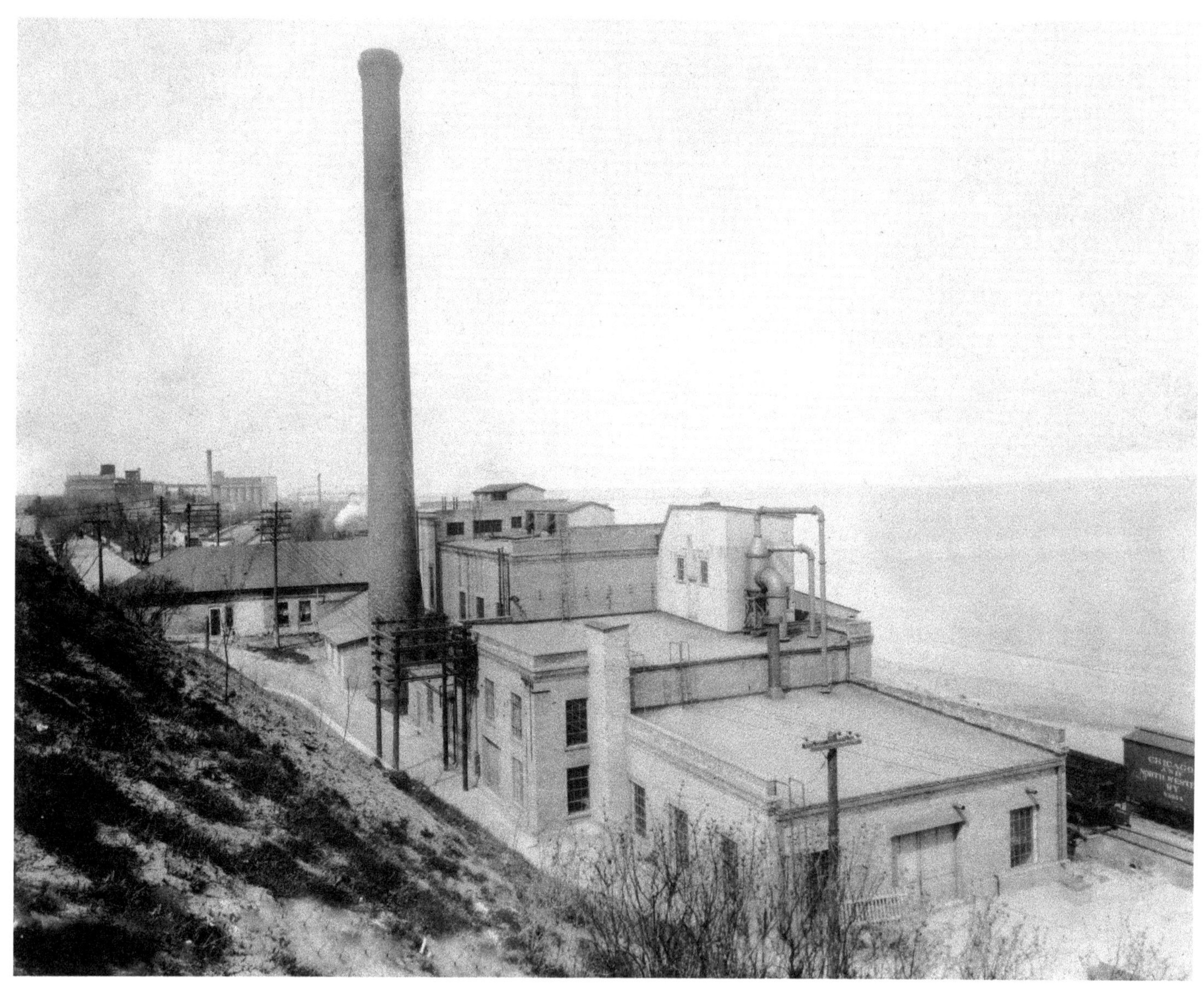

A hilltop view, captured in 1927, of Manitowoc, Wisconsin's Municipal Electric and Water Plant overlooking Lake Michigan.

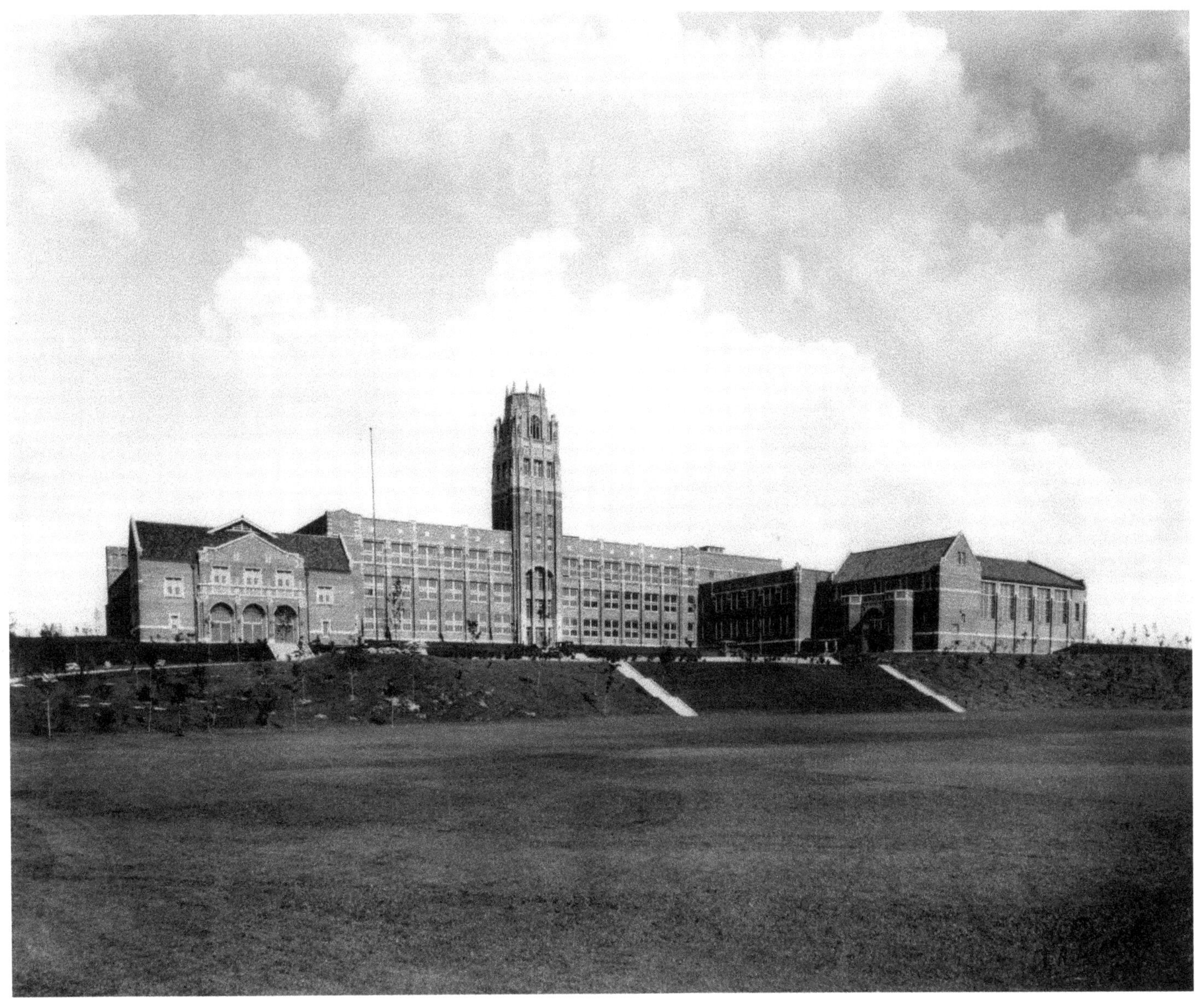

Lincoln High School pictured in 1926, just three years after its construction. The Gothic-style building, designed by Jen Jensen, a landscape architect and former superintendent of Chicago's sublime West Park System, perches atop Roeff's Hill, overlooking Lake Michigan in Manitowoc.

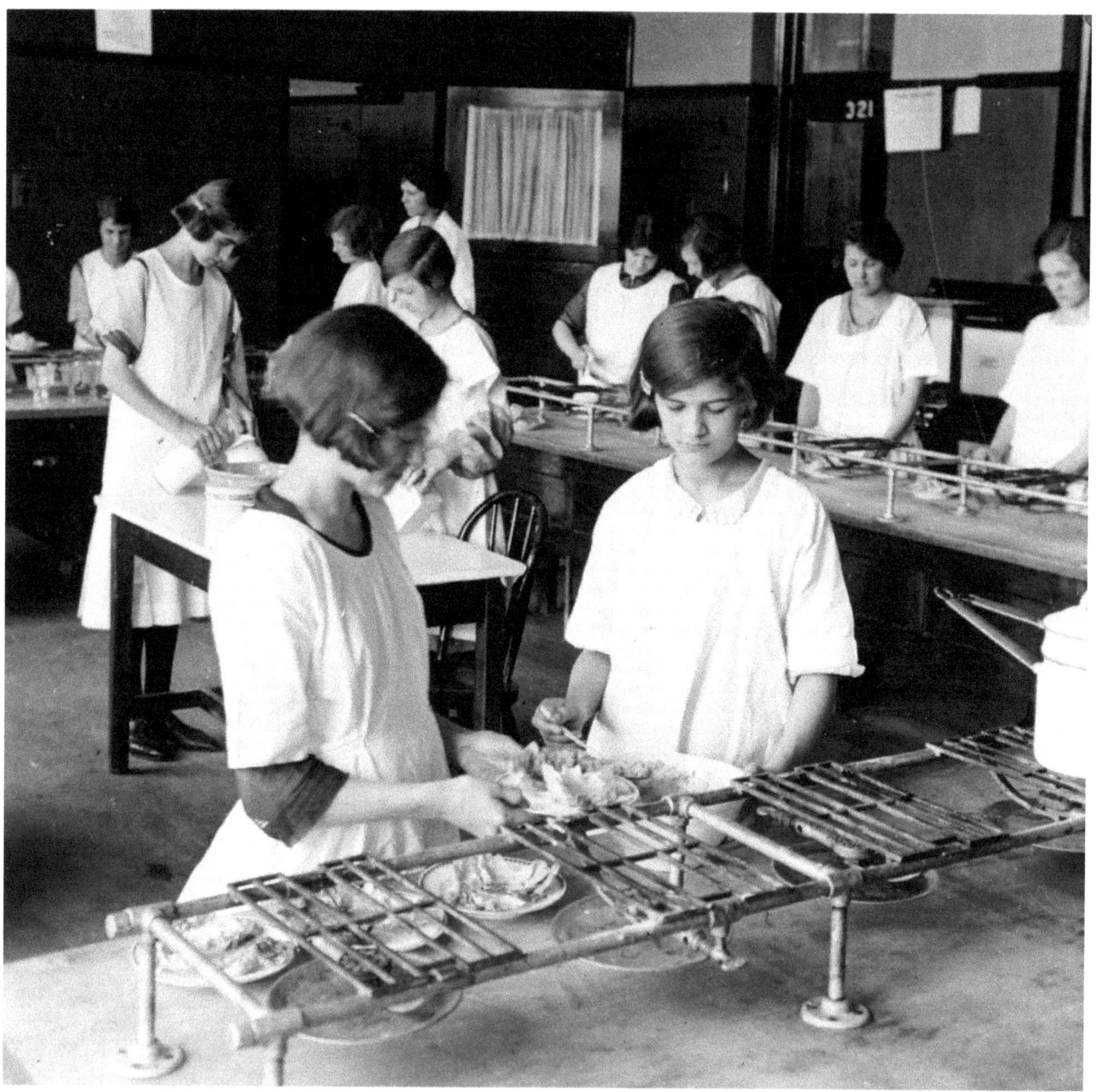

Students in a cooking class at the John Hay School in Chicago make salads in 1929. In 1959, the school would accept several students no longer able to attend the city's Our Lady of the Angels School, which had caught fire on December 1, 1958, killing 92 students and three nuns.

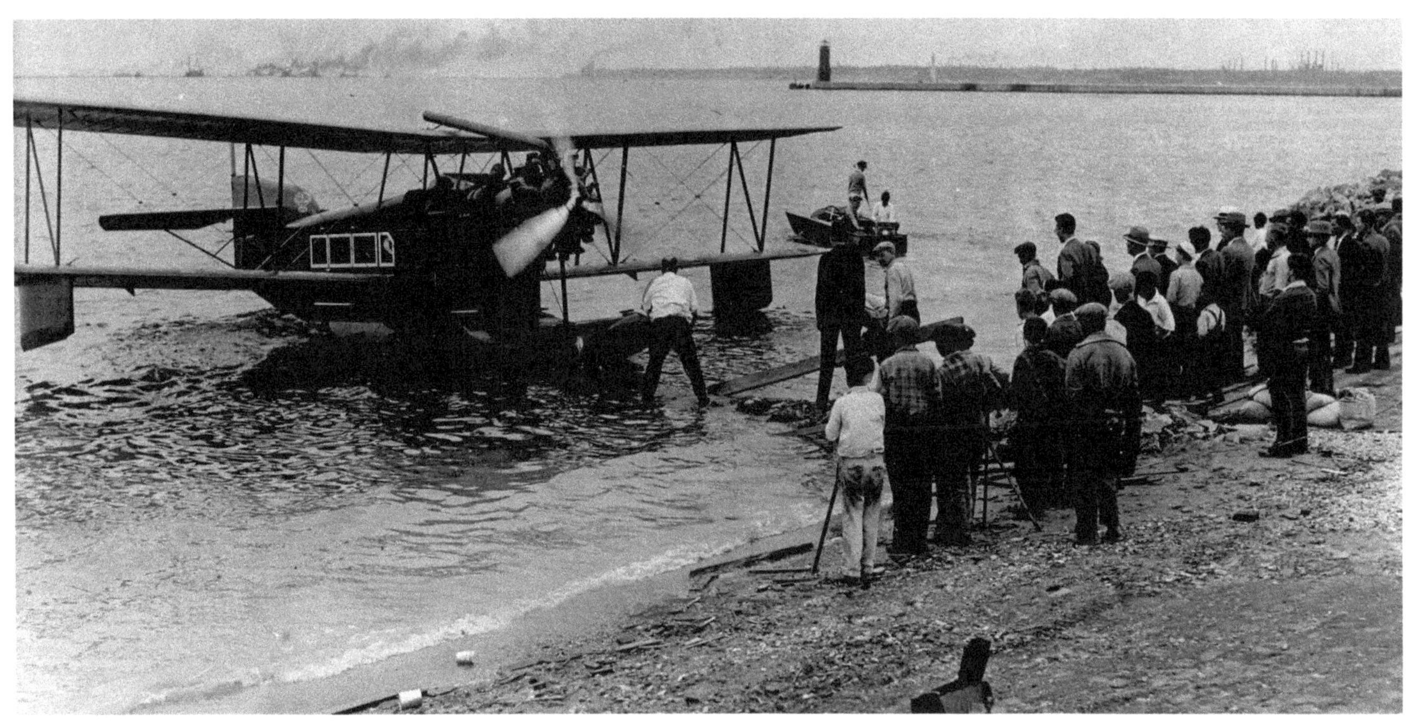

Based in Grand Rapids, Michigan, the Kohler Aviation Company provided passenger flights across Lake Michigan from Milwaukee's Maitland Field to Grand Rapids and Detroit. The key to Kohler's popularity? Its Loening amphibian planes, which the public—who believed flight over water was more dangerous than over land—considered safe and reliable. Shown here is one of the amphibious planes in 1929, shortly before the Great Depression and the airline's demise.

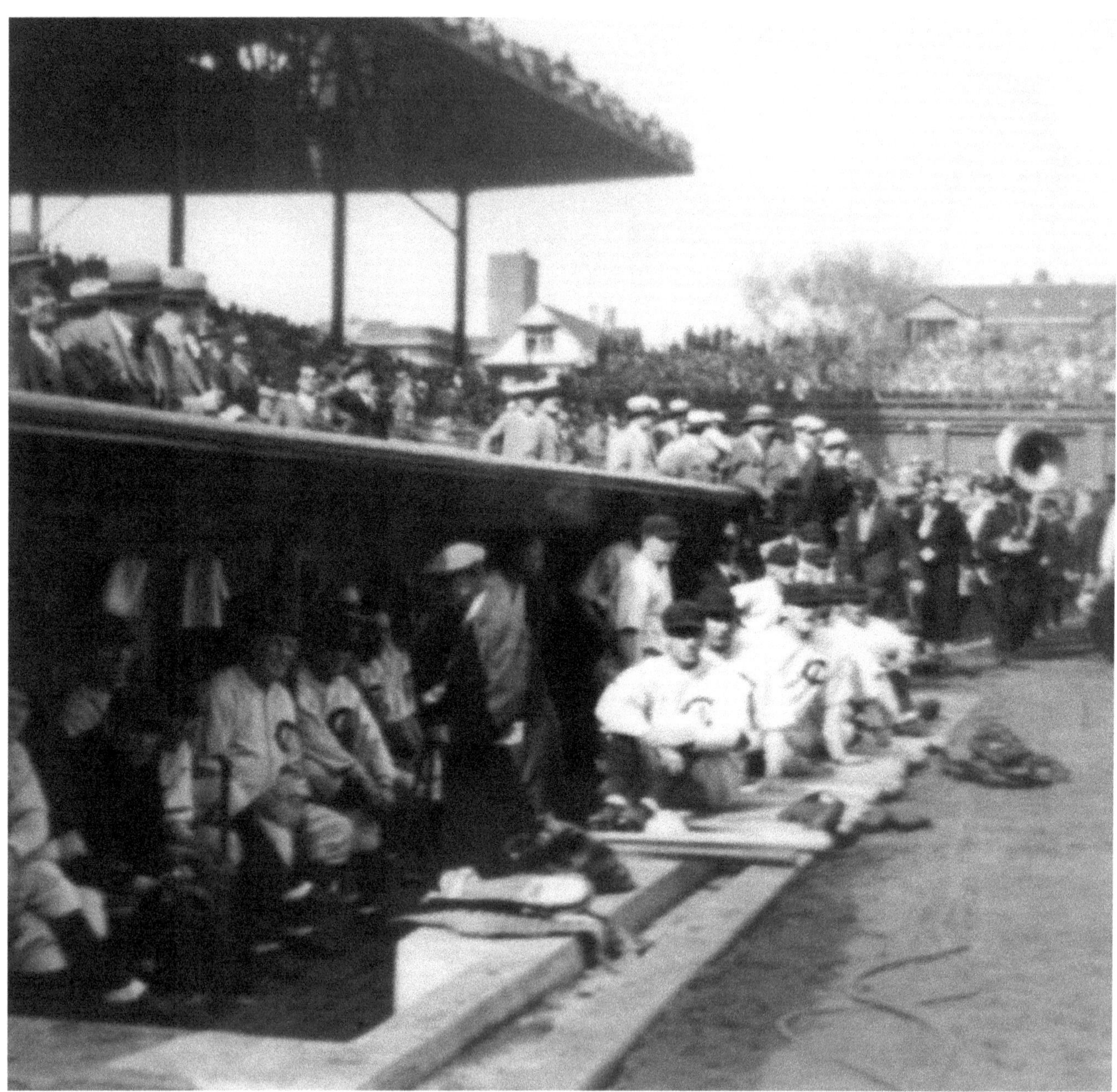

Chicago Cubs players watch from their Wrigley Field dugout during an early game in the World Series against the Philadelphia Athletics in October 1929. The Cubs lost both Game 1 and Game 2 on their home field. Although the Cubs would win Game 3 at Philadelphia's Shibe Park, the Athletics would ultimately reign supreme, overcoming a record 8-run deficit to win Game 4 and then Game 5 to become World Series champions.

Hard Times and Postwar Prosperity (1930–1965)

Many older Chicagoans associate the first chapter of the Great Depression with the Cubs' World Series loss on October 14, 1929. But folks of the Lake Michigan region at large could rightly say the grim story of the Great Depression actually began October 22, 1929, the day the first railroad car ferry sank.

The SS *Milwaukee* set sail from its namesake city to Grand Haven, Michigan, with a load of 25 freight cars. Out on the water the boat hit northeast gales blowing at 37 M.P.H. Pitching and rolling amid monstrous waves, the *Milwaukee* turned back toward home, but it was too late: she took on too much water and sank. All 52 men on board perished. An ominous foreshadowing of what was to come, the loss of the SS *Milwaukee* came just days before the stock market crash. As the rest of the nation sank into the Depression's early years, so too did the region around Lake Michigan. By 1932, railroad freight revenues were barely half of what they had been in 1930, forcing some railroads into receivership and others into bankruptcy. Whereas 15 different car ferry routes crossed the Great Lake before the Great Depression, so many boats were laid off or taken out of service during that decade that by the 1940s only three railroads offered ferry service—and only on seven routes. The people of the coastal cities and towns struggled to keep their industries and themselves alive.

The times weren't wholly without hope, however. The nation's new president, Franklin Delano Roosevelt, promised Americans a new deal. Among the early New Deal government programs was the creation of the Civilian Conservation Corps, which provided thousands of men across the nation with jobs related to conserving the nation's natural resources. In the Lake Michigan region, these jobs included reforesting the lands cleared of trees in the nineteenth century to build the region's towns, cities, and railroads. When America entered World War II, unemployment was still running at depression-era levels, but the region was ready, gearing up its once-thriving farms, orchards, and automobile and manufacturing plants for the war effort. Women around the region went to work, reshaping the workforce and with it, society.

The return to normalcy in the years after the war brought renewed prosperity and progress—a way of life that had defined the region around Lake Michigan since the Civil War, and would continue to do so, anchored by the constancy of the glacial footprint at its center, for decades to come.

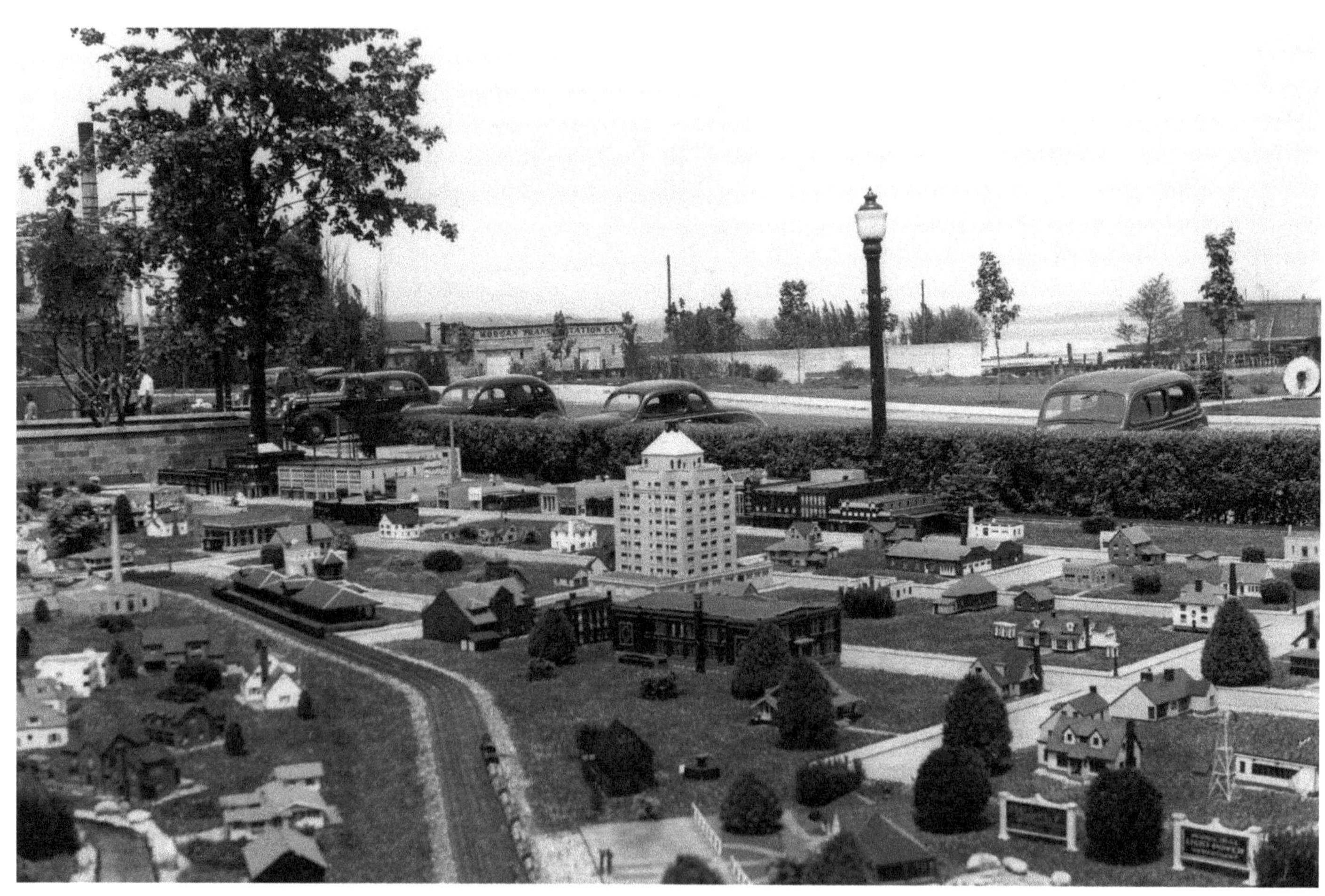

Sometime after 1930 in Traverse City, Michigan, in what would later become Clinch Park Zoo, artisans created a city in miniature, replete with streets, a river, and a miniature railroad.

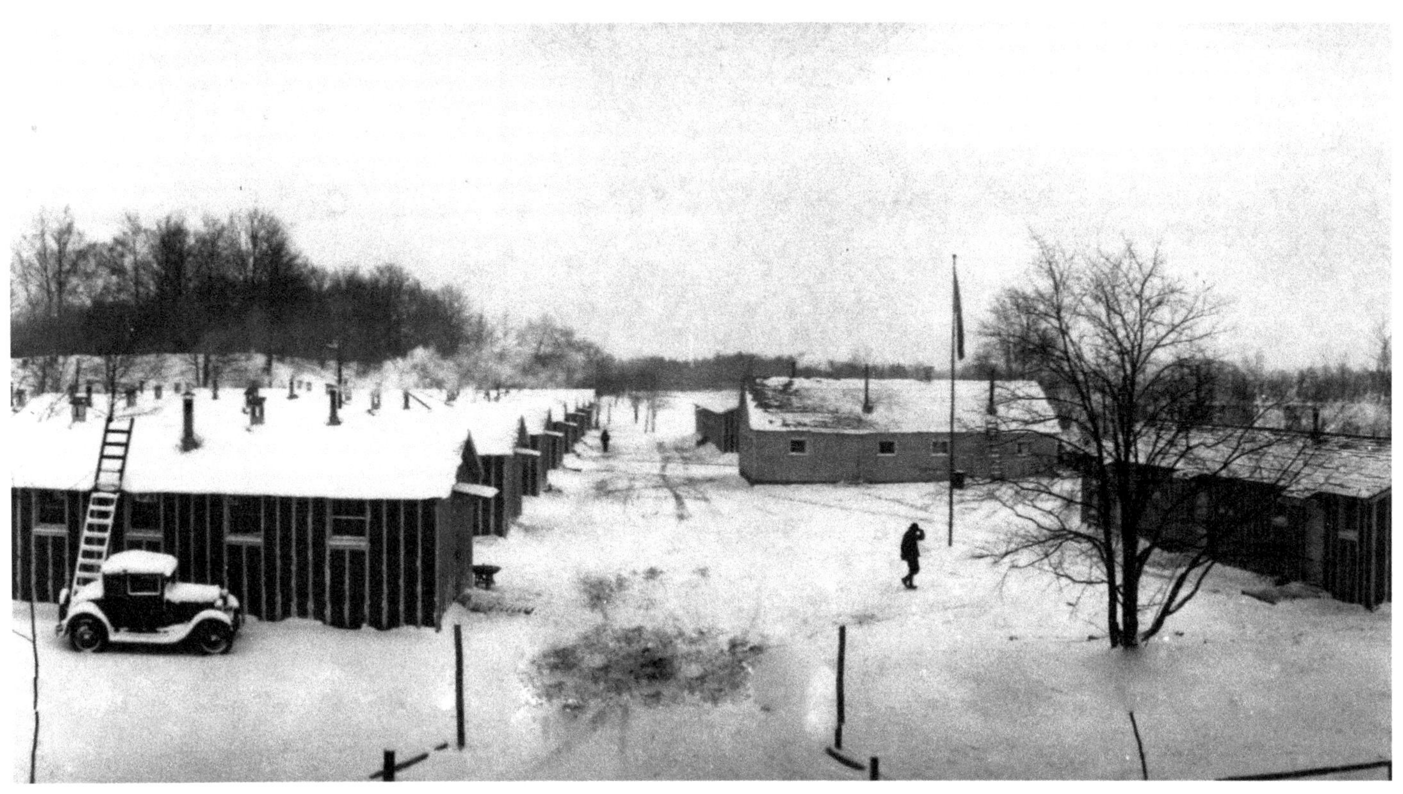

With Michigan's once-vast forests stripped to the stumps and the nation mired in the Great Depression, it was inevitable that President Franklin Delano Roosevelt's "tree army" program, the Civilian Conservation Corps, would arrive in Michigan. Shown here is the 1666th company's Pere Marquette Forest base, CCC Camp Ludington, in 1934. Today buildings and roads from the camp are still in evidence on the site, which is now part of Ludington State Park.

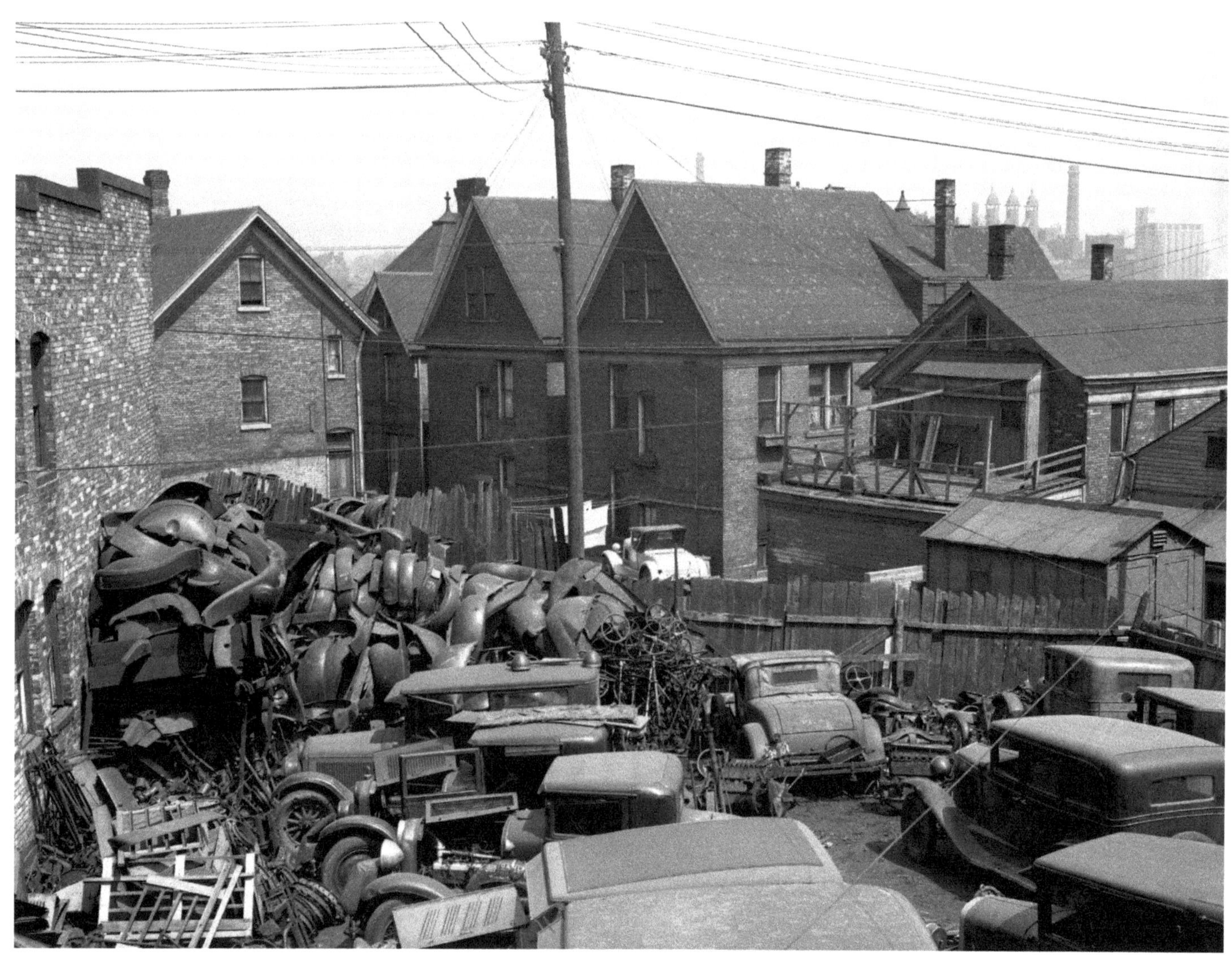

A Milwaukee junkyard, pictured here in 1936, is squeezed in among the city's brick tenements.

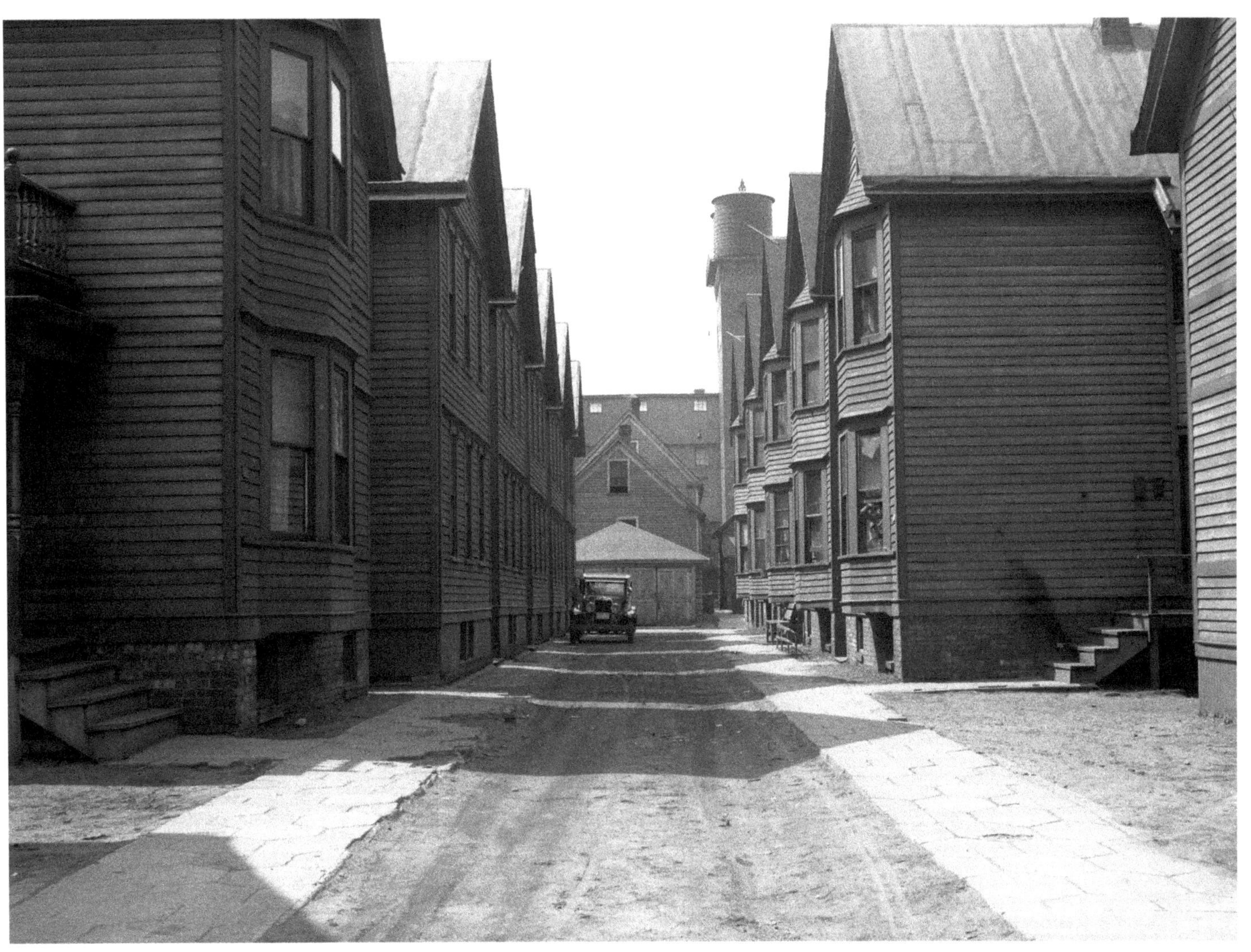

A 1936 photograph taken from the living quarters at 730 West Winnebago Street in Milwaukee looks out over an unpaved alley.

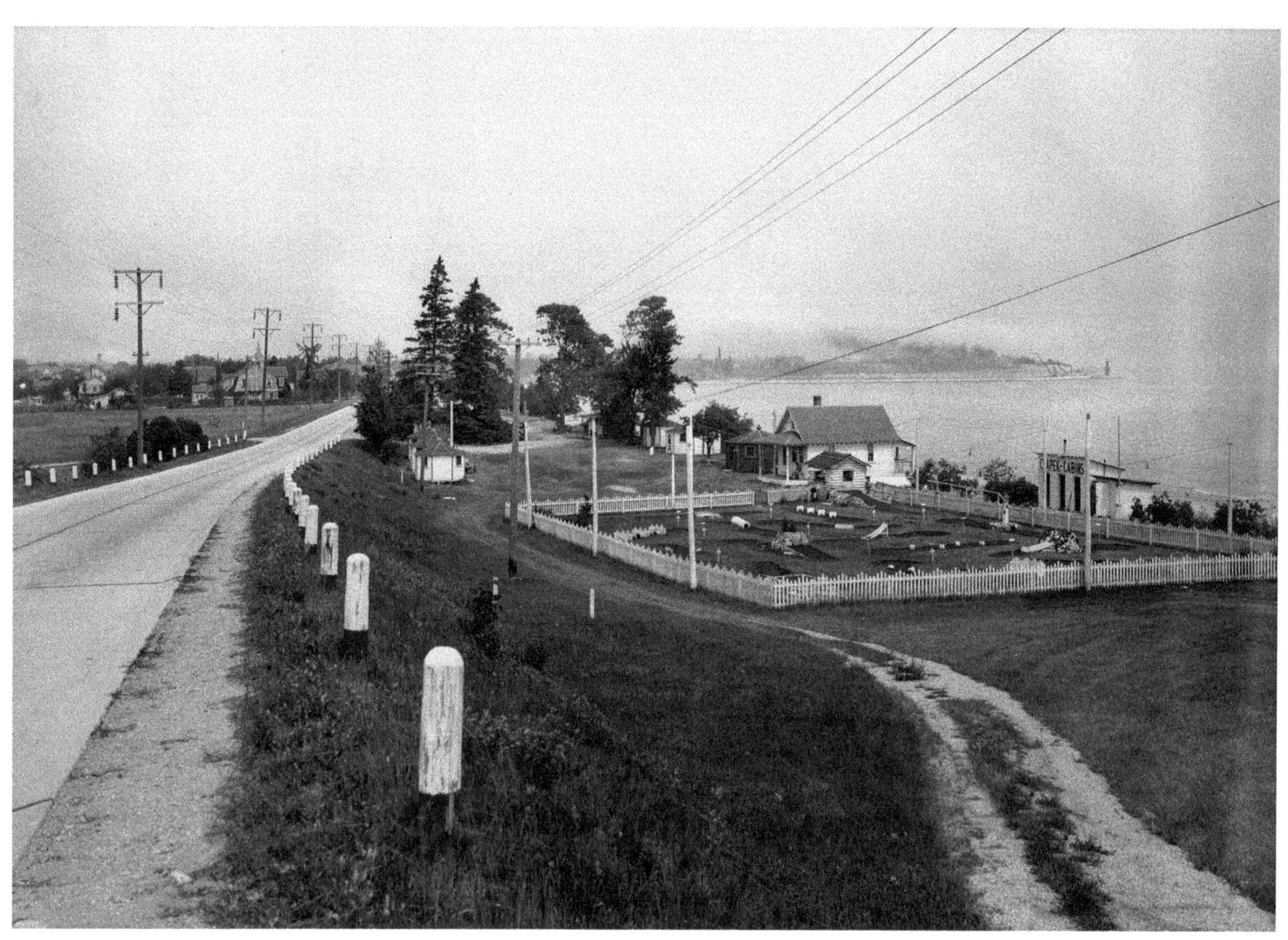

A classic 1936 scene along Crescent Beach, part of the Lake Michigan harbor town of Algoma, Wisconsin: a campsite with cabins and a miniature-golf course—all overlooking the Great Lake.

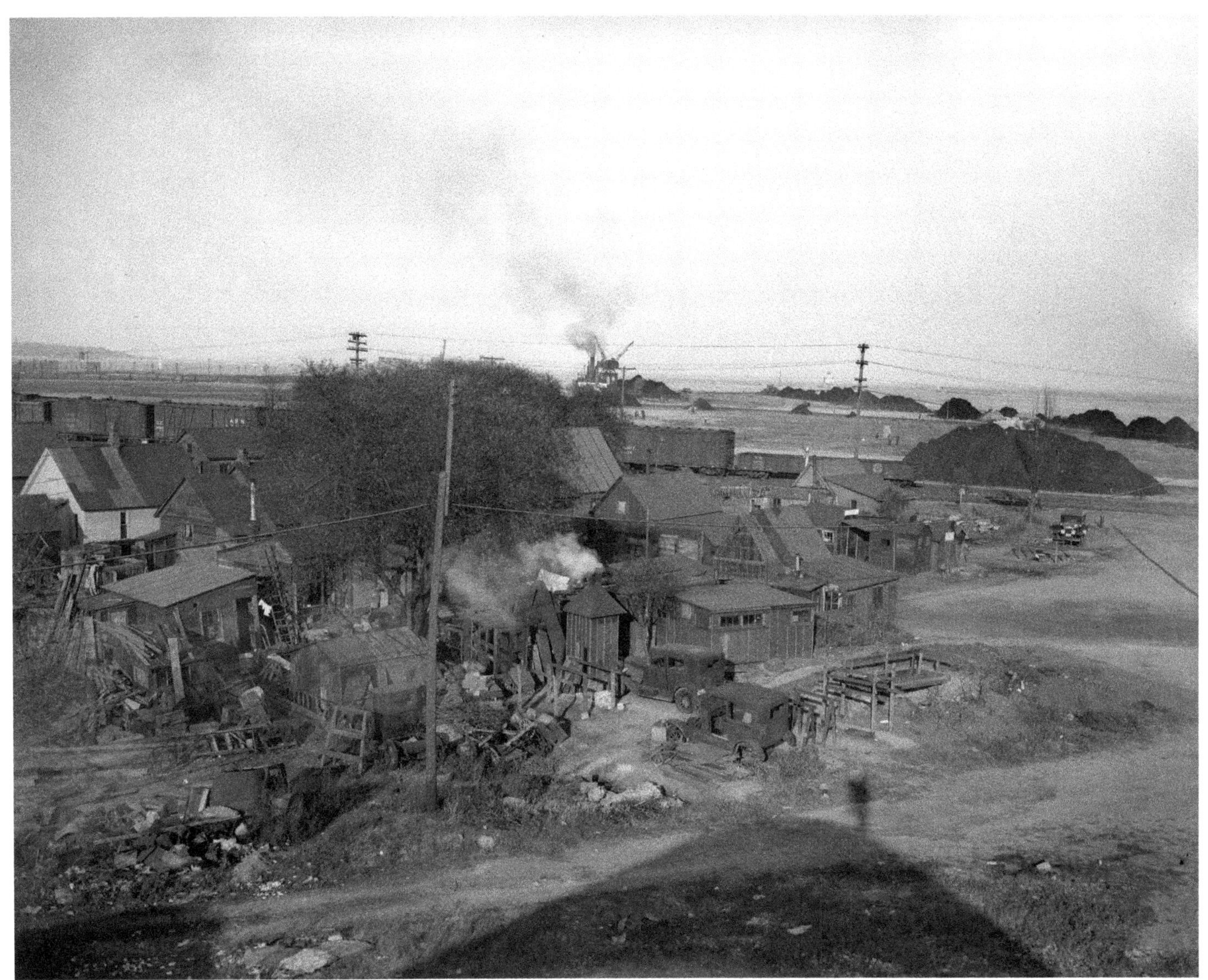

Originally a marshy island between Milwaukee's Milwaukee and Kinnickinnic rivers settled mostly by Polish and German immigrants, Jones Island was eventually filled in to accommodate the railroad. Shortly after this photograph was taken in 1938, the settlers—considered squatters by the city of Milwaukee—were evicted and their fishing village torn down.

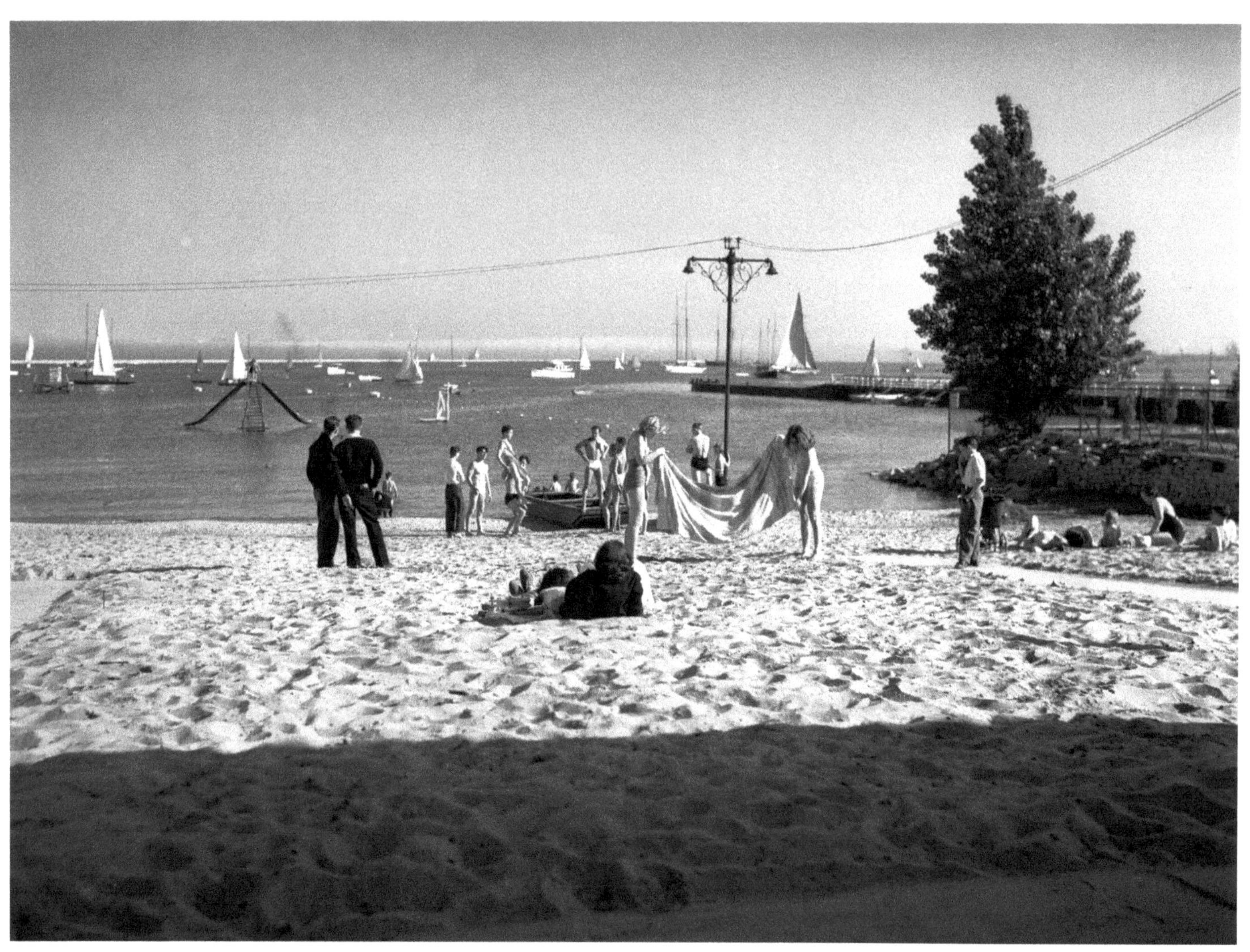

With the waters of Lake Michigan and the billowing sails of pleasure cruisers in the background, and the Milwaukee Yacht Club nearby, families enjoy a leisurely afternoon in 1939 Milwaukee.

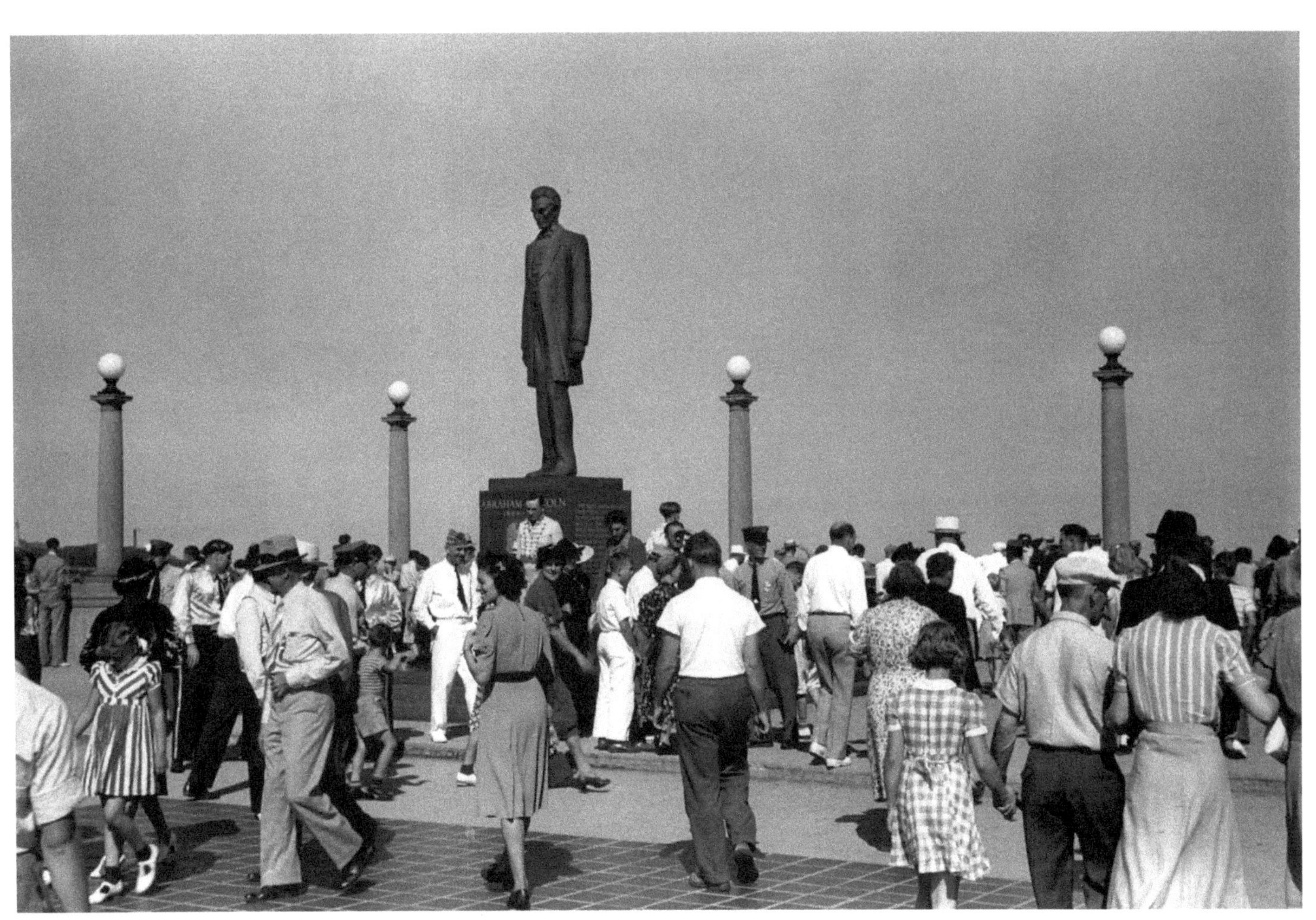

Crowds mingle in an unnamed Milwaukee park during a Labor Day celebration in 1939.

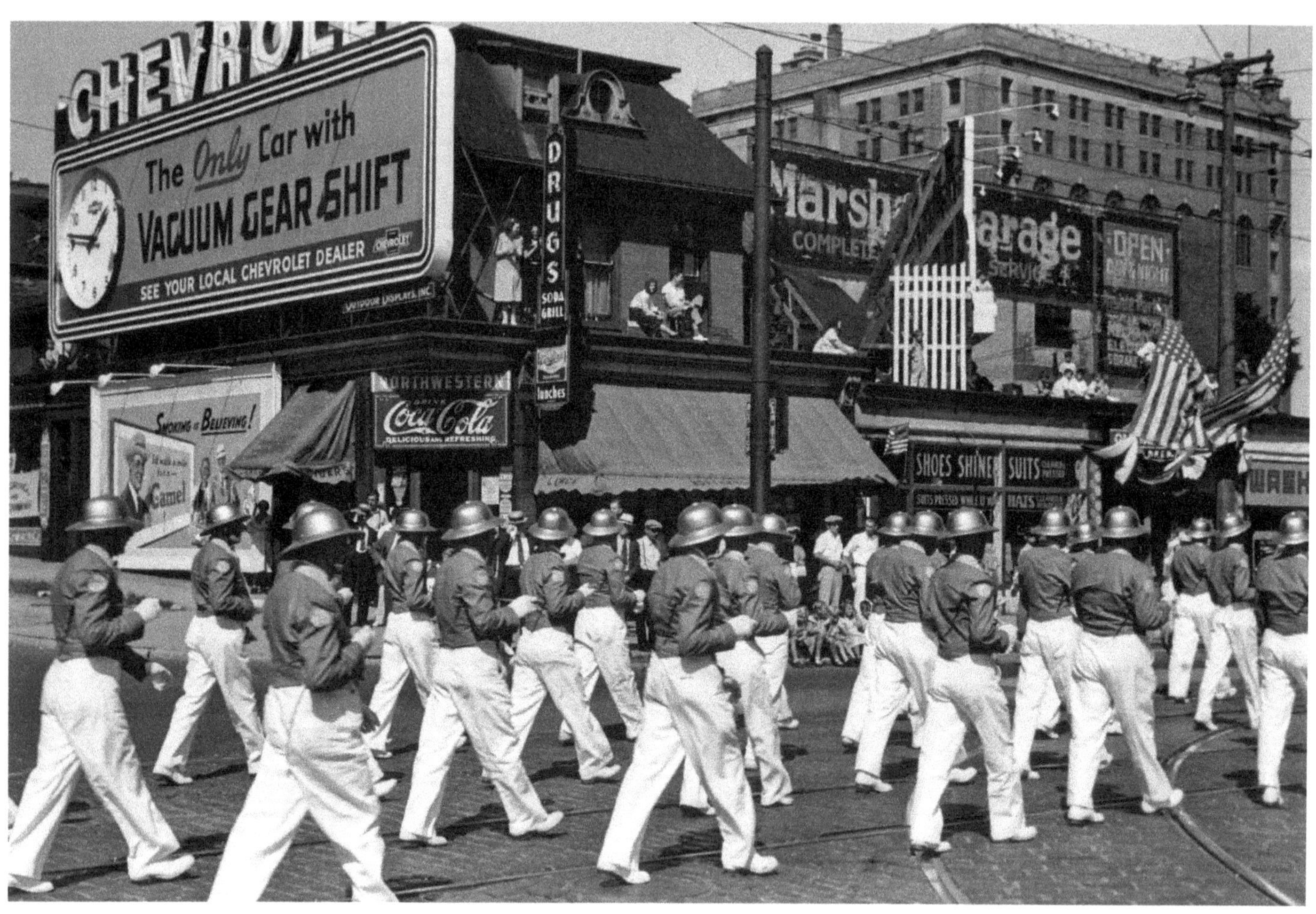

A parade makes its way down Milwaukee streets during the 1939 Letter Carriers Convention. The National Association of Letter Carriers, the union of city-delivery carriers working for the United States Postal Service, was founded in 1889 by a group of 60 letter carriers representing 18 states during a gathering in the city's Schaefer's Saloon.

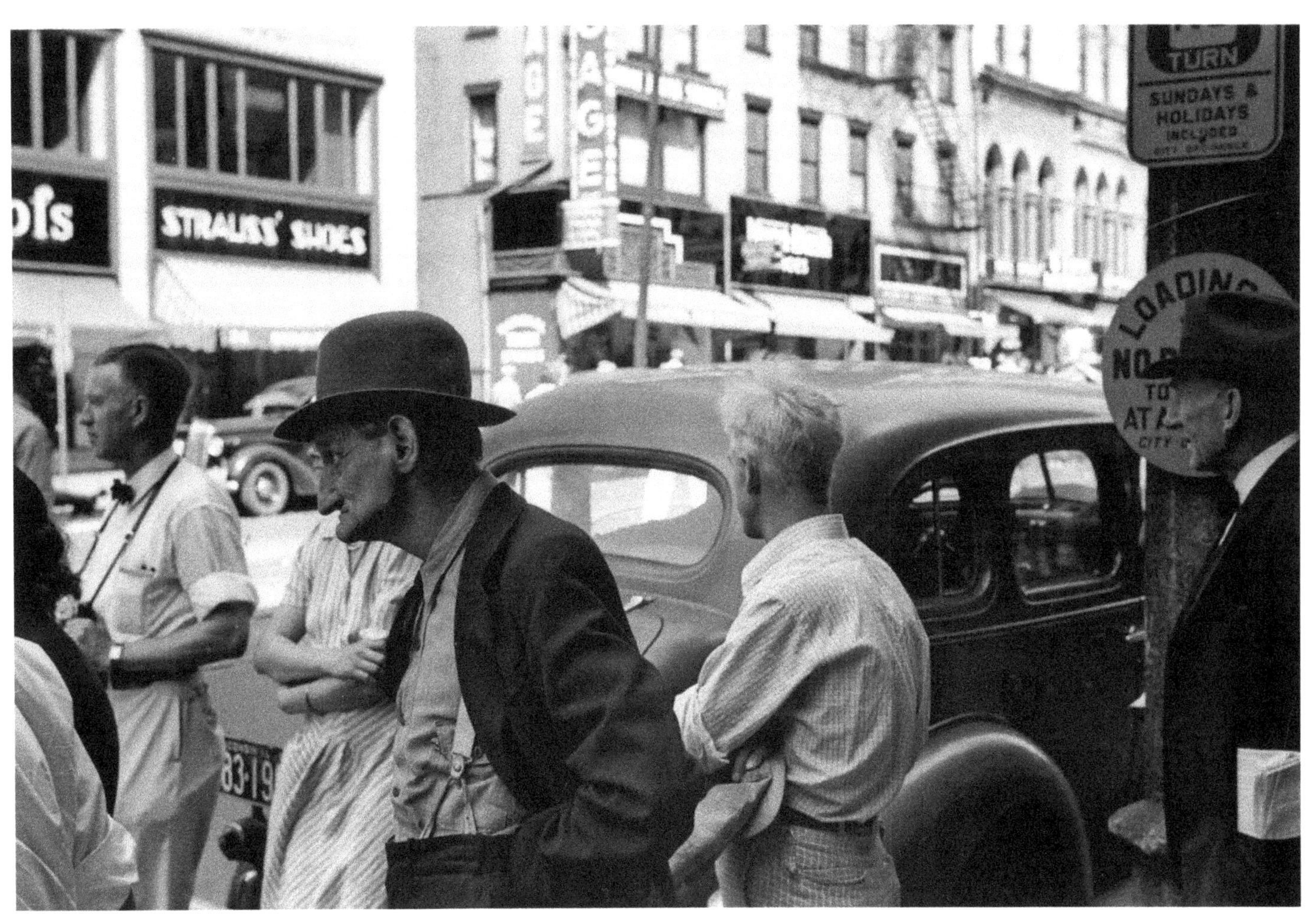

Spectators watch the parade during the 1939 Letter Carriers Convention in Milwaukee.

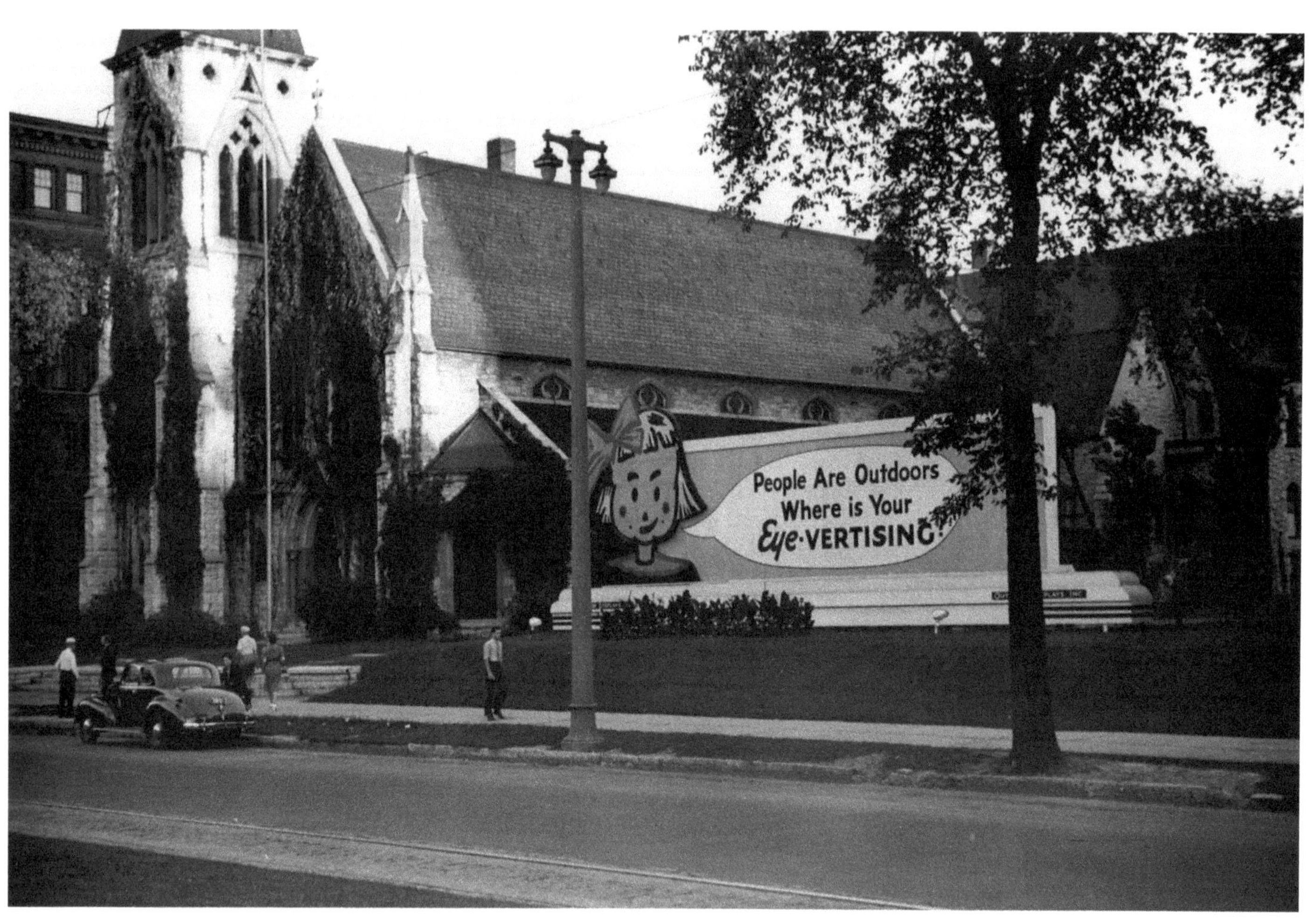

Giving rise to the question of anything being sacred, a monstrous signboard promoting billboard advertising looms beside a Milwaukee church.

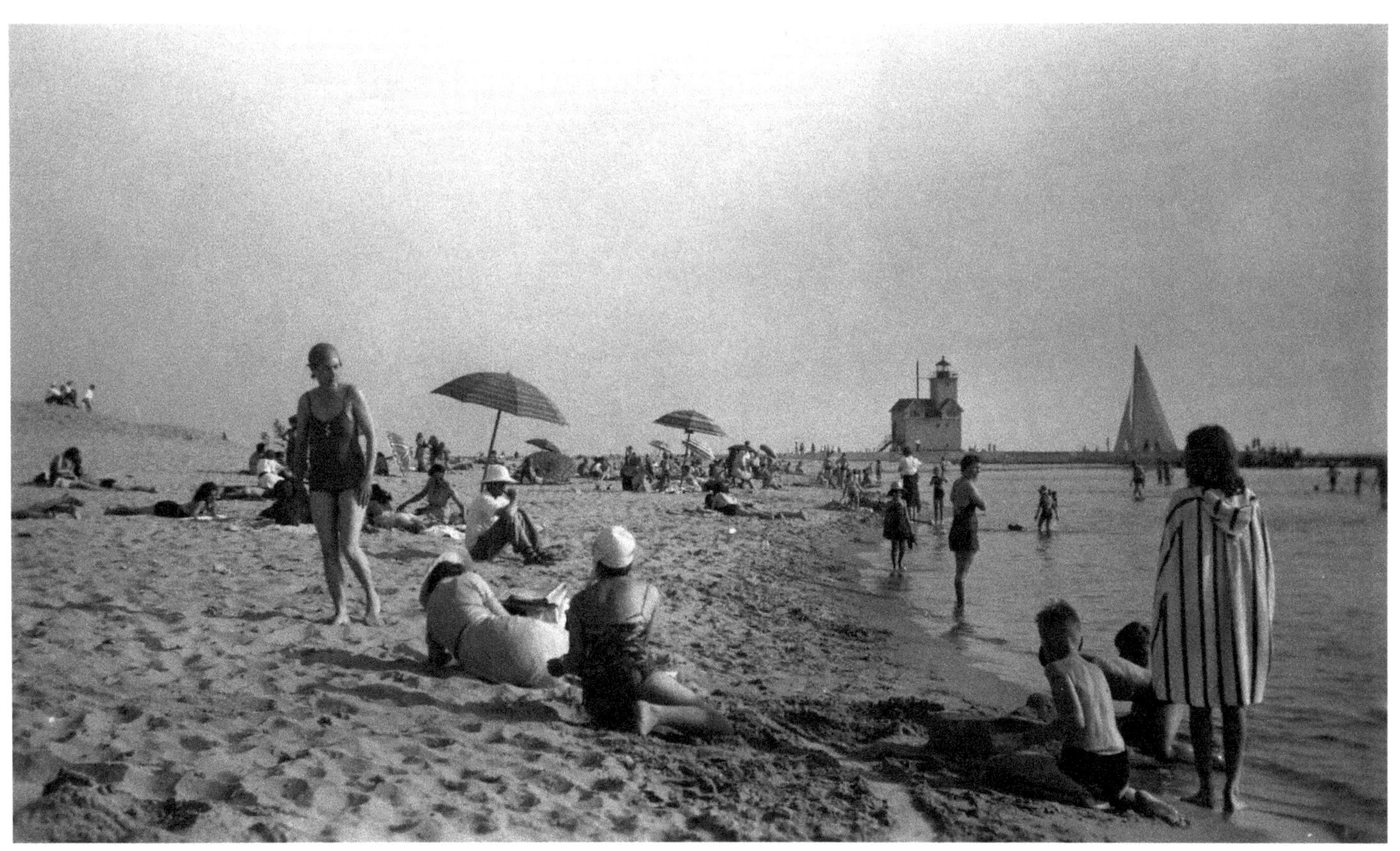

Beachgoers frolic along the Lake Michigan shore at Holland, Michigan. In the background is "Big Red." The third incarnation since 1872 of the original lighthouse built in Holland, Big Red earned its name in 1956 when the Coast Guard painted the formerly pale-yellow structure bright red. This was done to abide by the navigation rule that any structure standing on the right side of a harbor entrance must be red.

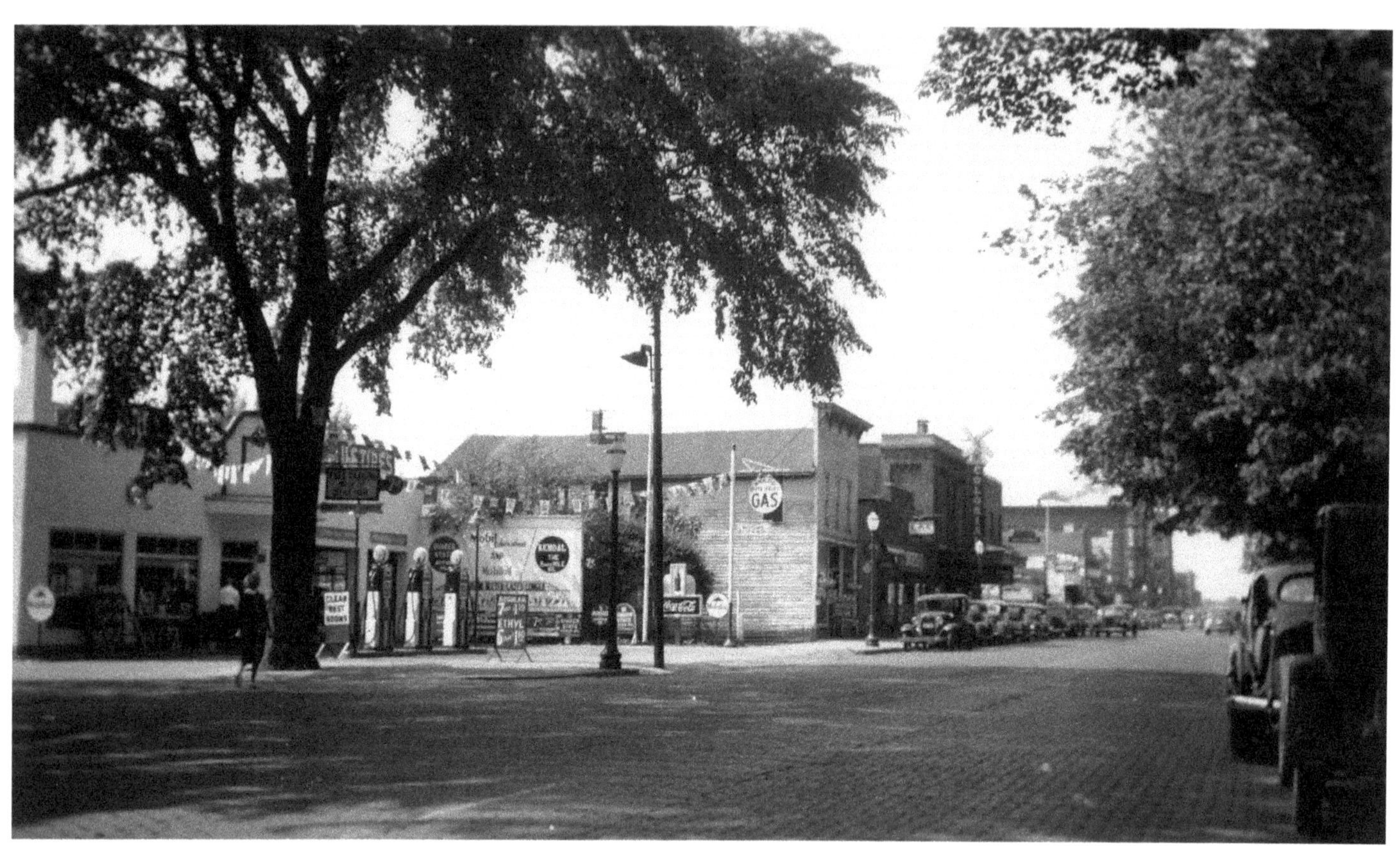

On the streets of Holland, Michigan, in 1940. The town was settled in 1847 by a group of Dutch Calvinist men, women, and children escaping religious oppression in Rotterdam, the Netherlands. Over the next century the group and the immigrants who followed transformed their swampy, forest-choked colony on Lake Michigan—hand-dredging a channel between the big water and Black Lake (later Lake Macatawa), pioneering what would become Hope College, and giving rise to a successful furniture manufacturing industry.

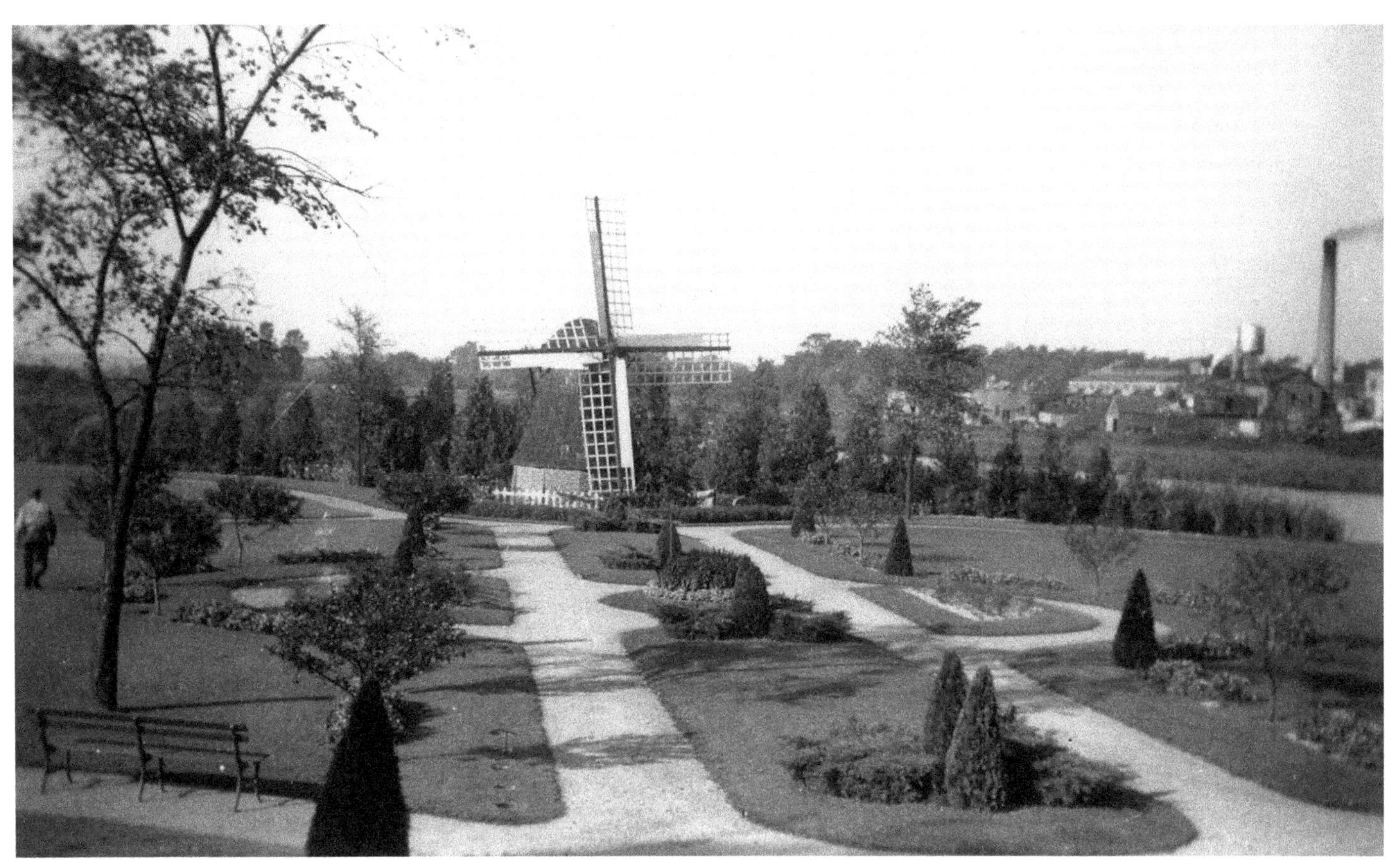

An icon and ode to Holland's Dutch heritage, the historic Dutch windmill, De Zwaan, meaning "graceful bird," perches in 1940 above Windmill Island's park-like setting of gardens, dikes, and canals.

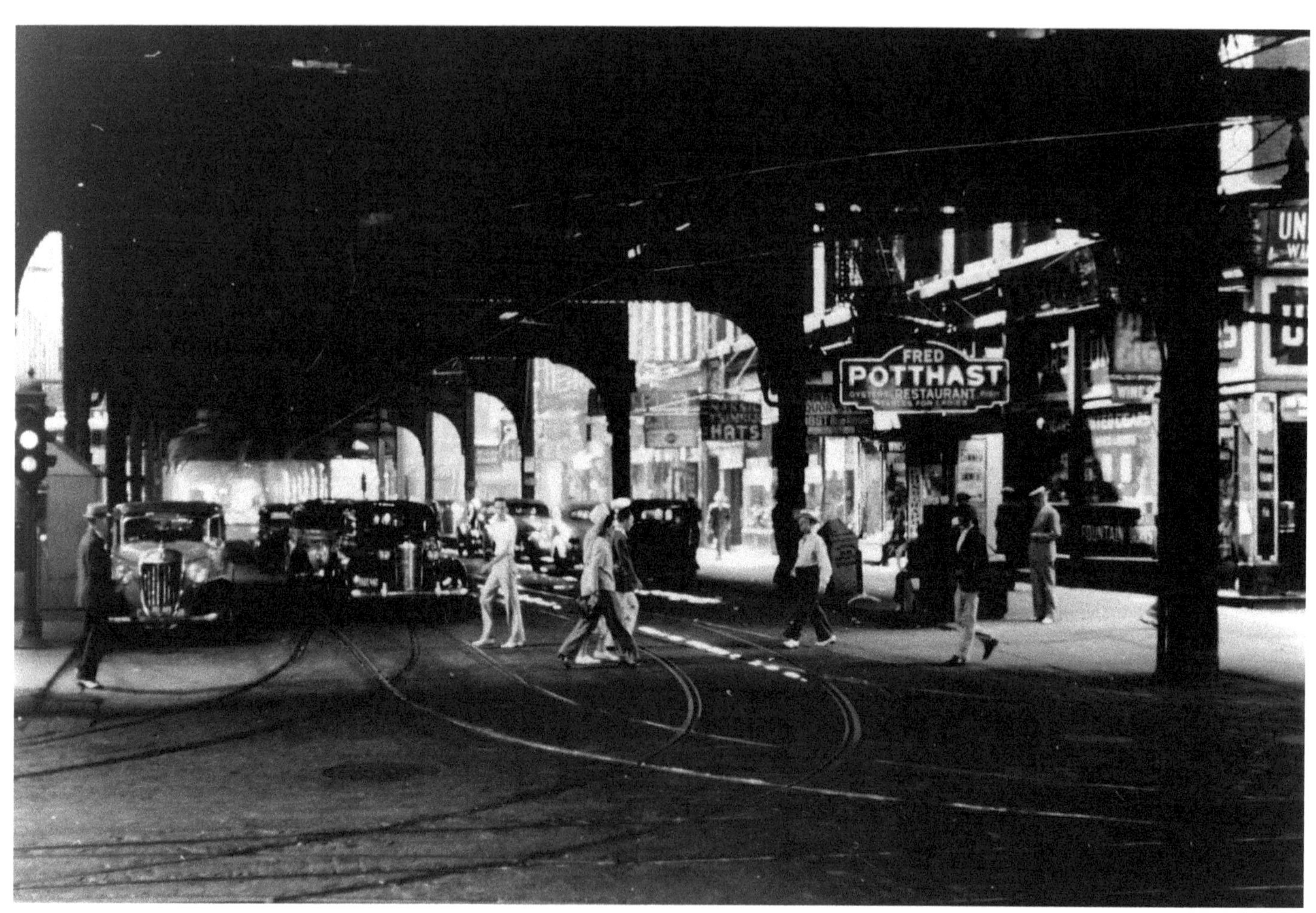

Pedestrians slip under Chicago's elevated tracks on a July day in 1940.

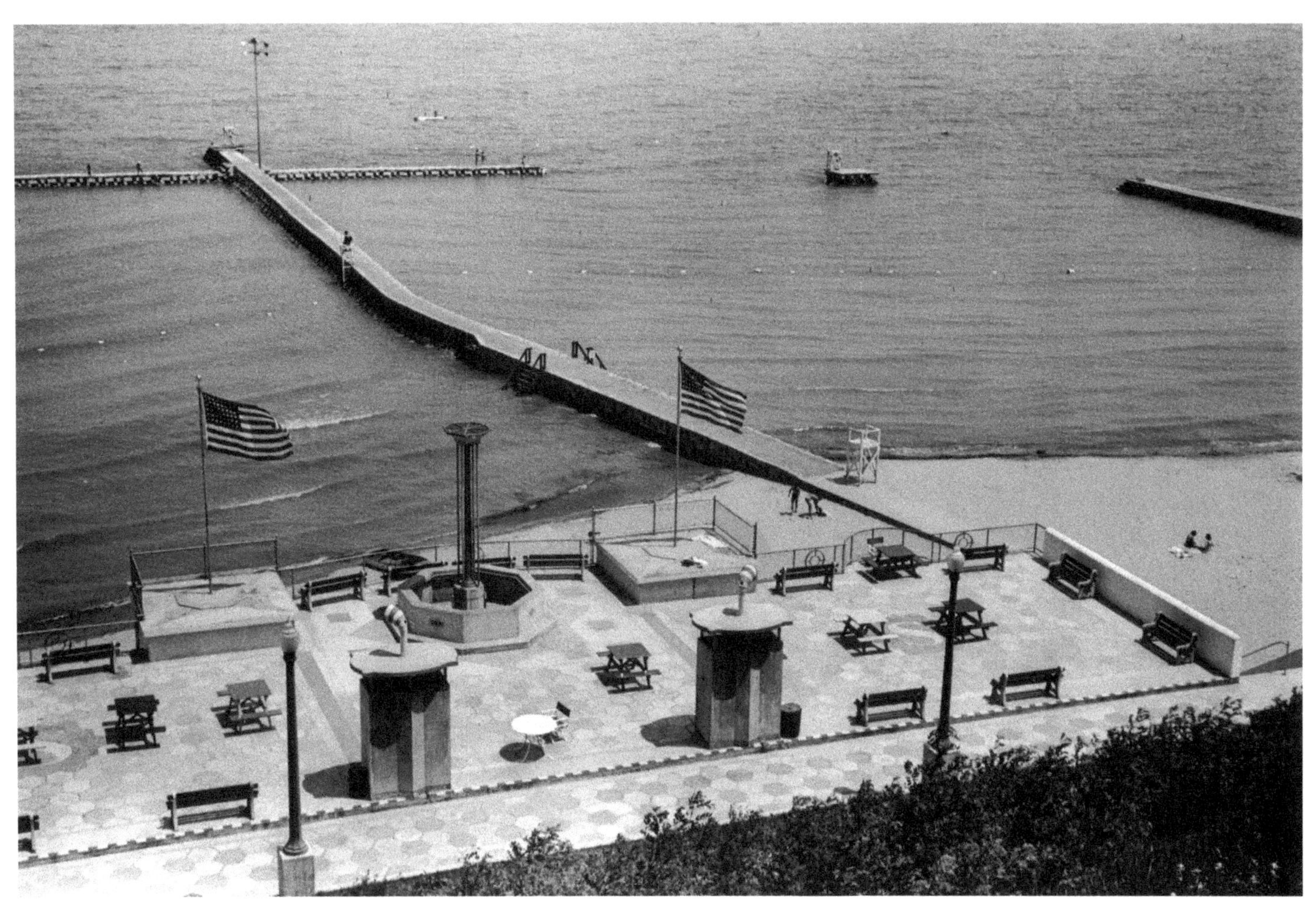

A serene Lake Michigan awaits swimmers at Milwaukee's bathing beach.

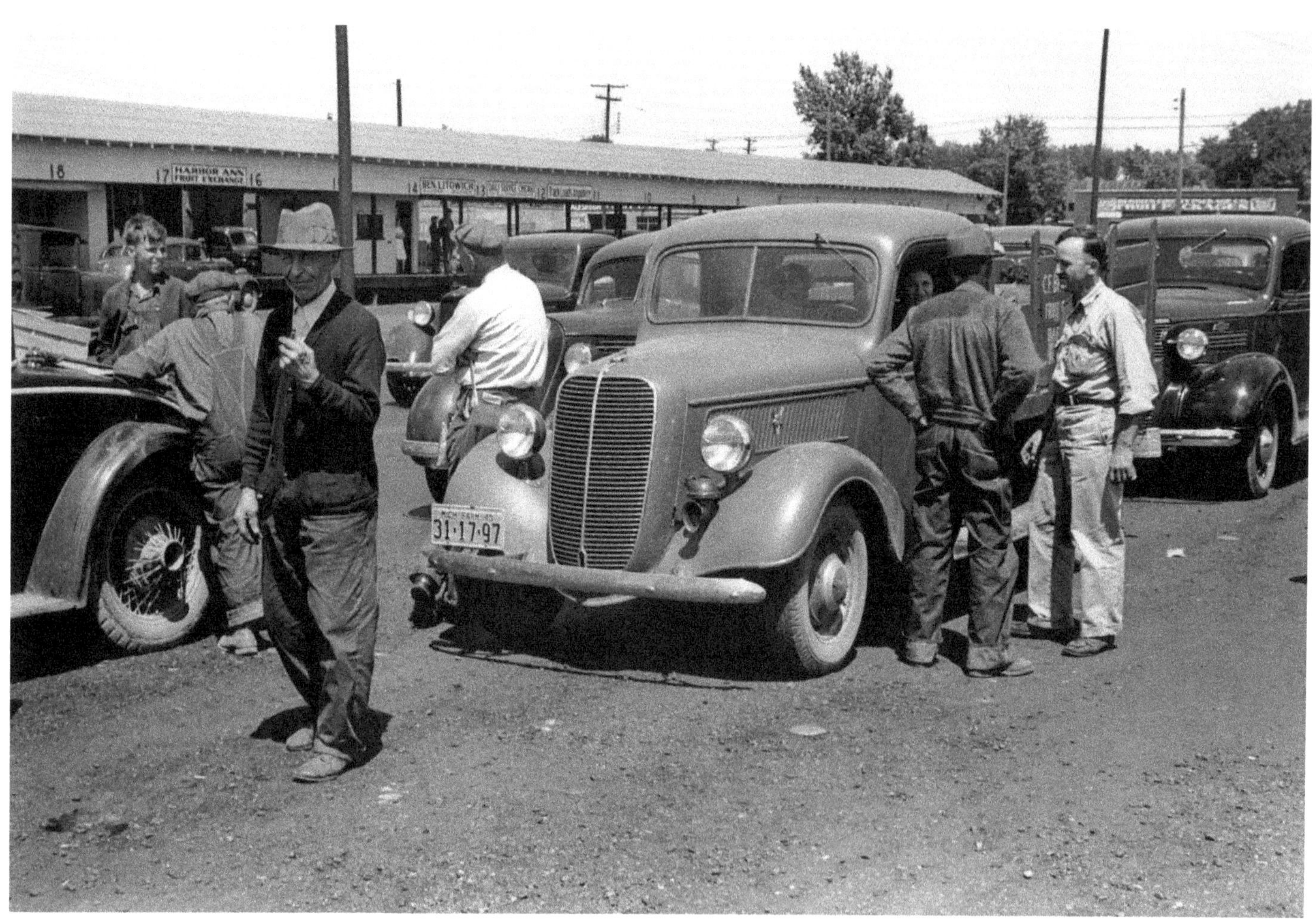

Farmers mingle outside Michigan's Benton Harbor Fruit Market in 1940. The market originated in 1860, and though it has moved locations several times, it is today one of the largest cash-to-grower wholesale markets in the world.

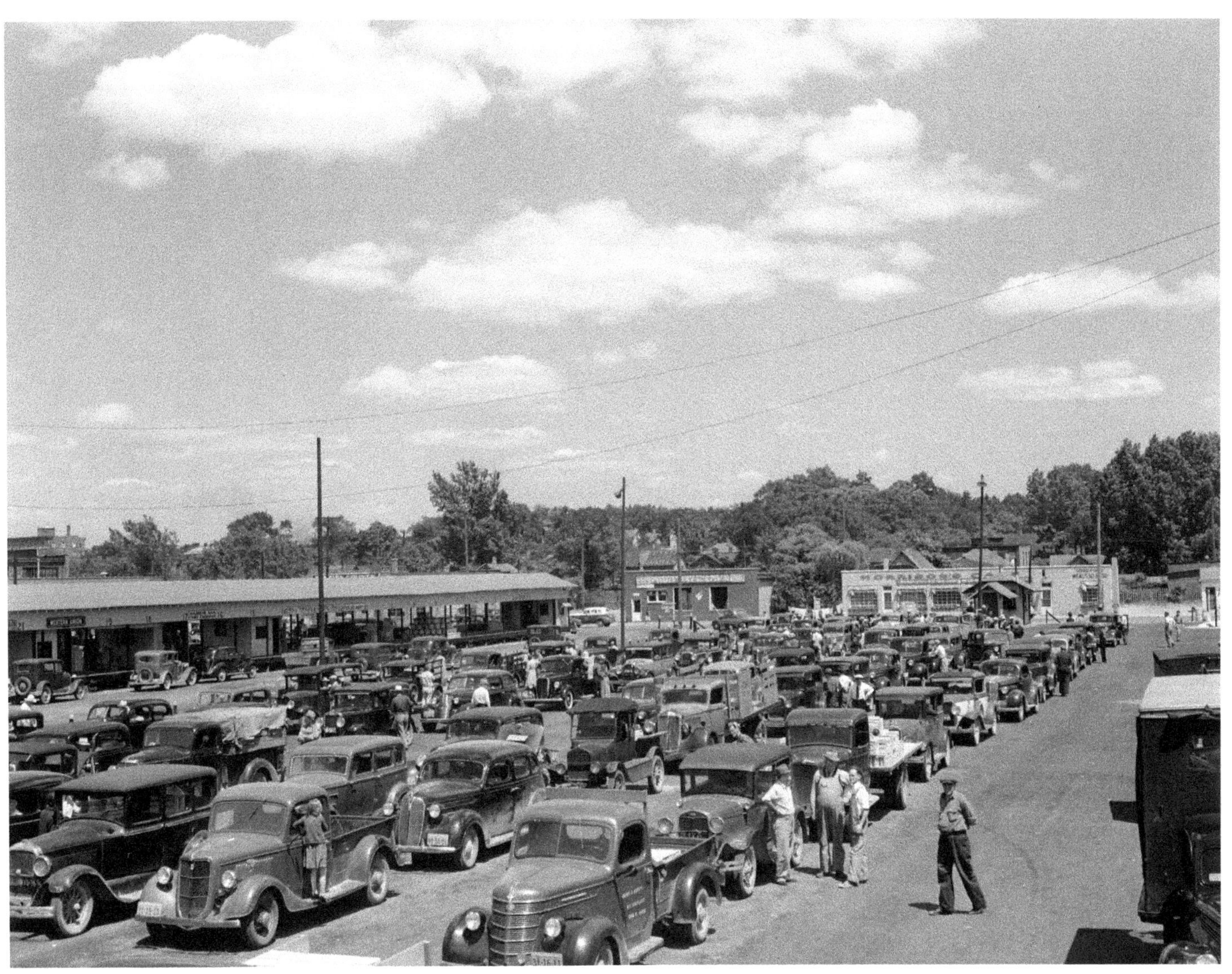

The Benton Harbor Fruit Market worked like this in 1940: growers paid 10 cents to drive their truck of produce through the market. If their produce wasn't sold at the end of the line, the grower would have to enter the gate again.

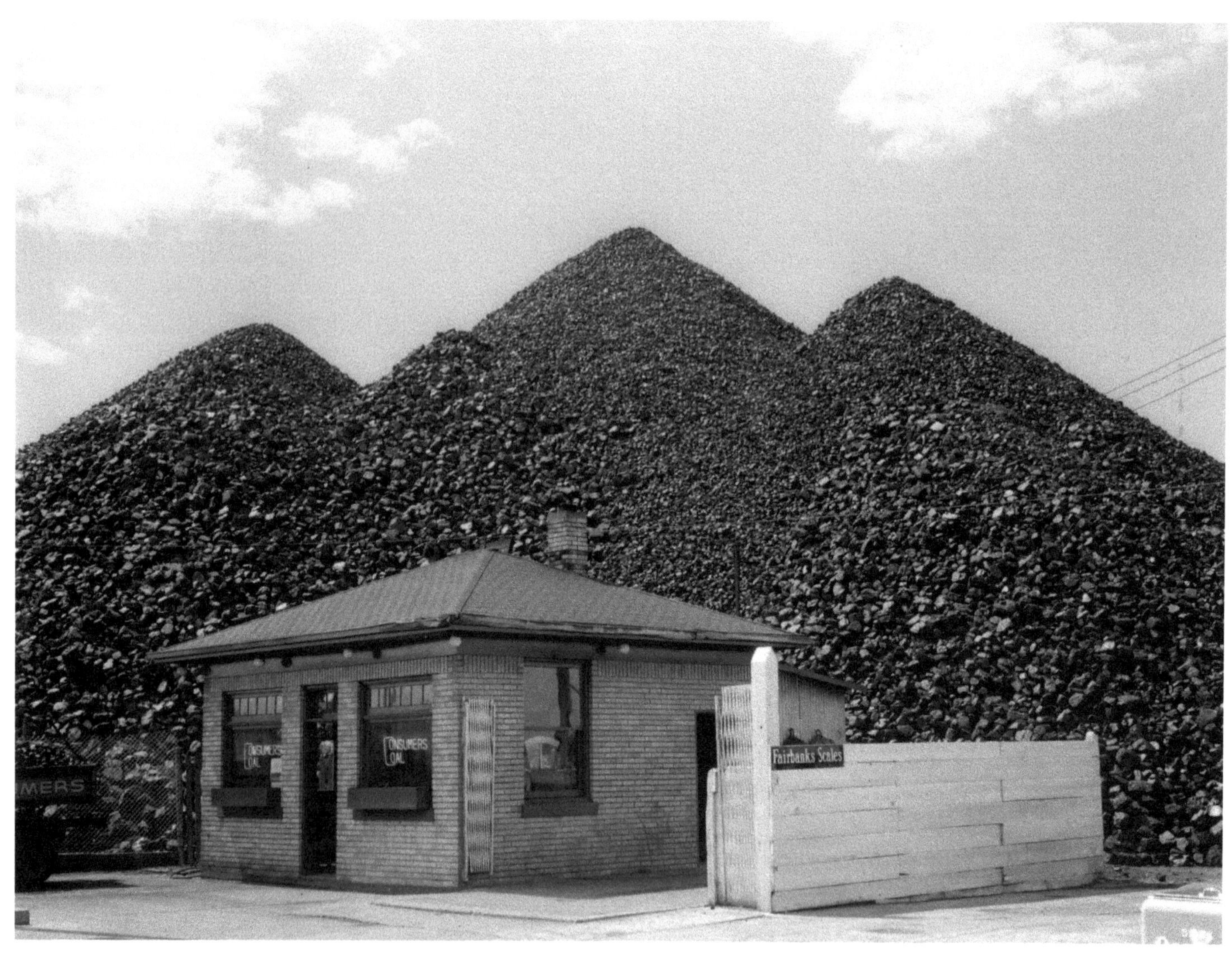

Besides produce, Benton Harbor was home to several coal operations over the last century. Benton Harbor's House of David colony, founded by Benjamin Purnell in 1903, owned and operated coal mines—among its many other businesses. Here, hillocks of coal sparkle under a 1940 July sun.

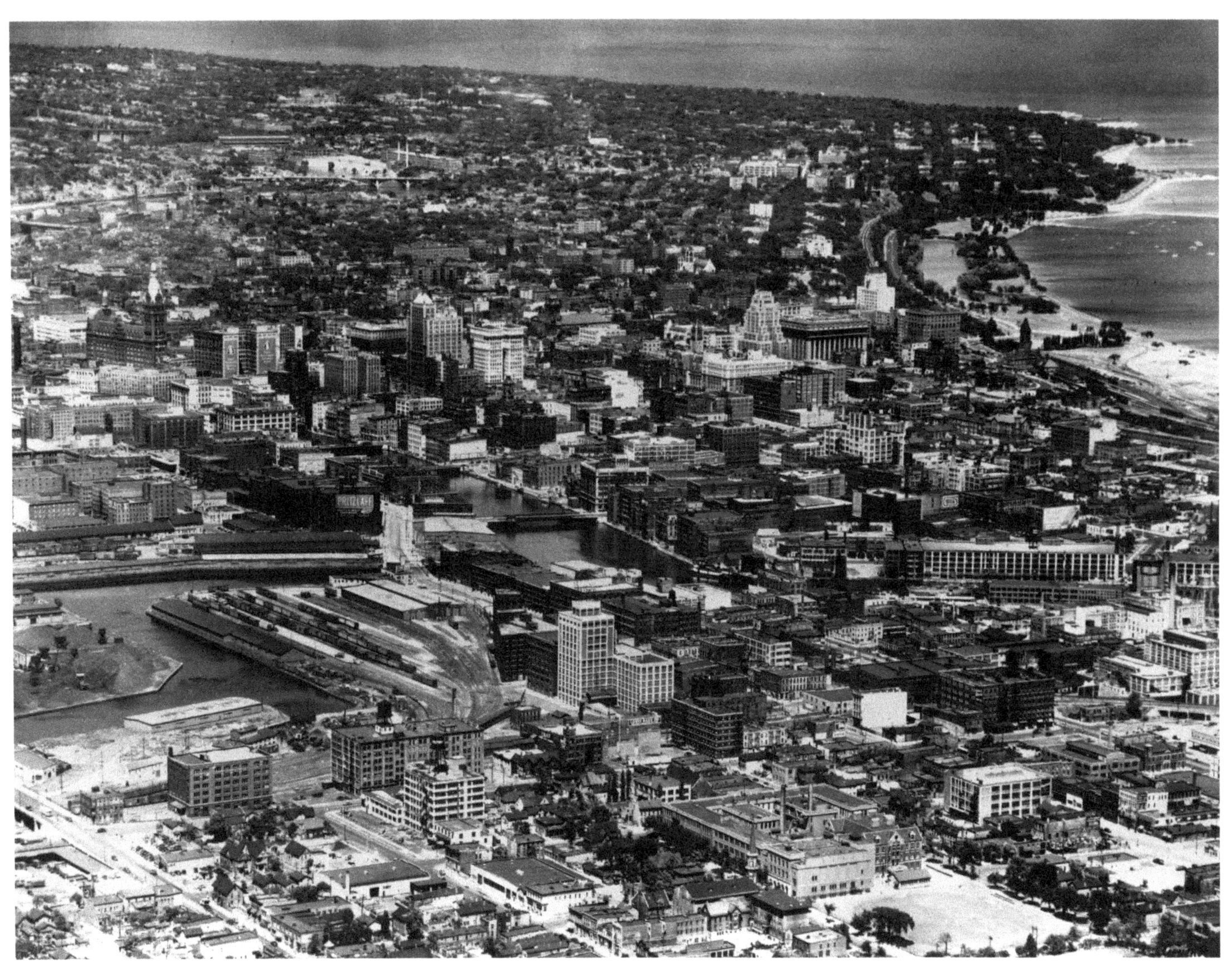

An aerial view of downtown Milwaukee, including the Milwaukee River and Lake Michigan, as the city appeared prior to World War II.

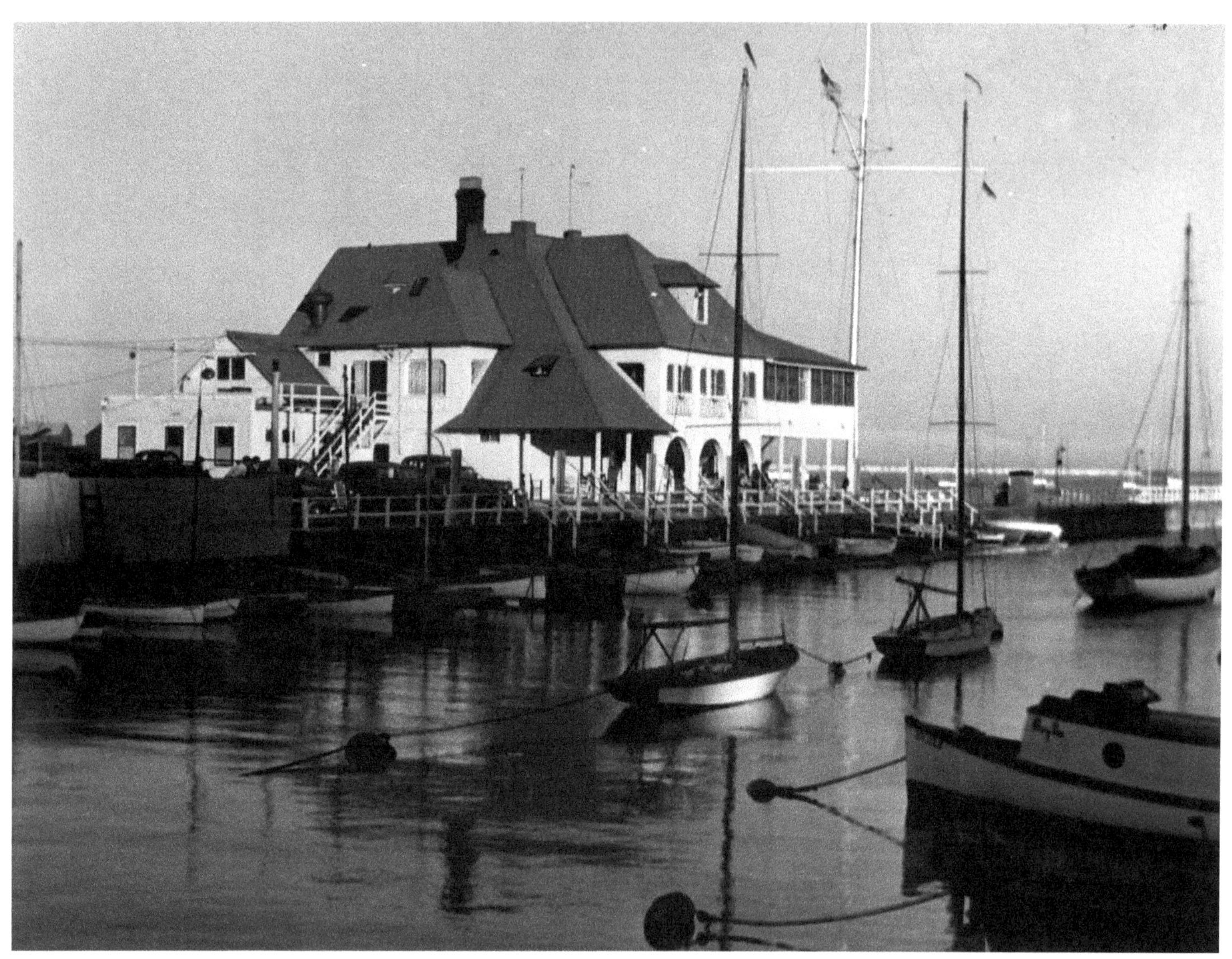

Although the Milwaukee Yacht Club was organized in 1871, its first permanent clubhouse—the elegant two-story structure captured in this pre-1940 photograph—wasn't erected until 1896. It was destroyed by fire during World War II.

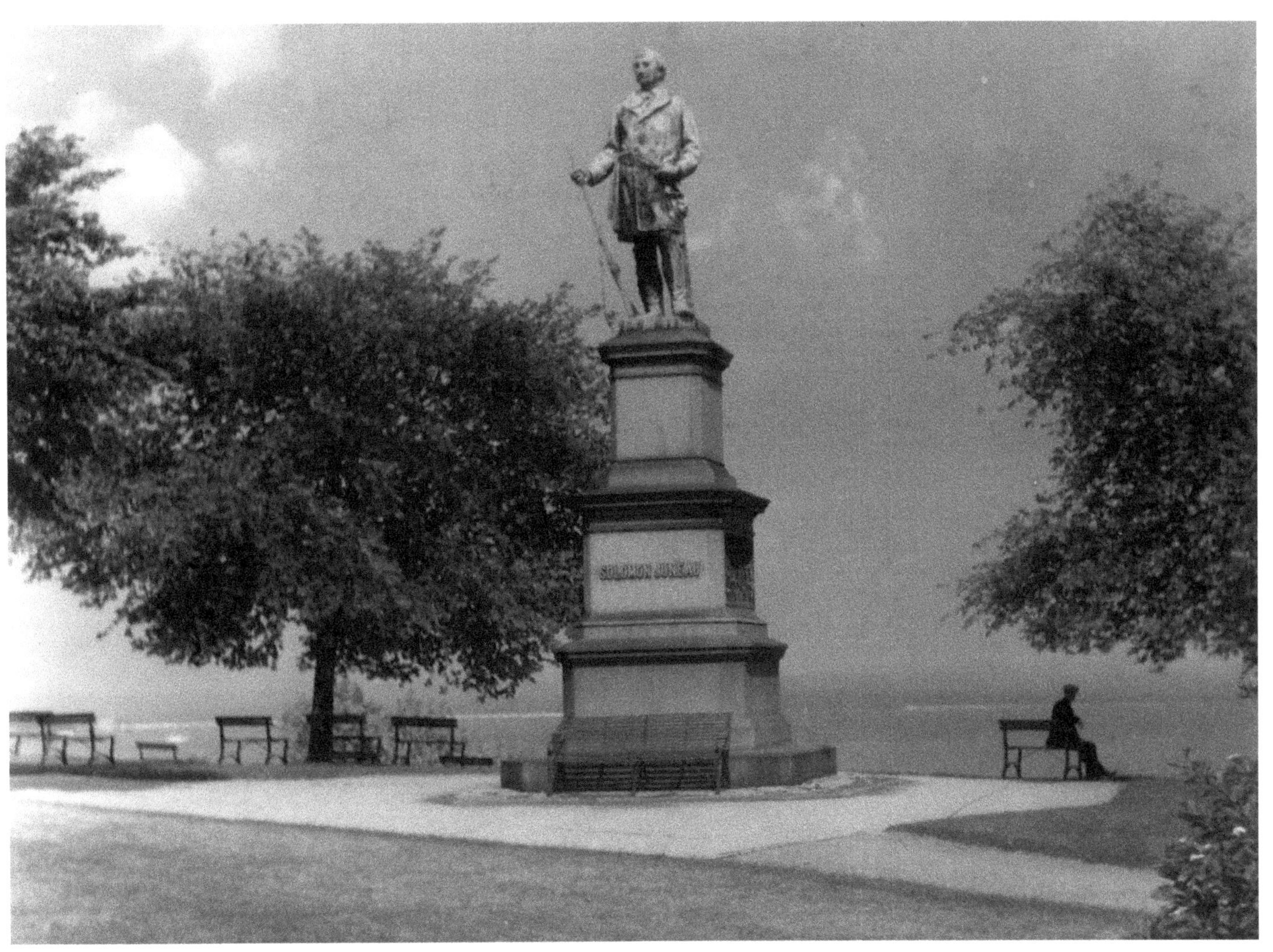

A 1940 view of the monument celebrating Solomon Laurent Juneau, the Quebec-born fur trader who settled Juneautown (now known as East Town) east of the Milwaukee River in 1818 and eventually merged it with land owned by George H. Walker and Byron Kilbourn to incorporate the city of Milwaukee. Juneau was the city's first mayor and first postmaster.

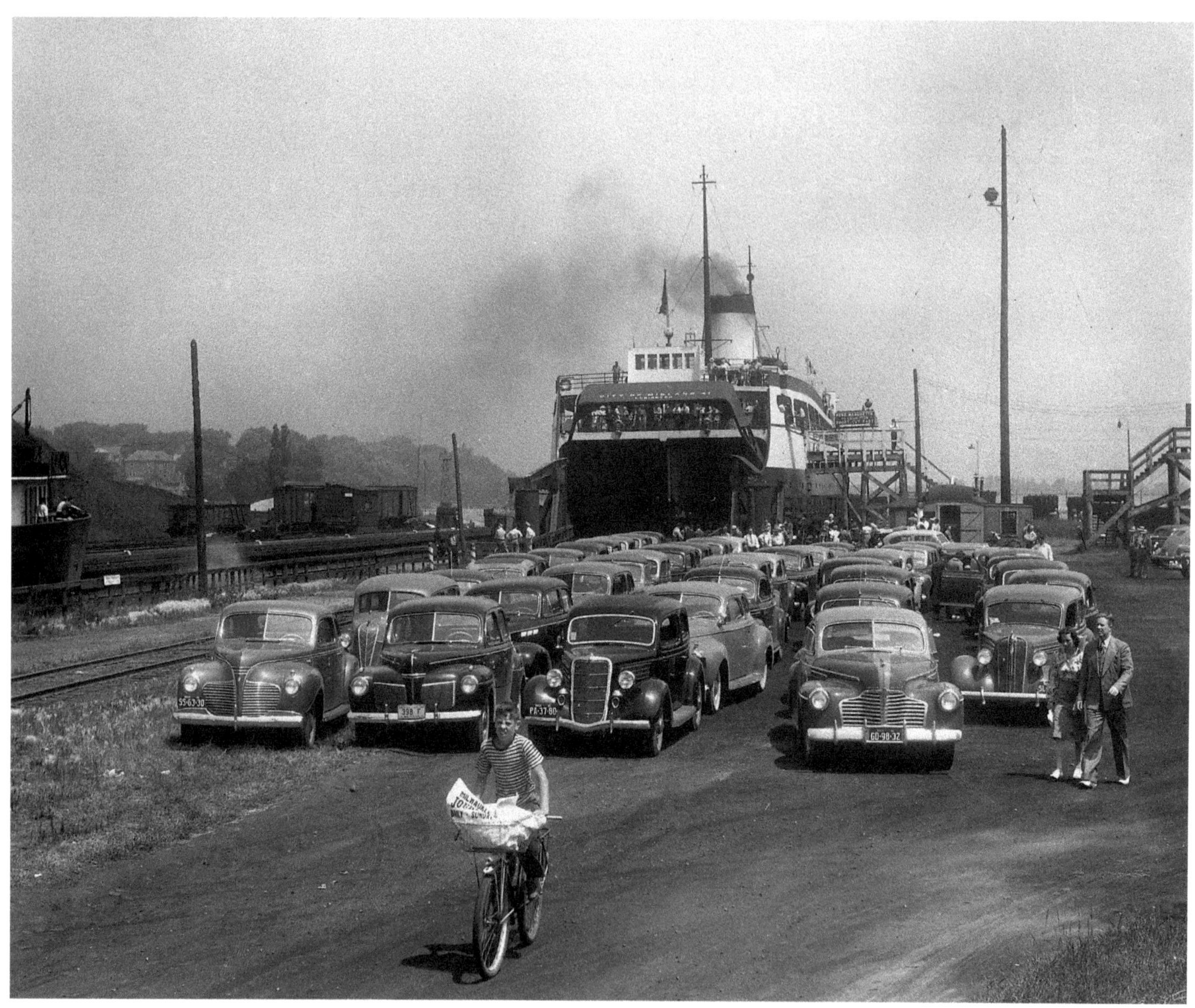

Automobiles wait in line to board a Lake Michigan car ferry at Manitowoc, Wisconsin. Although Lake Michigan car ferries fell out of favor as the Midwest's railroad system crumbled in the 1970s, the SS *Badger*—the largest car ferry ever to sail Lake Michigan and the only coal-fired steamship remaining in operation in North America—still plies the lake, crossing 60 miles of open water in four hours and transporting passengers and cars between Manitowoc and Ludington, Michigan, each summer. Threatened in 2008 by the federal government's Environmental Protection Agency, the future of the historic ferry is now in question.

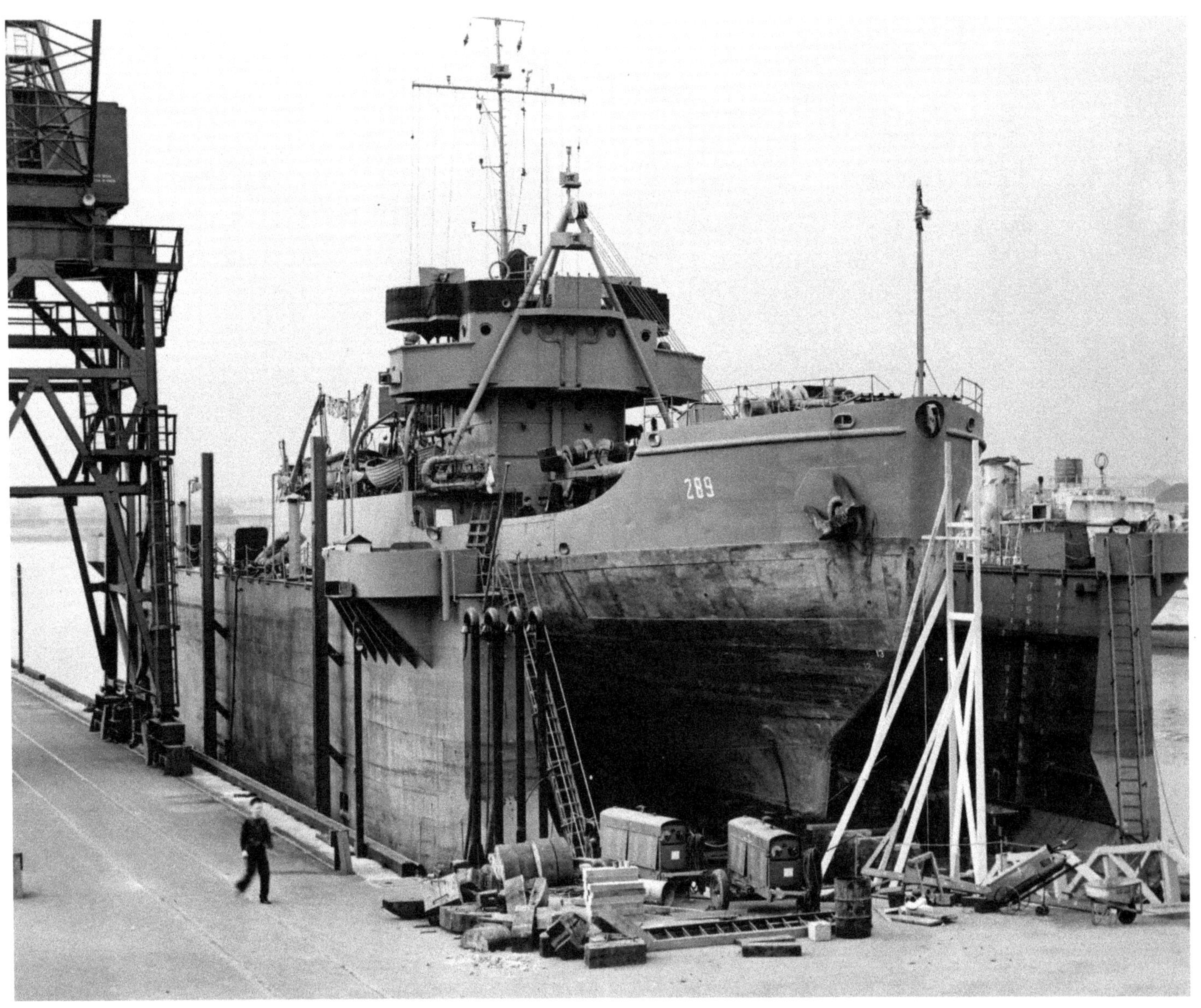

Built in Duluth, Minnesota, by the Zenith Dredge Company in 1942, the 180-foot U.S. Coast Guard Cutter *Woodbine* was stationed in Norfolk, Virginia; San Juan, Puerto Rico; and San Francisco, California, before being deployed to the Pacific Theater of Operations during World War II. Following her war duties, *Woodbine* was stationed in Grand Haven, Michigan, in 1947, where she spent the rest of her career primarily as an ice cutter on Lake Michigan.

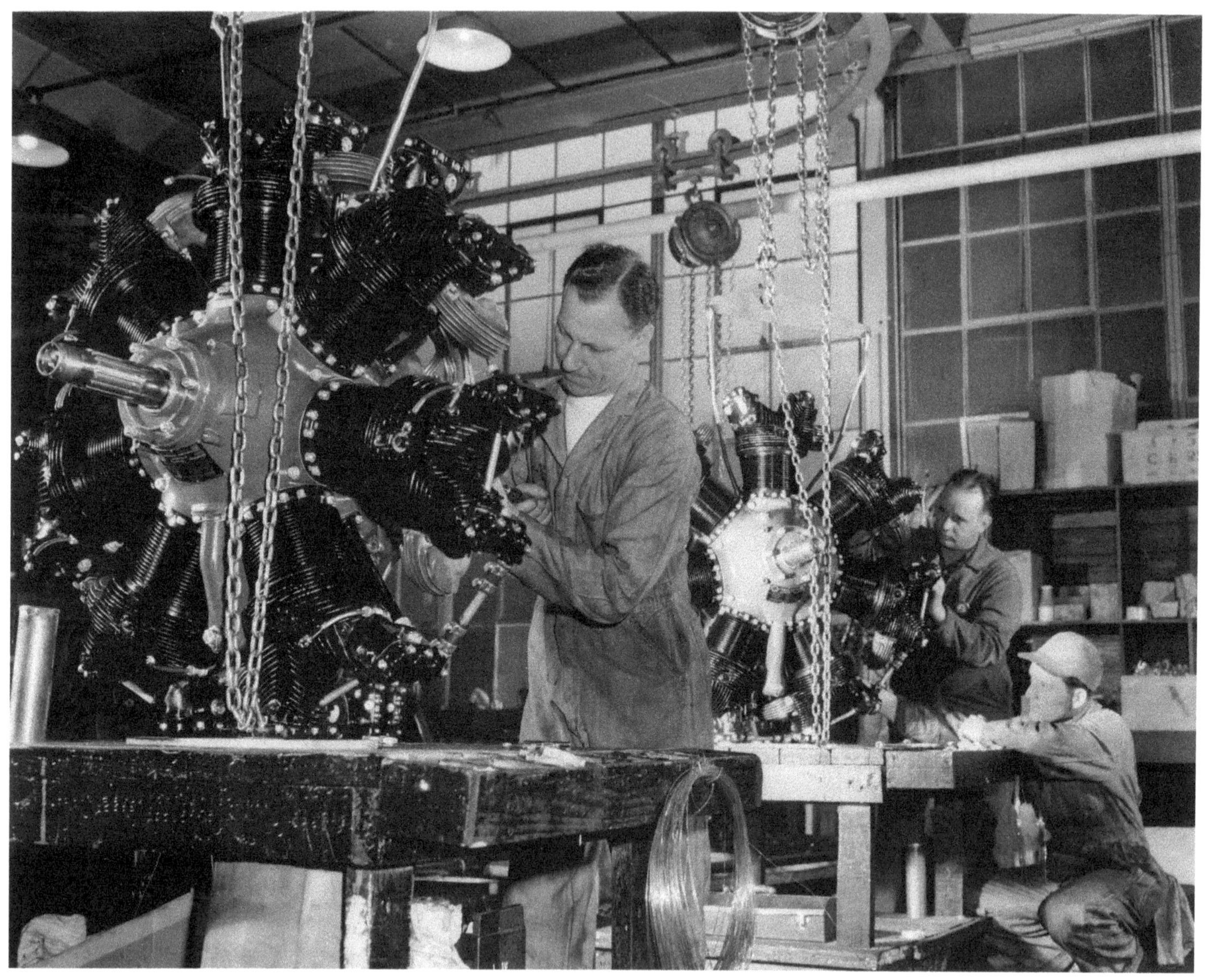

Workers at Continental Aircraft Engine Company in Muskegon, Michigan, assemble engines in February 1942 to be shipped to aircraft factories for the production of wartime planes. The Continental Aircraft Engine Company was created in 1929 as a subsidiary to Muskegon's Continental Motors Company, whose full automobile production efforts began—and ended—during the Great Depression.

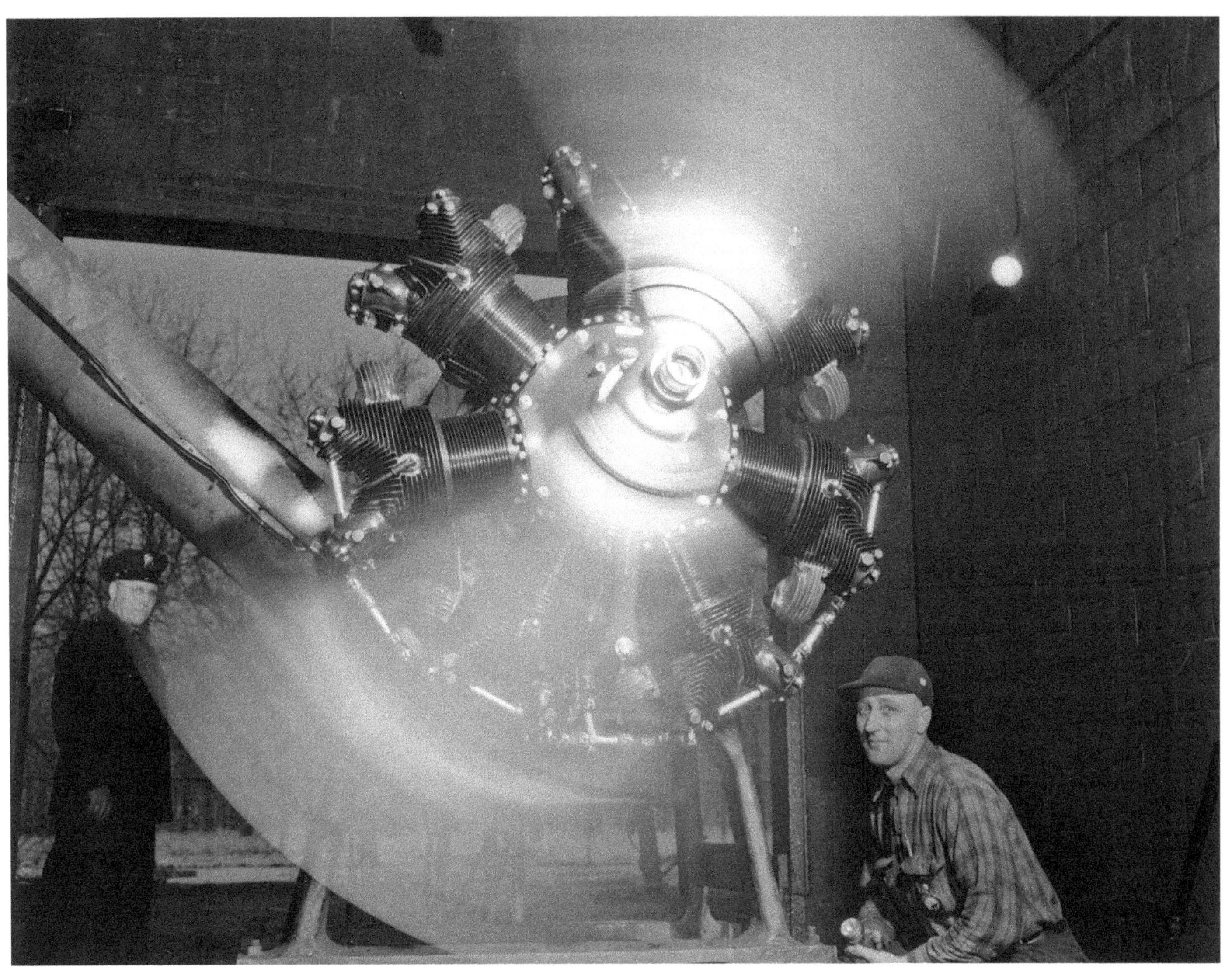

A testing engineer for Continental Aircraft Engine Company tests one of the company's airplane engines in a guarded forest near Muskegon in 1942. If satisfactory to the exacting requirements of the test engineers, the results of the test would be used to guide the construction of other engines.

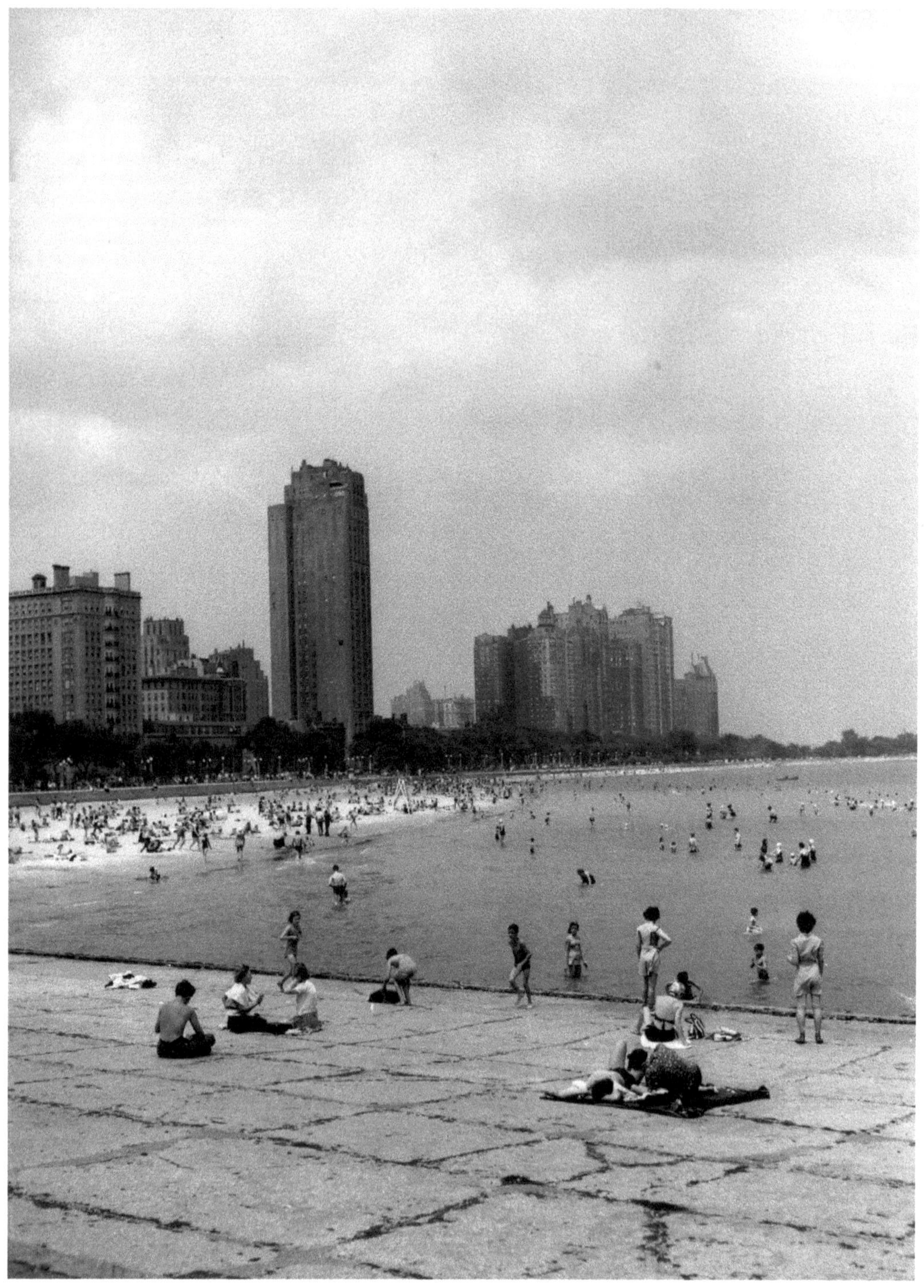

With World War II raging on the other side of the world, Chicagoans take respite on the Lake Michigan beach alongside downtown Chicago on a peaceful July day in 1942.

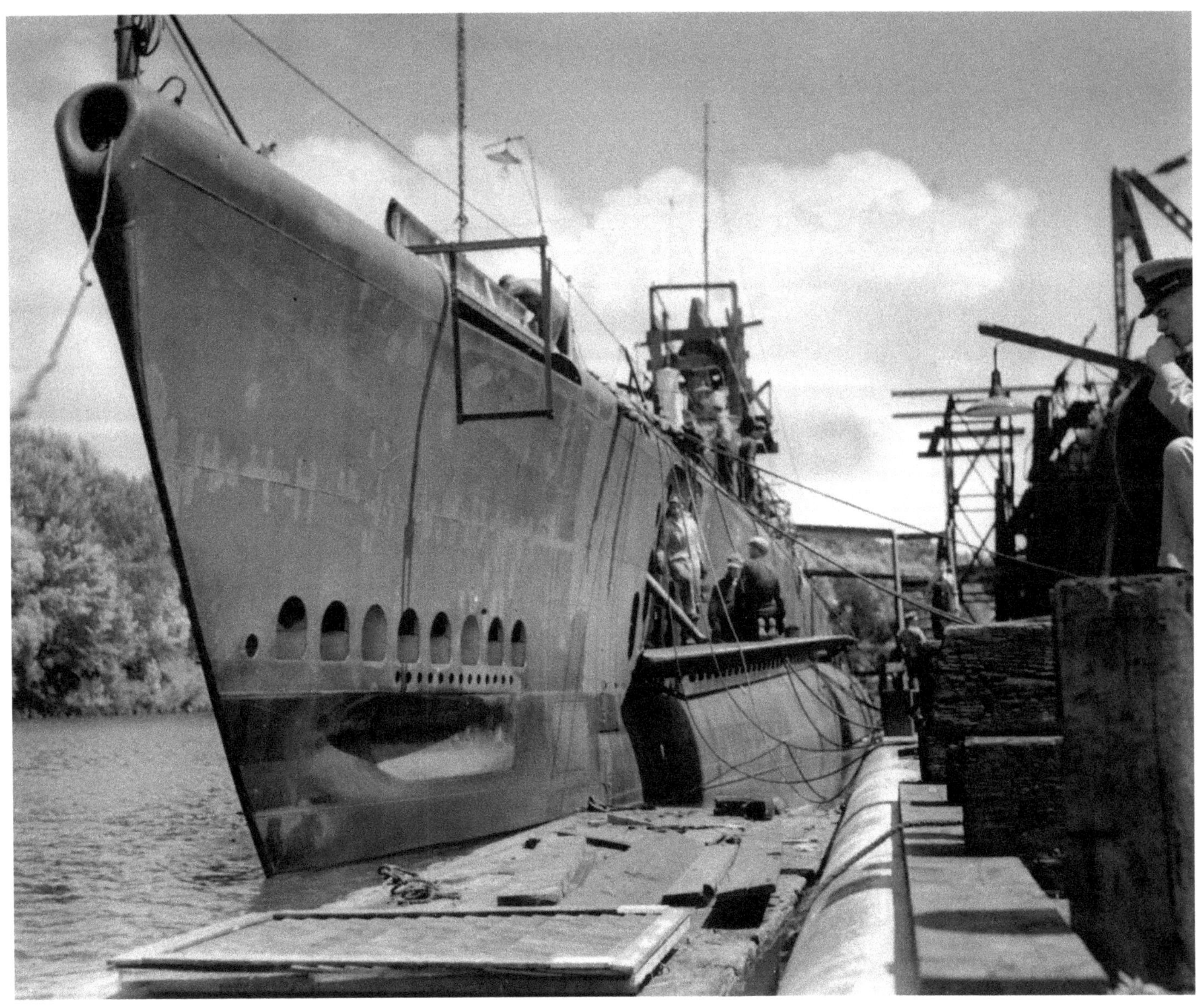

Like many of America's inland waterways during World War II, a small bay at Manitowoc, Wisconsin, served as a construction site for an underwater military craft. This submarine is undergoing finishing touches in August 1942.

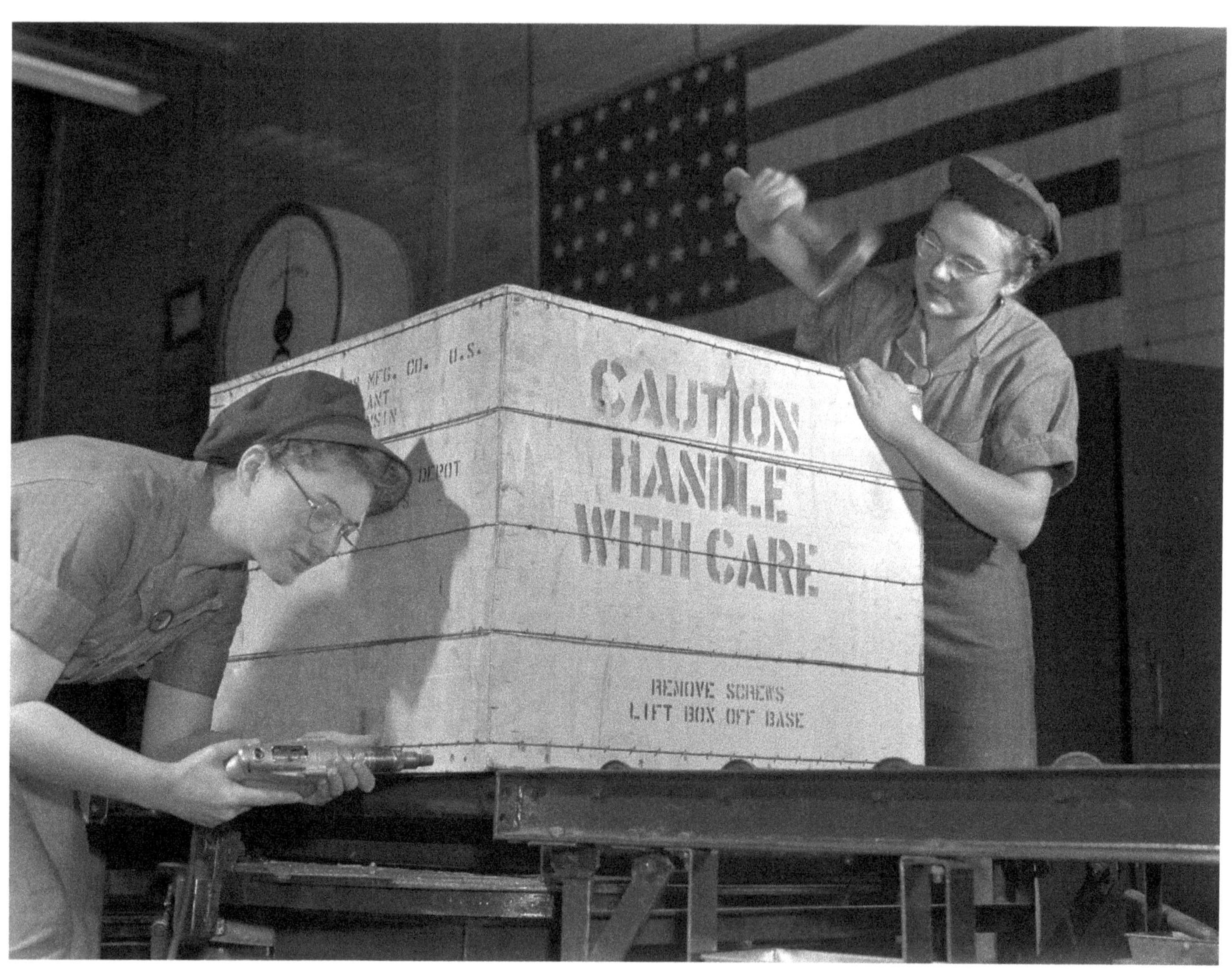

In the shipping department of a supercharger plant in Milwaukee during October 1942, two women ready a crate for transport. The woman at left, Betty Hinz, left her job at a local bank to join the war effort; her husband was in the Army Air Corps.

A rare look inside a repair shop for steam locomotives of the Chicago and Northwestern railroad, captured in December 1942. Although diesel locomotives first appeared in the 1920s, reliance on steam power for hauling heavy loads of freight would not end until after the war.

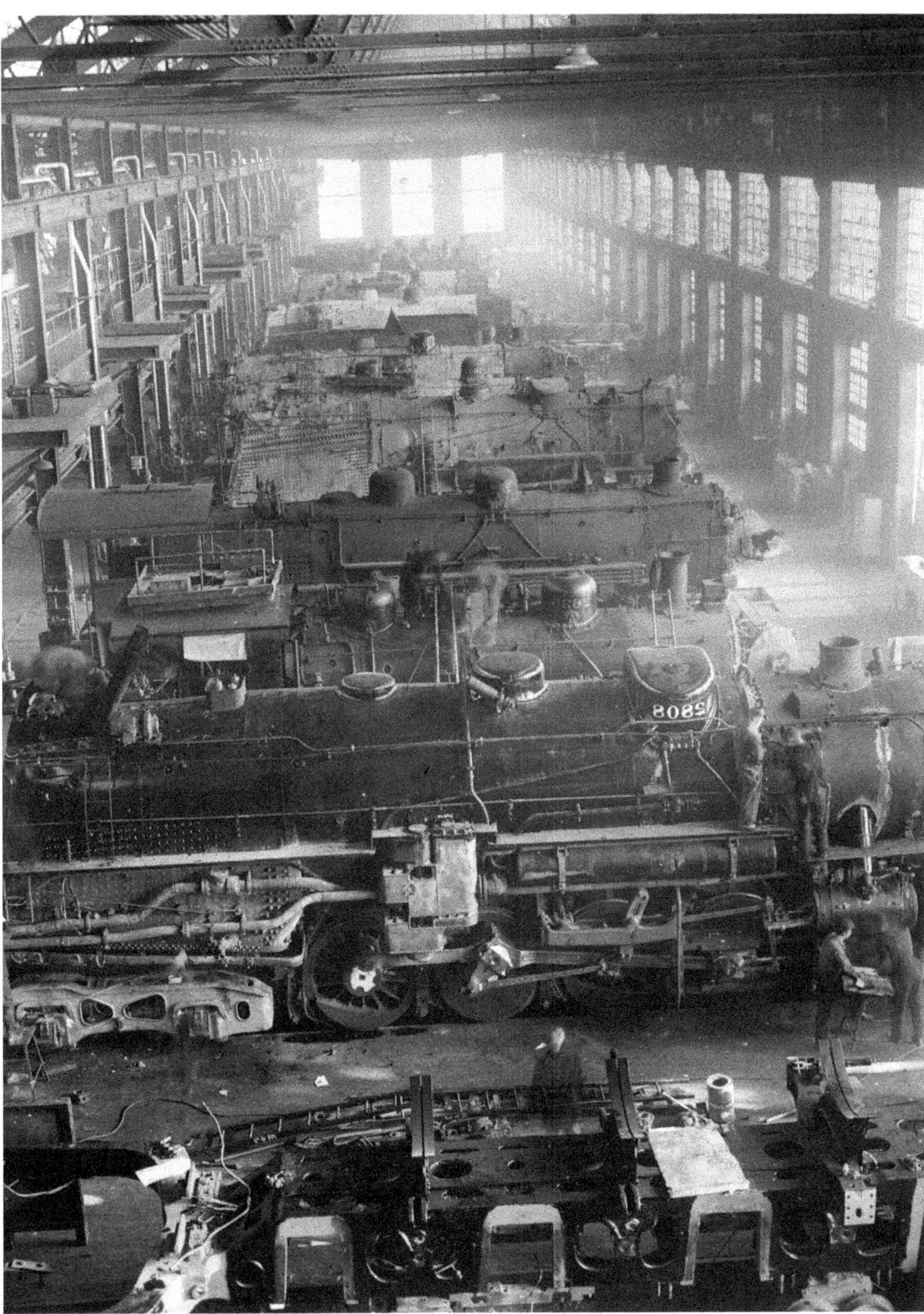

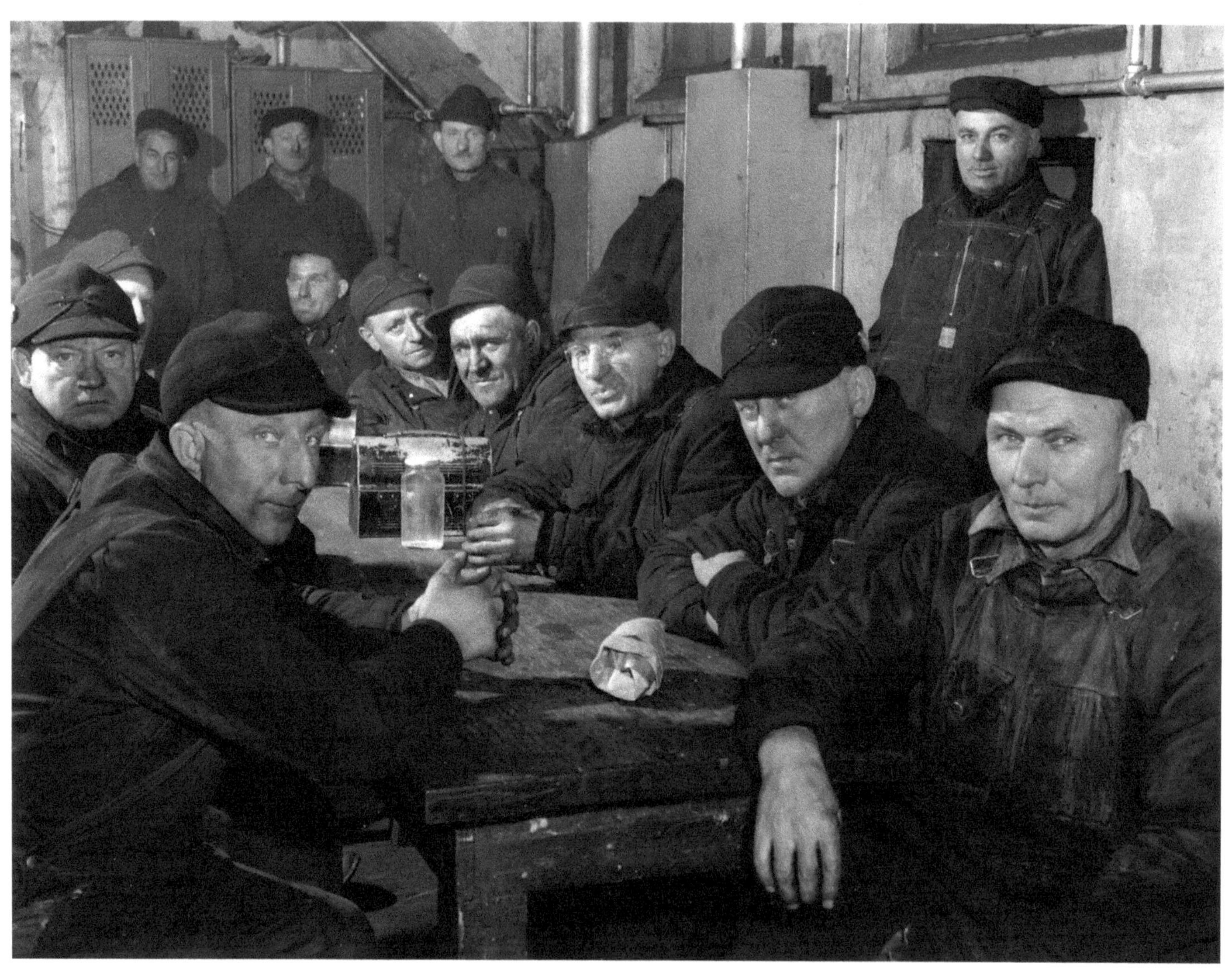

A burly crew of truck drivers and other employees gather for lunch in the locker room of the Seventeenth Street office of the Milwaukee Western Fuel Company in 1942. News from the war fronts was undoubtedly the main topic of conversation.

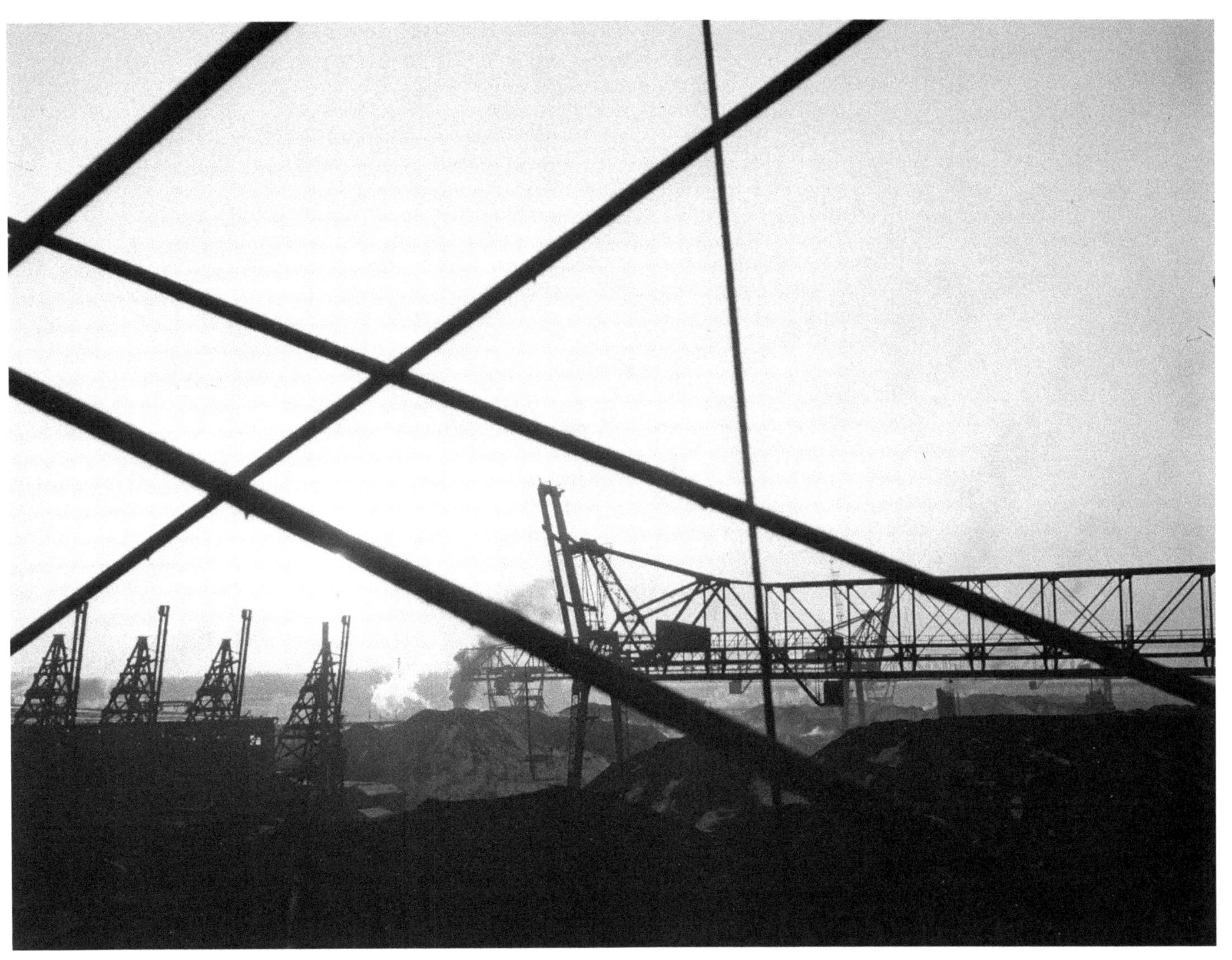

This view from January 1943 shows the Milwaukee Western Fuel Company coal docks silhouetted against Lake Michigan and the sky.

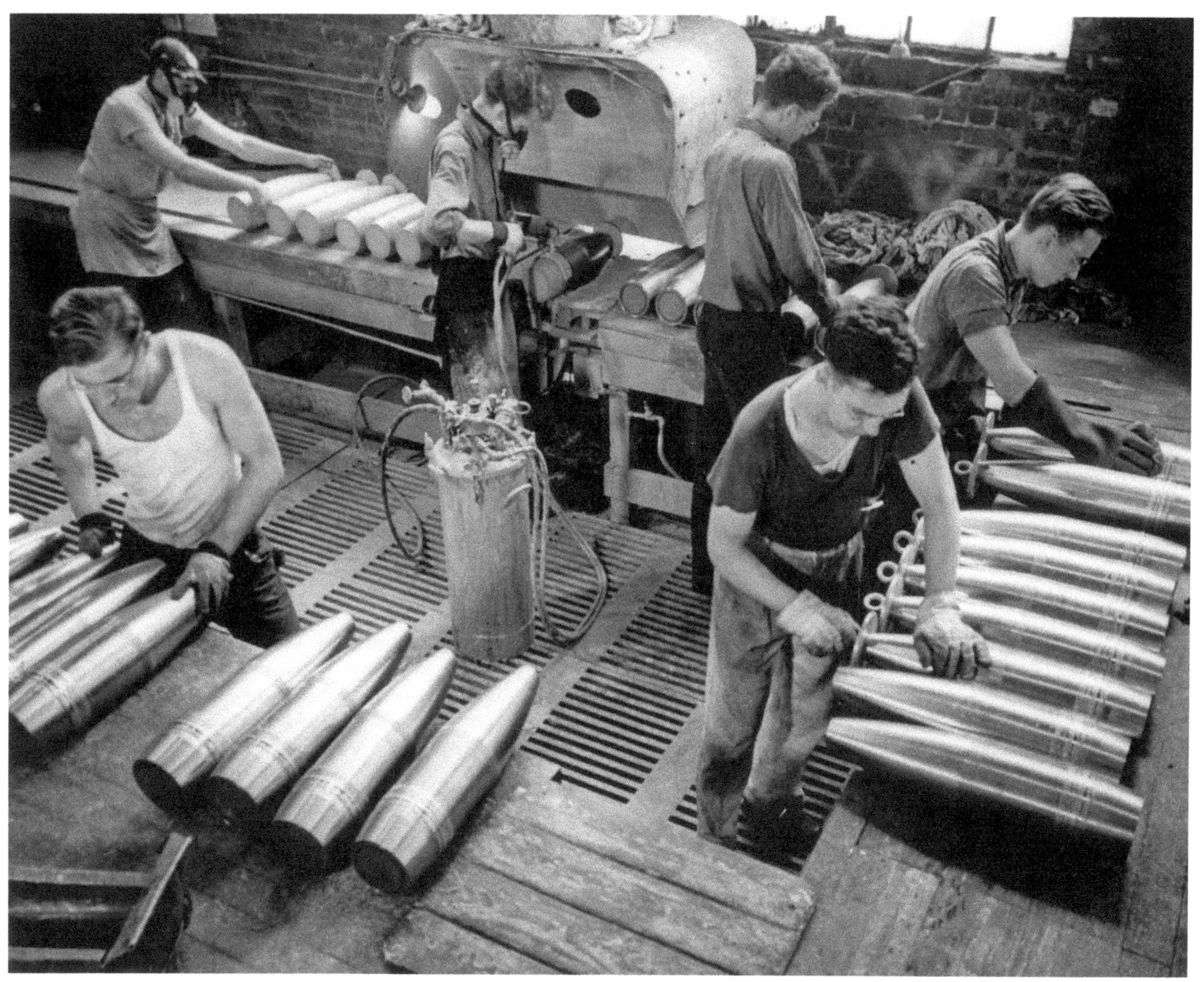

Formerly the site where freight cars were constructed, Hammond, Indiana's Pullman Standard Car Plant was transformed for the war effort. The men shown here are inspecting and painting 155 mm. shells. The fellow in the right foreground is screwing small disks onto the shells, which will act as wheels to ensure that the shells roll correctly along the production bench.

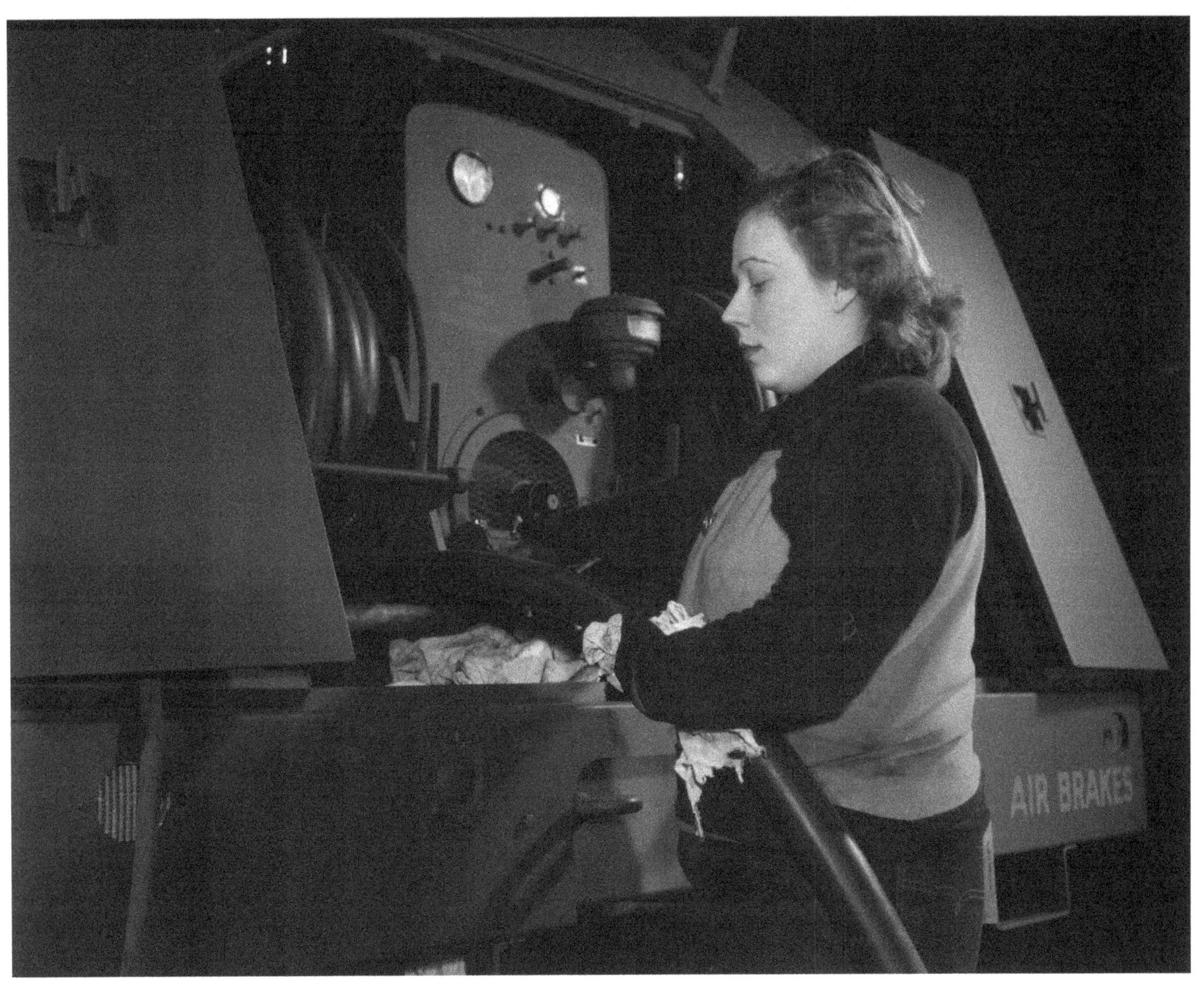

Having left her job in a Milwaukee department store, 23-year-old Agnes Cliemka supports the United States Air Force, checking the gasoline hoses of gasoline trailers as an employee of the city's Heil and Company, which fabricated steel tank cars.

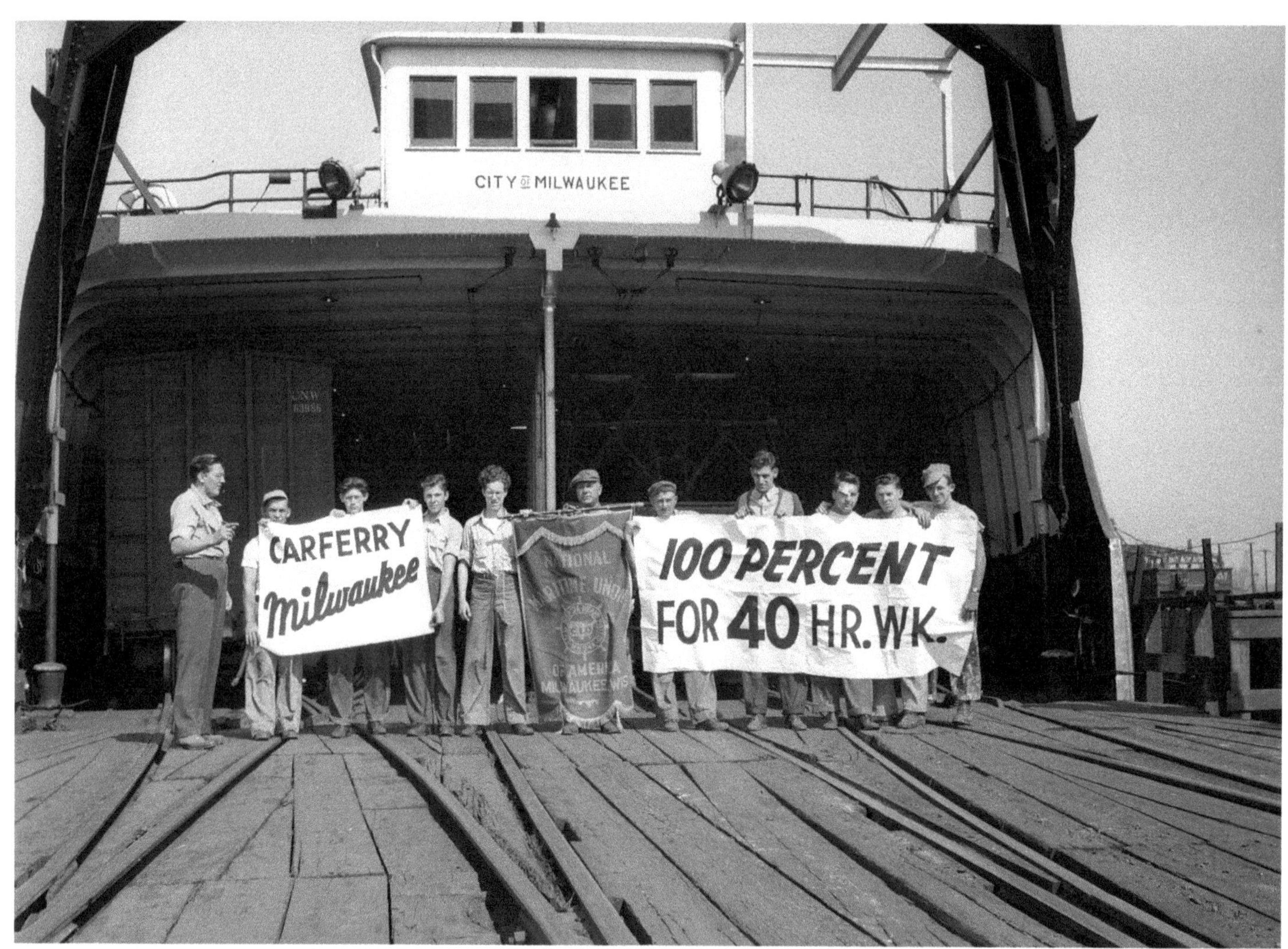

Members of the National Maritime Union of America, the crew of the SS *City of Milwaukee* car ferry demonstrates for a 40-hour workweek and overtime pay in August 1946. The *City of Milwaukee* ferried railroad cars of the Grand Trunk Western and those of other railroads across Lake Michigan until she was retired in 1981. Today she is permanently docked in Manistee, Michigan.

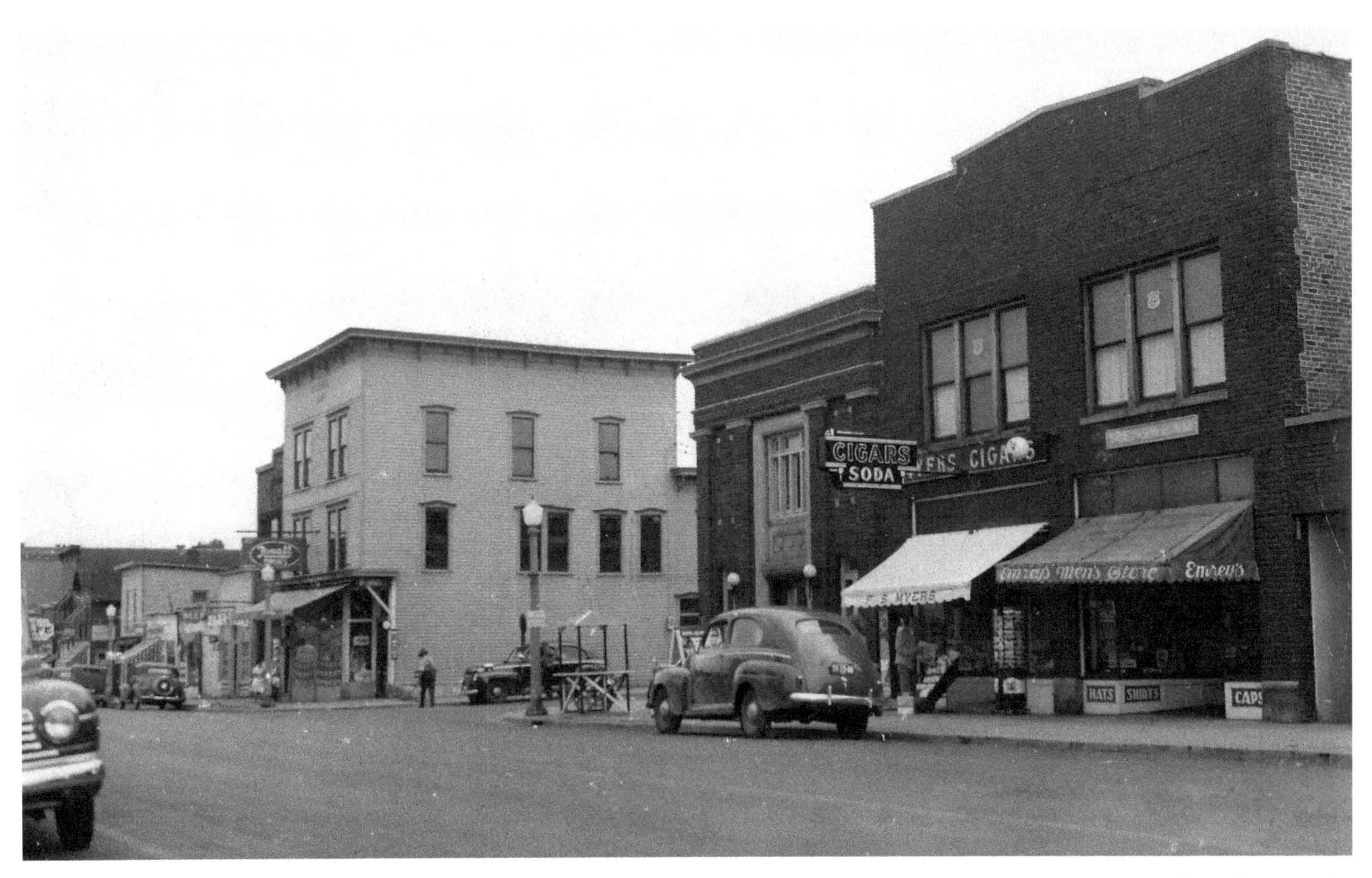

Downtown Charlevoix, Michigan, captured on film in 1947.

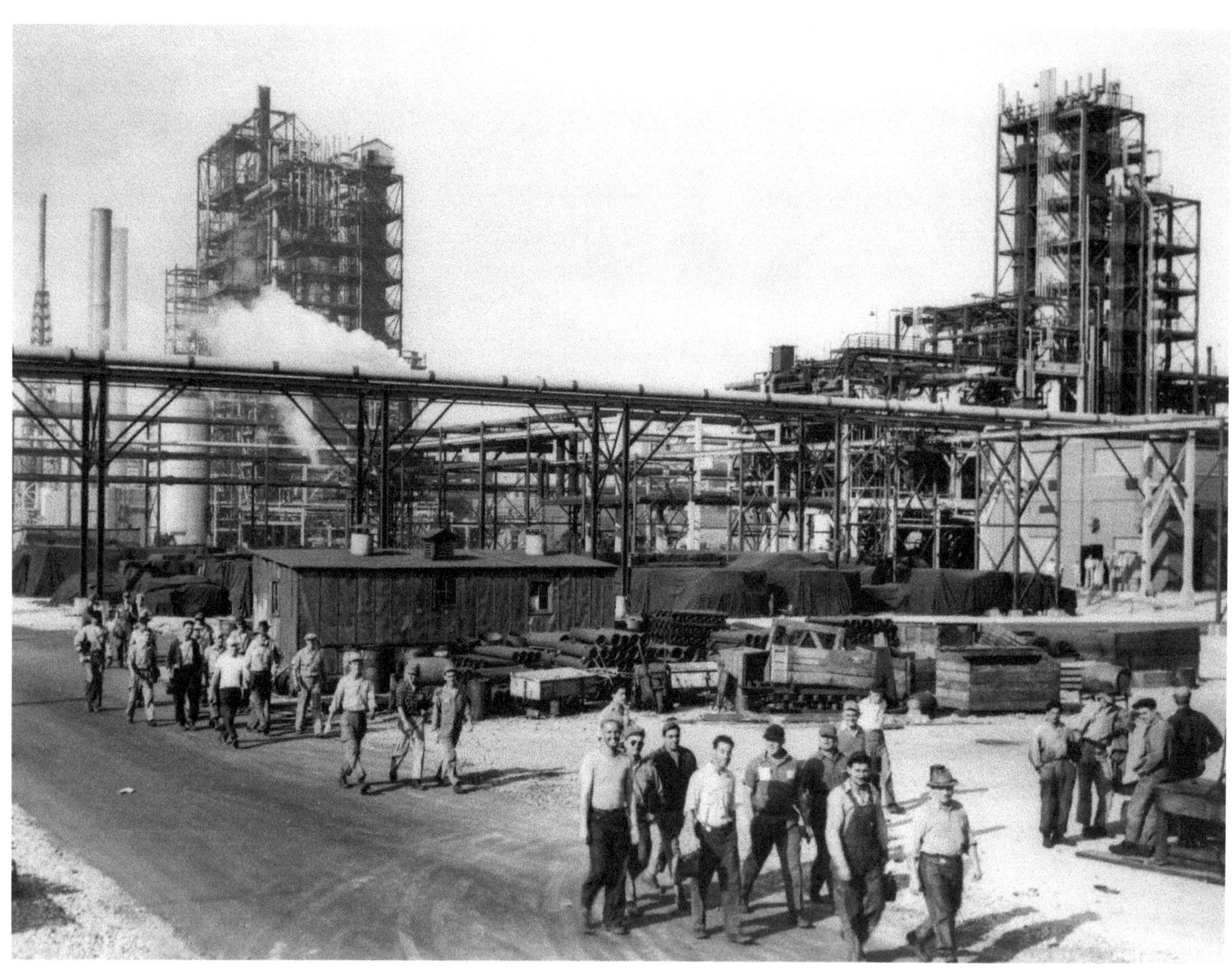

Workmen are shown outside the Indiana Standard Oil refinery in Whiting, Indiana, in 1952. The early 1950s were excellent years for Standard Indiana. The company grossed roughly $1.5 billion in annual sales and was ranked as the second-largest American oil company.

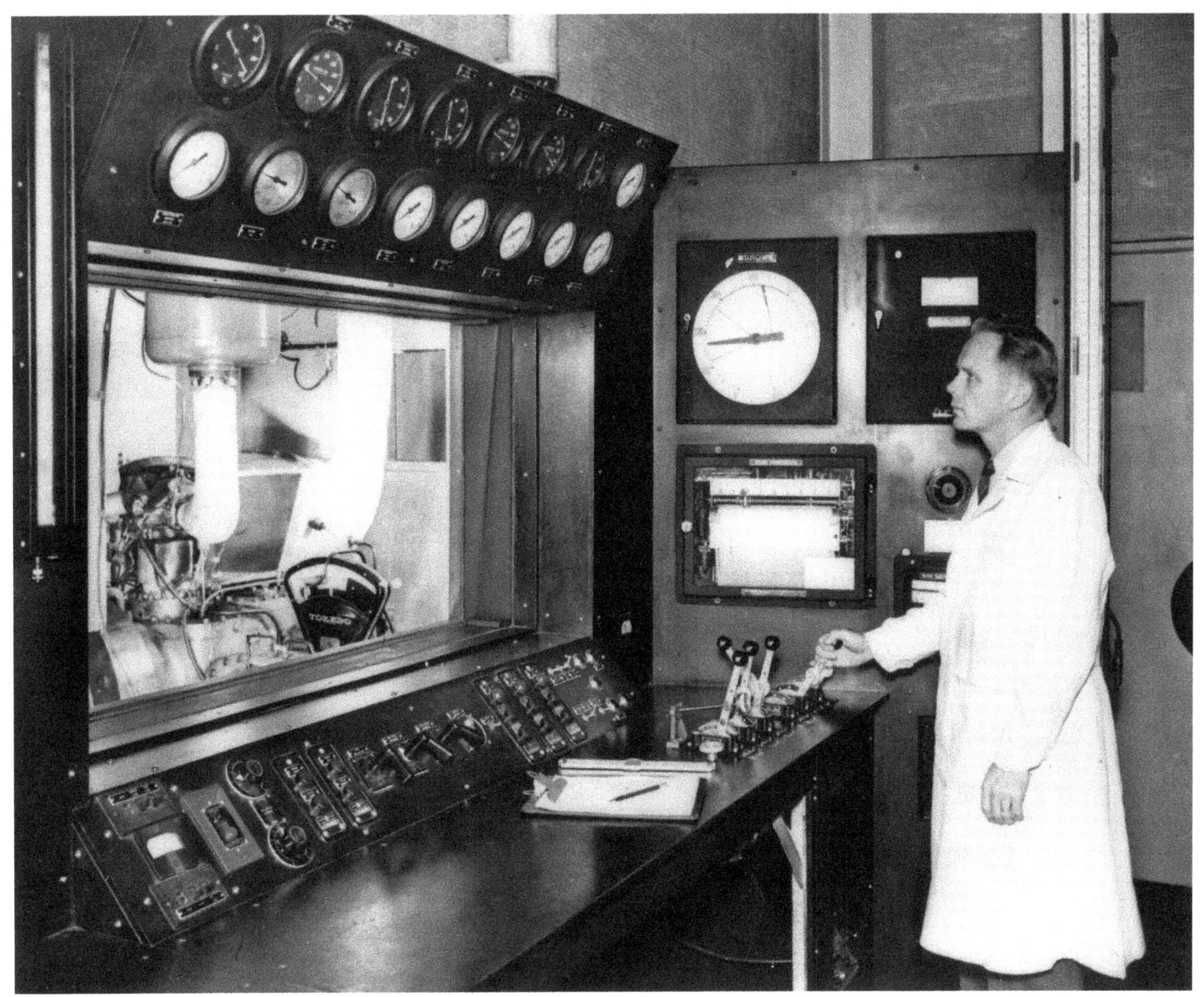

This employee is shown managing the control board at the Indiana Standard Oil Company in Whiting, Indiana, in 1952.

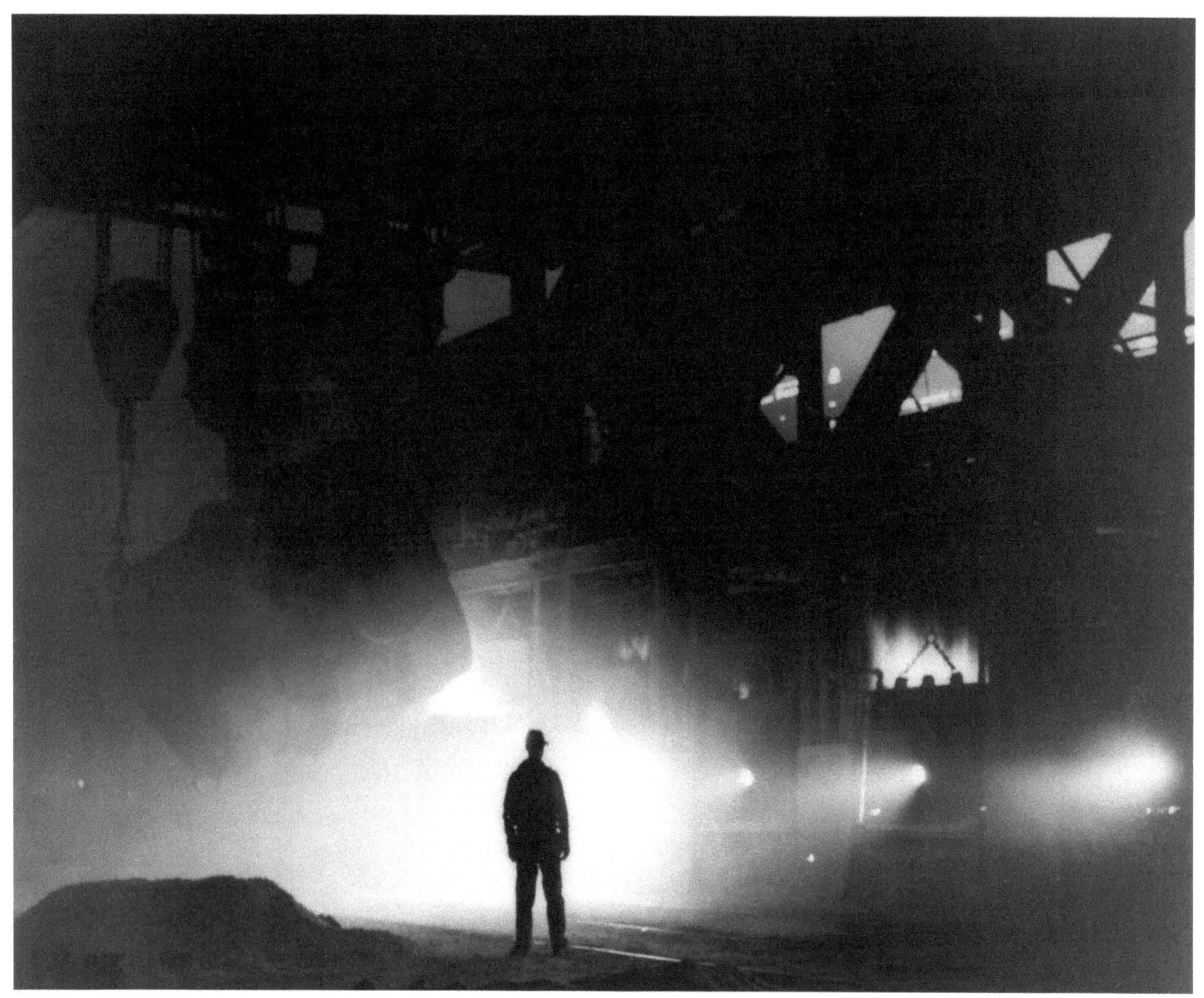

The inner workings of the U.S. Steel plant in Gary, Indiana, as it appeared in 1952.

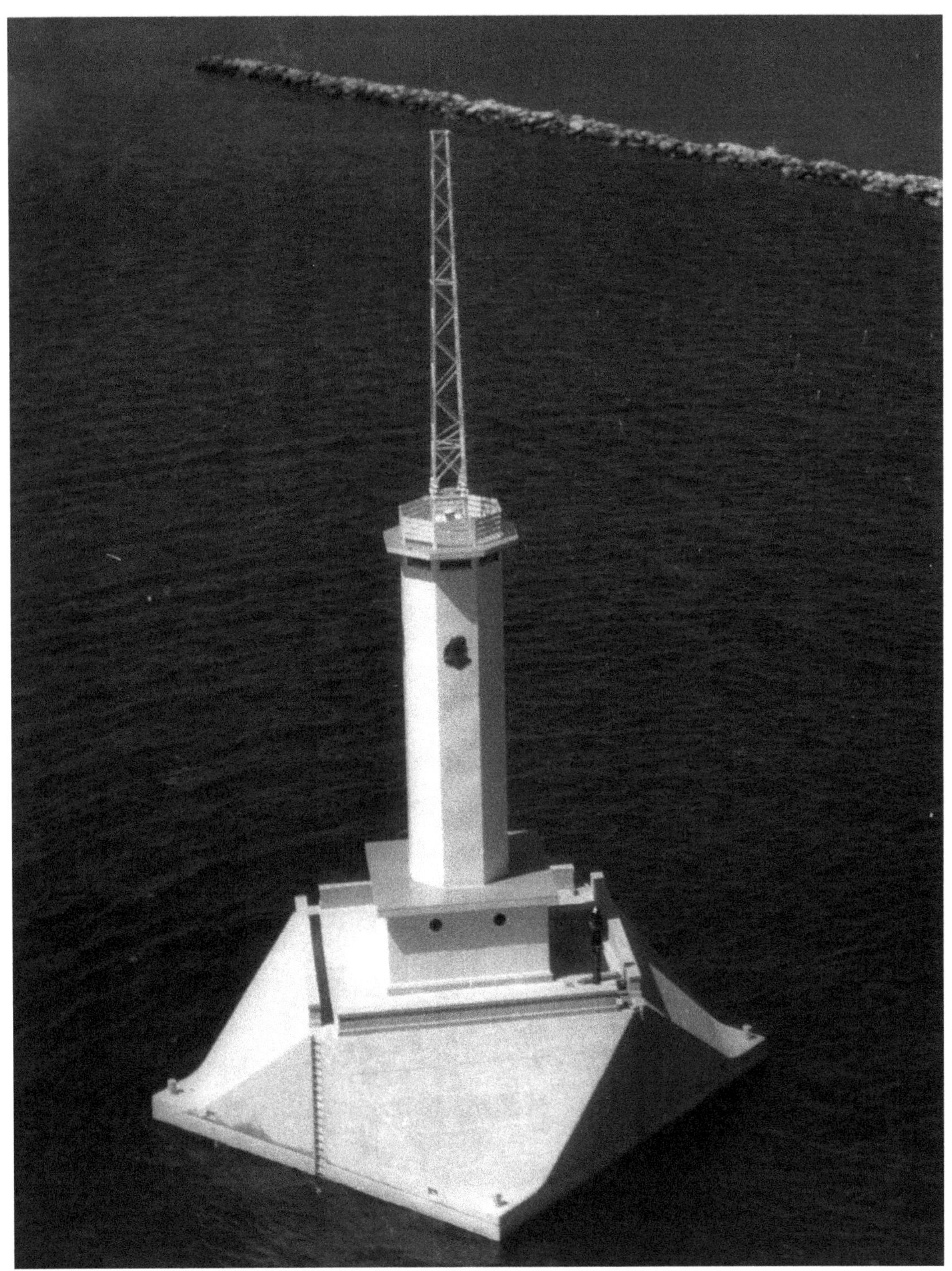

Located roughly 600 meters from the Round Island Lighthouse in the Straits of Mackinac—the waters where Lake Michigan and Lake Huron meet between Michigan's Upper and Lower Peninsulas—the Round Island Signal Light was erected in 1948, one year before this photograph was taken. The profile showcased on the light is that of Ottawa Indian chief Pe-to-se-ga, otherwise known as Chief Petoskey, founder of nearby Petoskey.

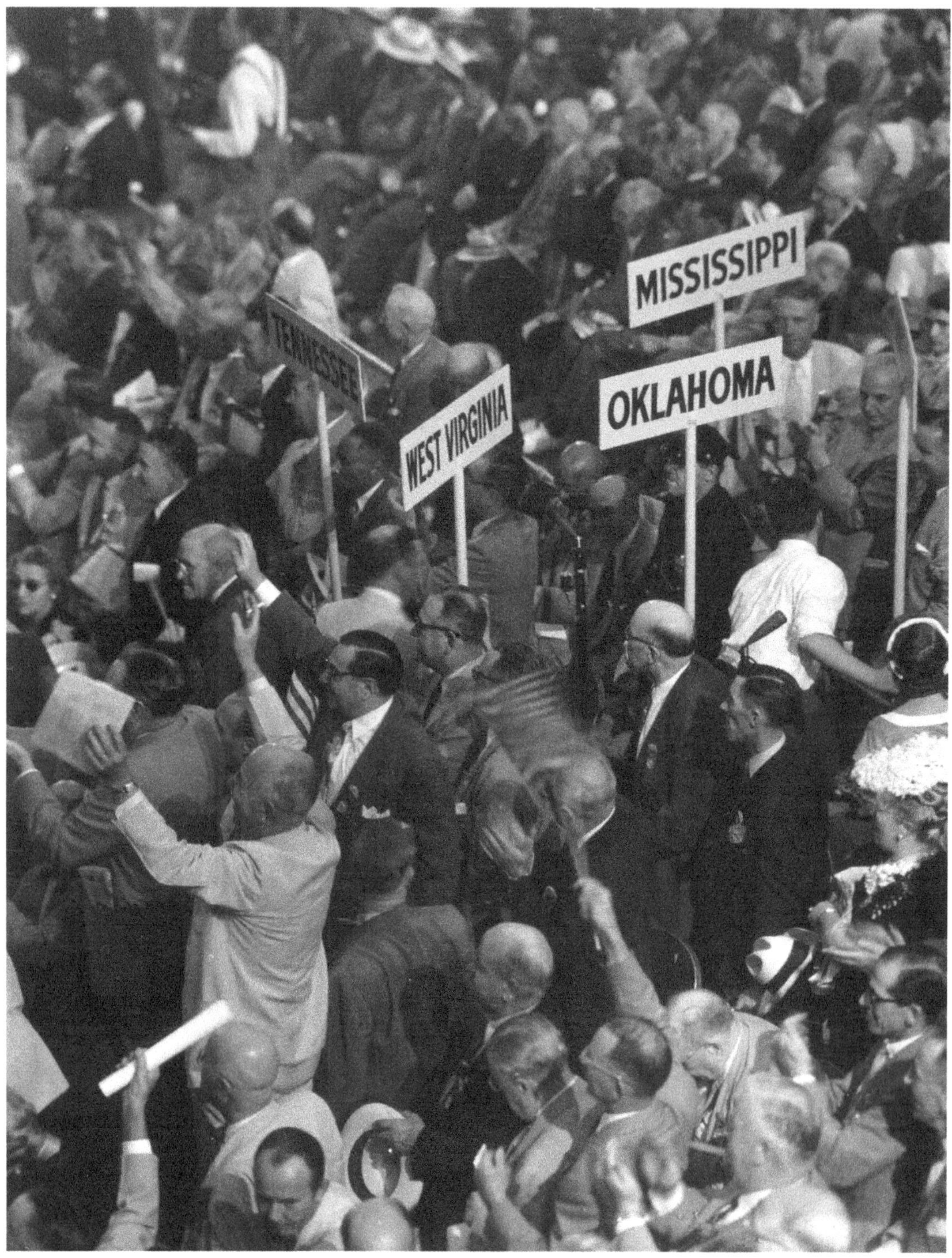

Following decades in the Chicago Coliseum and Chicago Stadium, the Republican National Convention held in Chicago in 1952 took place in the city's International Amphitheatre, adjacent the Union Stock Yards. War hero Dwight D. Eisenhower of Kansas was nominated by his party to run for the presidency. He won by a landslide, putting to end 20 consecutive years of Democratic control of the executive office.

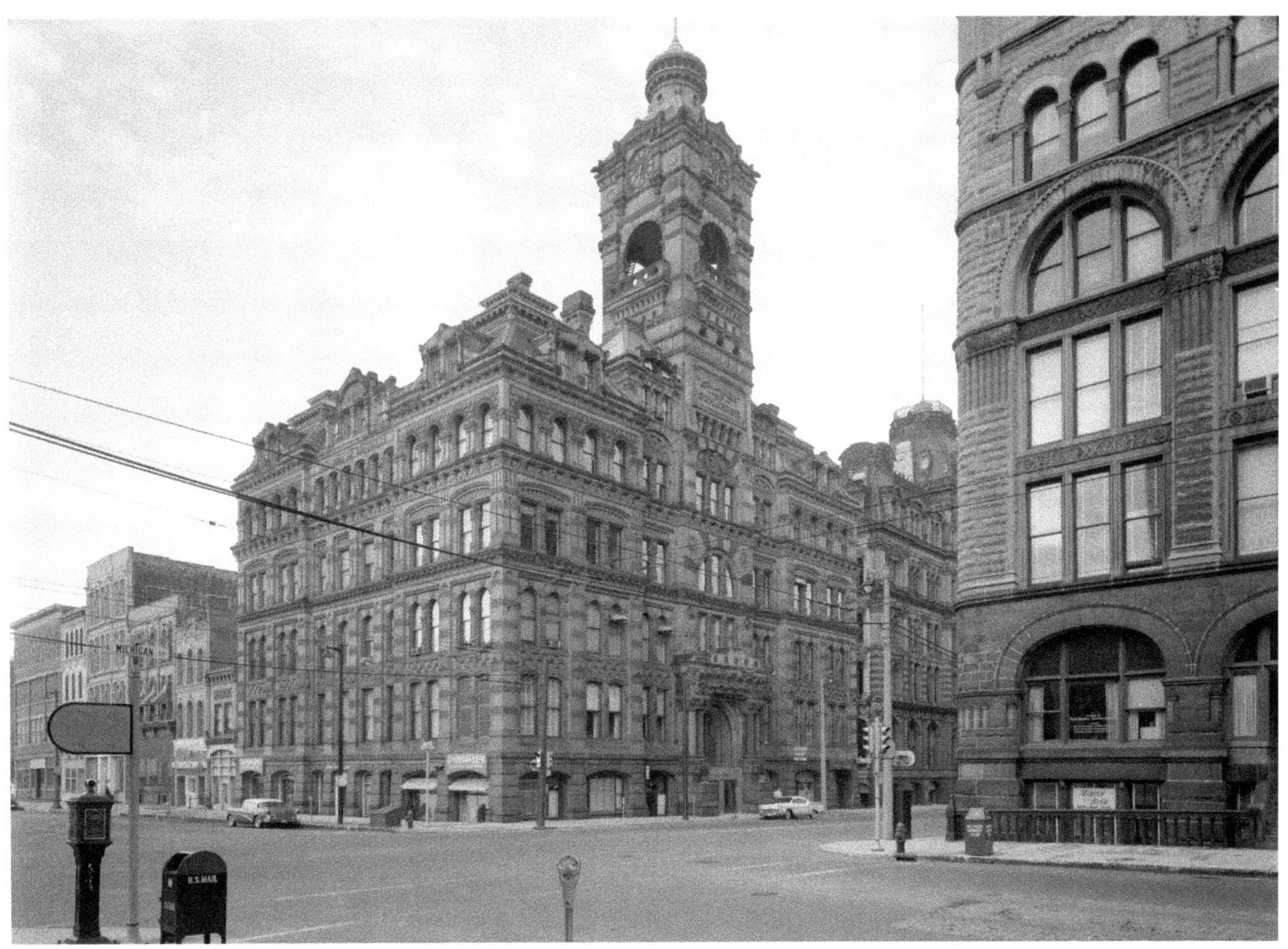

Originally constructed in 1879 for Alexander Mitchell, a wealthy Milwaukee banker and businessman, the ornate and imposing structure at 611 North Broadway is an excellent example of Milwaukee's rapid growth and commercial development following the Civil War. Known for decades simply as the Mitchell Building, the structure would eventually house one of the world's largest grain exchanges, and later, the city's Chamber of Commerce.

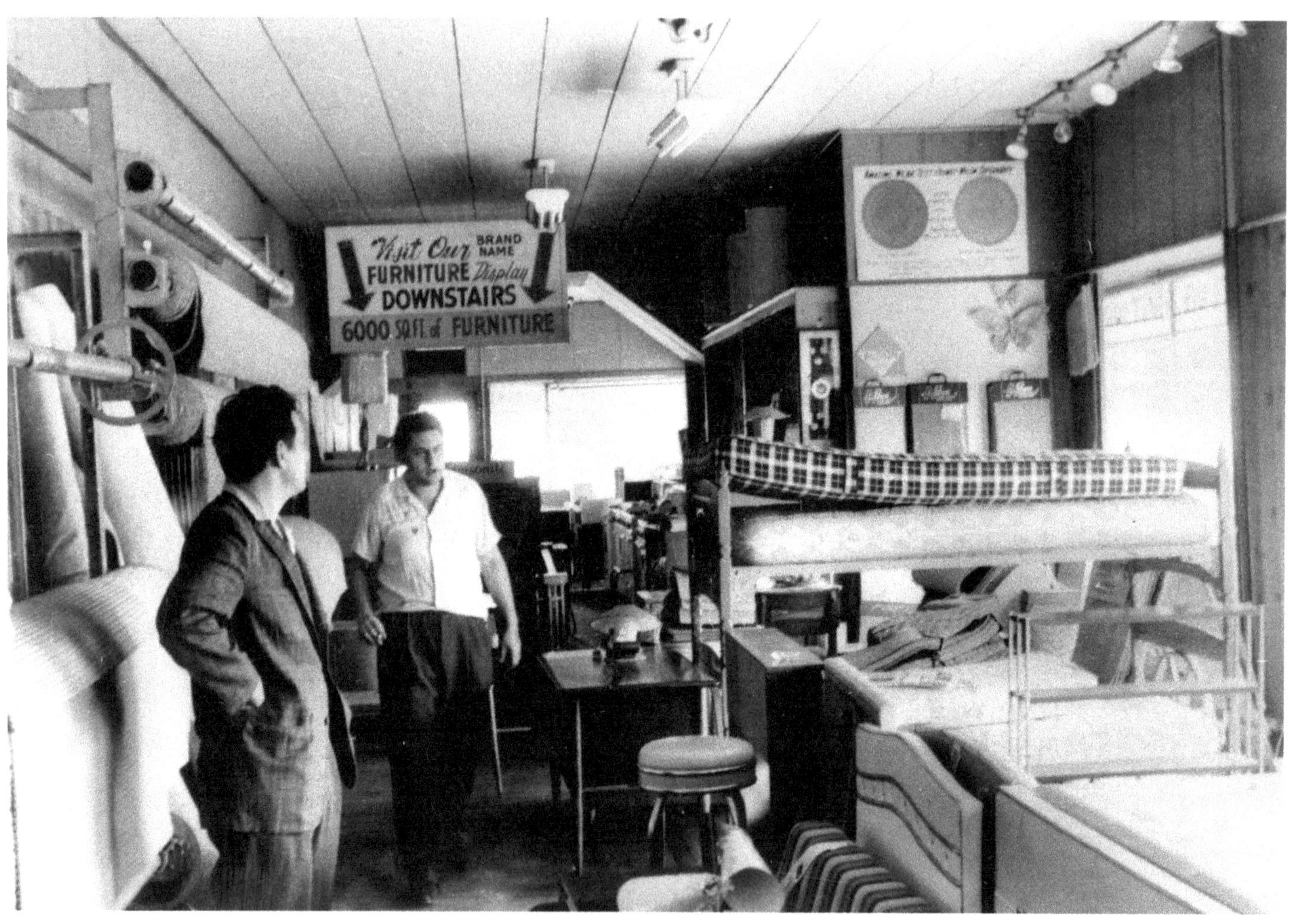

Brothers Edward and Mendel "Manny" Chulew stand inside the family furniture store, Chulew Furniture, in Kenosha, Wisconsin, in 1958. During World War II, the brothers fled with their family from Poland to Siberia. They arrived in New York City in 1951 and soon traveled to Kenosha, where an uncle who had immigrated decades earlier helped them start their store.

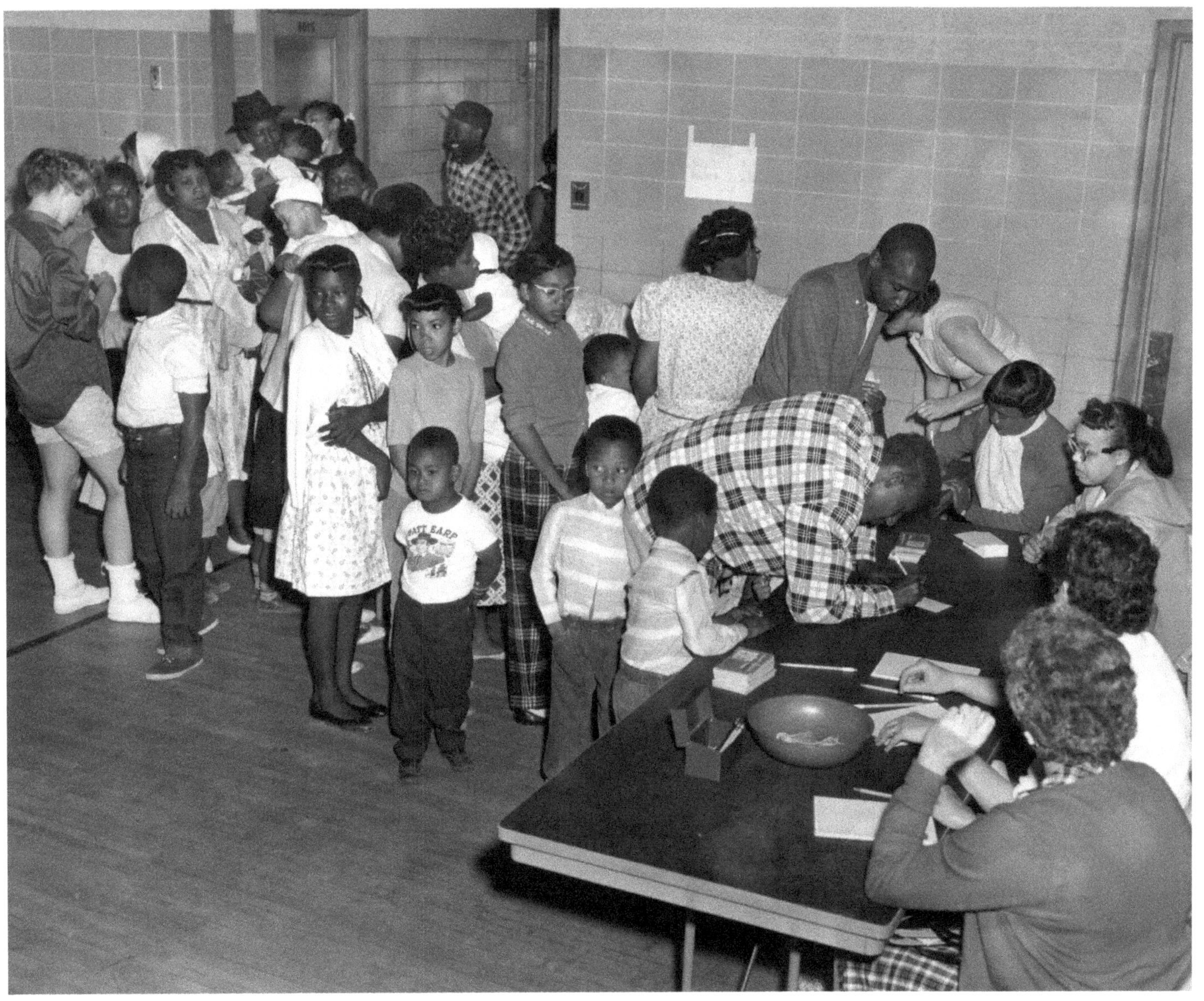

The Urban League of Greater Muskegon sponsors a polio clinic to vaccinate area children against poliomyelitis. In the 1950s Michigan was among the first states in the nation to vaccinate children against the crippling virus.

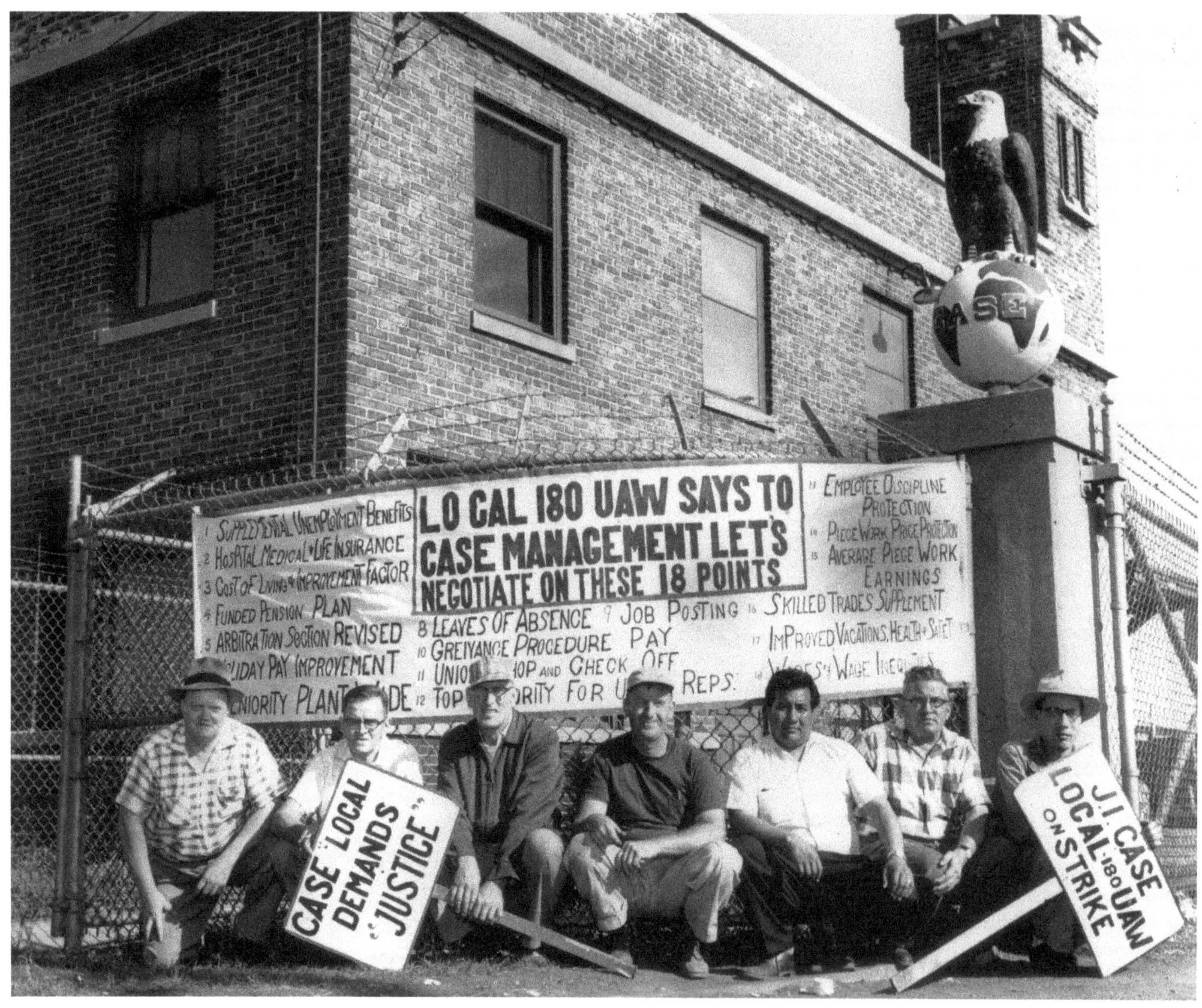

In 1960, striking members of the Racine, Wisconsin, United Automobile Workers Union, Local 180, pose below a banner stating their demands. They are squatting outside one of the J. I. Case Company's three farm-machinery manufacturing plants.

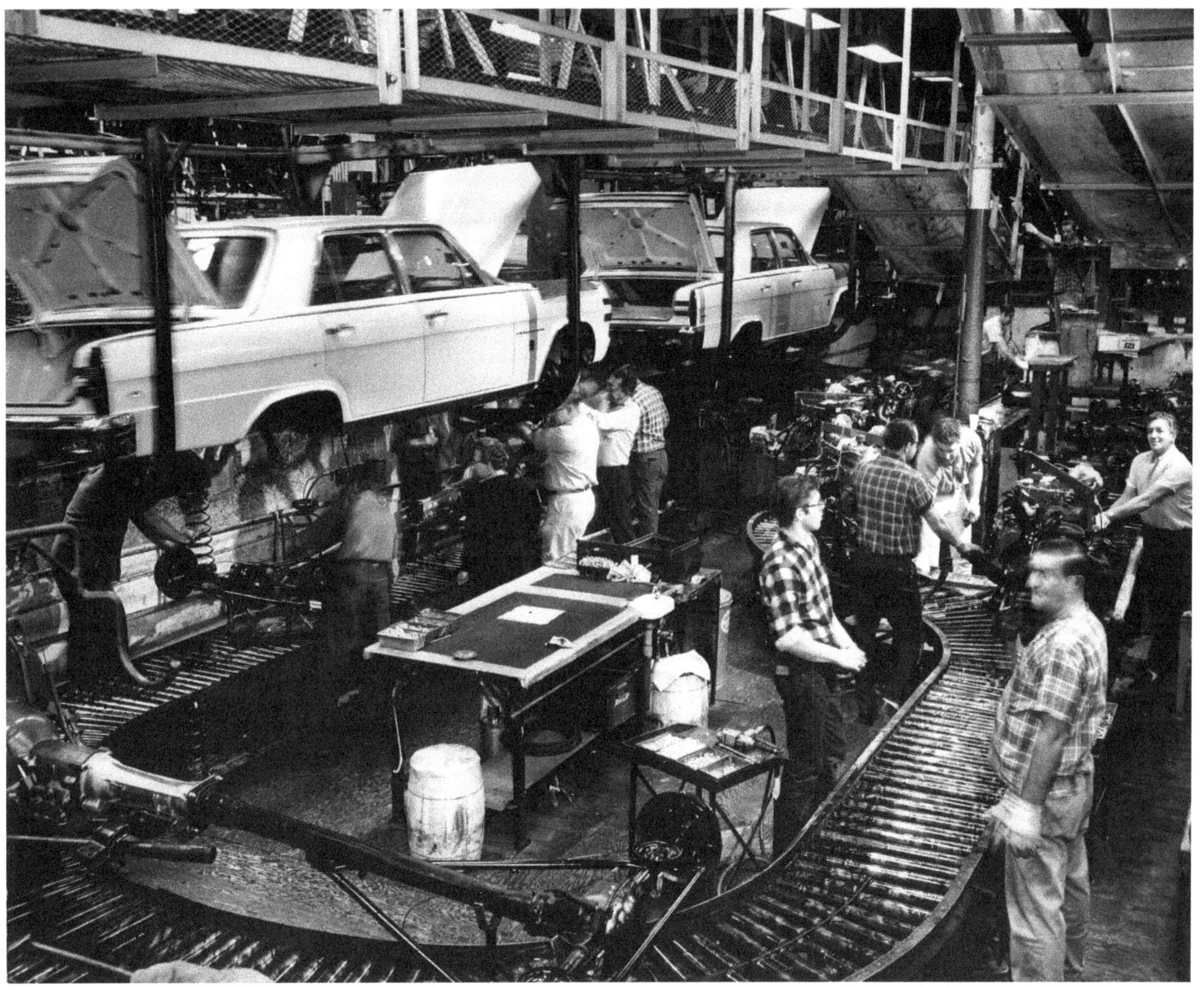

A 1965 snapshot of the assembly line inside the American Motors Company of Kenosha, Wisconsin—the year AMC began phasing out its Rambler line. Formerly Nash Motors, the American Motors Company was formed following Nash's merger with the Hudson Motor Car Company, and was ultimately acquired by the Chrysler Corporation in 1987.

With its early century settlers removed, Milwaukee's Jones Island, located between the Milwaukee and Kinnickinnic rivers, evolved into a heavily industrialized commercial fishing community and peninsula. Shown here is a relatively serene stretch of its Lake Michigan shoreline in 1961.

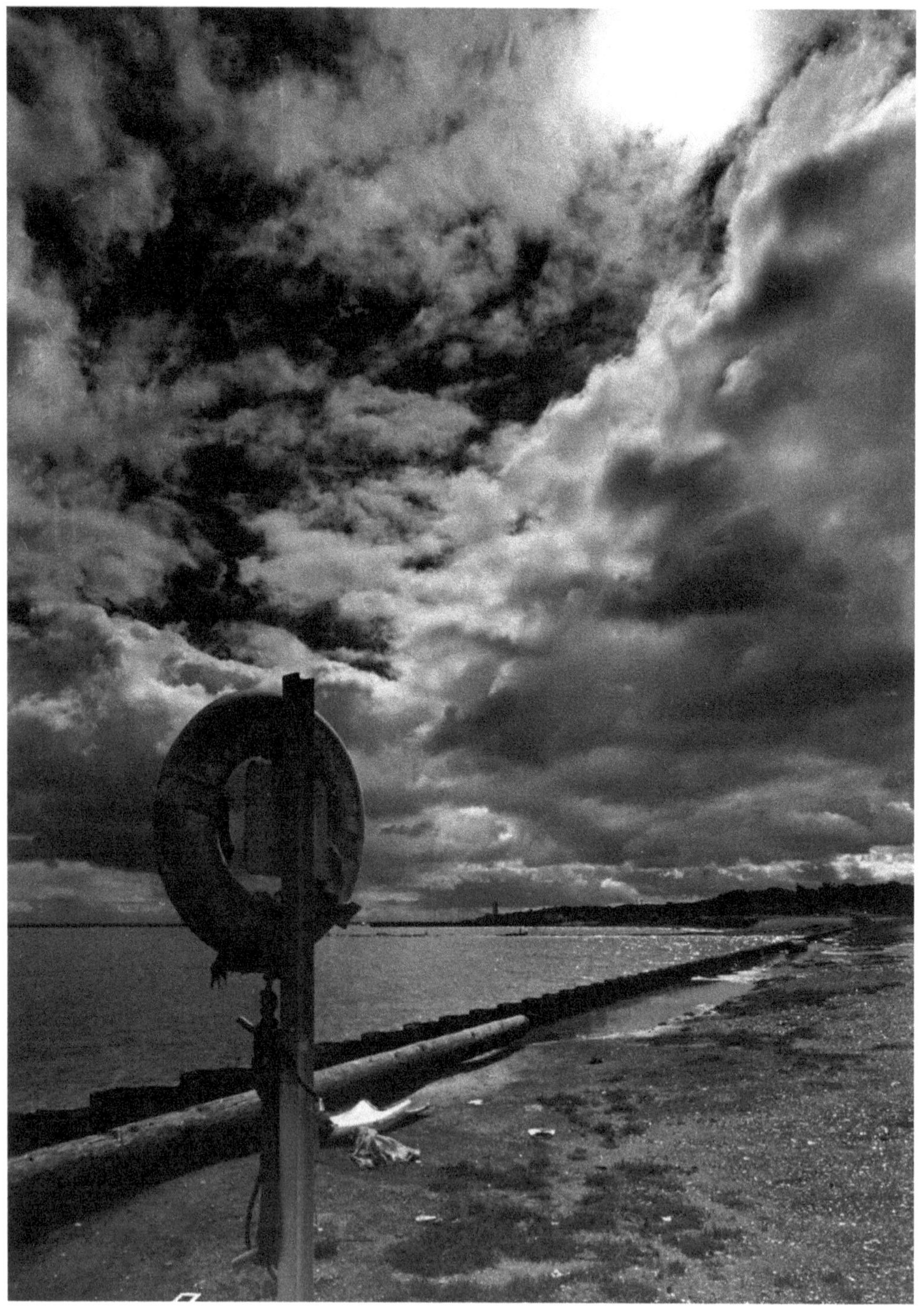

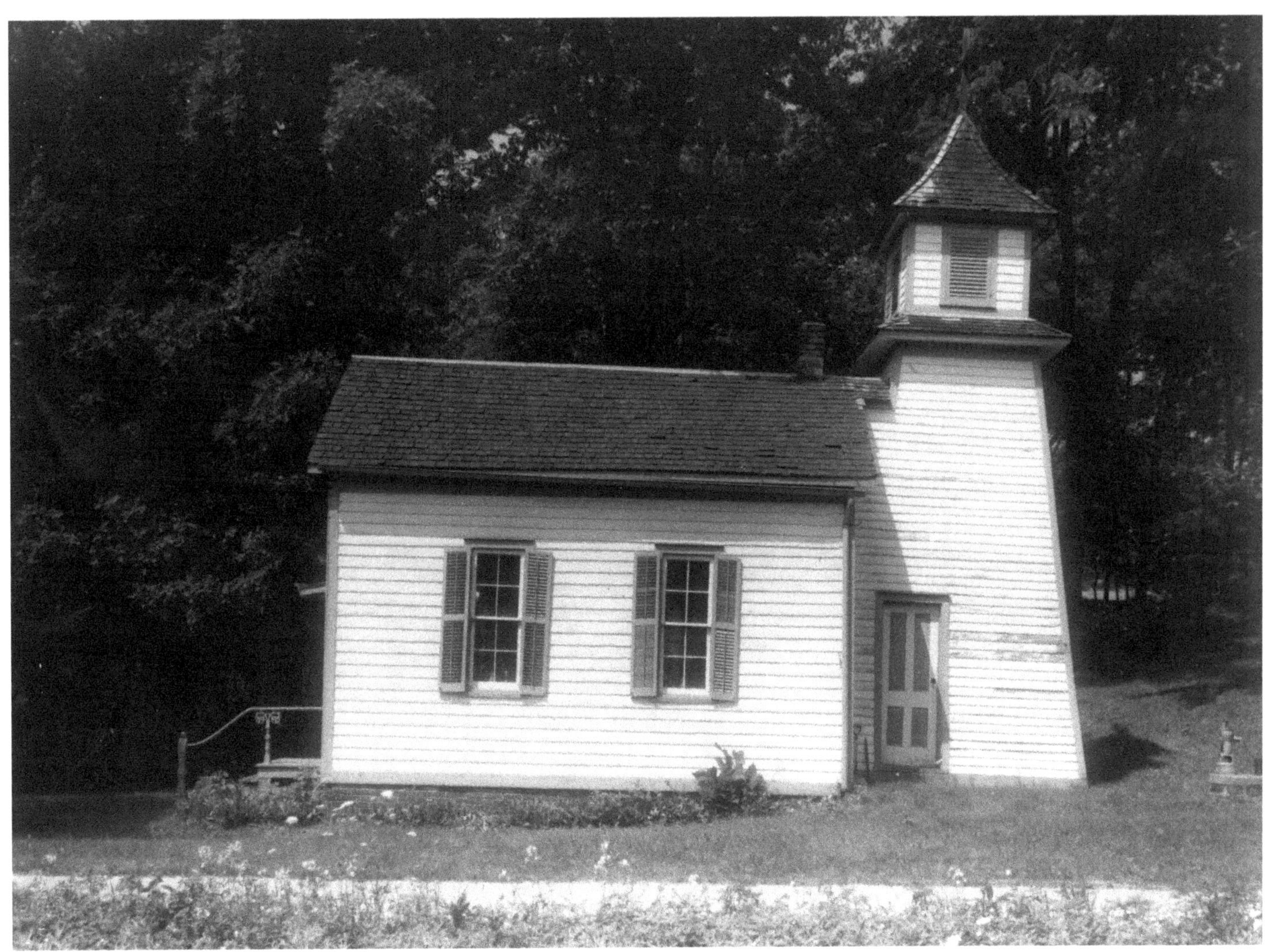

The Augsburg Swensk Skola, a church structure built by nineteenth-century Swedish immigrants near Chesterton in Porter County, Indiana. Notable is the off-center placing of the section that houses the bell, an architectural tradition of Scandinavian nations.

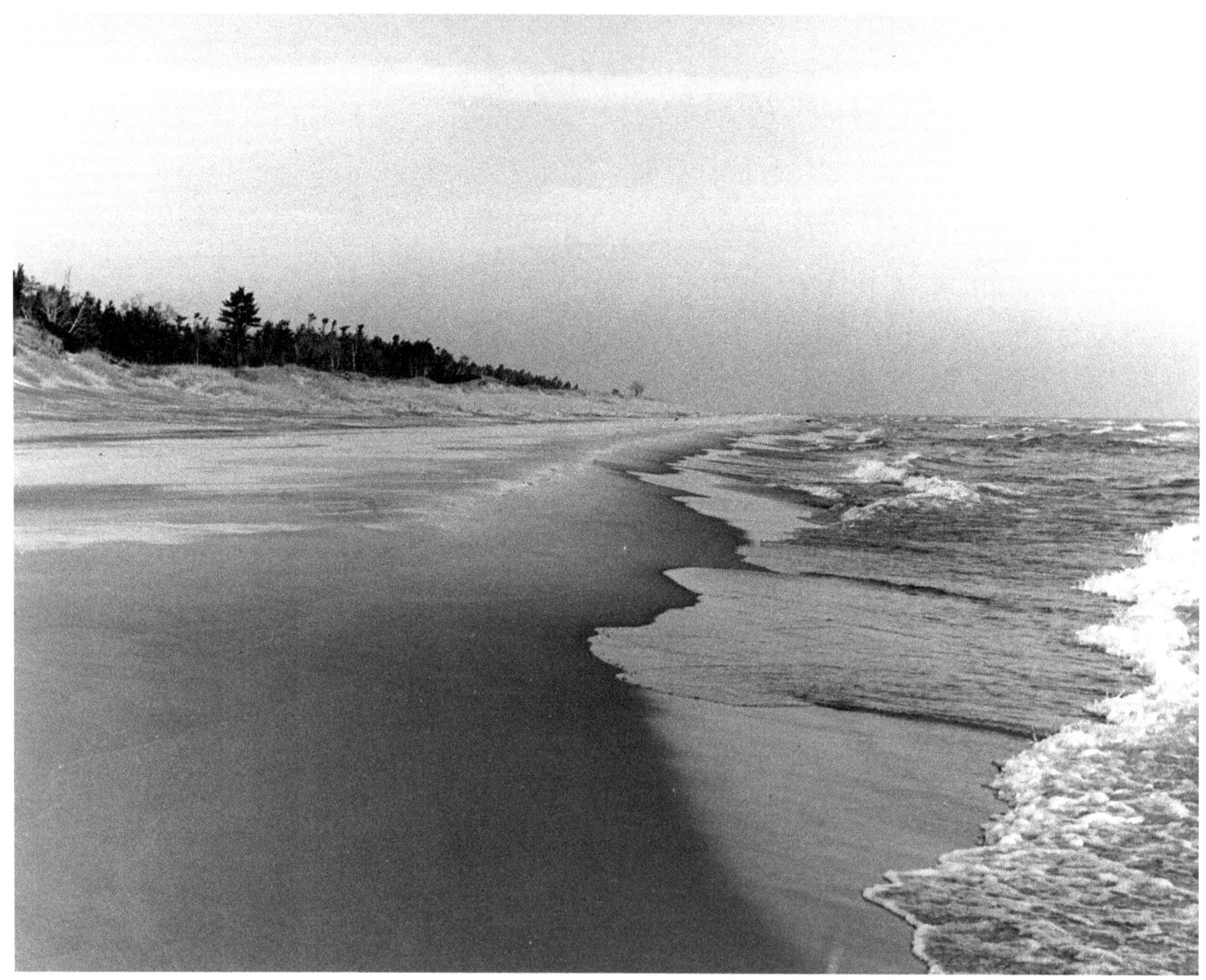

A view of the Lake Michigan shoreline a few miles south of Sheboygan in what is now Kohler-Andrae State Park, named after John Michael Kohler, scion of the Kohler plumbing-fixture empire and inventor of the "bubbler" drinking fountain, and Terry Andrae, president of Milwaukee's Julius Andrae and Sons' Electric Supply Company. Both men owned significant acreage here, which was donated to the state of Wisconsin following their respective deaths. This photo from 1965 was taken shortly before Kohler's 280-acre contribution.

Notes on the Photographs

These notes, listed by page number, attempt to include all aspects known of the photographs. Each of the photographs is identified by the page number, photograph's title or description, photographer and collection, archive, and call or box number when applicable. Although every attempt was made to collect all data, in some cases complete data may have been unavailable due to the age and condition of some of the photographs and records.

II **Sheboygan County's Crystal Lake**
Library of Congress
pan 6a12427

VI **Floating Boardinghouse at Elk Rapids Harbor**
Bentley Historical Library, University of Michigan
BL005716

X **Charlevoix Merchant Store Interior**
Bentley Historical Library, University of Michigan
BL005757

2 **Chicago's Great Central Depot, 1863**
Library of Congress
LC-DIG-stereo-1s01449

3 **Downtown Milwaukee, 1868**
Wisconsin Historical Society
54888

4 **Steam Locomotive at Kenosha**
Wisconsin Historical Society
24761

5 **Lake Michigan Coast at Milwaukee, 1870**
Wisconsin Historical Society
53759

6 **Little Fort Lighthouse**
Library of Congress
HABS ILL,49-WAUK,2-1

7 **Aftermath of the Great Chicago Fire**
Library of Congress
LC-USZ62-137823

8 **Elk Rapids Iron Company**
Bentley Historical Library, University of Michigan
BL005720

9 **Chicago Interstate Industrial Exposition Booth**
Library of Congress
LC-DIG-ppmsca-08921

10 **Grand Haven Shipyard and Dewey Hill**
Bentley Historical Library, University of Michigan
BL005970

11 **Rooftop View of Milwaukee and Lake Michigan**
Wisconsin Historical Society
54887

12 **Milwaukee's Lakeshore, 1877**
Wisconsin Historical Society
6949

13 **Chicago Traveling Club Encampment**
Wisconsin Historical Society
27146

14 **Sunset on the Lake, at South Haven, 1880s**
Bentley Historical Library, University of Michigan
BL006004

16 **Black Lake at Norton Shores**
Library of Congress
HAER MICH,61-NOSHO,1-8

17 **View of the Lake from Racine Court House Tower**
Wisconsin Historical Society
39979

18 **Milwaukee Residential Street, 1889**
Wisconsin Historical Society
53909

19 **Main Street in Pentwater**
Bentley Historical Library, University of Michigan
BL005954

20 **Muskegon's Western Avenue, 1889**
Bentley Historical Library, University of Michigan
BL005941

21 **Knickerbocker Ice Works at Harbor Springs**
Bentley Historical Library, University of Michigan
BL005795

22 **South Haven**
Bentley Historical Library, University of Michigan
BL006005

23 **Green Bay and Courthouse**
Wisconsin Historical Society
31411

24 **Green Bay Cyclists**
Wisconsin Historical Society
2001

25 **Betsie Bay from Frankfort**
Bentley Historical Library, University of Michigan
BL005733

26 **Charlevoix**
Bentley Historical Library, University of Michigan
BL005758

27 **Muskegon River Loggers**
Bentley Historical Library, University of Michigan
BL005914

28 **Charlevoix Life Saving Station**
Library of Congress
LC-USZ62-74427

29 **Brick Kiln at Manistee**
Bentley Historical Library, University of Michigan
BL005902

30 **Hines Machine Shop in Traverse City**
Bentley Historical Library, University of Michigan
BL005813

31 **Manistee River Sawmill**
Bentley Historical Library, University of Michigan
BL005900

32 **Handcar and Men on Manistee and Luther Railroad**
Bentley Historical Library, University of Michigan
BL005901

33 **Racine Horse-drawn Trolley**
Wisconsin Historical Society
24971

34 **Chicago World's Fair Parade**
Library of Congress
LC-USZ62-99660

35 **Railroad Connections at Petoskey**
Library of Congress
LC-USZ62-91996

36 **Chicago's Haymarket Square, 1893**
Library of Congress
LC-USZ62-134212

37 **World's Columbian Exposition, 1893**
Library of Congress
LC-USZ62-98684

38 **World's Fair Fisheries Building**
Library of Congress
LC-USZ62-113927

39 **World's Fair Hot-air Balloon**
Library of Congress
LC-USZ62-97666

40 **World's Fair International Exhibit**
Library of Congress
LC-USZ62-103077

41 **World's First Ferris Wheel at World's Fair**
Library of Congress
LC-USZ62-50927

42 **Milwaukee City Hall**
Wisconsin Historical Society
43074

43 **Chicago's South Water Street**
Library of Congress
LC-USZ62-95802

44 **Charles F. Gardner Repair Shop**
Library of Congress
LC-USZ62-61736

45 **Chicago's State Street, 1899**
Library of Congress
LC-USZ62-93763

46 **Pere Marquette Depot at Little Traverse Bay**
Library of Congress
LC-DIG-ppmsca-18181

47 **Wooden Crib Pier at Charlevoix**
Library of Congress
LC-DIG-det-4a18516

48 **Fishing at White Lake**
Bentley Historical Library, University of Michigan
BL005948

50 **Moravian Church at Green Bay**
Library of Congress
HABS WIS,5-GREBA,1-1

51 **River Street in Elk Rapids, 1900**
Bentley Historical Library, University of Michigan
BL005718

52 **Cutting Wood at Harbor Springs**
Bentley Historical Library, University of Michigan
BL005794

53 **Burning Lumber Mill at Boyne City**
Bentley Historical Library, University of Michigan
BL005756

54 **Milwaukee River from Sycamore Street**
Library of Congress
LC-D401-12563

55 **Schlitz Brewery's Director's Room**
Library of Congress
LC-USZ62-60528

56 **Milwaukee Public Library**
Library of Congress
LC-DIG-ppmsca-13671

57 **Harbor Point on Little Traverse Bay**
Library of Congress
LC-DIG-ppmsca-18179

58 **Royal Frontenac Hotel at Frankfort**
Bentley Historical Library, University of Michigan
BL005735

59 **State Street in 1903**
Library of Congress
LC-USZ62-57355

60 **John Dowie's City of Zion, 1904**
Library of Congress
LC-USZ62-53421

61 **Zion Parade**
Library of Congress
LC-USZ62-53423

62 **Milwaukee Central Library Interior**
Library of Congress
LC-DIG-det-4a20333

63 **Chicago River from the Rush Street Bridge**
Library of Congress
LC-DIG-det-4a12889

64 **Crew at Lifesaving Station in Michigan City**
Library of Congress
LC-USZ62-93045

65 **Theatrical Production at Chicago Coliseum**
Library of Congress
LC-USZ62-53430

66 **Maroons Thanksgiving Day Game, 1905**
Library of Congress
LC-USZ62-128940

67 **Milwaukee ABC Bowling Tournament, 1905**
Library of Congress
pan 6a29791

68 **State Street in 1906**
Library of Congress
LC-USZ62-70762

69 **Mary Crane Nursery Open-air School**
Library of Congress
LC-DIG-ppmsca-18483

70 **Arion Musical Club at Pabst Theatre**
Library of Congress
LC-USZ62-52876

71 **Northwestern Mutual Offices**
Library of Congress
HABS WIS,40-MILWA,32-10

72 **Fraternal Order of Eagles Convention**
Library of Congress
LC-USZ62-137401

73 **Vacationers on Logging Train**
Library of Congress
LC-USZ62-76127

74 **Lagoon at Central Park**
Library of Congress
LC-USZ62-94032

75 **Visitors at Garfield Park**
Library of Congress
LC-USZ62-101615

76 **Milwaukee Hippodrome**
Library of Congress
LC-USZ62-53437

77 **Ryerson Laboratory at University of Chicago**
Library of Congress
LC-USZ62-95571

78 **International Harvester, 1907**
Library of Congress
LC-USZ62-41393

79 **Chicago Mounted Police**
Library of Congress
LC-USZ62-117653

80 **Panorama of the Chicago Waterfront**
Library of Congress
LC-USZ62-126635

81 **Muskegon Sewer Laborers**
Bentley Historical Library, University of Michigan
BL005940

82 **Lawrence Captive Airship with a View**
Library of Congress
LC-USZ62-51725

83 **Summer Day at the Chicago Shore**
Library of Congress
LC-USZ62-61670

84 **Petoskey Paper Mill, 1908**
Library of Congress
LC-D4-70723

85 **Young Conkey Printers**
Library of Congress
LC-DIG nclc-04499

86 **Frank Betz Surgical Supply**
Library of Congress
LC-DIG-nclc-04466

87 **Front Street in Traverse City**
Bentley Historical Library, University of Michigan
BL005811

88 **Crowds at Chicago Coliseum**
Library of Congress
LC-USZ62-53440

89 **International Ballooning Contest, 1908**
Library of Congress
LC-USZ62-24415A

90 **Gary Surveyors**
Library of Congress
HABS IND,45-GARY,2-4

91 **Gary Land Company Office**
Library of Congress
HABS IND,45-GARY,2-5

92 **Gary Police Force**
Library of Congress
LC-USZ62-103289

93 **Cubs vs. White Sox in City Championship Game**
Library of Congress
pan 6a29751

94 **Armour & Company Assembly Line**
Library of Congress
LC-USZ62-97322

95 **Rockefeller's Standard Oil Refinery in Whiting**
Library of Congress
LC-USZ62-109339

96 **Northpoint Public School Chemistry Class**
Bentley Historical Library, University of Michigan
BL005884

97 **Ladies at Great Warren Dunes**
Bentley Historical Library, University of Michigan
BL000361

98 **The City That U.S. Steel Built**
Library of Congress
pan 6a19366

100 **Belt Line Train at Sheboygan**
Library of Congress
LC-USZ62-127103

102 **Students at Gary's Emerson School**
Library of Congress
LC-USZ62-43661

103 **Boyne City Docks**
Bentley Historical Library, University of Michigan
BL005754

104 **Chicago Skyline, 1911**
Library of Congress
LC-USZ62-123211

105 **Chicago International Aviation Meet, 1911**
Library of Congress
LC-USZ62-45023

106 **Racine Country Club**
Library of Congress
LC-USZ62-125092

107 **Bird's-eye View of Chicago and Lake Michigan**
Library of Congress
pan 6a04115

108 **Outside the 1912 Republican National Convention**
Library of Congress
LC-DIG-ggbain-10587

109 **Convention Goers Listening to Teddy**
Library of Congress
LC-DIG-ggbain-10567

110 **On the Street in Evanston**
Library of Congress
LC-USZ62-49259

111 **Ray Freeland with Dragon Fly**
Bentley Historical Library, University of Michigan
BL005793

112 **Gladstone Fire Fighters Tournament, 1912**
Library of Congress
LC-USZ62-122802

113 **Milwaukee from the Bay**
Library of Congress
pan 6a12468

114 **Milwaukee's Gipfel Union Brewery**
Library of Congress
HABS WIS,40-MILWA,11-5

115 **Baseball Legend Guy Harris White**
Library of Congress
LC-DIG-hec-02785

116 **W. W. Rice Leather Company Workers**
Library of Congress
pan 6a26151

117 **July 4th Parade at Manistee**
Bentley Historical Library, University of Michigan
BL000381

118 **Gary Fire Fighters at Police Headquarters**
Library of Congress
pan 6a26193

119 **Harbor Springs Men Aboard an Overland**
Bentley Historical Library, University of Michigan
BL000349

120 **Chief Wawatum at Mackinaw City**
Bentley Historical Library, University of Michigan
BL005761

121 **Rosenwald Colored Y.M.C.A.**
Library of Congress
LC-USZ62-137807

122 **Lake Forest Country Fair, 1916**
Library of Congress
LC-USZ62-127503

123 **Lake Forest's Market Square**
Library of Congress
LC-DIG-ppmsca-12662

124 **Elgin Six Scout Car in Chicago**
Library of Congress
LC-USZ62-108394

125 **Students at Chicago's Franklin School**
Library of Congress
LC-DIG-ppmsca-11778

126 **Benjamin Purnell's House of David at Benton Harbor**
Bentley Historical Library, University of Michigan
BL005738

127 **Traverse City Storefront**
Bentley Historical Library, University of Michigan
BL005810

128 **Contraband Seizure at Zion**
Library of Congress
LC-USZ62-95895

129 **Disposal of Contraband by Mayor Clendein**
Library of Congress
LC-USZ62-96024

130 Toothbrush Drill at Chicago's Franklin School
Library of Congress
LC-USZ62-94390

131 On the Beach at Sturgeon Bay
Wisconsin Historical Society
4583

132 The Morgan Club House in Kenosha
Wisconsin Historical Society
35507

133 Lily E. as Floating Clubhouse for S.S.Y.C.
Wisconsin Historical Society
47772

134 The Dempsey-Miske Fight at Benton Harbor
Library of Congress
pan 6a28690

135 Jack Dempsey in Michigan City
Library of Congress
LC-USZ62-94046

136 Radio Hobbyist John Iringle
Library of Congress
LC-USZ62-93539

137 Harbor Scene at Leland
Bentley Historical Library, University of Michigan
BL005880

138 Warren Harding Funeral Train
Library of Congress
LC-USZ62-102860

139 Lakeside in Milwaukee
Wisconsin Historical Society
53881

140 Baseball Legend Sam Rice
Library of Congress
LC-USZ62-135439

141 Northwestern and Illinois at Dyche Stadium, 1927
Library of Congress
pan 6a28990

142 President and First Lady Coolidge at Hammond
Library of Congress
LC-USZ62-106667

143 Ajax Rubber Company Assembly Line at Racine
Wisconsin Historical Society
40812

144 Manitowoc Electric and Water Utility
Wisconsin Historical Society
55030

145 Manitowoc's Lincoln High School, 1926
Library of Congress
LC-USZ62-98658

146 Cooking Class Students at Chicago's John Hay School
Library of Congress
LC-USZ62-107068

147 Koehler Aviation Company Amphibious Plane
Wisconsin Historical Society
10689

148 Wrigley Field Dugout During World Series, 1929
Library of Congress
LC-USZ62-94924

150 Miniature City at Traverse City
Bentley Historical Library, University of Michigan
BL005809

151 CCC Camp Ludington, 1934
Bentley Historical Library, University of Michigan
BL005912

152 The Cedarburg Covered Bridge
Library of Congress
HABS WIS,45-CEDBU.V,1-1

153 Milwaukee's Detroit and Van Buren Streets
Library of Congress
LC-DIG-fsa-8b28645

154 Milwaukee Junkyard
Library of Congress
LC-DIG-fsa-8b28651

155 West Winnebago Street in Milwaukee, 1936
Library of Congress
LC-DIG-fsa-8b28650

156 Scene at Crescent Beach in Algoma
Wisconsin Historical Society
24365

157 Jones Island Dwellings
Wisconsin Historical Society
56151

158 At the Beach in 1939
Wisconsin Historical Society
60350

159 Labor Day Celebration, 1939
Library of Congress
LC-USF33-T01-001418-M3

160 NALC Convention
Library of Congress
LC-USF33-T01-001430-M1

161 Observers of NALC Parade
Library of Congress
LC-USF33-T01-001429-M2

162 Billboard Beside Milwaukee Church
Library of Congress
LC-USF33-T01-001423-M5

163 Beachgoers at Holland
Bentley Historical Library, University of Michigan
BL005968

164 A Street in Holland
Bentley Historical Library, University of Michigan
BL005969

165 Holland's Windmill Island
Bentley Historical Library, University of Michigan
BL005967

166 Beneath Chicago's Elevated Tracks, 1940
Library of Congress
LC-USZ62-125455

167 Milwaukee's Bathing Beach
Library of Congress
LC-USF33-T01-001915-M4

168 Benton Harbor Fruit Market
Library of Congress
LC-USF33-T01-001950-M2

169 Benton Harbor Fruit Market no. 2
Library of Congress
LC-USF34-061207-D

170 Coal Operation at Benton Harbor
Library of Congress
LC-USF34-061210-D

171 Aerial View of Milwaukee and Lake Michigan
Wisconsin Historical Society
52835

172 Milwaukee Yacht Club Clubhouse
Wisconsin Historical Society
54091

173 Statue Honoring Solomon Juneau
Wisconsin Historical Society
53655

174 Lake Michigan Car Ferry at Manitowoc
Wisconsin Historical Society
24570

175 U.S. Coast Guard Cutter Woodbine
Library of Congress
HAER MI-326-1

176 The War Effort at Continental Aircraft in Muskegon
Library of Congress
LC-USE6-D-005086

177 Engine Test at Continental Aircraft
Library of Congress
LC-USE6-D-005026

178 Respite at the Beach, 1942
Library of Congress
LC-USW3-005779-D

179 Submarine Construction at Manitowoc
Library of Congress
LC-USE6-D-006233

180 Milwaukee War Plant Workers
Library of Congress
LC-DIG-fsa-8b07727

181 Steam Locomotive Repair Shop
Library of Congress
LC-USW33-014769

182 Truck Drivers for Milwaukee Western Fuel Company
Library of Congress
LC-USW3-020002-D

183 Milwaukee Western Coal Docks
Library of Congress
LC-USW33-017615-D

184 War Materiel Production at Hammond
Library of Congress
LC-USZ62-90357

185 The Home Front at Heil and Company
Library of Congress
LC-DIG-fsac-1a34976

186 NMUA Strikers
Wisconsin Historical Society
3040

187 Downtown Charlevoix, 1947
Bentley Historical Library, University of Michigan
BL005755

188 Indiana Standard Oil at Whiting
Library of Congress
LC-USZ62-65715

189 Managing the Indiana Standard Control Board
Library of Congress
LC-USZ62-93229

190 U.S. Steel Works at Gary
Library of Congress
LC-USZ62-53452

191 Round Island Signal Light
Library of Congress
LC-DIG-ppmsca-09101

192 Inside at the 1952 Republican National Convention
Library of Congress
LC-DIG-ppmsca-03099

193 Milwaukee's Mitchell Building
Library of Congress
HABS WIS,40-MILWA,7-1

194 Edward and Mendel of Chulew Furniture in Kenosha
Wisconsin Historical Society
56475

195 Polio Clinic at Muskegon
Bentley Historical Library, University of Michigan
BL006834

196 UAW Squatting Strikers
Wisconsin Historical Society
41268

197 Assembly Line at American Motors in Kenosha
Wisconsin Historical Society
40739

198 Milwaukee's Jones Island
Wisconsin Historical Society
53638

199 Swedish Immigrant Church near Chesterton
Library of Congress
HABS IND,64-CHEST.V,1-2

200 Lake Michigan Shoreline
Wisconsin Historical Society
35881

HISTORIC PHOTOS OF LAKE MICHIGAN

The vast lingering remnant of an ice age that came to a close more than 10,000 years ago, Lake Michigan has shaped the history of the settlements along its surrounding shores for centuries. Its storied waters have seen schooners, luxury steamships, and modern freighters, its lakeshores the rise of the railroads that helped to carve a way of life into the surrounding wooded wilderness for the Americans who called the region home. Through high times and lean, the lake's 1,640 miles of coastline have clung to their untamed beauty even as bustling harbor hamlets and booming cities like Chicago and Milwaukee rose in their midst.

Historic Photos of Lake Michigan chronicles portions of two centuries on and around Lake Michigan—the only great lake entirely within United States borders, the third-largest of the five Great Lakes, and the fifth-largest freshwater lake in the world—showcasing the ever-changing life and landscape along its quartz crystal coast.

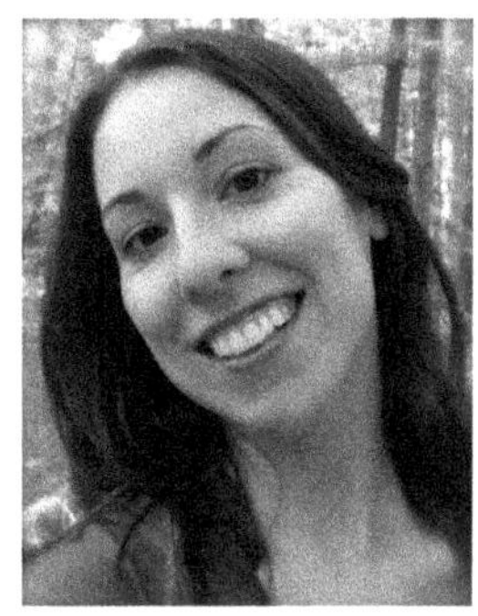

Born and raised in Michigan, Lynda Twardowski spent nearly a decade of her post-college years living on the West Coast but realized that life back home along Lake Michigan—the nation's "Third Coast"—was better and more beautiful than on any other shore. Ever since, she's been singing the praises of Great Lake-side paradise as travel editor of *Traverse, Northern Michigan's Magazine,* and MyNorth.com.

A 1997 graduate of Michigan State University's journalism program, Twardowski has written more than a dozen published books, as well as hundreds of articles for regional and national magazines. She lives in Traverse City, Michigan, on the Lower Peninsula.

WWW.TURNERPUBLISHING.COM